THE UNIVERSITY OF CONNECTICUT

AVERY POINT

★ 1881 ★

ALUMNI
BOOK
FUND

THE SOVIET UNION AND THE THIRD WORLD

THE LAST THREE DECADES

THE SOVIET UNION AND THE THIRD WORLD

THE LAST THREE DECADES

EDITED BY

Andrzej Korbonski and
Francis Fukuyama

A BOOK FROM THE RAND/UCLA CENTER FOR THE
STUDY OF SOVIET INTERNATIONAL BEHAVIOR

CORNELL UNIVERSITY PRESS

ITHACA AND LONDON

First published 1987 by Cornell University Press.
First published, Cornell Paperbacks, 1987.
Second printing 1988.

International Standard Book Number (cloth) 0-8014-2032-6
International Standard Book Number (paper) 0-8014-9454-0
Library of Congress Catalog Card Number 86-47974
Printed in the United States of America
*Librarians: Library of Congress cataloging information
appears on the last page of the book.*

CONTENTS

[v]

PREFACE

In July 1955 Egypt received a consignment of arms manufactured chiefly in Czechoslovakia but negotiated for and delivered under the aegis of the Soviet Union. This event is generally accepted as having been the opening volley of Moscow's postwar effort to expand its influence outside the traditional theaters of Europe and the Far East.[1]

The countries of the so-called Third World were at that point midway through the process of decolonization. The struggle for independence was frequently traumatic and led to sharp conflicts between former colonies and the West; the resentment that the Third World felt toward the United States and Western Europe provided an easy and obvious entree for the Soviet bloc. The apparent opportunities led to sudden hopes on the part of Khrushchev and his colleagues and to equally extravagant fears on the part of the West. The program of the Soviet Communist party asserted that "the rise of socialism marks the advent of the era of liberation of oppressed peoples," that "a mighty wave of national-liberation revolutions is sweeping away the colonial system and undermining the foundations of imperialism," and that socialism is capable of "transforming a backward country into an industrial country within the lifetime of a single generation."[2] Western statesmen, reading similar statements and watching the growing Soviet relationship with Egypt, believed that Moscow had "leapfrogged" the containment barrier they were trying to erect in the Northern Tier and had established its influence in the heart of the Middle East, where it would be in a position to control the region's vital resources and communications routes. The Suez crisis of 1956 was the first of many Third World conflicts into which the states of the West would be drawn, in large measure from fear of Soviet expansionism.

Thirty years later, Third World conflicts in Central America, Southern

---

[1]As chapters by Stephen Sestanovich and Shahram Chubin point out, however, the Soviets undertook important initiatives in the Third World during Stalin's reign, the importance of which is often underrated.

[2]The party program was published in *Pravda*, November 2, 1961.

Africa, the Middle East, and Southeast Asia, as well as the war in Afghanistan, continue to vex U.S.-Soviet relations. Whether the United States ought to aid the Contras in Nicaragua or Jonas Savimbi's UNITA in Angola are central foreign policy concerns for the administration and Congress, and in October 1985 President Ronald Reagan put the matter of regional negotiations on the agenda of his summit with Soviet general secretary Mikhail Gorbachev. Although issues of nuclear war and strategic arms control still occupy center stage in East-West relations, it is only in the Third World that the superpowers have consistently been drawn into very real and frequently costly conflicts: Korea, Vietnam, and, more recently, Lebanon and Central America for the United States, Angola and Afghanistan for the Soviet Union. With stalemate in Central Europe since the early 1950s, the Third World has been, as Stephen Sestanovich points out in his chapter, the only arena to present both superpowers with the possibility of substantial gains and losses. Indeed, so large are potential gains and losses in the Persian Gulf, for example, that they make all too plausible the prospect of direct superpower confrontation and ultimately an escalation that might destabilize the Central Front itself and lead to nuclear war.

It is clear that the West's nightmare of the mid-to-late 1950s, namely, that the Soviets would ride the wave of anti-Westernism in the formerly colonial world to undermine Western positions everywhere and establish a series of communist satellites, was not realized. After initial successes in the 1950s, in such countries as Egypt, Indonesia, and India, Moscow was faced with setbacks in the mid-1960s as coups overthrew its clients. Like Washington, Moscow found it difficult to anchor its influence; its position proved vulnerable to wars, coups, changes of heart on the part of local leaders, and simple outbidding by the other superpower. The continuing search for stable influence led to a new series of tactical innovations during the expansionist surge of the mid-1970s, involving Marxist-Leninist regimes and vanguard parties. But only in Cuba and Vietnam did Soviet-style Marxism-Leninism take root, and the regimes of the 1970s did not fare noticeably better than those of an earlier generation.

At the same time, through a patient policy of two steps forward, one step back, the Soviets were achieving a steady net increase in their influence in the Third World. From the vantage point of the mid-1980s one sometimes forgets that "containment" in its Dulles-era form was intended to create an actual physical barrier to Soviet freedom of movement by land, sea, and air through interlocking alliances with countries bordering on the USSR. This plan was realized, however briefly, to a remarkable degree. Now, by contrast, the Soviets have allies in virtually every part of the globe, providing them with concomitant political, economic, and in places military access. As Harry Gelman points out in the concluding chapter of this book, from the first years of their postwar involvement in the Third World the Soviets have experienced setbacks and frustrations for which they have patiently and with some success sought to compensate themselves. Thus although the defection of Egypt in the mid-1970s was a major loss for Moscow, the Soviets moved quickly to shore up their relationship with Syria and to establish new outposts in South Yemen, Ethiopia, and Libya.

Western analyses of these developments have tended to mirror the ups and downs of Soviet policy. Following the period of intense Soviet activism in the Third World which began with the October 1973 Middle East War and culminated in the December 1979 invasion of Afghanistan, many observers took the pessimistic view that Soviet willingness and capabilities to intervene in local crises were following a secular upswing. Studies of Soviet policy done in the 1960s and early 1970s tended to focus on arms transfers;[3] those from later in the decade began to look at the full range of instruments that the Soviets had developed and were just beginning to employ, such as a blue-water navy and other power projection forces (including transport aircraft and airborne forces), and various proxy or cooperative forces, including the Cubans and East Germans used in Angola, the Horn of Africa, and elsewhere.[4] In addition to this expansion in capabilities came what many regarded as an equally troubling increase in Soviet risk-taking propensities in support of foreign policy objectives in the Third World.[5] The precedents broken by the invasion of Afghanistan (the first massive use of ground forces outside the Warsaw Pact area) suggested a monotonically increasing willingness to intervene all over the world. This apparent willingness, together with the chaotic situation brought on by the collapse of the Shah's regime in Iran, raised sharp fears that the Soviets might use Afghanistan as a springboard for a far more dangerous move on the Persian Gulf.

Analysts in this period tended to concentrate on Soviet strategy and tactics as expressed in behavior, on such questions as how the Soviet-Cuban relationship worked, what the mechanics were for coordinating the operations of Soviet bloc forces, what were the capabilities of Soviet power projection forces and how those capabilities might evolve, how Moscow evaluated the risks and benefits of an operation against Iran, and the like. Such analyses were based for the most part on empirical observation of Soviet operations in the preceding decade.

Five years after the invasion of Afghanistan, the picture drawn by Western observers looked entirely different. The Soviet Union had not, after all,

[3]Examples include Uri Ra'anan, *The USSR Arms the Third World* (Cambridge: MIT Press, 1969), and Jon Glassman, *Arms for the Arabs: The Soviet Union and War in the Middle East* (Baltimore: Johns Hopkins University Press, 1975).
[4]On power projection see Bradford Dismukes and James McConnell, *Soviet Naval Diplomacy* (Elmsford, N.Y.: Pergamon, 1979). More generally, good studies include Stephen Hosmer and Thomas Wolfe, *Soviet Policy and Practice toward Third World Conflicts* (Lexington, Mass.: Lexington Books, 1982), and Bruce Porter, *The USSR in Third World Conflicts* (New York: Cambridge University Press, 1984).
[5]For example, see Donald Zagoria, "Into the Breach: New Soviet Alliances in the Third World," *Foreign Affairs*, Spring 1979.

undertaken another large-scale intervention or established new precedents in the use of force. Moscow appeared rather to be in a phase of consolidation, pouring considerable resources into established clients such as Angola and Afghanistan while avoiding new commitments where possible. Indeed, there was a remarkable reversal of roles between the superpowers. Whereas in the 1960s and 1970s the Soviet Union had supported a variety of national liberation movements and insurgencies against pro-Western regimes (Vietnam being the prototypal example), in the early 1980s for the first time there were anti-Marxist insurgencies being conducted by local "national liberation" forces sympathetic to the West against Soviet-sponsored regimes in Afghanistan, Angola, Mozambique, Cambodia, and Nicaragua. Indeed, Moscow's prolonged counterinsurgency war against the Afghan mujahedeen has prompted numerous comparisons with the American experience in Vietnam.

As Soviet policy moved from expansion to consolidation, some Western observers began to notice that the way in which the Third World was perceived and debated within the Soviet Union had begun to shift as well. Elizabeth Valkenier was one of the first scholars to note that even in the 1970s Soviet economists had begun to reject the traditional Stalinist model of development, which stressed the need for autarkic industrialization along Soviet lines.[6] Instead, they started to emphasize the potential benefits to developing countries of mixed economies with market sectors that remained open to the global capitalist economic order. In the political sphere, other observers have noted growing Soviet disenchantment with the types of organizational structures and clients promoted in the 1970s as the solution to the problem of stable influence, such as the vanguard party.[7] Soviet specialists demonstrated considerable skepticism as to whether the quick transformation from feudalism to socialism implicit in the earlier concept of the noncapitalist path of development was possible—that is, whether developing societies, just like the countries of Europe, did not have to pass through a lengthy bourgeois stage before reaching socialism. By the mid-1980s the second thoughts expressed by Soviet academic specialists on the reliability and prospects for many Soviet Third World clients were reflected in authoritative policy pronouncements. Both Yuriy Andropov and Mikhail Gorbachev signaled Moscow's allies that the Soviet Union regards economic development as the responsibility primarily of the local regime and that there are strict limits to Soviet largess. Indeed, Gorbachev in his address to the Twenty-seventh Congress of the Soviet Communist party in February 1986 made no special mention of the Third World at all, in stark contrast to Brezhnev's practice; the

[6]Elizabeth Valkenier, *The Soviet Union and the Third World: An Economic Bind* (New York: Praeger, 1983).
[7]See Jerry Hough, *The Struggle for the Third World* (Washington, D.C.: Brookings, 1986); Francis Fukuyama, *Moscow's Post-Brezhnev Reassessment of the Third World*, R-3337-USDP (Santa Monica: Rand Corporation, 1986), as well as his chapter in this book; and Galia Golan's forthcoming book on Soviet policy toward national liberation movements.

failure to celebrate the successes of Moscow's socialist and socialist-oriented allies and to promise them further support, in the presence of such representatives as Fidel Castro and Mengistu Haile Mariam, seemed strongly to signal a lessened degree of commitment.

Unlike the Western analyses of the 1970s, studies of the 1980s have tended to be more Kremlinological in nature, focusing on what the Soviets themselves were saying and writing about the Third World rather than what they were actually doing. These studies pointed out that even as Moscow was intervening in Angola, Ethiopia, and Afghanistan, Soviet specialists were expressing reservations and second thoughts about the consequences of such policies, reservations that eventually would be echoed by top officials and, presumably, reflected in policy.

Clearly the superpower competition in the Third World looks considerably different in the mid-1980s from the way it looked at the close of the previous decade. The dynamism and initiative displayed by the Soviet Union in the mid-to-late 1970s has passed, it seems, to the United States, which in many regions is challenging the status quo. Moscow, by contrast, seems absorbed by a multitude of domestic political and economic concerns, and reluctant to bear the costs of an overseas empire. How long is this situation likely to continue? Is it possible to speak of secular changes in Soviet objectives and behavior? Or are we witnessing a cyclical period of consolidation in Soviet foreign policy which will be followed by a new expansion when the appropriate opportunities arise? Can one even speak of the Soviet Union being in a period of consolidation? It may be, for example, that what appears deliberate Soviet quiescence in fact reflects mere lack of opportunities and that Soviet "policy" will change when the international environment changes. What can the history of Soviet policy in the Third World tell us about its likely evolution?

Such questions form the background to this book. To avoid the parochialism inherent in an orientation overly focused on the present and the immediate past, the authors of the individual chapters have sought to place the current situation in the broader context of Soviet policy in the past three decades and to see if larger historical patterns are at work which might help us predict future Soviet behavior. In each geographical or functional area they tried to examine certain common questions and to determine which applied to the whole of Soviet Third World policy. They had several issues to consider.

The first concerns the appropriate periodization of Soviet policy, both from the standpoint of an outside observer and from that of the Soviets themselves. It is clear that the conventional transitions from Stalin to Khrushchev to Brezhnev do not apply in all Third World theaters; Robert Horn's chapter suggests that Soviet policy toward India has been remarkably stable and for the most part unaffected by external events over the entire three decades that concern us here. Nonetheless, as Abraham Becker's chapter on the economic dimension indicates, major and relatively clear-cut shifts have taken place in the distribution and character of Soviet military and economic assistance. There is, moreover, the interesting question of the nature of the current period, whether it represents a passing phase or an evolutionary direction.

The second issue concerns the tactical principles that govern Soviet activities. Nearly all observers have outgrown earlier debates on whether the Soviets have been following some "master plan" for the Third World. But even if no such plan exists, most analysts would concede that Moscow has reasonably consistent objectives and that the means used to achieve them (such as the "cooperative interventions" of the 1970s involving Soviet, Cuban, and other bloc participation) often bear the marks of systematic planning. As Melvin Goodman's chapter on military matters points out, the Soviets have sought concrete military objectives in their Third World activities, though their resulting ability to project power around the world relative to that of the United States remains in doubt.

The third issue concerns the character of Soviet influence. It is clear that Soviet influence over such clients as Syria, Iraq, and India is weak and in the cases of Egypt and Somalia has disappeared altogether. It is equally clear that the Soviets, too, are aware of this problem and have taken measures to improve the reliability and permanence of their influence, through such measures as providing personal bodyguards to protect leaders (for instance, Libya's Qadhdhafi), creating popular militias to guard against military coups, and using the East Germans to remake the security apparatus. How successful have these measures been?

A fourth issue, of particular relevance to the United States, concerns the Soviet view of the relationship between regional policies and overall superpower relations. Does Moscow take into account Washington's likely reactions when it formulates its Third World strategies? The Soviets' activism in the 1970s at the same time as they were seeking detente and strategic arms control with the Americans suggests that it did not, a conclusion borne out in Galia Golan's chapter on the Middle East. Nonetheless, the question remains as to whether the Soviet leadership has learned any lessons from the 1970s. In the future, will Moscow understand the inevitable linkage in American policy between detente in the central relationship and "good behavior" in the Third World?

The final issue concerns the changing perceptions of the states of the Third World themselves regarding the potential benefits and costs of association with the Soviet bloc. It is clear that the Soviets accumulated gains in the 1950s from their support of decolonization with an ease that will not recur; as many Soviet observers themselves point out, the age of European colonialism ended with the collapse of the Portuguese empire in 1974, and the current task in the Third World is no longer national but social liberation. But in the struggle for economic development the Soviet bloc offers benefits much less obvious than the security-related ones that underpinned Soviet influence in earlier years; who will find Moscow appealing in the next decade?

Individual authors raise many other points that can be applied more generally, of course. Harry Gelman's concluding chapter seeks to synthesize these into a set of broader conclusions, though those conclusions represent his own views rather than a consensus of the different contributors. Overall we hope that these essays will provide valuable historical perspective on an issue of great concern to American foreign policy and to the future course of U.S.-Soviet relations.

ANDRZEJ KORBONSKI
FRANCIS FUKUYAMA

Los Angeles and
Santa Monica, California

ACKNOWLEDGMENTS

This book is the second major publication in a new series on various aspects of Soviet foreign and military policy to be issued by the RAND/UCLA Center for the Study of Soviet International Behavior (CSSIB). CSSIB, a joint center for advanced research and training in Soviet studies, was established in October 1983 by The RAND Corporation and the University of California at Los Angeles, with major grant assistance from the Rockefeller Foundation. The Center supports a broad program of analytic and policy-relevant research in Soviet international behavior, provides training leading to a doctoral degree at UCLA or the RAND Graduate School, and disseminates its research findings to the public.

This book is based on papers delivered at a conference sponsored by CSSIB at the Villa Serbelloni in Bellagio, Italy, in November 1985. This collection follows on the first CSSIB volume, *U.S.-Soviet Relations: The Next Phase*, edited by Arnold L. Horelick and published by Cornell University Press in 1986, and it attempts to address many of the same policy concerns raised there.

The Bellagio conference brought together not only the authors of the essays included here but other prominent scholars and specialists on various aspects of Soviet Third World policy, representing American, European, and Third World points of view. Among the conference participants who provided useful suggestions and comments shaping the present book we particularly thank Cole Blasier of the University of Pittsburgh; Larry Caldwell of RAND/UCLA CSSIB and Occidental College; Edmé Dominguez Reyes of CIDE, Mexico City; Mark Falcoff of the American Enterprise Institute; Pierre Hassner of the Fondation Nationale des Sciences Politiques in Paris; Arnold Horelick, director of CSSIB; Hiroshi Kimura of Hokkaido University; Klaus Lange of the Hans Seidel Stiftung in Munich; Marie Mendras of the Centre Nationale de la Recherche Scientifique in Paris; Bhabani Sen Gupta of the Center for Policy Research, New Delhi; Sarah Terry of Tufts University; Elizabeth Valkenier of Columbia University; Augusto Varas of FLACSO, Santiago, Chile; and Peter Wiles of the London School of Economics. The chapters have been revised under the general supervision of the two editors to take account of the comments and discussion they provoked at the conference.

The editors thank the Ford and Rockefeller Foundations and the UCLA Center for Russian and East European Studies for their support of the conference on which this book was based. Lubov Fajfer, the Conference Coordinator, deserves special credit for long hours spent in organizing the conference arrangements and attending to a host of administrative details. We express our appreciation to Roger Haydon, the editor of both this and the earlier CSSIB volume at Cornell University Press, for his valuable editorial advice, and to Constance Greaser, head of RAND's Publications Department, who gave us unfailing help and advice in bringing this book to publication. We also thank Nancy Giggy and Linda Tanner for their assistance in putting together both the conference and the book.

A.K.
F.F.

THE SOVIET UNION AND THE THIRD WORLD

THE LAST THREE DECADES

I

The Third World in Soviet Foreign Policy, 1955–1985

STEPHEN SESTANOVICH

What place has Moscow's policy toward the Third World had in its diplomatic and security strategy as a whole? Has policy toward the Third World had high priority or low? How has it influenced, or been influenced by, the pursuit of other Soviet objectives?[1] This chapter explores these issues by examining three structural transformations that defined Soviet foreign policy between 1955 and 1985.

First, in the course of thirty years, a combination of political changes, diplomatic accommodations, and military investment made Soviet security concerns in Europe significantly less acute. Over the same period the strategic nuclear balance became much more favorable to the Soviet Union. How were these trends—which taken together marked a major improvement in the "correlation of forces"—related to more ambitious Soviet policies outside Europe?

Second, the world communist movement suffered blows in this period from which it did not recover. Both the ideology of "internationalism" and the Soviet-dominated organization that supported it were weakened. How was this decline affected by the parallel expansion of Moscow's relationships with radical states of the Third World? To what extent did the latter compensate for the former?

Third, after 1955 Soviet policy displayed strong interest in reaching understandings with the West on a series of contentious political questions. Such arrangements were intended to protect past gains and create a more stable international environment for the exercise of Soviet power. How was this

---

[1]The Soviets usually speak of the "Third World" only when they are adopting Western terms for convenience. In this chapter the phrase is used more or less interchangeably with "developing nations," "LDCs," and "extra-European regions." Although its meaning has necessarily changed over time, with few exceptions it includes all of Latin America and Africa and all of non-Soviet Asia except China, Japan, and Korea.

continuing interest, which thirty years ago seemed barely realistic as an approach to European questions, applied to Third World issues that divided East and West?

A close look at these three transformations can help us place Moscow's Third World policy in the context of its principal successes and failures on the international scene. A favorable European settlement and attainment of strategic parity were surely Soviet postwar policy's foremost successes. This chapter reviews the extra-European ramifications of these achievements. At the same time Moscow's strategy in the Third World was closely related to the outstanding failure of its policy: the broken alliance with China and resulting loss of international communist unity. Finally, this strategy should also be seen in the light of what arguably has been the overarching theme of Soviet policy in recent years—the attempt to acquire and institutionalize a steadily larger international role.

Seen from all three vantage points, the decisive feature of the Soviet Union's efforts in the Third World has been the unstable environment in which Moscow must operate. Such instability illuminates the most important discontinuities between these efforts and the rest of Soviet strategy.

Security in Europe: A Quieter Western Front

Whatever else might be won or lost in the bargain, Soviet policy after World War II aimed to prevent the renewal of a major security threat from Germany, whether independently or through Germany's incorporation into an anti-Soviet alliance under American leadership. This was the minimal Soviet goal, which once achieved could become the basis for a more ambitious objective: ousting the United States from a major role in European affairs. Judged by either standard, Moscow's balance sheet was still in the red at the outset of the period examined here. In 1955 the Federal Republic was the newest member of NATO and, despite the opening that same year of diplomatic relations with Moscow, its anti-Soviet Christian Democratic leadership marched in near lockstep with Washington and was strongly committed to German rearmament. "Massive retaliation" and "rollback" were the West's principal strategic slogans.[2]

By the mid-point of the period, however, the picture had been fundamentally altered. Not only was a peace treaty signed in 1970 by which the FRG recognized the postwar status quo, but a new Social Democratic leadership appeared to believe that Germany's diplomatic vocation lay in greater independence from the United States. The status of Berlin was soon thereafter fixed by treaty, and arms control talks with the United States were on the

---

[2]See Samuel P. Huntington, *The Common Defense* (New York: Columbia University Press, 1961), pp. 64ff.

verge of agreement. After another fifteen years, of course, the outlook had changed yet again: in 1985 a Christian Democrat was again chancellor; he spoke of reunification and offered a home for U.S. missiles to an American leadership that was less arms control–minded. Nevertheless, for the Soviet Union many of the accomplishments of the detente period remained intact.

What part did extra-European policies play in the Soviet strategies that produced this result? If they did not help produce it, how much did they benefit from it? President Reagan's frequent misquotation of Lenin—that by "taking" Asia, Latin America, and so forth the Soviet Union could make the United States and Western Europe fall into its lap like ripe fruit—reflects a common Western assessment of Soviet calculations.[3] Whatever Moscow's postwar "blueprint," Soviet conduct in the interwar period had clearly established that policies beyond Europe were formulated with Europe in mind. (And not only Soviet practice but Soviet theory as well: Bukharin's categories—the "global city" and the "global countryside"—were but one expression of an analytical tradition that began with Lenin.)[4] The young Soviet state approached both the independent states of Asia and imperial European holdings in hopes of compensating for its own weakness in the Great Power balance and for the failure of its revolutionary efforts in Europe. Conversely, although the "Third World" could be a lever against a hostile concert of capitalist European powers, the Soviets had shown that they could deliberately put the lever aside, as when they sought to cooperate with Britain and France during the search for "collective security" against Hitler in the 1930s.[5]

Events of the interwar period showed a trade-off, or alternation, between European and extra-European concerns in Soviet policy. After World War II, although better tools and increased opportunities made the relationship of these concerns more complex, the basic pattern persisted. Postwar Soviet interest in the Third World was spurred by weaknesses and failures in dealing with the United States and Western Europe; the same weaknesses, of course, also limited what could be achieved. Only Soviet policy in the seventies revealed a major departure from this pattern: activism in the Third World for the first time reflected success and strength in the central East-West balance. This new pattern may not have taken firm hold, however: there is some evidence that higher East-West tensions and domestic resource stringencies

[3]Trotsky's well-known remark gave permanent life to this Western assessment of Soviet strategy: "There is no doubt at all that the Red Army constitutes an incomparably more powerful force in the Asian terrain of world politics than in the European terrain. . . . The road to Paris and London lies via the towns of Afghanistan, the Punjab, and Bengal." Quoted in Richard Pipes, *Survival Is Not Enough: Soviet Realities and America's Future* (New York: Simon & Schuster, 1984), p. 57.

[4]Stephen Cohen's *Bukharin and the Bolshevik Revolution* (New York: Knopf, 1973) contains an excellent discussion of early Soviet thinking on the relation between revolutions in Europe and among what Bukharin referred to as "Hottentots and bushmen."

[5]See Robert Legvold, *Soviet Policy in West Africa* (Cambridge: Harvard University Press, 1970), pp. 6–13; and Bruce Porter, *The USSR in Third World Conflicts: Soviet Arms and Diplomacy in Local Wars* (New York: Cambridge University Press, 1984), pp. 6–12.

led to a lower priority in the eighties for Soviet policy toward the Third World.

Stalin, it is sometimes argued, showed a "lack of interest" in an active Third World policy, particularly in what anticolonial revolutions could do to strengthen Soviet security.[6] Perhaps because of the more important East-West confrontation in Europe, Stalin committed few resources and took few risks to distract the West's attention and undermine its strength. A weak position in Europe obliged him to be cautious beyond it.

This description, however, does not fully capture the outlook of a man who sought holdings in Libya and the Horn of Africa in 1945, pursued the partition of Iran in 1946, gave the go-ahead for communist insurrections in Southeast Asia after 1947, and (at a distance, to be sure) waged the Korean War to a stand-still from 1950 to 1953.[7] Stalin conducted these policies while tension was growing in Europe, and he may have been aiming in some fashion to exploit Western vulnerabilities outside the principal theater of action. If so, however, his policies proved counterproductive: they galvanized Western governments to meet what they came to regard as a global danger. Soviet Third World policy may have reflected the high level of East-West tension, but it also helped raise tensions further.

Compared to Stalin, Khrushchev had an ambitious and far more activist strategy in the Third World. Here he would, in one analyst's phrase, "crack the chrysalis of containment."[8] Revising Zhdanov's "two-camps" doctrine (in which the world was either socialist or capitalist), he saw two "zones," of war and peace.[9] The world, in short, was now divided into looser ideological categories, between those who could promote the goals of Soviet foreign policy and those who hindered them; the former group, while more diverse than the socialist "camp," was also far larger. This shift was reflected in the growing flow of Soviet resources (both development funds and military equipment) into the Third World, not to speak of propaganda rhetoric, diplomatic initiatives, and leadership trips.

These involvements paralleled Khrushchev's policy of increasing tensions in Europe. (The Soviet commitment to oppose the Baghdad Pact, from which flowed the Czech arms deal of 1955, coincided with German membership in NATO.) Yet his Third World activism clearly took second place to crisis

---

[6]E.g., S. Neil MacFarlane, *Superpower Rivalry and Third World Radicalism: The Idea of National Liberation* (Baltimore: Johns Hopkins University Press, 1985), p. 148. See also Mark Katz, *The Third World in Soviet Military Thought* (Baltimore: Johns Hopkins University Press, 1982), p. 16.

[7]For accounts of Soviet policy in these cases, see Ruth T. McVey, "The Southeast Asian Revolts," and Glenn D. Paige, "Korea," in Cyril E. Black and Thomas P. Thornton, eds., *Communism and Revolution* (Princeton: Princeton University Press, 1964) and George Lenczowski, *Russia and the West in Iran* (Ithaca: Cornell University Press, 1949).

[8]Alvin Z. Rubinstein, *Red Star on the Nile* (Princeton: Princeton University Press, 1977), p. 4.

[9]The text of Khrushchev's speech appears in *Current Digest of the Soviet Press* 8, no. 4 (1956). See also Legvold, *Soviet Policy*, pp. 30–31.

mongering close to home. The risks associated with a half-decade of "Berlin crises" may have been one reason for this priority, but there were others. The Soviets appeared to believe that they could win tactical advantages on European issues by displaying moderation on issues beyond it. At the Geneva Conference on Indochina, for example, they had pushed Ho Chi Minh to accept half a loaf, the better to encourage France to oppose the European Defense Community.[10] Later, for similar reasons, the Soviets kept their aid to the Algerian independence effort strictly limited. As Mikoyan put it when asked (in Iraq) whether Moscow would help the Algerian rebels, "Some people who heard your question will hasten to declare that the Bolsheviks want to occupy Algeria by volunteers and make it [their] colony."[11] The same anxiety was suggested in Khrushchev's memoirs, where he admitted concern lest Soviet aid to Indonesia be publicly revealed.[12]

For the Soviet leader, there was considerable frustration in this situation. In mid-1962, for example, he complained that the West did not see how the global balance of power had shifted against it.[13] Yet as long as the West refused to see reason, Soviet policy had no choice but to take its obduracy into account in two ways. First, as long as Khrushchev sought to deal with European disputes by raising tensions, Soviet interest was not served by also raising tensions elsewhere. (Cuba is the important exception.) Second, once he sought to resolve difficulties (above all, the status of Germany) by detente, then he did not poison the process by challenging the West outside Europe.[14]

Khrushchev's successors began from the latter starting point. The Third World had not been clearly shown to be an arena in which the correlation of forces could be strengthened to Soviet advantage. In the first third of the Brezhnev era, through about 1970, the flow of resources to Third World states (particularly Vietnam) may have increased, but it appeared to bring few benefits for Moscow in return. Moreover, in Europe itself this was a highly fruitful period for Soviet diplomacy, culminating in a detente that commanded strong support throughout the Western alliance. Soviet activities outside Europe did not aid this result, except to the extent that assistance to North Vietnam helped to wound the United States strategically, but they did not detract from it. Early in the Nixon administration—with the first enunciation of "linkage"—the United States did attempt to make the Soviets pay a

[10]Robert F. Turner, *Vietnamese Communism: Its Origins and Development* (Stanford: Hoover Institution Press, 1975), pp. 89–90.

[11]Quoted in Donald Zagoria, *The Sino-Soviet Conflict, 1956–61* (Princeton: Princeton University Press, 1962), pp. 274–275.

[12]Strobe Talbott, trans. and ed., *Khrushchev Remembers: The Last Testament* (Boston: Little, Brown, 1974), p. 327.

[13]*Pravda*, May 26, 1962, p. 1, in *Current Digest of the Soviet Press* 14, no. 21, p. 17.

[14]Donald Zagoria argues that in 1964—a year in which Khrushchev was casting about for a rapprochement with the West, especially for a resolution of the German problem—he cut off aid to Vietnam. See his *Vietnam Triangle: Moscow/Peking/Hanoi* (New York: Pegasus, 1967).

Third World price for detente. But the concept enjoyed little support and was not consistently backed even by its authors.[15] One reason for the lack of strong U.S. support was perhaps that the policy seemed unnecessary: in this period the Soviet Union appeared unlikely to gain any enduring edge from the policies it followed in the Third World.

Under the surface, however, changes were taking place that enlarged Soviet policy in the Third World and made it a much more contentious East-West issue after the early seventies, in the second phase of Brezhnev's foreign policy. First, Soviet conventional military capabilities were growing. Airlift capability, for example, grew 132 percent between 1965 and 1977.[16] Soviet forces, as a result, were now more available for use in extreme situations. Here the 1970 War of Attrition was a major turning point. Second, in the latter half of the decade new regimes committed to Leninist social and political forms came to power in Africa, Asia, and Central America; they proved more reliable partners for Soviet cooperation than earlier, "bourgeois nationalist" parties.[17] Finally, Soviet strategic nuclear forces were growing rapidly toward parity with those of the United States. Soviet analysts began to argue that this change in the nuclear balance narrowed American freedom of action in the Third World:

> Experience has shown that capitalist countries, when engaged in direct aggression, were often forced to limit the scale of utilization of their armed forces and weapons, in order not to provoke a major international outcry. In all these instances they were deterred by the political, economic and military might of the socialist countries, and *in the first place* by the nuclear missile might of the Soviet Union.[18]

Soviet missiles, according to another analysis, "reduce the former invulnerability of the territory of the United States to nought."[19]

The concluding phase of Brezhnev's foreign policy, within which we may also include the policies of Andropov and Chernenko, saw Western support for detente unravel. Resentment of Soviet policies in the Third World had accumulated in the course of the seventies, but a dramatic rupture came only with the Soviet invasion of Afghanistan. The Soviets paid for this enterprise twice over, both in battle on the ground with the Afghan resistance and in sharply reduced Western receptivity to Soviet offers in arms control bargaining. As a result the SALT II treaty was withdrawn from the U.S. Senate and

---

[15]See Henry Kissinger, *White House Years* (Boston: Little, Brown, 1979), pp. 127, 129–30.

[16]Stephen Kaplan, *The Diplomacy of Power* (Washington, D.C.: Brookings, 1981), p. 199.

[17]See Chapter 3 of this volume by Francis Fukuyama.

[18]I. Ye. Shavrov, *Local Wars: History and the Present* (Moscow: Voyenizdat, 1981), p. 229; see also p. 288.

[19]A. A. Gromyko and B. N. Ponomarev, eds., *Soviet Foreign Policy, 1945–80*, vol. 2 (Moscow: Progress, 1981), p. 638.

NATO intermediate-range missile deployments sailed through the legislatures of the alliance with only minor difficulty.

The Soviet response was an attempt to generate a war hysteria in the West fueled by the most extreme anti-American polemics in decades. Activities in the Third World—support for the Sandinistas in Nicaragua, and for Syria in the wake of the 1982 Lebanon war—may have played some small part in the Soviet campaign to counter resurgent Western policies. But for the most part, Moscow did not see—and did not seek—opportunities in the Third World for major gains at Western expense. Instead, Soviet analyses emphasized the strong priority of Euro-strategic issues. The judgment of *Kommunist* was quite typical:

> Is it not clear that were the Soviet Union to allow the existing correlation of military forces in Europe to be disrupted, a dangerous illusion could spread in Washington that it is possible to raise the military fist for action in relation to real socialism, and not in relation to it alone? It is easy to imagine with what adventurism and scorn for the life of peoples the American military would act in the vast regions of the world in such a case.[20]

This thirty-year overview suggests a series of conclusions about how the Soviet leadership related different theaters of action to one another in the pursuit of security and diplomatic advantage.

As a factor in the East-West balance, the Third World stood in contrast to the increasingly stable equilibrium between the blocs in Europe and even to the comparatively slow-moving strategic nuclear competition. Rivalry in the latter areas became highly routinized. The Third World, by contrast, was not only a regular source of conflict in East-West relations; it was also the theater where the West had the least confidence in its ability to control or correct potential changes in the correlation of forces.

Ironically, these opportunities in the Third World were at their peak when the Soviets were least able to exploit them. In the middle and late fifties, when many in the West feared that decolonization might spin completely out of control, Moscow's ability to act was strictly constrained. Its own military capabilities were limited, and the European security issues it cared about most were unresolved. In light of these constraints Soviet involvements tended to be marginal, enough to arouse and hamper Western governments but not enough to dominate events.

Chronic political instability and recurrent conflict in the Third World have meant that Soviet policy had to reckon with gains there but also with major defeats. Soviet commitment of large number of troops and new equipment into an active war zone (in the Middle East, for instance, both in the War of Attrition after the humiliation of 1967 and in the SA-5 deliveries to Syria in

---

[20]"The World at a Responsible Crossroads," *Kommunist*, no. 2 (February 1984).

late 1982, after the war in Lebanon) were efforts needed to protect a regional position against near-total reverse. In such instances the Soviet Union was willing to act decisively no matter what the overall strategic climate was. In 1970 and again in 1973 the Soviet Union acted against a background of improving relations with the West; in 1982–83, against a background of sharply deteriorating relations. The record suggests that although differences in the strategic environment had weight in Soviet decisions about whether (and how) to pursue gains, these differences were made largely irrelevant by the prospect of severe local defeats.

Defensive Soviet interventions were independent of the international environment not only in their origins but also in their *effects*. Their defensive purpose seemed to neutralize the damaging East-West impact.

The same was not true of actions—for example, the interventions in Angola and Ethiopia—that were plainly more discretionary and that brought more pronounced Soviet advantages: new clients, new bases, and so forth. Against the background of an improved correlation of forces and lower tensions in Europe, Soviet policy in the 1970s appeared ready to pursue gains in the Third World at much higher levels of direct involvement than previously. These actions raised the risk of a superpower military confrontation only obliquely and involved far fewer Soviet forces than were deployed to the Middle East in 1970 (or than Moscow threatened to deploy in 1973). Nevertheless, they had a far more lasting negative impact on East-West relations. Had Soviet behavior in the Third World not extended beyond the pattern of "defensive" interventions, detente would almost certainly not have been so thoroughly undermined. (From a Soviet perspective the Western reaction to the invasion of Afghanistan may disprove this point, for few in the West took account of the fact that the move was, in a narrow sense, defensive. The scale of the invasion overwhelmed the distinction: to the Western eye, 6,000 air-defense technicians can be defensive, 120,000 combat troops cannot.)

Did the Soviet leadership *expect* greater activism in the Third World to upset East-West relations? The question has some importance, for it involves the relative priority of different tracks of Soviet policy. At a minimum, the posture of wounded incomprehension that Soviet spokesmen have often adopted on this point is utterly ahistorical. The entire record of Soviet foreign policy, virtually since 1917, refutes it. This history repeatedly shows Soviet leaders aware of the potential connection and ready to make adjustments when necessary. The moderation of the Soviet line in the thirties, to promote unity against Hitler, is but one example; innumerable others make the same point.

The historical record, however, does not by itself settle the question. The Soviets may have believed that a major break with this past pattern had already been made. The West appeared to be in strategic retreat during the seventies, seemingly disinclined to make Soviet boldness a sticking point in detente. As noted above, the unprecedented deployment of large numbers of Soviet military personnel, including pilots flying combat missions, to the Middle East war zone in 1970, *before* the full flowering of detente, had aroused no special American outrage.[21] If in the remainder of the decade the West did not counter Soviet policies in the Third World as tenaciously as it had in the past, the Soviets probably saw this not as a matter of justice or a mark of tacit agreement but simply as a consequence of weakness.

Finally, if Soviet policy traditionally relates its European to its extra-European tracks, does this mean that Soviet Third World assets can be bargained away? The record reveals a Soviet readiness to restrain activities in the Third World and compromise assets there so as to improve its footing in East-West bargaining of various kinds. The most open examples are from the fifties, a time of Soviet strategic weakness, but later instances are also noteworthy. Soviet restraint on Sadat during the preparation for the 1972 summit is one example.[22]

Despite readiness to bargain Third World assets for advantages in the East-West competition, Soviet policy has never manipulated a European asset to advance a Third World goal. The Soviets have not yielded such assets, nor do they appear to have jeopardized or even invoked them in diplomatic bluffs. To take a frequently cited case, no retaliation was made in Soviet-American relations for the U.S. mining of Haiphong harbor on the eve of the 1972 summit.[23] Similarly, although many in the West expected Soviet troops to go on alert around West Berlin during the Cuban missile crisis, they did not do so.[24]

These two patterns obviously confirm the overall priority of Europe in Soviet policy. They may also suggest one of the less obvious reasons for this priority: the Third World is too unstable to justify Soviet concessions on European issues. But because of such instability, today's restraint need not be permanent—as it was not in Indochina, for example. This feature of the East-West competition in the Third World is important to the concluding section of this chapter, on the Soviet Union's efforts to institutionalize a role for itself in the Third World.

---

[21]See Rubinstein's discussion of the War of Attrition, *Red Star*, pp. 87–112.

[22]Jon D. Glassman, *Arms for the Arabs* (Baltimore: Johns Hopkins University Press, 1975), contains a fine account of Soviet policy. See also Rubinstein (*Red Star*, pp. 160, 201), who argues that interest in detente was one reason for the Soviets' weak response to their expulsion by Sadat.

[23]Soviet acquiescence in American policy may not simply have reflected the priority of relations with the United States. It surely mattered that in Vietnam the United States was, while tactically on the offensive, strategically on the defensive. See my "Linking Politics to SALT," *Wall Street Journal*, July 25, 1979.

[24]Stephen Hosmer and Thomas Wolfe, *Soviet Policy and Practice toward Third World Clients* (Lexington, Mass.: Lexington Books, 1983), p. 141. See also Kaplan, *Diplomacy of Power*, p. 131. The public record does not make clear whether Soviet strategic nuclear forces went on alert during the crisis (ibid., p. 54).

Internationalism: The Communist Movement in Decline

A second distinguishing mark of Soviet diplomacy after the mid-fifties was the decline of internationalism. Soviet policy did not necessarily become less ideological as a result of this decline, but it took less of its structure and correspondingly less of its strength from the existence of a world communist movement.

International communism underwent almost as much and as fundamental change in this thirty-year period as it had in the thirty years between 1925 and 1955.[25] To be sure, the first decade after World War II brought a transformation that the world communist movement was still assimilating by 1955. This transformation, the source of much subsequent internal difficulty, was the appearance of new communist states in addition to the Soviet Union, in both the Far East and Eastern Europe. These nominally sovereign states had the same potential conflicts of interest as other states. Few of them (most of them near-identical replications of the Soviet political order) enjoyed any real independence in either domestic matters or foreign policy, but one apostasy occurred almost immediately. Yugoslavia's defection warned of what might be in store: Soviet domination could, in the right circumstances, be challenged and thrown off.

Despite this portent, in 1955 the world communist movement remained relatively strong and at least superficially cohesive. The Soviet Union was, as member-parties (ruling and otherwise) affirmed in 1957, the "head" of this grouping.[26] Khrushchev had not yet launched the drive for de-Stalinization, which would before long let loose enormous pressures on still Stalinized governments. And communist parties loyal to Moscow still retained some strength in the industrial West.

Thirty years later the strength and cohesiveness of the world communist movement had largely vanished. Without question the most significant event in its disintegration was the Sino-Soviet split. China was routed as a contender for leadership of the movement by the late-sixties, if not earlier; the congress of pro-Soviet parties in 1969 was called almost solely for the purpose—not fully realized—of expelling China from the movement's ranks. Yet the impact of this challenge and of other difficulties was not undone. By the 1970s, to take one simple measure, many members of the world communist movement were virtually denying that the movement existed, and it became nearly impossible for the organization to hold a meeting.[27] The once vig-

---

[25]The period 1925–55 included virtually the entire history of the Comintern (after the failure of its revolutionary enterprises in Europe in the twenties through its demise during World War II) and of its "successor," the Cominform (one of the first of many institutions for the management of the Soviet Union's new bloc).

[26]See Zbigniew Brzezinski, *The Soviet Bloc: Unity and Conflict*, rev. ed. (Cambridge: Harvard University Press, 1967), pp. 302–303.

[27]In 1976, in the months leading up to the European Conference of Communist Parties (June

orous "Eurocommunist" parties fell back from the peaks of their strength in the seventies, but they did not become more susceptible to Soviet control in consequence. And while both sides made much less of it in public, the Chinese ideological challenge to Soviet authority remained potent, reinvigorated by the evident success of structural innovations in the Chinese economy.[28]

What has been the place of the Third World in this change? Has Soviet Third World policy *hastened* the decline of internationalism or *slowed* it? A plausible case can be made for either view. Certainly the latent divisions between Soviet and Chinese policy were brought to the surface as disagreements over the "national liberation struggle." Mao believed himself uniquely qualified to lead this stage of the world revolution and without this point of conflict some of the intensity of Sino-Soviet disagreements would obviously have been lost.

As for the impact on Soviet policy, Adam Ulam has written that Khrushchev's dispute with Mao spurred greater Soviet involvement with the radical leftist movements of the Third World than would otherwise have taken place.[29] This is doubtless true, for while Soviet involvements in the Third World promised to improve the correlation of forces vis-à-vis the United States, preservation of the correlation of forces within the world communist movement required that Soviet policies also be ideologically correct. Hence Khrushchev's justification of an active Third World policy in internationalist terms: "We would be poor internationalists if we thought only of ourselves. . . . It is better to have a hundred friends than a hundred rubles."[30] Similarly, at the time of Khrushchev's fall in 1964 a more elaborate and defensive insistence on the Soviet Union's internationalist purity was made by Boris Ponomarev:

> "Internationalism in action," wrote V. I. Lenin, "can have only one meaning: selfless labor on the development of the revolutionary movement and of the revolutionary struggle in one's *own* country, the support (through propaganda, sympathy, material help) of the same struggle, the same party line *without any deviation*, in all countries without exception." Lenin taught our party to be a deeply internationalist one. Soviet communists, all Soviet people, never forget their class brothers, their brothers in struggle for the common goal. We shall

---

29–30), Soviet spokesmen made much of the importance of "proletarian internationalism" as an organizing principle of the world communist movement. Threats of nonattendance by the European parties (including the Yugoslavs) forced the Soviet leaders to water down their use of the term. The final document of the conference made no mention of a leading role for the CPSU, did not criticize Maoism, and upheld each party's right to pursue its own road to socialism.

[28]This is presumably why Soviet analysts insisted so strenuously that Deng Xiaoping's reforms were being reconsidered by the Chinese. A NEP, some of these analysts said (with the experience of Lenin's more liberal New Economic Policy in mind), cannot go on forever.

[29]Adam Ulam, "The Soviet Union and the Rules of the International Game," in Kurt London, ed., *The Soviet Union in World Politics* (Boulder, Colo.: Westview, 1980), p. 42.

[30]Quoted in Legvold, *Soviet Policy*, p. 233.

support with all available means the holy struggle of peoples against their oppressors. Assistance to protect the freedom and independence of socialist Cuba, the decisive support of the United Arab Republic during its most critical moments, help for heroic Algeria, support for Indonesia, help for the peoples of Vietnam and Korea in their struggle against American imperialist aggressors—these and hundreds of other examples are the brightest testimonial of Soviet internationalism in action.[31]

In addressing the Twenty-fifth Congress of the Soviet Communist party in 1976, Brezhnev also invoked the standard of internationalism, both to affirm the ideological foundations of Soviet foreign policy and to call for loyalty to the Soviet Union by other communist parties:

[Proletarian internationalism] is one of the main principles of Marxism-Leninism. Unfortunately some people are trying to make out that almost nothing remains of internationalism. One even encounters people who oppose, openly at that, and reject internationalism. . . . In our view, to repudiate proletarian internationalism would mean depriving communities parties and the workers' movement in general of a powerful and tested weapon. . . . We Soviet Communists consider defense of proletarian internationalism the sacred duty of every Marxist-Leninist.[32]

The Third World was, in the course of the Sino-Soviet split, the arena in which the Soviets were most pointedly asked to validate their Leninist credentials. In large part they failed to do so. Despite claims like that of Ponomarev just quoted, the heart of the Soviet position throughout the dispute with China was that solving its security problems in Europe had to take precedence over any other involvement. As one *Pravda* writer put it at the time, it was wrong to regard the Soviet Union "merely as an instrument of the national liberation movement and a source of aid to the young national states rather than as the main force of the revolutionary transformation of *all* human society."[33]

This was also party ideologue Mikhail Suslov's meaning in 1964 when he declared that the socialist countries retained the main role in the world revolutionary process. National liberation movements were important, he said, but they were not the vanguard nor was theirs the main theater of action, as some seemed to be arguing.[34] As the source of such conflicts, the Third World hastened the dissolution of Soviet-led internationalism.

By the early seventies this conclusion could hardly have been questioned. The record of the past decade, however, suggested that it be reexamined. The

---

[31]Speech of September 28, 1964, in *Selected Works* (Moscow: Politizdat, 1977).

[32]Brezhnev's report to the Twenty-fifth Congress of the CPSU appears in *Foreign Broadcast Information Service: Daily Report (Soviet Union)*, February 25, 1976; see p. 26.

[33]Quoted in William E. Griffith, *The Sino-Soviet Rift* (Cambridge: MIT Press, 1964), p. 63.

[34]Ibid., pp. 339, 452.

only expansion of the Soviet bloc since the rise of Fidel Castro (and apart from Cuba, since the late forties) took place in this period—in the Third World. The resultant grouping began to appear as a kind of restored International and as the ideological reflection of increased Soviet strength.[35]

This is a tempting way to describe the activism of Soviet policy in the seventies. It clarifies the greater reliance placed on radical movements and governments rather than on those with no ideological affinity to the Soviet Union. But as a measure of Moscow's *achievement*, talk of a new International is highly misleading. The new bloc, at the very least, did not restore the crucial attributes of the old. The Soviet Union was not able, for example, to use the members of the bloc to build and secure its dominance over the whole, as it had when Khrushchev and his colleagues sought Chinese support for their policies in suppressing autonomy in Eastern Europe after 1956. Soviet success in manipulating Mao to this end helped Moscow ride out the storm of de-Stalinization.

Such an effort was unthinkable in 1985. The Third World states of the new bloc commanded no political weight within the old bloc (and very little with each other).[36] Admittedly, this detachment had its comforting side for Moscow. These new states did not, as the Chinese did, try to subvert the movement as a whole. The furthest thing from the mind of, say, José Dos Santos or Mengistu Haile Mariam was to comment on Soviet agriculture or to debate the correct policy on consumer goods before the Twenty-seventh Party Congress. In fact, apart from matters that directly concerned their own security, these leaders spoke up on issues of Soviet foreign policy only to offer rhetorical support. (Typical were the ritualized communiqué denunciations of U.S. strategic nuclear policies during these leaders' visits to the Soviet Union.) If measured by open challenges to its authority, the Soviet Union's leadership was more nearly unquestioned in 1985 than fifteen years earlier, with fewer sources of future discord than were present thirty years ago.

All the same, one has to ask, leadership of *what*? The differences between the old bloc and the new went beyond internal political dynamics. For every Soviet statement about the need to affirm internationalism, it was easy to find another reflecting the frustration and setbacks of Soviet policy and a desire to keep some ideological distance between Moscow and its clients. There could be hardly any doubt that the ideological advantages accruing from Moscow's relations with radical Third World states were more limited than in the past.

The International Department's Roftislav Ulyanovskiy, for example, offered a tirade about what happens to Third World anti-imperialist move-

---

[35]As a mark of the novelty of these relationships, it became Soviet policy to institutionalize them in a string of "friendship treaties." See the discussion by Galia Golan in Chapter 8 of this book.

[36]Some analysts have detected patterns of mutual military support within this grouping, but such cooperation neither reflects a political identity nor lays the basis for one. See Avigdor Haselkorn, *The Evolution of Soviet Security Strategy, 1965–1975* (New York: Crane & Russak, 1978).

ments of nationalist (i.e., bourgeois) orientation. What was wrong with them
only *started* with nationalism. They then became "isolationaist, separatist,
exclusive, messianic, and in the final analysis chauvinist, which consequently
opposes the national to the international."[37]

Yuriy Andropov's pessimistic analysis probably represented the low point,
certainly in Soviet leadership statements, of ideological respect for the Third
World:

> The young states that have flung off the colonial yoke are at present going
> through a difficult period of national self-assertion and social development. They
> are *hampered by their colonial heritage of backwardness, internal strife and conflict.*
> Not yet strong enough, they are in danger of falling into the numerous neo-
> colonialist traps. However we are confident that resolute resistance to imperial-
> ism, a well-defined strategy of economic and socio-political development, mu-
> tual respect for each other's interests and rights will enable their peoples to
> overcome these difficulties, which we might describe as growing pains. *Soviet
> people wish them great success* in consolidating their independence, and in their
> fight for prosperity and progress.[38]

As had been true during the Sino-Soviet polemics, the Third World remained the area of Soviet foreign policy that most acutely raised the validity
of Marxist-Leninist ideology. It was the only part of Soviet diplomacy that
retained any easily describable ideological impetus but was also the only part
that could *in*validate the ideology. This risk may be the principal source of
much of Moscow's attraction/repulsion in dealing with the Third World. It
represents an ideological parallel to the place of the Third World in Soviet
security policy. On security issues the Third World is the only arena for
scoring big *successes*, but over the past two decades it has also been the main
arena in which Soviet policy can sustain major *defeats*.

A full parallel to security issues might also imply a more cautious ideological approach to the Third World. Two particular difficulties in Third World
policy certainly suggest that the Soviets may seek ideological legitimacy elsewhere in the future. First, costs will be more sharply scrutinized in light of
the poor performance of the Soviet economy. The same Lenin quotation
(that Soviet economic performance has the greatest effect on the world revolutionary process) so current around the fall of Khrushchev once more was
regularly invoked.[39] This theme expressed the apparent view of Soviet leaders

---

[37]*Present Day Problems in Asia and Africa*, pp. 48–49, as quoted in MacFarlane, *Superpower
Rivalry*, p. 156.

[38]"Sixty Years of the USSR," in *FBIS Daily Report: Soviet Union*, December 21, 1982. The most
comprehensive survey of this more negative theme in Soviet leadership statements on the Third
World is in Francis Fukuyama, *Moscow's Post-Brezhnev Reassessment of the Third World* (Santa
Monica: RAND Corporation, 1986).

[39]Abraham Becker in his chapter in this volume is right to speak of this quotation as "canonical." Yet the lesson extracted from it is not always the same. Brezhnev, for example, in addressing
the 1969 congress of world communist parties, employed the formula to observe that the Soviet

that economic success does more to legitimize Leninist ideology and their own rule than political achievements in the Third World.

A second reason for ideological distance was the growing vulnerability of these states to overthrow by insurgencies. This prospect was obviously much more troubling than, say, diplomatic realignment of friendly nationalist states like Egypt; it involved the potential overthrow of regimes of a socialist orientation and as such the reversal of historical progress.

The Third World presented acute problems and opportunities for the attainment of both the security and the ideological objectives of Soviet foreign policy, and the reason in both cases was the same: its instability, what Andropov called its "heritage of backwardness, internal strife and conflict."[40] The most important validation that Marxism-Leninism can gain is the demonstration of history's relentless advance. Setbacks can always be—and had been—rationalized in ideological terms: history, Soviets are practiced at saying, does not move forward at an even pace.[41] Nevertheless, the Soviet leadership must have feared the internal reverberations of these reverses. There was much exaggeration in the claim that the successes of Soviet foreign policy help cow the populace at home.[42] The converse claim, however, was convincing: the demonstration that other communist regimes may fall can stir the most dangerous thoughts among the Soviet people.

A Stable Environment for Soviet Power?

Among the many changes in East-West relations over the past thirty years, few put down deeper roots than the presumption that problems should be resolved by negotiation between the two sides, and especially between the Soviet Union and United States. This principle had become nearly instinctive by the seventies and eighties, but in the early fifties it was not a given of Western thinking on how to deal with the Soviet Union. On the eve of his departure for Geneva in June 1955, for example, President Eisenhower believed that he had to justify to the American people his decision to take part in an East-West conference "at the summit."[43] His motives apparently were not self-explanatory.

Union's economic achievements made it possible to increase its military strength (*Selected Works*, vol. 1: *1960–70* [Moscow: Politizdat, 1981], p. 381). By contrast, when Andropov used the quotation in addressing the Central Committee on taking office in 1982, he argued that "improvement of the welfare of the [Soviet] people" was "our internationalist duty" (Tass, November 22, 1982). The latter formulation is closer to the use made of Lenin's statement both by Kosygin in the mid-sixties and by Gorbachev in his report to the Twenty-seventh Party Congress.

[40]See "Sixty Years," note 38 above.

[41]Soviet commentaries on the "counter-revolution" in Chile after 1973 exemplified this theme.

[42]See Pipes, *Survival Is Not Enough*, pp. 40–41.

[43]*Public Papers of the Presidents of the United States: Dwight D. Eisenhower, 1955* (Washington, D.C., 1959), pp. 701–703.

Thirty years later, the imperative of "dialogue" was strong. Talk was conducted partly for its own sake but also because it was expected to culminate in agreements and formal understandings, giving structure to the relationship as a whole. This expectation receded during the Reagan administration, but even in tattered form it retained considerable authority.[44]

In three decades of talk, however, the only East-West military agreements—for that matter, the only sustained and serious *negotiations*—of any consequence concerned nuclear weapons; the only political agreements, European affairs. The Soviet Union seemed to regard the European settlement (the complex of treaties relating to German boundaries, the status of Berlin, and the recognition of East Germany, plus the Conference on Security and Cooperation in Europe [CSCE] and its offshoots) as a model for structuring the global competition. Certainly the outlines of this model were to be found in certain Soviet proposals for joint diplomatic approaches on the Third World. Yet the European settlement did not become the basis for a true stabilization of the East-West competition or for understandings of major value to either side.

Major examples of inconclusive efforts at institutionalization include the nuclear nonproliferation regime; regional conflict resolution, and above all the recurrent Soviet proposal for an international conference on the Arab-Israeli conflict; efforts to regulate conventional arms traffic; and the development of rules of engagement to promote "crisis management" and prevent superpower confrontations in the Third World. All have been regarded at different times as promising areas of accommodation or cooperation between the United States and the Soviet Union. It is important, therefore, to consider why the results have been so marginal.

Nonproliferation

As initially conceived in the 1950s, the Nuclear Nonproliferation Treaty (NPT) was to be an East-West arms control pact regulating the central balance; then it was to be extended to cover parties either not aligned with or peripheral to the two alliance systems. The NPT was to govern the status of the most important ally of each superpower—Germany and China, both still without nuclear weapons. Agreement seemed impossible to reach as long as the terms of the pact were likely to prejudice other disputed East-West issues. Two events eventually made the treaty negotiable between Moscow and NATO. The first was the abandonment by the Western alliance of operational "nuclear sharing" schemes, which satisfied the Soviets that West Germany would remain a subordinate member of NATO, except perhaps for the figleaf of nuclear planning. The second was the emergence in the second half of the sixties of a Western consensus in favor of experimenting with detente, which

---

[44]This was why the administration and its supporters and critics alike attached so much importance to middle-level discussions on so-called regional issues.

satisfied the West Germans that they would receive some political reward for accepting subordinate military status. Meanwhile, the Sino-Soviet split made Chinese acquisition of nuclear weapons irrelevant as an East-West negotiating issue. These events removed the most important obstacles to striking a deal.[45]

By contrast, the NPT's relationship to the Third World, while recognized, was never a matter of real controversy between the United States and the Soviet Union. In fact, the NPT had very little to do with the extra-European competition at all. Once the terms of the treaty were hammered out, the rest of the world, to put it bluntly, signed on for the ride with comparatively little fuss. Like the Americans, the Soviets welcomed this broad support, but the accession or, for that matter, nonaccession of other states posed no choices for the superpowers comparable to those involving European security issues.

Since the negotiation of the NPT, the proliferation problem has become relevant to the Third World above all. Superpower consultation and limited cooperation have become institutionalized, reflecting apparently strong interest on the Soviet side. Technical and commercial issues have predominated, and gains and losses in the consolidation of the NPT regime have been marginal and incremental. In contrast to the European precedent, in no case has the settlement of a proliferation problem been an element of a larger political process in which states weigh their nuclear options against the opportunity to solve fundamental security concerns by waiving these options. As a result nuclear proliferation issues have acquired little political substance in East-West relations, even though some important states in regions of Soviet interest are near-nuclear (or crypto-nuclear) powers.[46]

In one region, of course, nuclear issues *are* a crucial obstacle to a grand accommodation: South Asia. If an Indo-Pakistani accommodation took shape, it would throw Soviet dilemmas into high relief. The Soviet leadership would have to ask itself how much it could, would, or should contribute to an understanding, for in the 1980s the nuclear anxieties of both India and Pakistan seem objectively to strengthen Soviet policy. The Soviet Union did not necessarily foster these anxieties or openly reject efforts to allay them.[47]

---

[45]I have presented this analysis more fully in "Nuclear Proliferation and Soviet Foreign Policy, 1957–1968: The Limits of Soviet-American Cooperation" (Ph.D. diss., Harvard University, 1978).

[46]The former category includes South Africa and Pakistan; the latter, Israel. The problems raised by acquisition of nuclear weapons by any and all of these states are a staple of Soviet rhetoric; their rhetorical prominence bears little relation to the way the problem is treated in practice by the two sides.

[47]To the contrary, Soviet writings and official statements express strong support for the cause of nuclear nonproliferation in South Asia and incorporate the idea into proposals for Asian security. See I. I. Kovalenko, "On a Complex Approach to the Problem of Asian Security," *Problems of the Far East* no. 1 (January 1986). At Vladivostok, Gorbachev also referred to nuclear-free-zone proposals for the Korean peninsula, Southeast Asia, and the South Pacific. "Speech by Mikhail Gorbachev in Vladivostok, July 28, 1986" (Novosti Press Agency Publishing House), p. 36.

But the constellation of political forces that they produced—and even perhaps the constellation that a true regional nuclear arms race would produce—served Soviet diplomatic objectives. Pakistan's nuclear option provided extra support for the Soviet-Indian connection. It was also the most plausible ground on which the U.S.-Pakistani security relationship could be ruptured. A rupture, in turn, would have radically improved Soviet prospects in Afghanistan. Finally, nuclear suspicions helped keep Sino-Indian relations at a low level.

These considerations suggest that the Soviet Union is not likely actively to promote a resolution of the South Asian proliferation problem. Unlike the detente that took hold in Europe around 1970, an accommodation between India and Pakistan would not necessarily bring major benefits (whether equal or not) for both the United States and the Soviet Union. Instead, the nuclear future of the subcontinent will probably involve terms that favor one of the superpowers much more than the other. This fact hampers the emergence of stabilizing understandings.

Regional Peace Making

The proposal for an international conference on the Middle East became a perennial of Soviet diplomacy after the October War. It was in relation to this region, after all, that Soviet foreign minister Gromyko announced that no important problem could be resolved without the Soviet Union's participation and assent.[48] Similar in form was the Soviet suggestion, offered after 1980, to negotiate East-West understandings on the Persian Gulf, either in conjunction with or independent of an agreement on Afghanistan.[49] And in 1985 Gorbachev revived a long-standing proposal for a conference on security in Asia (first put forward as part of Moscow's campaign against China, now curiously transformed to court the PRC).[50] Like the CSCE, this forum would probably include the United States.

These Soviet proposals were usually resisted by the United States; in fact, Washington's opposition to a Middle East conference seemed to be a special Soviet grievance.[51] The one exception—the brief Geneva Conference of 1974—suggested that the United States was willing to join with the Soviets in multilateral peacemaking only when little meaningful cooperation was involved, when the serious work had been completed or would be done in other forums, subsequently and separately.[52]

---

[48]Rubinstein, *Red Star*, p. 294.

[49]See the discussion by Henry Trofimenko in "America, Russia and the Third World," *Foreign Affairs*, Summer 1981, pp. 1039–1040.

[50]Gorbachev first alluded to this plan during the visit to Moscow of Indian prime minister Rajiv Gandhi in May 1985. He compared the would-be conference explicitly to Helsinki. The proposal has repeatedly reappeared; see "Vladivostok speech," p. 34.

[51]Hence the enduring bitterness of Soviet references to the October 1, 1977, agreement.

[52]For a participant's discussion, see William Quandt, *Decade of Decisions: American Policy*

Here again is a contrast between East-West interactions in Europe and in the Third World. In Europe a long chain of negotiating mechanisms was created with the advent of detente (and was extended after its fall). Whatever the tensions of the moment, the international political setting of these talks was far more stable, their substance less consequential, and the purpose of the meetings frequently to allay the popular anxieties that arose when the two sides were not talking. In the Third World, by contrast, the anxieties of America's friends were often aroused not by the breakdown of communication but by the idea that the United States and the USSR might reach an agreement over their heads.

The string of Soviet proposals and the apparent Soviet desire to be included should not obscure the fact that the Soviet side faced comparable problems with its clients. Since the seventies American insistence on discussing the Soviet-Cuban presence in southern Africa has brought the reply that the Soviet Union cannot address the matter for another state and that the United States should take up the matter with Havana. Similarly after 1982, when Brezhnev initiated an effort at rapprochement with China, the Soviet leadership punctuated its initiatives with regular statements that rapprochement could not be achieved at the expense of third parties (i.e., Vietnam).[53] And the Soviets probably had no choice but to reject President Reagan's proposal for resolving regional conflicts because, as formulated by the United States, exchanges between the superpowers would begin only after negotiations between Soviet clients and groups leading insurrections against them.[54]

This problem of protecting client relationships existed not only in the regional forums that the Soviets *opposed* but even in those that they *supported*. Soviet policy was committed to a Middle East conference, but Moscow could have gained little from involvement in one unless it could also guarantee its regional clients that their interests would not be sacrificed. Soviet participation that estranged Syria would have become meaningless, for Moscow would then have had no bargaining hand to play. Like that of the United States, its regional role depended on the military and political base provided by its clients.

Constrained in this way—and, to make matters worse, having fewer clients than the United States—the Soviet Union appeared to find it extremely

---

toward the Arab-Israeli Conflict, 1967–1976 (Berkeley: University of California Press, 1977), pp. 213, 223–224.

[53]See Gorbachev's comments at Vladivostok: "Through its suffering, [Vietnam] has earned the right to choose its friends and allies. . . . [T]he normalization of Sino-Vietnam relations . . . is a sovereign matter of the governments and the leadership of both countries." "Vladivostok Speech," p. 35.

[54]Without referring directly to the Reagan proposal, Gorbachev characterized U.S. public statements as "an attempt to cover up real U.S. interference in the affairs of these states and hinder their free and independent development." *Pravda*, November 3, 1985; reprinted in *FBIS Daily Report: Soviet Union*, November 4, 1985, p. J1. The occasion was the visit of Ethiopian leader Mengistu, whose speech in reply included a far more open, heated attack on the U.S. proposal.

difficult to decide *how much* to pay for participation in diplomatic forums on Third World conflicts. Participation was clearly a Soviet objective, but its priority was not clear, less because the United States did not haggle energetically enough about the price of participation than because the USSR was necessarily uncertain what the appropriate price should be. The instability of the Third World can easily make any price seem exorbitant, either because the goods purchased are never delivered or because, with a little patience, they can be acquired free of charge.

Conventional Arms Transfers

On his March 1977 trip to Moscow, Secretary of State Cyrus Vance agreed with Gromyko on the formation of nine U.S.-Soviet "working groups," including one on international arms transfers. At their Vienna summit meeting in 1979, Carter and Brezhnev declared that their representatives would soon meet to consider yet another round of talks on the same subject, and Soviet suggestions to continue these discussions have reappeared from time to time ever since.[55]

The role of arms sales as the opening wedge of Soviet involvement in the Third World in the fifties made it ironic that proposals to regulate such sales by superpower agreement became a staple of the Soviet diplomatic repertoire. The theme, of course, had its propaganda value in driving home the message that the United States—under both the Carter and the Reagan administrations—had turned its back on arms control. Yet although the Soviets doubtless favored these talks and would readily have resumed them had the United States agreed, it was highly doubtful that the Soviet Union would have any greater practical interest than would the United States in reaching a formal or informal agreement on conventional arms transfers. (Moscow might feel that it could circumvent such a regime more easily than Western countries could, but that is another matter.) The income lost from foregone sales would be only part of the reason for Soviet hesitation.[56] A

---

[55]Cyrus Vance, *Hard Choices: Critical Years in America's Foreign Policy* (New York: Simon & Schuster, 1983), p. 54. Vance referred to this issue as "an extremely important area which vitally affects our foreign policy." The Vienna agreement appears in *Public Papers of the Presidents of the United States: Jimmy Carter, 1979* (Washington, D.C.), 2:1085. The idea of mutually agreed restraints on arms transfers had appeared before in U.S. statements. See "U.S. Foreign Policy for the 70's," *Department of State Bulletin*, February 18, 1970, p. 304. Nixon's reference was specifically to the Middle East; even under the Carter administration (which proposed to discuss global restraints) this was the region where superpower agreement had the greatest potential meaning. For a discussion of this issue by participants, see Barry Blechman, Janne Nolan, and Alan Platt, "Negotiated Limitations on Arms Transfers: First-Steps toward Crisis Prevention?" in Alexander George et al., *Managing U.S.-Soviet Rivalry* (Boulder, Colo.: Westview, 1983).

[56]Arms are a larger share of Soviet exports than of any other country's. According to U.S. government estimates, Soviet arms deliveries between 1978 and 1982 totaled $44.5 billion. See the series published annually by the Arms Control and Disarmament Agency, *World Military Expenditures and Arms Transfers*.

more serious obstacle was that such a regime would lack political content. Unless the regime could be negotiated as a purely one-sided restriction on the United States, it would do little to protect the interests of Soviet clients in conflicts with their neighbors or to protect Soviet influence, which has rested so heavily on arms.

A still more important obstacle to agreed limits on arms transfers was, once again, the instability of the Third World. Such understandings are likely to be workable only where some underlying political stability supports them. Such stability made it possible to pursue an almost endless array of initiatives to bolster or improve the European status quo. Limits on arms sales have little or no relevance to Europe, but the deep stability of the political and military stand-off between the blocs makes such concepts more thinkable. (How else can we explain something like the Stockholm Conference on Security and Confidence Building Measures in Europe, a negotiating forum tolerated because thought to be largely meaningless?) They were virtually unthinkable in the turbulence of Third World politics.

Rules of Engagement

Even amid turbulence, of course, certain de facto norms of mutual safety may emerge.[57] East-West military encounters in the Third World have appeared to some observers as confirmation that the status quo is the principal factor in defining for each side what is an acceptable risk.[58] That is, a superpower patron finds it necessary, if at all possible, to prevent a client from suffering a strategic defeat; once the balance has been restored, however, the patron seeks to limit the risks of its own involvement.

The importance of the status quo as a guide to conduct in the Third World suggests a potential parallel to the stability created in Europe by each side's recognition, grudging and hedged though it was, of the other's bloc. Certainly the most dramatic instances of Soviet commitment—sudden insertion of troops into a war zone—have had as their immediate goal the protection of a client threatened with a strategic loss. Soviet actions in the War of Attrition and in the wake of the Lebanon war fit this pattern, as argued earlier, and in each case the mission the Soviets intervened to perform was the same—ground-based air defense. There is, of course, nothing selfless in this self-limitation; nor is there in Europe. It merely reflects each side's assessment that the other is more likely to be drawn in once the tide begins to turn

[57] See Frank Fukuyama, "Escalation in the Middle East and Persian Gulf," in Graham Allison, Albert Carnesale, and Joseph Nye, eds., *Hawks, Doves and Owls* (Cambridge: Harvard University Press, 1985).

[58] E.g., James McConnell, "The Rules of the Game: A Theory on the Practice of Superpower Naval Diplomacy," in McConnell and Bradford Dismukes, eds., *Soviet Naval Diplomacy* (Oxford: Pergamon, 1979). Stephen Kaplan broadens this discussion in *Diplomacy of Power.*

decisively against its client. The patron's warnings gain credibility as the client's trouble deepens.

Did this system of tacit restraint represent a superpower modus vivendi based on support for the status quo? Was it the ground on which the Soviets could build either formal or informal understandings that protected the use of their power and their political role in the Third World?

The answer appears to be no. These "rules of the game" may have governed Soviet and American conduct in the heat of Third World crises, but they did not reflect a shared interest in stabilizing the broader balance of power. One side might respect these rules of the game, strictly speaking, at the same time as it was making broader strategic advances.[59] Although Soviet-Cuban intervention in both Angola and Ethiopia perhaps fit within these tacit rules, each incident also represented an unquestionable victory for the Soviet side and a setback for the United States. In the Yom Kippur War the United States also played by the rules in trying to block a complete Israeli victory over Egypt. Yet the outcome of the war revealed a further erosion of the Soviet position in the Middle East—one that could appropriately be called strategic.[60]

A second reason that the tactical rules of military engagement did not amount to true rules of the game for competition in the Third World was that each side had so many other instruments available for waging the contest. (In Europe, by contrast, the status quo gained acceptance, especially in West Germany, precisely because the West seemed unable to conceive a workable policy for altering it.) The growth of Soviet military reach created new options for Soviet policy, but Moscow has by and large preferred to extend its power in other ways—through the proxy activities of clients such as Cuba, through covert action, through the supply of arms. Where these other instruments were successful, moreover, they created a new status quo to constrain the actions of the superpowers. The same was obviously true of the United States. In the early eighties, policy debate in the United States suggested that covert action against exposed Soviet positions would be increasingly important in the future.

The rules of the game have proved to be completely consistent with major Soviet gains in the past. They may prove equally consistent with Soviet reverses in the future. In any one case the two superpowers comported themselves, and will likely continue to comport themselves, with a keen sense

[59]See Trofimenko, "America, Russia." Having spoken of certain norms that should be respected by both sides in their conduct in the Third World, he added, "it is obvious that elaboration of certain more specific rules of conduct stands little practical chance of success in view of the objective factors leading to revolutionary changes in the Third World, and in light of the conflicting evaluations given to these phenomena by the capitalist and socialist countries."

[60]McConnell, "Rules of the Game," pp. 274–276, emphasizes the common U.S. and Soviet interests served. This is persuasive as long as one focuses on the dangerous tactical situation; the argument becomes less persuasive with a broader strategic focus, which makes clear that one-sided benefits could be derived from an apparently cooperative process.

of the risks involved, but this element of stability has been primarily tactical. It did not guarantee a secure, much less an expanding, base for Soviet action. It did not create strategic stability (in the non-nuclear sense) between East and West.

Conclusion

In the three decades after 1955 Soviet diplomacy and security strategy appeared to aim at creating what might be called a dynamic status quo—that is, a stability that gradually but steadily tilts to Soviet advantage. At least from the mid-sixties onward, this appeared to be the central theme of Soviet efforts in Europe—to create an orderly environment for efforts to gain influence, improve the correlation of forces, and weaken the global presence of the United States. An interest in an advantageous stability also governed Soviet management of its own bloc and even its direct dealings with the United States. Given the rigidity of the Soviet system itself, this drive to institutionalize gains is not surprising.

Similar efforts were seen in Soviet policy beyond Europe, but the Third World was and remains in most respects far less congenial to them. Soviet policy there has clearly enhanced the broader Soviet claim to a kind of dynamic equality with the West—an equality both active and challenging. But critical differences between Europe and the Third World have made for equally critical discontinuities between Soviet efforts in the two arenas. The lack of political stability in the member-states of the Third World and the absence of a more or less clear line of demarcation between the blocs meant that more dramatic Soviet gains were often possible in the Third World (particularly when they could be conducted in the shelter of favorable East-West relations). These gains were, however, individually more precarious, and they did not bring the Soviet Union the broader legitimacy that it won for its objectives and its role in Europe.

2

Soviet Strategy
in the Third World

Francis Fukuyama

It is common for Western observers of the USSR to characterize the Soviets as longtime practitioners of realpolitik in their strategy toward the Third World. Moscow, it is asserted, has been largely indifferent to the ideological character or internal political organization of its friends and allies in the developing world, being ready to work pragmatically with virtually anyone who can further its state interests. Concomitantly, the Soviets are said to believe that their own influence and appeal are based primarily on hard-headed calculations of their ability to supply whatever their clients need, mainly military security but also political and economic aid in the overall competition with the United States.

Although this proposition contains a great deal of truth, both objectively with regard to past Soviet policy and subjectively with regard to the Soviets' self-understanding, it is an inadequate and in many ways misleading description of what the USSR has been up to in the Third World, particularly during the 1970s. Indeed the twin issues of ideology and internal political organization have been central preoccupations of Soviet policy makers, and changing Soviet views on the subject delineate the major phases in the evolution of Moscow's strategy toward the Third World in the postwar period. It is beyond question that Soviet leaders regard foreign policy broadly in the context of power politics; but they have at different times and with varying emphases regarded ideology and political organization as among the most powerful of the tools available to them for furthering their realpolitik ends. In particular, Soviet Third World strategy during the late Brezhnev period was characterized by a pronounced emphasis on one specific form of political organization, the Marxist-Leninist vanguard party (MLVP). From the Soviets' perspective, the MLVP was a far more significant tactical innovation than any of the commonly noted policy instruments that first appeared during the late 1960s and early 1970s, such as Cuban or East German proxy forces, a bluewater navy, tactical transport aviation, and other military power projection capabilities. Indeed, Soviet expectations may have been *too* high: between 1975 and 1985 the MLVP had a highly chequered record, with a growing number of Soviet observers openly acknowledging its problematic character. Much of the future course of Soviet Third World strategy is likely to be shaped by the ongoing Soviet reevaluation of the MLVP.

The Soviet focus on political organization and ideology rather than military force as the basis for global influence and power is not surprising given the history of the Bolshevik movement and the Soviet Communist party (CPSU). The Bolsheviks succeeded in November 1917 not because they were the most numerous or militarily powerful—indeed, they were one of the smaller parties represented in the Petrograd Soviet—but because of their superior discipline and political organization. Lenin's primary legacy to the communist movement was the concept of a small, centralized elite party that could be used as a highly effective means of seizing and consolidating political power. The utility of the concept was demonstrated by the Nazi party in Germany, which came to power by the same organizational principles (invested, of course, with an entirely different ideological content). It is not surprising, then, that the Soviets should have regarded the MLVP as an important route to political power in the Third World.

In this chapter I trace the evolution of the Marxist-Leninist vanguard party in both Soviet theory and Soviet practice. This evolution falls into four broad phases, the first three corresponding roughly to the tenures of the first three postwar general secretaries of the CPSU. Soviet policy appears to have entered a fourth, new phase starting with the accession of Yuriy Andropov to the leadership of the party. The contours of this most recent period are as yet not fully determined and will be influenced heavily by the ongoing succession process at both the top and the middle levels of the Soviet leadership, as well as by the preferences and inclinations of the new general secretary, Mikhail Gorbachev.

The First-Generation "Bourgeois Nationalists"

In the immediate postwar era the Soviet Union placed very heavy emphasis on ideology as a means of determining who were its friends and enemies in the colonial world (most of the Third World still being under European domination at the time). With the deepening of the Cold War and the commencement in 1947 of a period of heightened militancy in the USSR known as the *Zhdanovshchina*, Stalin and other Soviet spokesmen began to adopt an extremely polarized view of international relations, one in which countries not firmly in the socialist camp were written off as belonging to the imperialists. Stalin's definition of the socialist camp included only formal communist parties, and of them only parties directly dependent on and tied to the Soviet Union. He regarded all noncommunist nationalists opposing the colonial system, and leaders of newly independent countries such as Jawaharlal Nehru of India, as no more than bourgeois puppets of the former metropolises; their sham independence masked only a continuing, neo-colonial dependency. Hence the two major initiatives undertaken by the USSR in the Third World between the end of the war and Stalin's death, the attempt to break off parts of northern Iran in 1946 and the encouraging of Kim Il-Sung to unify the Korean peninsula in 1950, involved the use of formal communist parties in countries directly contiguous with the Soviet Union. As these formal parties, with the exception of the Chinese Communists, tended to be very weak, Soviet influence in the Third World was restricted throughout the period.

Khrushchev's Opening to the Third World

Postwar Soviet policy toward the Third World really began with Khrushchev's opening to the so-called bourgeois nationalists,[1] a heterogeneous collection of newly independent states whose leaders eschewed Marxism-Leninism but whose memory of colonial domination led them to adopt strongly anti-imperialist foreign policies. The shift in strategy was evident in policy before its announcement or development in the theoretical literature, through the Soviet Union's approbation for the first Afro-Asian conference of nonaligned states in Bandung, Indonesia, in April 1955; the Czech-Egyptian arms deal of July of that year; and the well-publicized visits by Khrushchev and Bulganin to Afghanistan, Burma, and India in August. The Soviet Union thus inaugurated a prolonged period during which it lent strong support to such leaders as Gamal Abdul Nasser of Egypt, Sukarno of Indonesia, India's Nehru, Kwame Nkrumah in Ghana, and Modibo Keita in Mali.

The theoretical justification for this shift in strategy was initially laid out in Khrushchev's address to the Twentieth Congress of the CPSU in February 1956; then in the reports to the Twenty-first and Twenty-second Congresses in 1959 and 1961 and the meeting of eighty-one communist parties in Moscow in 1960, as well as in a wide variety of books and articles on the Third World. By admitting at the Twentieth Congress that the transition to socialism could be made in a variety of ways, Khrushchev legitimized a range of noncommunist progressive forces in the Third World whose tremendous anti-imperialist potential the Soviet Union had previously not tapped. As Rostislav Ul'yanovskiy, the longtime deputy chief of the Central Committee's International Department, put it, "In contemporary conditions, as the CPSU program decrees, the national bourgeoisie in colonial, former colonial, and dependent countries, detached from imperialist circles, is *objectively* interested in under-

---

[1] I use the terms "bourgeois nationalists," "national bourgeoisie," "national democrats," and "first-generation revolutionary democrats" here interchangeably, following Soviet practice. All of these terms are a subset of the larger category "revolutionary democrats."

taking the basic tasks of anti-imperialist and anti-feudal revolution."[2] This line was not without its theoretical problems. Stalin, after all, had a point when he denounced bourgeois nationalists: by conventional Marxist analysis, societies had to pass through a capitalist period of development, which included the creation of a large and well-organized industrial proletariat, before a socialist revolution became possible. Opportunistic cultivation by the USSR of countries at an essentially feudal level of development for the sake of short-term foreign policy gains might backfire if those countries eventually followed a capitalist path of development.

The response of Khrushchev and the theorists who supported him was to argue that the bourgeois nationalists would not simply serve the ends of Soviet foreign policy in the short run but would eventually evolve ideologically in the direction of orthodox Marxism-Leninism. Interest revived in the idea of the so-called noncapitalist path of development. Proponents of this theory were highly optimistic (excessively so, as they later recognized) about the possibility that underdeveloped states might skip the capitalist phase altogether, making the transition to socialism in a relatively short period of time and ultimately arriving at a full acceptance of orthodox Marxism-Leninism. Khrushchev himself made some extravagant claims about the ideological development of his preferred clients, declaring the United Arab Republic's Nasser a "Hero of the Soviet Union" and congratulating Algeria's Ben Bella on "the determination of the Algerian people to embark upon the socialist path."[3] Khrushchev touted his own successes for essentially political reasons, but his optimism was shared at the time by prominent theorists later known for their skepticism, among them Georgiy Mirskiy and Rostislav Ul'-yanovskiy.[4]

Implementing the Khrushchevian Policy

The implementation of Khrushchev's policy of support for bourgeois nationalists had several characteristic features. In the first place, the Soviets found themselves compelled to conduct relations with established governments on a state-to-state basis and to drop their support for local communist parties and other nonstate opposition forces. This is not to say that the Soviets were indifferent to the fate of their ideological brethren; Khrushchev engaged in open invective with Nasser in 1958 and Iraq's Abdul Karim Kassem in 1959 when the two Arab leaders began persecuting local Communists.

[2]Ul'yanovskiy, "Ekonomicheskaia nezavisimost'—blizhaishaia zadacha osvoboditel'nogo dvizheniia v Azii," *Kommunist* no. 1 (1962), p. 106, my emphases.
[3]Quoted from Robert Legvold, *Soviet Policy in West Africa* (Cambridge: Harvard University Press, 1970), pp. 190–192.
[4]On Mirskiy see ibid., pp. 177–178. On Ul'yanovskiy see his articles, "Nekotoriye voprosy nekapitalisticheskogo razvitiya osvobodivshikhsya stran," *Kommunist* no. 1 (1966); "Birmanskii narod nakhodit pravil'nyi put'," *Kommunist* no. 16 (1964); and "Programma natsional'nogo vozrozhdeniye," *Narody Azii i Afriki* no. 4 (1964).

But while Moscow might have wanted to walk both sides of the street, its bourgeois nationalist clients compelled it to stand by helplessly as local Communists were jailed and in many cases shot.[5]

A second characteristic of Khrushchev-era policy was the Soviets' tendency to cultivate ties with individual nationalist leaders—Nasser, Sukarno, Nkrumah—and to be largely indifferent to the political structures and institutions beneath them. Although the Soviets sought to promote economic development and gave a lot of gratuitous advice to their clients, they did not seek to direct their political development directly by, for instance, helping them create cohesive party organizations or by taking control of coercive mechanisms such as the internal security forces.[6] Indeed, they tended to be indifferent to the client's internal ideological character as long as the client provided a modicum of cooperation on foreign policy issues, and they were forced to show at least outward respect for a variety of syncretic nationalist doctrines, including African socialism, pan-Arabism, and in later years Islamic Marxism.

The third characteristic of the Khrushchev period was its heavy reliance on arms transfers and (secondarily) economic assistance as sources of leverage. In arms transfers the Soviet Union proved to be fully competitive with the United States in the Third World, supplying large quantities of cheap and technologically up-to-date weapons from its own enormous inventories.[7] Economic aid, while relatively large in dollar volume, tended to be concentrated in a small number of high-visibility development projects in the United Arab Republic (UAR), Afghanistan, and India. Apart from political support during crises, the Soviet Union had little to offer its Third World clients in the way of more direct military support and intervention.

The Second-generation Marxist-Leninists

The Problematic Character of Bourgeois Nationalism

There is no question that Khrushchev's shift of Soviet policy away from orthodox Communists toward bourgeois nationalists vastly increased Soviet

[5]Although the Soviets have chosen to work through existing states, they have consistently made the fate of local communist parties an issue in their relations with noncommunist clients. The Soviets warmly approved the outcomes in Syria and South Yemen, where orthodox communist parties were accepted into fronts with ruling nationalist parties, and bitterly attacked the Iraqi Ba'ath party for persecuting Communists in 1977.

[6]Ul'yanovskiy, for example, argued in 1966 that in some cases it was possible for the broad masses to choose "the path of noncapitalist development, beginning the movement toward socialism *in the absence of* proletarian dictatorship and an organized vanguard party." "Nekotorye voprosy nekapitalisticheskogo razvitiia osvobodivshikhsia stran," *Kommunist* no. 1 (1966).

[7]The Soviets were able to rebuild the inventories of their Arab clients in a matter of months, if not weeks, following the Middle East wars of 1956, 1967, 1973, and 1982.

influence and prestige in the Third World. From a position of virtual isolation under Stalin, by the mid-1960s the Soviets had major footholds in the Middle East, Africa, South Asia, the Far East, and on the island of Cuba. This broadening of influence had a concrete military payoff as well, undermining U.S. positions of strength in, for example, the Middle East's northern tier and providing the Soviet Navy with anchorages or facilities in Egypt, Syria, and Somalia.

But there were critical weaknesses in the Khrushchevite policy of support for bourgeois nationalists as well. First, many of Moscow's Khrushchev-era allies proved highly unstable and vulnerable to sudden shifts in political fortunes. Soviet clients were overthrown in military coups in Indonesia and Algeria (1965), Ghana (1966), and Mali (1968). As the rule of many of these clients tended to be highly personalistic, the removal or defection of a single leader undermined the entire Soviet position in the country concerned.

Second, even when those clients stayed in power, they tended to be highly unpredictable and often uncooperative with Soviet aims. It would be impossible to catalogue all the instances of a Soviet client acting contrary to Moscow's wishes; every study of Soviet dealings with particular countries and regions lists several. In high-stakes areas such as the Middle East and South Asia, the Soviets found themselves getting dragged into local conflicts that involved the risk of confrontation with the United States. In other cases Soviet Third World allies tried deliberately to flaunt their independence from Moscow, as when the Syrians refused for over ten years to conclude a friendship and cooperation treaty, or when the Iraqis signed an accord with the Shah of Iran in 1975 and turned increasingly to France for arms. With the sole exception of Cuba, not a single bourgeois nationalist ally of the Khrushchev era adopted orthodox Marxism-Leninism as its governing ideology. The worst case, from the Soviet standpoint, was Egypt, the centerpiece of Soviet Third World policy in the fifties and sixties and the recipient of a total of over $4 billion in aid, which between 1972 and 1976 defected altogether to the Western camp.

Third, arms transfers and economic aid proved to be an extremely poor source of leverage over intractable clients, as the United States has discovered in its dealings with such allies as Turkey and Israel. Soviet efforts to force Nasser and then Anwar Sadat into a negotiated solution of the Arab-Israeli dispute by withholding arms deliveries backfired; when Sadat expelled Soviet advisers from Egypt in July 1972, Moscow was compelled to resume shipments and in effect give the go-ahead for the October 1973 war to retain a position there. In other cases, Syria, for instance, the Soviets found themselves forced to provide ever greater quantities of ever more sophisticated weapons simply to stay in their clients' good graces; their provision of SA-5 air-defense missiles to Syria after the 1982 Lebanon War is only the most recent example of this pattern.

The Rise of the MLVP: Theoretical Development

Soviet disillusionment with bourgeois nationalist clients began to appear in the mid-1960s. Indeed, some evidence suggests that Khrushchev's colleagues, including Mikhail Suslov, Boris Ponomarev, and Aleksei Rumyantsev, were dubious about his grandiose claims on behalf of favored Third World clients while Khrushchev was still first secretary.[8] Policy toward the Third World was evidently one of the charges held against Khrushchev when he was deposed in 1964, and following his ouster an internal policy review held in high Kremlin circles decided to provide support somewhat more selectively. As the decade progressed, Khrushchev-era optimism about the likelihood of quick transition to socialism along the noncapitalist path of development gave way to increasing skepticism about the reliability of noncommunist Third World states. Looking back on the period of the late 1950s and early 1960s in 1984, Ul'yanovskiy noted that "excessively optimistic researchers wanted to see in the personalities of Nasser or Ben Bella a Chernyshevskiy who would change into a Plekhanov. Occasionally wishes were presented as reality."[9] The particular problem with these Khrushchev-era clients was their insufficient institutionalization of political power and their consequent inability to make permanent revolutionary change: "in a number of countries (Egypt, Mali, Sudan, Zaire, Ghana) [progressive forces] failed to create a revolutionary-democratic organization which would ensure the reliability of truly revolutionary-democratic accomplishments . . . [relying instead] on a national leader who, in turn, relied on the army, the security organ, his clan or his tribe."[10] As another academic commentator noted, "the problem of the necessity of changing a broad-scale organization into a vanguard organization was particularly critical after revolutionary democrats, first in 1966 in Ghana and then in 1967 in Mali, were removed from power."[11]

In the late 1960s and early 1970s Soviet theoreticians began developing a twofold solution to the weaknesses that came to be closely associated with the late Brezhnev period. The first aspect was the promotion of parties or national liberation movements that explicitly based themselves on Marxist-Leninist ideology;[12] second was the encouragement of these groups to transform themselves into formal vanguard parties once they came into power. The first aspect of the solution was in some sense a return to Stalin's preference for

---

[8]Legvold, *Soviet Policy in West Africa*, pp. 198–201.

[9]Ul'yanovskiy, "O natsional'noy i revolyutsionnoy demokratii: puty evolyutsii," *Narody Azii i Afriki* no. 2 (March–April 1984). This statement is somewhat ironic because Ul'yanovskiy shared much of this optimism when it was fashionable.

[10]Ibid., p. 14.

[11]Yuriy N. Gavrilov, "Problems of the Formation of Vanguard Parties in Countries of Socialist Orientation," *Narody Azii i Afriki* no. 6 (1980) (Joint Publications Research Service [JPRS] J-8 IIII), p. 3.

[12]Or scientific socialism; the terms, synonymous for Soviet authors, are used interchangeably here.

orthodox communist parties, though in its Brezhnev-era incarnation this principle of selectivity was applied much less rigidly.[13] Soviet theoreticians recognized that, all things being equal, a self-proclaimed Marxist-Leninist state would be more likely to cooperate with the Soviet bloc reliably than, say, an African socialist, pan-Arab nationalist, or Islamic Marxist one, no matter how left-wing their doctrines (Karen Brutents was an important dissenting voice, however, as noted below). The heterodox ideologies tolerated by Khrushchev were nationalist at the core and ultimately led to an unwillingness on the part of the countries that espoused them to cooperate fully with Soviet foreign policy. Unadulterated scientific socialism, by contrast, is an explicitly internationalist doctrine. As one author notes, the second generation of self-proclaimed Marxist-Leninists "differs from the revolutionary-democrats of the 1960's (or national democracy) in that it more consistently speaks out from antiimperialist and anticapitalist positions, cooperates with the world communist movement and the world socialist system, and relies on the working masses."[14] Or as Ul'yanovskiy put it, "in the practical aspect [groups or parties oriented toward scientific socialism] enhance cooperation with the socialist countries to a new level and deliberately promote the expansion of such cooperation. They do not mistrust the socialist commonwealth or fear a 'communist penetration.' "[15]

It should be noted that throughout the 1970s the Soviets themselves never took at face value the claims of the second-generation states to have actually adopted Marxism-Leninism (except for Cuba and Vietnam, which were classified as genuinely "socialist"). Together with a couple of non-Marxist-Leninist regimes, such as in Algeria and Tanzania, the second generation was lumped together as "socialist-oriented" or "revolutionary democratic" states[16] and said to be "approaching the positions of Marxism-Leninism." Our use of "Marxist-Leninist vanguard party" is therefore somewhat misleading, as it refers to the client's rather than the Soviets' perception. As one Soviet author put it, the most accurate description would be the "vanguard revolutionary-democratic worker party," to indicate that it is "not yet a communist party."[17] Although these distinctions may seem meaningless from a

[13]In contrast to Stalin, the Soviets in the 1970s continued to support first-generation bourgeois nationalists in such countries as Syria, India, Iraq, and Libya, where there was no obvious Marxist-Leninist alternative. The Soviets today do not regard any of the new regimes that emerged during the 1970s as genuine socialist states or their ruling parties as orthodox communist ones (with the exception of Cuba and Vietnam), and for this reason it is not clear than Stalin would have supported them.

[14]Yu V. Irkhin, "Formation of the Vanguard Parties of the Working People in Socialist-Oriented Countries," *Nauchnyy Kommunizm* no. 1 (January–February 1985) (JPRS-UPS-85-059, July 30, 1985), p. 9.

[15]Ul'yanovskiy, "O natsional'noy i revolyutsionnoy demokratii," p. 16.

[16]These two terms are synonymous in Soviet parlance, though Brutents's use of "revolutionary democrat" is considerably more expansive than that of most Soviet writers.

[17]Irkhin, "Formation of the Vanguard Parties," p. 10.

noncommunist perspective, they eventually provided the basis for a serious Soviet critique of the second-generation states.

The second and perhaps more important aspect of the solution lay in the sphere of political organization. As one Soviet author put it, "in conditions of a backward multisectoral country . . . no group of revolutionaries, however sincere and consistent, can insure the socialist orientation of the bulk of the population and the work of the entire state apparatus without the presence of a vanguard revolutionary party of fellow-thinkers."[18] Particularly during the 1970s, there was a great upsurge in Soviet writings on vanguard parties and their importance to the revolutionary development of Third World states.[19] Vanguard parties were seen as a means of stabilizing revolutionary power, and consequently pro-Soviet orientation, by providing the local regime with a firm organizational base, "a well-organized party uniting representatives of the working people, supporters of the socialist road, a party free of pro-bourgeois and anti-socialist elements, a party guided by a progressive ideology."[20] A vanguard party would institutionalize the socialist orientation and permit it to survive the whims or the passing of individual Third World leaders like a Nasser or a Sukarno, and it would provide the Soviets with multiple points of entry as an alternative to the single leader at the top. Vanguard parties were seen as one way to make local revolutions in some sense irreversible and to avoid the "voluntarism" of the Khrushchev generation of bourgeois nationalists.[21]

Centralization of power in the hands of a reliable political organization was particularly important in view of Moscow's declining ability to assist and control the economic development of its client states. As Elizabeth Valkenier and others have noted, Soviet development economists in the 1970s increasingly concluded that the traditional socialist formula for economic development, calling for rapid nationalization of foreign and private property and isolation of the local economy from the world capitalist economic system, was inadequate; developing countries would actually benefit from a policy of "gradual" transition to socialism similar to those followed during

---

[18] Nodari Simoniya, "The Present Stage of the Liberation Struggle," *Asia and Africa Today* no. 3 (May–June 1981), p. 4.

[19] There is no end to Soviet writings on the importance of Marxist-Leninist vanguard parties. For a representative sample in addition to the sources quoted, see P. Manuchka, "The CPSU and Revolutionary-Democratic Parties," *Socialism: Theory and Practice*, October 10, 1976; G. I. Shitarev, "Nekotorye problemy evolyutsii revolyutsionno-demokra ticheskoy organizatsii v napravlenii partii-avangarda," *Narody Azii i Afriki* no. 2 (1976); A. S. Kaufman, "Strategiya i taktika marksistsko-leninskikh partiy v osvobodiv-shikhsya stranakh," *Rabochiy Klass i Sovremenny Mir* no. 3 (May–June 1984); as well as Vadim Zagladin, ed., *The World Communist Movement* (JPRS UPS-84-034-L, August 29, 1984). For further discussion see also David Albright, "Vanguard Parties in the Third World," in Walter Laqueur, ed., *The Pattern of Soviet Conduct in the Third World* (New York: Praeger, 1983), pp. 208–225.

[20] Alexei Kiva, "Revolutionary-Democratic Parties: Some Trends of Development," *Asia and Africa Today* no. 4 (1978), pp. 43–44.

[21] See Gavrilov, "Problems of the Formation"; V. F. Li, ed., *Partii i revolyutsionnyy protsess v stranakh Azii i Afriki: Sbornik Statei* (Moscow: Nauka, 1983); and Ul'yanovskiy, "O natsional'noy i revolyutsionnoy demokratii."

the period of the New Economic Policy (NEP) in the USSR during the 1920s.[22] Whatever the Soviet leadership thought of this argument on its merits, the notion provided a convenient justification for the Kremlin's increasing reluctance to foot the bill for large-scale economic development. But the retention of a private sector and continuing integration with Western economies poses potentially grave dangers for a state's future political orientation unless there is a reliable party in charge. As Boris Ponomarev put it, "the experience of many socialist oriented countries shows that a useful role can be played by private enterprise—*with corresponding supervision by the state.*"[23] Existence of a strong vanguard party potentially allows Moscow to have its cake and eat it too, with the West assisting the economic development of Marxist-Leninist states that remain in political terms closely aligned with the USSR.

The MLVP in Practice

In a remarkable convergence between theory and practice, the Soviet Union undertook the promotion of MLVPs during its intense period of Third World activism that began in the early-to-mid 1970s. Soviet writers themselves are quite explicit about the change that resulted in their client base and speak of a second generation of states very different from those of the Khrushchev era. This shift is described in the 1984 edition of the *World Communist Movement*, a handbook of official Soviet positions concerning the worldwide revolutionary process edited by Ponomarev's first deputy in the International Department, Vadim Zagladin. The section on the Third World states:

> It is possible today to speak of two groups of countries of a socialist orientation and of a *second generation of revolutionary democrats, who are closer to scientific socialism.* The distinctiveness of the new group of countries of a socialist orientation (Angola, Ethiopia, Afghanistan, Kampuchea, the PDRY [People's Democratic Republic of Yemen], and others) is that they have to build the economy virtually from scratch, and that a working class is springing up in them together with industry. *The political regimes of this group of countries are distinguished by great clarity of class positions. A process in which new revolutionary parties are coming into being, parties which at their congresses have declared their adoption of Marxist-Leninist ideology, is under way there. It is these parties which are heading the revolutionary development.*[24]

---

[22]See particularly Elizabeth Valkenier, *The Soviet Union and the Third World: An Economic Bind* (New York: Praeger, 1983), and Jerry Hough, *The Struggle for the Third World* (Washington: Brookings, 1986).

[23]Boris Ponomarev, *Information Bulletin* nos. 23–24 (1980), p. 68, my emphases.

[24]Zagladin, *The World Communist Movement*, p. 363, my emphases. The section on the Third World was written by S. I. Semenov. Division of Third World clients into two generations is quite common in Soviet writings; for example, Ul'yanovskiy (O natsional'noy i revolyutsionnoy demokratti," p. 13) refers to a "second echelon" of states advancing to the proscenium "approximately during the mid-1970s." See also Georgiy Kim, "National Liberation Movement: Topical Problems," *International Affairs* no. 10 (September 1984), p. 48.

The list of second-generation Marxist-Leninist clients is actually longer than the one Zagladin gives; between 1964 and 1984 the number of regimes proclaiming scientific socialism as their guiding ideology climbed from three (North Korea, North Vietnam, and Cuba) to sixteen (those three plus Angola, Mozambique, Ethiopia, the PDRY, Afghanistan, Nicaragua, Laos, Kampuchea, Madagascar, Guinea-Bissau, Cape Verde, Benin, and the People's Republic of the Congo).[25] In addition, Marxist-Leninists were in power in Grenada until the American invasion in October 1983, and there were reports of a Communist coup attempt in Iraq in 1977. Beyond new regimes brought to power, the Soviets also provided substantial support to two of their existing Marxist-Leninist allies, Cuba and Vietnam. Moscow's underwriting of their expansionist foreign policies led to a rapid growth in allotments of military and economic assistance, to the point where Cuba was receiving an annual subsidy on the order of $5 billion and Vietnam $1 billion. Although Soviet authors tend to treat this sudden proliferation of Marxist-Leninist regimes as an autonomous sociopolitical phenomenon, the truth of the matter is that the USSR and its socialist allies—particularly Cuba and East Germany—helped a number of them come to power (as in the case of the MPLA in Angola) or stay in power once there (as in Ethiopia, Afghanistan, Mozambique, and Nicaragua).

A case could be made for the Soviet point of view, that is, that Moscow acquired self-proclaimed Marxist-Leninist clients simply as the result of the Soviet habit of responding to available opportunities rather than as the consequence of a deliberate policy choice. But such an argument ignores the real margin of choice available. In Angola, for example, the Soviets could have waited for the three-way civil war between the MPLA, UNITA, and the FNLA to resolve itself and then cultivate ties with the winner—such would have been the *typical* policy of an earlier decade.[26] Similarly, the Soviets had no need to intervene massively on behalf of the Ethiopian Dergue when it was attacked by Somalia in 1977 were it not for the apparent concern for the character of the regime in Addis Ababa and the quality of their relations with it. Even if the Dergue had fallen, the Soviets would likely have maintained some foothold in Ethiopia, and moreover, they would not have jeopardized their position in Somalia.

The Soviets and their allies did not, of course, abandon their ties with the earlier generation of non-Marxist clients such as Syria, Libya, or India. The Soviets had invested considerable prestige in these countries, which were in any case highly important to Moscow by virtue of their size, wealth, or

---

[25]This trend was noted in Donald Zagoria, "Into the Breach: New Soviet Alliances in the Third World," *Foreign Affairs*, Spring 1979. See also my "A New Soviet Strategy," *Commentary*, October 1979.

[26]Jonas Savimbi's current ties with the West do not imply that he would have been unwilling to accept Soviet patronage in 1975 had he emerged on top.

geostrategic position. Being relatively stable states, they did not give the Soviets the option of encouraging alternative, Marxist-Leninist leaderships. Nonetheless, where the Soviets had a choice, their behavior clearly indicated a preference for national liberation organizations or parties proclaiming adherence to orthodox scientific socialism.

With the exception of the People's Democratic Party of Afghanistan (PDPA), none of the second-generation clients began their existence as orthodox communist parties but evolved out of a variety of national liberation fronts or military juntas that only later proclaimed their adherence to Marxism-Leninism. In these cases the Soviets then implemented the second half of their theoretical solution: to encourage these groups, once in power, to reorganize themselves as formal Leninist vanguard parties, which is what happened in Mozambique (February 1977), Angola (December 1977), the PDRY (October 1978), and Ethiopia (September 1984). Soviet pressure to form a vanguard party was most evident in Ethiopia, where the ruling Dergue formed the Committee for Organizing the Party of the Working People of Ethiopia in 1979, largely to satisfy Soviet demands, prior to the actual establishment of the Workers' Party of Ethiopia. Indeed, there is evidence that Mengistu Haile Mariam and the other military leaders of Ethiopia understood full well the Soviet motives in pressing for a vanguard party and resisted the idea for as long as they did precisely to avoid giving Moscow an extra source of leverage.[27] Soviet writers have criticized the Sandinista National Liberation Front (FSLN) in Nicaragua for not having a vanguard party organization; the fact that it has not yet adopted such an organization has led to a lower ranking for Nicaragua in Soviet priorities among Third World clients.

In contrast to the somewhat distant state-to-state relationships maintained with first-generation bourgeois nationalists, promotion of MLVPs requires a much greater willingness by the Soviets to interfere in the internal affairs of their clients. This is so because Moscow has to be concerned not only with a second-generation client's foreign policy but with its domestic character as well. Interference has involved not only military intervention to ensure the client's initial coming to power—Marxist-Leninist groups being, by and large, more narrowly based than their bourgeois nationalist counterparts and therefore less likely to do so on their own—but also active participation in what might be called "Leninist state-building," that is, the creation of powerful, centralized institutions to help consolidate the regime's control.[28] Beyond simple exhortations to establish vanguard parties, the Soviets have helped their clients in many concrete ways, through the training of party cadres in party-organizational work, establishment of internal security

[27]See Paul Henze, "Communism in Ethiopia," *Problems of Communism* 30, no. 3 (1981).
[28]See Alex Alexiev, *The New Soviet Strategy in the Third World*, N-1995-AF (Santa Monica: Rand Corporation, June 1983).

organs, seizure and control of at least the "commanding heights" of the economy, purging of unreliable elements, agitational and propaganda activities, and so forth.

Moscow's socialist allies have been particularly important to the building of Leninist states because they bring to bear special capabilities that conveniently complement those of the Soviets themselves. Many aspects of the Cuban role are well-known and do not need to be detailed here. The Cubans have provided military manpower (in what is in most Third World contexts substantial amounts) for direct intervention on behalf of clients, being less provocative to the United States and other Western countries than Soviet troops and at the same time more acceptable to Third World audiences.[29] But in addition to their military role, the Cubans have provided a variety of other services designed to preserve the *character* of a particular regime and to encourage it to develop along Marxist-Leninist lines. Following the military coups in Algeria in 1965 and Ghana in 1966, Cuban forces began concentrating on the problem of regime security. They served in the presidential guards of Alphonse Massamba-Débat in the People's Republic of the Congo and Sékou Touré in Guinea-Conakry and were credited with having suppressed a Congolese army revolt in June 1966.[30] The Cuban General Directorate of Intelligence was reorganized by the KGB in 1971 and is reportedly controlled to a large degree by Soviet intelligence officials. The two intelligence services (together with the East Germans) collaborate extensively in Latin America and Africa, helping keep vulnerable client regimes in power. The Cubans also assisted in the establishment of popular militias in Sierra Leone, Equatorial Guinea, and the PDRY, providing the regime with a counterweight should the regular military seek to stage a coup. Other Leninist state-building activities are more mundane, among them the training of party cadres, the reception of innumerable party delegations in Havana, and the indoctrination of some 10,000 Angolan children on the Isle of Youth off the southern coast of Cuba.

Moscow's other major proxy, the East Germans, specialize in two areas: internal security and party-organizational work. Though less visible than the Cubans, the East Germans in providing these services are critical to the building of MLVPs. The East German Ministerium für Staatsicherheit has played a key role in organizing the security apparatus in several states: the MPLA's Department of Information and Security, the National Service for Popular Security in Mozambique, the General Directorate of State Security in Nicaragua, the Libyan Mukhabarat, and other organizations in Ethiopia,

---

[29]The Cubans also serve as Moscow's eyes and ears, being more attuned to Third World developments and readier to recognize revolutionary opportunities than the Soviets. The Cubans, for example, understood the potential of the Sandinistas in Nicaragua long before the Soviets and were instrumental in uniting the three FSLN tendencies prior to the fall of Somoza in 1979.

[30]Brian Crozier, "The Soviet Satellitization of Cuba," *Conflict Studies* no. 35 (May 1973), pp. 14–16, and "The Surrogate Forces of the Soviet Union," *Conflict Studies* no. 92 (1978), p. 9.

the PDRY, Guinea-Bissau, São Tomé, and Grenada.[31] Penetration of client security services provides the Soviets with not only up-to-date intelligence but also a means of removing a recalcitrant or deviationist client. In the PDRY the East Germans built up the internal security apparatus under the leadership of Muhsin al-Sharjabi, which was instrumental in helping oust Rubai Ali when he appeared to be moving the country out of the socialist camp in June 1978.[32] Moscow's ability to control unreliable clients through direct police methods should be contrasted to the Soviet lack of options when expelled from Egypt in 1972. East Germans have served in the personal bodyguards protecting Ethiopia's Mengistu, Mozambique's Samsra Machel, and Libya's Muamar Qadhdhafi.[33] The East Germans have also been very active in party-organizational matters. They have established schools for the training of party cadres in Mozambique and the PDRY (the latter school had produced more than 10,000 graduates by 1979). Moreover, large numbers of Third World Communists have been brought to Germany for study, and the East Germans have assisted in such esoteric tasks as the writing of South Yemen's lengthy socialist constitution. These specialized services come in addition to more mundane operations such as military training and economic assistance.

Second Thoughts on MLVPs

In practice, promotion of MLVPs has been a mixed blessing. On the one hand, such parties indeed cooperated closely with the Soviet bloc, signing friendship and cooperation treaties with Moscow, permitting relatively free air and naval access to the Soviet military, supporting sympathetic national liberation movements and participating in the socialist "collective security system," voting with the USSR in the United Nations, and so forth. On the other hand, these regimes have tended to be weak and narrowly based, lacking the broad nationalist legitimacy of the first generation of clients and heavily dependent on Soviet bloc support for their initial rise to power or their ability to remain in place, or both. As a result, Angola, Mozambique, Afghanistan, Nicaragua, Kampuchea, Ethiopia, and South Yemen have all faced indigenous opposition guerrilla movements, forcing the Soviets to assist in costly counterinsurgency wars.[34] The Soviet political leadership has

[31]Crozier, "Surrogate Forces," pp. 9–10, and Melvin Croan, "A New Afrika Korps?" *Washington Quarterly* 3, no. 1 (Winter 1980), p. 31.

[32]For more on South Yemeni–East German relations, see Laurie Mylroie, *Politics and the Soviet Presence in the People's Democratic Republic of Yemen: Internal Vulnerabilities and Regional Challenges*, N-2052-AF (Santa Monica: RAND Corporation, December 1983), pp. 12–29.

[33]Qadhdhafi's personal bodyguard over the past few years has been trained by the East Germans and is responsible for saving the Libyan leader's life on at least two occasions. *L'Expres*, November 4–10, 1983, pp. 104–105.

[34]See Francis Fukuyama, "The New Marxist-Leninist States and Internal Conflict in the Third World," in Uri Ra'anan et al., *Third World Marxist-Leninist Regimes: Strengths, Vulnerabilities, and U.S. Policy* (Cambridge, Mass.: Institute for Foreign Policy Analysis, 1985).

demonstrated a growing awareness of the problematic character of their recent achievements. Brezhnev's report to the Twenty-sixth Congress of the CPSU, delivered in March 1981, had a distinctly more sober tone than the one he had presented to the Twenty-fifth Congress in 1976. Although he noted in 1981 an increase in the number of countries having chosen the socialist orientation, he added that "the development of these countries along the progressive path does not, of course, proceed uniformly" but is "taking place in complex conditions." As a whole, "the period after the Twenty-fifth Congress was not an easy one. There were many difficulties both in the economic development of the country and in the international situation."[35]

Largely as a result of the second generation's mixed record, Soviet theorists, as well as important members of the Soviet leadership, began to take another look at the political development strategies undertaken during the Brezhnev years and to posit other courses of action. Most important was a rethinking of the Marxist-Leninist vanguard party. Soviet writers (with some important exceptions) did not question the concept of the MLVP itself as the theoretically ideal form of political organization for Third World states but rather expressed increasing skepticism that existing revolutionary democratic groups could make a successful transition to true Marxist-Leninist vanguard parties or that those groups which already had formally made the transition had done so in practice. Moreover, countries of the second generation started out from an even lower level of political and economic development than their predecessors, making yet more complicated the bypassing of the capitalist stage. Many of the criticisms leveled by Soviet authors were reminiscent of those expressed during the 1960s and early 1970s, only this time their targets were not the bourgeois nationalists but the new, self-proclaimed Marxist-Leninists.

Typical of the skepticism about Third World MLVPs expressed in the early 1980s is an article by Nodari Simoniya, a section head at the Oriental Institute in Moscow. Simoniya notes five conditions that must be met before countries can successfully make the transition to full-fledged socialist soceites, including the eschewing of "leftism" and a solution to national-ethnic problems, and implies that few if any of Moscow's Third World allies have managed to meet them. He openly criticizes the PDPA in Afghanistan, where "a part of the former Afghan leadership tried without justification to accelerate social transformations and to raise them immediately to the level of the people's democratic revolution." While he underlines the importance of vanguard parties, he takes a slap at such countries as Angola and Mozambique by noting that the fact that they created formal parties "does not mean, of course, that such parties immediately become communist ones."[36]

[35]*Dvadtsat' Shestoi S'ezd Kommunisticheskoy Partii Sovetskogo Soyuza, 23 fevrala–3 marta 1981 goda. Stenograficheskii otchet*, p. 29.
[36]Nodari Simoniya, "The Present Stage of the Liberation Struggle," *Asia and Africa Today* no. 3 (1981).

Similar warnings about the dangers of mistaking declarative socialism for the real thing can be found in the writings of a wide variety of Soviet authors. In a collection of essays by prominent Soviet experts on the Third World published in 1982, a Soviet reviewer notes, "the authors underscore the complex and contradictory nature of [the stage of socialist orientation] and warn about the dangers of attempts to 'accelerate it . . . into socialist ones, to identify it with socialist reconstruction and to thereby view national democrats as confirmed adherents of scientific socialism.' "[37] As noted previously, Soviet authors have always been careful to distinguish between radical socialist-oriented countries, including those with formal vanguard parties, and genuine socialist countries.[38] As one writer put it: "Does the designation of the socialist-oriented states as 'communist' or even 'socialist' really correspond to the truth? Of course not. The leaders of Socialist Ethiopia, the only socialist-oriented country in Africa where the official state name contains the word 'socialist,' have repeatedly noted that it is not an appraisal of the existing social and political order but a goal sought by the people."[39]

Reservations about MLVPs have been expressed by the two Central Committee International Department deputies responsible for the Third World, Rostislav Ul'yanovskiy and Karen Brutents. The former, in two articles published in 1984, notes that there is no reason to think that the changes going on in Angola, Mozambique, or the PDRY should resemble the positive example of Vietnam, where the transition to socialism was led by an orthodox communist party.[40] Indeed, observation of these cases suggests that "the idea of advancing toward socialism without a firm communist vanguard . . . is today no less topical than it was twenty years ago." "Declarative radicalism" does not automatically produce a transition to socialism; indeed, it may exacerbate the situation by triggering sharp internal opposition to the regime. The shortcomings of the new MLVPs lie precisely in their poor party-organizational work: they have not laid the groundwork for socialism by securing mass support, with the result that in many of these countries they have incurred the hostility of the majority. Mongolia and some of the central Asian

[37] M. M. Avsenev, review of *Sotsialisticheskaya orientatsiya osvobodivshikhsya stran: Nekotoryye voprosy teorii i praktiki*, by Karen Brutents, Anatoliy Gromyko, Alexei Kiva, G. F. Kim, G. I. Mirskiy, Yevgeniy Primakov, V. F. Stanis, Gleb Starushenko, G. V. Smirnov, and Rostislav Ul'yanovskiy, in *Narody Azii i Afriki* no. 5 (October 1984), p. 184.

[38] Kiva, p. 46, "Revolutionary-Democratic Parties," is careful to distinguish between "vanguard revolutionary democratic parties and a party of the proletarian vanguard (i.e., a genuine Communist party)"; formation of the vanguard party is a step, but only a step, toward a true Marxist-Leninist party.

[39] Irkhin "Formation of the Vanguard Parties," p. 11. Irkhin goes on to say: "Also unscientific is the attempt to declare that the vanguard worker parties are communist." Irkhin's view of Ethiopia is somewhat disingenuous, as Mengistu Haile Miriam has on occasion referred to himself as "the Communist leader." See Henze, "Communism in Ethiopia."

[40] R. Ul'yanovskiy, "O revolyutsionnoy demokratii, ee gosudarstve i politicheskoy sisteme," *Voprosy Filosofi* no. 4 (April 1984), pp. 27–28.

republics are cited as more appropriate models for the Third World; there the transition to socialism was much more gradual and cautious than in European Russia, owing to the backwardness of socioeconomic systems at the time of the revolution.[41] Like Simoniya, Ul'yanovskiy criticizes the Afghan Communists explicitly: "Four or five years ago some leftist leaders in Afghanistan had proclaimed the existence of a proletarian dictatorship in a country under feudalism, believing that this assertion was an important contribution to scientific socialism."[42]

Skepticism about the viability of MLVPs is even more pronounced in the case of Karen Brutents, who is twenty years younger than the octogenarian Ul'yanovskiy and likely to inherit overall responsibility for the Third World in the Central Committee when the latter passes from the scene. Brutents does not criticize the MLVPs explicitly but rather damns them with faint praise and shows a considerably greater interest in the non-Marxist parts of the Third World. A survey of his writings over the past twenty-five years indicates that he was consistently skeptical about the ability of Third World states to make a successful transition to socialism and never seems to have been persuaded that the MLVP would be a meaningful alternative to the first-generation bourgeois nationalists. Indeed, it may be fair to characterize him as a neo-Khrushchevite in his emphasis on the foreign policy potential of the noncommunist or non-Marxist states of the Third World, but he lacks Khrushchev's illusions about the likelihood of eventual conversion to orthodox communism.[43] In a February 1982 *Pravda* article, for example, Brutents makes a nod toward the socialist-oriented countries but quickly notes that under modern conditions "the position and role of a country in the world arena are determined not only by the socioeconomic forms which hold sway" (that is, by whether or not the regime is Marxist), but by other factors as well, particularly its attitude toward imperialism.[44] Brutent's focus then shifts quickly to "the solid base for the Soviet Union's cooperation with those liberated countries where capitalist relations are developing but which pursue a policy of defending and strengthening national sovereignty in politics and economics." Rather than attack the shortcomings of these capitalist-oriented

[41]Ul'yanovskiy (ibid., pp. 28–29) notes that the Bukhara and Khorezm Soviet people's republics were not admitted into the USSR upon its foundation in 1922 because there is no "automaticity" in the transition from revolutionary-democratic to socialist state power.

[42]Ul'yanovskiy, "O natsional'noy i revolyutsionnoy demokratii," p. 19. Note that this criticism applies to the Percham faction headed by Babrak Karmal as much as it does to the Khalq faction of Hafizullah Amin, which since the Soviet invasion has been attacked in the Soviet press quite regularly.

[43]In contrast to Ul'yanovskiy, Brutents has never written directly on the socialist-oriented states, concerning himself instead in recent years with such varied topics as the Falklands crisis and the nonaligned movement. See "Konflikt v yuzhnoy atlantike: nekotorye posledstviya i uroki," *SShA: Ekonimika, Politika, Ideologiya* no. 11 (November 1982), and "Dvizheniye neprisoedineniya v sovremennom mire," *MEiMO* no. 5 (1984).

[44]Karen Brutents, "Sovetskiy Soyuz i osvobodivshiesya strany: voprosy teorii," *Pravda*, February 2, 1982.

countries, he takes note of the many "contradictions" that exist between them and the imperialist states. He points to the Soviet Union's growing cooperation with such countries as India, Brazil, and Mexico, suggesting that they and not the socialist-oriented states ruled by MLVPs will provide the more fertile ground for Soviet policy. Brutents takes these themes even further in a 1984 article in which he defends the anti-imperialist posture and credentials of several capitalist-oriented Third World states.[45] He again points out the contraditions that exist between these countries and imperialism, and he states that "as long as it does not reach the monopolistic stage, even the development of capitalist relations in the liberated countries does not nullify [these contradictions] and does not directly contribute to consolidating the positions of imperialism." In 1984 he gave a highly positive evaluation of the 1955 Bandung nonaligned countries' conference, inspiration for Khrushchev's move away from a narrow emphasis on communist parties.[46]

The final and in some ways most important source of skepticism about the MLVP came from Secretary General Yuriy Andropov himself, who in his June 1983 Plenum speech echoed the line of many Soviet Third World theoreticians: "It is one thing to proclaim socialism as one's aim and quite another to build it. For this, a certain level of productive forces, culture, and social consciousness are needed." While sympathizing with states of a socialist orientation, he noted "the complexity of their position and the difficulties of their revolutionary development"[47]—common Soviet euphemisms for their poor performance on both a political and an economic level. This and other statements by Andropov suggest a consistent unhappiness with the sort of activist Third World policy that characterized the late Brezhnev years in general and a disillusionment with the socialist-oriented countries in particular.

It seems fairly clear that Mikhail Gorbachev has decided to associate himself with the Andropov line and with those calling for reassessment of the Brezhnev legacy. The new general secretary's early emphasis was on economic modernization and development of the Soviet Union's technological base, and his early pronouncements tended to downplay the Third World side of foreign policy. In his first speech as general secretary, for example, he stated: "The Soviet Union has always supported the struggle of the peoples for liberation from the colonial yoke and today, too, *our sympathies* are on the side of the countries of Asia, Africa, and Latin America that are following the path of strengthening their independence and social renewal."[48] The word

---

45Karen Brutents, "Osvobadivshiesya strany v nachale 80-kh godov," *Kommunist* no. 3 (February 1984), p. 109.

46Brutents, "Dvizheniya neprisoedineniya," pp. 26–41.

47"Rech' General'nogo Sekretariya Ts. K. KPSS tovarishcha Yu. V. Andropova," *Kommunist* no. 9 (June 1983), pp. 14–15.

48"Speech by Comrade Gorbachev, General Secretary of the CPSU Central Committee, at the CPSU Central Committee Plenum on 11 March," *Pravda*, March 12, 1985.

"sympathies" had been used on several occasions by Andropov to signal a diminished commitment to the Third World.

This inclination was confirmed in the two major policy documents published early in Gorbachev's administration, the new party program first issued in draft form in October 1985 and Gorbachev's report to the Twenty-seventh Party Congress in late February 1986. A downgrading of the importance of MLVPs was already evident in Brezhnev's report to the Twenty-sixth Congress in 1981, when he spoke only of "revolutionary democratic parties" rather than Communist or Marxist-Leninist ones. The 1985 party program retained this language by stating that

> the CPSU is deepening relations with the liberated countries' revolutionary democratic parties. Particularly close cooperation has taken shape with those of them striving to build their activity on the basis of scientific socialism. The CPSU favors the development of ties with all national progressive parties occupying anti-imperialist and patriotic stances.[49]

While making a nod toward Third World parties espousing scientific socialism, therefore, the program keeps open the door to non-Marxist-Leninist groups as well, provided they are anti-imperialist. Then, in a paragraph that seems to be directly inspired by Brutents, the program asserts that "real grounds exist for cooperation with young states which are traveling the capitalist road"—that is, that the Soviet Union can develop profitable relations in the Third World by turning away from the socialist orientation altogether.[50]

Gorbachev's address to the Twenty-seventh Congress of the CPSU is remarkable not so much for what it says about the Third World world as for what it omits. Gorbachev does not continue the practice of the past two Brezhnev addresses of including a long section on the Third World (apart from Afghanistan), makes no concrete offers of support for allies in the Third World, and fails to mention countries of a socialist orientation as being particularly close to the Soviet Union.[51]

Conclusions

The record of both Soviet theory and Soviet behavior over the past three decades makes it evident that questions of ideology and political organization have been critical in determining the basic course of Soviet Third World

---

[49]CPSU Draft Program, reprinted in FBIS *Daily Report, USSR National Affairs*, October 28, 1985, Supplement, pp. 24–25.

[50]Ibid., p. 25.

[51]Gorbachev's report is contained in FBIS *Daily Report*, USSR National Affairs, February 26, 1986.

policy. The Marxist-Leninist vanguard party played a particularly important role in the late Brezhnev period; it would be impossible to assert that ideology was irrelevant to Soviet concerns.

It is also clear that Soviet interest in MLVPs does not stem from a communist messianism but arises because the MLVP is regarded as a useful tool for furthering the state interests of the USSR, which are dictated in large measure by realpolitik concerns. The MLVP was never a universally applicable instrument; like any other tool, its utility depended on the circumstances of time and place, and in regions or countries where it was not viable, it was either discarded or not used in the first place. Hence the Soviets maintained relations with a variety of bourgeois nationalists in India, Syria, Algeria, and the like at the same time that they were cultivating vanguard parties in Angola and Afghanistan.

At the same time we should not underestimate the value to the Soviets of MLVPs as ends in themselves rather than as mere instruments of policy. The constant theme of Boris Ponomarev's speeches throughout the past two decades has been how each passing year shows us the ever-increasing vigor and dynamism of socialism, its superiority over capitalism as a social and economic system. It is likely that only in certain parts of the Third World is Soviet-style socialism still taken seriously, and the proliferation of Marxist-Leninist regimes in the developing world during the late 1970s reassured many in the USSR that their ideology was still relevant.

Recent Soviet writings on MLVPs leave the distinct impression that most Soviet theorists are at something of a loss regarding appropriate directions for future Soviet strategy in the Third World. Cultivation of first-generation bourgeois nationalists had its drawbacks and limitations, but the self-proclaimed Marxist-Leninists whom many in the USSR saw as an alternative in the early-to-mid 1970s have proved in key respects to be even weaker. Most Soviet writers go only so far as to point out the shortcomings of the second generation, without offering proposals for possible substitutes. The one major theorist who seems to have a clear idea of future directions for policy is Karen Brutents, who has openly advocated what amounts to a return to Khrushchevian policy, emphasizing the noncommunist Third World.

But Brutents's published views do not constitute Soviet policy. There is reason to think that the future role of the MLVP, as well as other broad questions such as the overall level of resource allocations to Third World clients, has been under debate in high Moscow political circles over at least the past three or four years.[52] That is, the debate has gone above academic and International Department theorists and has reached the Politburo and the Central Committee secretariat. Resolution of the debate has probably

---

[52]For evidence, see Stephen Sestanovich, "Do the Soviets Feel Pinched by Third World Adventures?" *Washington Post*, May 20, 1984, and my *Moscow's Post-Brezhnev Reassessment of the Third World*, R-3337-USDP (Santa Monica: RAND Corporation, February 1986).

been somewhat complicated by the ongoing succession uncertainties of the early 1980s, with no single general secretary remaining healthy or in office long enough to focus clearly on Third World issues. Although we have some idea of the terms of the debate, written sources do not indicate clearly whether and how it has been resolved. For that we have to look at behavior.

A case can be made that in the early 1980s the Soviet Union began to move away from promotion of MLVPs back to a Brutents-like strategy of building ties with large, geopolitically important Third World states. Soviet military assistance to second-generation clients including Ethiopia, the PDRY, and Mozambique has either remained flat or fallen slightly, while the rate of increase for established socialist allies such as Cuba and Vietnam has fallen. Yet at the same time Moscow substantially increased both the quantity and the quality of its aid to Syria, India, and Iraq, and initiated large economic agreements with Morocco, Argentina, and India. Some observers have cited Mozambique as a recent case of Soviet retrenchment. The Marxist-Leninist Frelimo regime was a charter member of the second generation, but since 1981 it has been allowed to slip into the South African orbit, a process culminating in the March 1984 Nkomati agreement whereby Pretoria and Maputo pledged noninterference in each other's internal affairs. Finally, Soviet policy may be more remarkable for what has not happened: there have been no large-scale Soviet interventions in the Third World since the invasion of Afghanistan in December 1979.

These trends, however, have not been consistent. At the same time that Mozambique was moving politically closer to South Africa, the Soviets negotiated a long-term, multibillion-dollar package of economic and military assistance with their other Marxist-Leninist client in southern Africa, Angola.[53] From a low level of perhaps 17,000, Cuban troop strength in Angola increased to 30–35,000 by the end of 1984, and in the late summer of 1985 MPLA forces, assisted by both Cuban and Soviet military advisers, undertook an ambitious offensive against Jonas Savimbi's UNITA.[54] The Soviets increased both the level of their "assistance" to Afghanistan and the scope of their military operations in 1984 and 1985, dramatically upped their commitments to Nicaragua, and for the first time in many years shipped modern tactical aircraft to North Korea.

The absence during the 1980s of large-scale Soviet interventions on behalf of Marxist-Leninist groups in the Third World is very difficult to interpret. Although it may be the result of deliberate policy, it may also reflect the simple absence of appropriate opportunities. As many Soviet observers have pointed out, Portugal's was the last of the European colonial empires to fall apart, and the era of easy gains from support of national liberation movements is now over. The only obvious opportunity to support a Marxist-

[53]U.S. Department of Defense, *Soviet Military Power* (Washington, D.C., 1984), p. 199.
[54]See Alan Cowell, "Enemy Blocked, Angolan Rebel Says," *New York Times*, October 9, 1985.

Leninist group in the early 1980s was provided by the Farabundo Martí National Liberation Front in El Salvador. Whatever "restraint" the Soviets have shown toward the FMLN is undoubtedly due to fear of unduly provoking Western opinion rather than a decision in principle to move away from MLVPs.

The case of Angola demonstrates that it would be difficult for the Soviets to reorient their policy even if a consensus within the leadership wanted to do so. As a result of its highly visible interventions in the mid-to-late 1970s, the Soviet Union has invested considerable money and presitge in the success of its new clients, and it cannot be seen to back away from them now that several of these enterprises have gone sour. One instance of the current bind for the Soviets is Afghanistan, where Soviet recognition of the mistakes of the Afghan Communists does not present a clear picture of how to settle the war through either military or political means. It may be that a major shift toward a Brutents-like policy would be virtually invisible to outside observers. Just as Moscow did not jettison viable Khrushchev-era bourgeois nationalists in the heyday of the MLVP, so there is unlikely to be a dramatic move away now from the second-generation clients. The most important manifestation of a new policy might be one quite beneficial to the West, a decreased willingness to intervene on behalf of small Marxist-Leninist groups hoping to come to power.

3

The Soviet Union and the Third
World: The Military Dimension

MELVIN A. GOODMAN

Mohamed Heikal, on the Arab experience with Soviet military assistance at the time of the 1956 Suez Crisis and the 1967 June War in the Middle East:

> Immediately on arrival Kuwatly [president of Syria] asked to see the Soviet leaders. He insisted that Egypt must be helped. "But what can we do?" asked Khrushchev.
>
> Zhukov produced a map of the Middle East and spread it on the table. Then turning to Kuwatly, he said, "How can we go to the aid of Egypt? Tell me! Are we supposed to send our armies through Turkey, Iran, and then into Syria and Iraq and on into Israel and so eventually attack the British and French forces?
>
> Khrushchev folded up the map and told Kuwatly, "We'll see what we can do. At present we don't know how to help Egypt, but we are having continuous meetings to discuss the problem."

> It was when Badran [Egyptian defense minister] and his party were leaving that the real misunderstanding took place. Marshal Grechko had come to the airport to see them off, and he was chatting to Badran at the foot of the aircraft steps. He said "Stand firm. Whatever you have to face, you will find us with you. Don't let yourselves be blackmailed by the Americans or anyone else." After the plane had taken off, the Egyptian ambassador in Moscow, Murad Ghaleb, who had heard Grechko's remarks, said to him, "That was very reassuring, Marshal." Grechko laughed, and said to him, "I just wanted to give him one for the road."[1]

Three decades ago the Soviet Union was a continental power whose military focus was the defense of the homeland and whose military reach was limited to regions contiguous with its own borders. Today it is a global power with worldwide naval deployments and the ability to monitor Western

---

[1] Suez Crisis, 1956, Mohamed Heikal, *The Sphinx and the Commissar* (New York: Harper & Row, 1978), pp. 70–71, 179–80.

naval forces; it has gained access to naval and air facilities in strategically located client states and is a factor to be considered in any regional crisis or conflict.

Moscow's success in achieving many of its Third World objectives—securing a military position in every major region of the globe, challenging the West and China, and influencing the governments of key regional states—has been accomplished almost entirely through the use of military instruments of policy. Through military assistance and the use of surrogate forces, the Soviets have served the national security needs of key Third World countries and have reaped the benefits.[2]

The evolution of the USSR's Third World policy since the mid-1950s has reflected its perceived national interests and its ability to capitalize on international developments. Although ideology has shaped Moscow's world view, it has not been a major factor in determining Soviet interests or behavior. And though its policy in the Third World has been keyed to its ambitions vis-à-vis the United States, Moscow has not allowed concern for bilateral relations with the United States to deter it from pursuing its global interests.[3]

In the decade following World War II the Soviets failed to capitalize on the collapse of Western imperial systems in Africa and Asia, the growth of radical nationalism, and the new responsiveness of "revolutionary democrats" in the Third World. Stalin remained oriented toward a European policy, and Moscow carefully avoided involvement in Third World conflicts and restricted its support to communist regimes contiguous to the USSR.

At the Twentieth Congress of the CPSU in 1956, the Soviets codified a new approach toward the Third World when Khrushchev described the "disintegration of the imperialist colonial system" as a "postwar development of historical significance." Khrushchev and his successors have viewed the Third World as the appropriate arena for competing with the West without running the risk of superpower confrontation and for supporting national liberation movements without getting drawn into regional battles.

Moscow's initial, and still more effective, approach was the provision of military assistance. And the pattern of Soviet arms to the Third World in the 1950s and 1960s clearly revealed the change in policy adopted under Khrushchev as most arms exports went to noncommunist countries. Soviet arms were shipped to Egypt and Syria before the Suez War in 1956, to Yemen before the border clashes with Aden in 1957 and 1958, to Algeria during its brief border struggle with Morocco in 1963, and to Indonesia during several internal conflicts from 1958 to 1965. The scale of these initial military assistance efforts was modest, but the political and military significance of Moscow's

[2]See Uri Ra'anan, Robert Pfaltzgraff, and Geoffrey Kemp, *Power Projection* (Hamden, Ct.: Archon, 1982).
[3]See Robert Donaldson, ed., *The Soviet Union in the Third World: Successes and Failures* (Boulder, Colo.: Westview, 1981); Carol Saivetz and Sylvia Woodby, *Soviet Third World Relations* (Boulder, Colo.: Westview, 1985).

shift in policy has proved to be considerable. Military assistance has provided the entree for Moscow in its courtship of Third World states; and it has earned a substantial bonus—hard-currency income that eases the economic burdens of Moscow's overall Third World involvement.[4]

The scope of Soviet military activities in the Third World expanded significantly in the 1960s, when the USSR began a steady increase in the size, capability, and range of operation of its forces in support of Soviet political goals. The rapid and impressive expansion of the Soviet Navy over the past twenty years has led to a continuous naval presence in the Mediterranean, the Indian Ocean, the South Atlantic Ocean off the coast of West Africa, and the South China Sea. Soviet naval forces now use facilities for a variety of purposes in about a dozen Third World countries that provide the USSR with intelligence and surveillance capabilities, various training opportunities, and support for Soviet interests abroad.[5]

During the 1970s, the period of Moscow's greatest success in the Third World, the Soviets appeared to believe that the larger setting of international relationships had become more favorable to them. In addition to the improvement in their own military position, they perceived a number of other favorable trends:

> Capitalist society was seen to be in crisis—possibly deeper and more long-lasting than past crises—with resulting erosion of the West's sense of common purpose.

> The USSR's growing strategic forces and improved capability for conventional warfare had increased its international stature.

> The Soviet position in Eastern Europe was strong and had been strengthened by a European security agreement that in effect confirmed the division of Europe.

> The United States had suffered international reverses and was experiencing domestic difficulties and, as a result, had lost prestige.

More recently the Soviets have encountered a range of obstacles in the Third World, but the growth of Soviet military power has paid important political and military dividends. The acquisition of naval access privileges bordering distant waters serves both operational and political purposes. The use of foreign facilities contributes to Moscow's ability to sustain worldwide deployments and monitor Western naval forces. Soviet naval forces abroad underscore Moscow's commitment to specific policies or local regimes and must be taken into account at times of regional crises. Major elements of the international community in South Yemen were evacuated by the Soviet Navy in January 1986 during the political and military upheaval in Aden. Every

---

[4]Cf. Roger Kanet, ed., *The Soviet Union and the Developing Countries* (Baltimore: Johns Hopkins University Press, 1975).

[5]Stephen Hosmer and Thomas Wolfe, *Soviet Policy and Practice toward Third World Conflicts* (Lexington, Mass.: Lexington Books, 1983).

Third World country with Soviet military facilities or providing military access has received substantial Soviet arms aid and political support, and certain Third World regimes have benefited from Soviet naval demonstrations of force during times of internal crisis.[6]

It is more difficult to assess the outcome of Moscow's operational planning and advisory role with its Third World clients. Soviet involvement certainly was a factor in Angolan military successes against UNITA in the 1980s, in Ethiopian successes against the Somalis in the 1970s, and in Vietnam's successes in Kampuchea in the 1980s. But Soviet operational planning has not helped Arab client regimes against the Israelis over the years, nor has it led to any sustained successes for Ethiopian forces against the Eritreans. Soviet inability to train and discipline the Afghan Army is a major reason for Moscow's inability to limit the insurgency in Afghanistan, which has become more pervasive since the Soviet invasion in December 1979.

The Soviets have had even less success in translating their limited military influence in key Third World states into political and diplomatic influence. Huge amounts of military assistance to Arab clients have not led to a Soviet role at various Arab-Israeli negotiations over the past fifteen years or in talks in southern Africa over the past decade that have dealt with Angola, Mozambique, Namibia, and Rhodesia. The Nkomati and Lusaka accords in 1984, moreover, appeared to catch the Soviets off guard, despite their military assistance efforts on behalf of Mozambique and Angola, respectively. Soviet military aid has led to a high degree of support for Soviet positions in such international forums as the United Nations, but it has not prevented Syria from pursuing policies that were not necessarily in Moscow's interest with regard to Israel, Lebanon, or the Palestine Liberation Organization. Cuba, India, and Vietnam have received billions of dollars in aid from the USSR over the past three decades but at the same time have displayed an extremely high degree of independence in pursuit of their own national interests.

Nevertheless, the steady increase in the size and capability of Soviet forces operating abroad, as well as the quantity and quality of Soviet weapons systems provided to Third World states, have added to Moscow's global military activities and its geostrategic position vis-à-vis the West. Soviet successes in Angola, Ethiopia, South Yemen, and Vietnam do not represent a major shift in the correlation of forces, but—in extending its military reach—the USSR has developed a global network of communications and intelligence collection sites, gained increased access to military facilities in a growing number of Third World states, and managed the military and advisory roles of its East European and Cuban allies in Africa, Central America, and the Middle East. The Soviets have not succeeded in eroding the predominant role of the West in the global system of Third World nation-states, but the

---

[6]So argues Bruce D. Porter, *The USSR in Third World Conflicts* (Cambridge: Cambridge University Press, 1984).

expansion of Soviet military power has led to a gradual expansion of Moscow's global role—particularly in the former colonial areas of Africa, the Middle East, and Asia—and to the consolidation of pro-Soviet Marxist governments in Afghanistan, Angola, Ethiopia, and South Yemen.[7]

Soviet Military Successes in the Third World

A number of indicators demonstrate that Moscow has acquired a significant capacity for global military involvement and power projection. Compared to its highly limited capabilities at the time of the Cuban missile crisis in 1962, or during the increase in U.S. action in Vietnam in the 1960s, the Soviet position in 1985 was considerably enhanced, with Moscow achieving its greatest gains in the mid-to-late 1970s. Over the past two decades, the Soviets have dramatically increased their military agreements and deliveries in the Third World, doubled the number of Soviet military personnel outside the Warsaw Pact countries and Afghanistan, and sharply increased naval deployments over an expanded area through access to naval facilities and ports of call.

Moscow's ability to project power has improved considerably over the past decade. Soviet naval reconnaissance aircraft now operate out of Cuba, Vietnam, Angola, Ethiopia, South Yemen, Syria, and Libya; ten years ago, only Cuba provided such access. Soviet military transport aircraft have use of Angola, South Yemen, Syria, Afghanistan, and Vietnam; only Syria was used ten years ago. Ground and air defense troops are in Cuba and the Middle East, and military technicians and security advisers are in the Middle East, Africa, Asia, and Latin America. The Soviet military presence in Syria, for example, has made Israel more tolerant of Syrian president Assad's recent maneuvering of mobile SAM sites in Lebanon. Israeli and South African forces will have to contend with more sophisticated air defense forces in planning any future operations against Libya and Angola, respectively.

The expansion of Soviet capabilities has had geostrategic benefits for the USSR, enabling it to break out of its traditional realm in the Baltic Sea and the Black Sea. Soviet air and naval power can now be projected virtually anywhere in the world, Moscow enjoys intelligence-gathering facilities in strategic regional locations, and Soviet military air transport can deliver tanks, troops, and self-propelled artillery into key outlying locations.

The USSR also has taken advantage of opportunities in several regions to use combined naval exercises to further its political and military goals in the Third World. Moscow's military and economic support for Vietnam, for example, has resulted in a substantial Soviet naval build-up in the South

---

[7]See Alex P. Schmid, *Soviet Military Interventions since 1945* (New Brunswick: Transaction, 1985).

China Sea, and a Soviet-Vietnamese exercise earlier this year demonstrated that Soviet interests and capabilities had to be taken into consideration by regional countries, particularly China and the United States. Soviet-Cuban exercises contribute to Cuban military capabilities, which far outdistance those of other Third World states in the region, while asserting Moscow's right to operate in the Caribbean and the Gulf of Mexico. Soviet exercises with allies in the Middle East and the Persian Gulf also demonstrate a Soviet commitment and presence.

Combined naval operations with the Soviet Union also enhance the prestige of a Third World navy. These exercises display the country's growing military capabilities to other nations in the region and signal that the country, given its strong military ties to the Soviet Union, is a power to be reckoned with. Such countries as Cuba, Syria, Libya, and Vietnam probably intend the exercises to counterbalance U.S. military operations in the region. Finally, Moscow's Third World clients probably realize that combined naval training helps sharpen their forces' military skills, particularly in countries with a limited military tradition.

There have been military and political gains in most regions of the world. In the *Middle East*, one of the USSR's top priority areas, the Soviets continue a close relationship with Syria through military weapons transfers. Moscow uses Syrian facilities for reconnaissance flights and has conducted several joint naval exercises with the Syrians. Moscow also has access rights to naval and air facilities in South Yemen. Such access enhances Soviet logistics and reconnaissance capabilities in both the Mediterranean and the Indian Ocean areas. The Soviets have a highly lucrative arms relationship with Libya, and arms sales to Iraq and Algeria provide the basis for ongoing bilateral ties. Moscow's limited entree to such moderate Arab states as Jordan and Kuwait has come through arms sales. Diplomatic relations were established recently with Oman. In *Southeast Asia* a Soviet military force has replaced the U.S. presence at Cam Ranh Bay, thus providing Moscow with direct leverage against Beijing and with logistical support for Soviet naval operations in the South China Sea and the Indian Ocean.

Indeed, the greatest gain for the USSR in Southeast Asia has been the acquisition of access to the American-built naval and air bases at Cam Ranh Bay and Da Nang in Vietnam, which provide Moscow with its only operating military base between Vladivostok and the east coast of Africa.[8] The USSR's growing presence in Vietnam includes naval units, a composite air unit, and a growing infrastructure for communications, intelligence collection, and logistics support. The three or four attack and cruise missile submarines operating from Cam Ranh Bay conduct patrols in the South China Sea and are well situated to operate against sea lines of communication in the region. If necessary, Soviet forces at Cam Ranh Bay can augment the Indian

[8]*Soviet Military Power* (Washington: U.S. GPO, 1986), p. 138.

Ocean Squadron. These facilities serve the twenty to twenty-five Soviet ships routinely deployed to the South China Sea.

For the past several years a Soviet air unit comprised of sixteen naval TU-16 Badger and eight TU-95 Bear aircraft, as well as a squadron of MiG-23 Flogger fighter aircraft, has been deployed at Cam Ranh Bay airfield. The Bear and Badger aircraft conduct reconnaissance, intelligence-collection, and antisubmarine warfare missions throughout the South China Sea. The Badger's strike range from Cam Ranh Bay includes not only regional states but also the Philippines, Guam, and the western portion of Micronesia. From 1978 to 1985, moreover, the Soviets provided over $5 billion in arms aid to Hanoi along with direct aid to Cambodia. Over 2,500 Soviet military advisers are in Vietnam to support this program, and a contingent of AN-12 Cubs has operated in Vietnam, Laos, and Cambodia since 1979 to deliver supplies to Vietnamese forces. In addition to more than $7 billion in Soviet economic assistance through 1984, Vietnamese membership in the Council for Mutual Economic Assistance obligates the Soviet Union's East European allies to provide aid to Vietnam.[9]

In *South and Southwest Asia* the Soviets have made little progress in defeating the Afghan insurgents, but their military policy has nevertheless demonstrated a perseverance in trying to wear down support for the resistance and defending a sensitive border region from a perceived security threat. Through its extensive security assistance ties to India, Moscow has reinforced the underlying coincidence of geopolitical interests and forged a strong bilateral relationship.

In *Africa* the Soviets have access to facilities in Ethiopia which expand their capabilities in the Indian Ocean area. In western Africa they have the use of Angolan facilities as well as the capability to use naval facilities in Guinea. These facilities bolster Moscow's ability to project force in southern Africa. Soviet backing of "national liberation" groups seeking Namibia's independence from South Africa and the overthrow of the South African government give Moscow credibility and prestige in the region. In the *Caribbean Basin*, Moscow enjoys port and air facilities in Cuba, as well as intelligence capabilities relative to U.S. activities in the Caribbean and North Atlantic region. These facilities allow Moscow to project power into international waters near the United States, to threaten potentially important U.S. shipping lanes, and to apply a kind of countervailing power to offset Soviet perceptions of the U.S. threat closer to Soviet borders. Soviet military aid to Nicaragua works in a similar manner—strengthening a regime whose activities divert U.S. attention, energies, and resources to the Caribbean Basin and away from regions more important from the Soviet perspective.

Soviet and Cuban efforts on behalf of the Popular Movement for the Liberation of Angola (MPLA) have led to numerous opportunities for the

---

[9]Ibid.

USSR to advance its influence in the region. Luanda is one of the largest and best natural harbors on the west coast of Africa and is the main support base for the Soviet Navy's West African Patrol. Other assets there include a floating drydock, a communications station, and access for TU-95 Bear Ds, which patrol the South Atlantic sealanes. The patrol's apparent mission is to maintain a Soviet presence and provide a contingency show of force with the six or seven ships based in Luanda. Other Soviet naval units have called on the Mozambican port of Maputo and on Port Louis in Mauritius.

Soviet arms transfers to Africa are a comparatively small percentage of total Soviet arms exports, but Moscow has significantly increased the amount of military aid provided to the MPLA. In 1985 the Angolans received MI-24 Hind and MI-17 Hip helicopters, additional SU-22 Fitters, MiG-23 Floggers, and SA13s to help detect and defend against alleged South African aircraft supporting the National Union for the Total Independence of Angola (UNITA). Previously the Angolans also received an early warning radar net that covers almost the entire southwestern part of the country and other equipment intended to improve intelligence-gathering capabilities against UNITA. A squadron of Soviet AN-12 Cub transports has been supporting Angolan government forces for several years.[10]

Renewed Emphasis on Northeast Asia

Most recently the Soviets have given increased attention to Northeast Asia, where they have concluded a military assistance package to North Korea which includes MiG-23 fighter aircraft.[11] The deliveries of MiG-23s represent the first major Soviet delivery of sophisticated aircraft to North Korea in more than ten years and take place in the wake of North Korean leader Kim Il-Sung's visit to Moscow in 1984. Kim's visit to Moscow followed Chinese party leader Hu Yaobang's trip to North Korea, which was marked by signs of strain in Sino-Korean relations. Pyongyang's treatment of the anniversaries of its defense treaties with Moscow and Beijing in 1986 also indicated an improvement in relations with the USSR and a cooling with China. And North Korea gave unusually high-level attention to the first anniversary of Kim's visit to the USSR, including Kim's attendance at an unusual anniversary banquet at the Soviet embassy in Pyongyang (such an event did not follow Kim's trips to the People's Republic of China in 1975 or 1982).

The Soviet willingness to provide MiG-23 fighter aircraft to Pyongyang signals that Moscow is determined not to be frozen out of broader political discussions of the Korean question and that the Korean peninsula may be-

[10]Ibid., pp. 131–32.
[11]Reuters reported on July 30, 1985, that North Korea had received fourteen to sixteen MiG-23 fighter aircraft from the USSR and that "large numbers" of North Korean officers had received training at Soviet military bases before and after the deliveries.

come less isolated from the larger strategic confrontation between the United States and the USSR in East Asia. The Soviets are countering Japan's willingness to accept F-16s, as well as the general augmentation of the U.S. military position in the region. Deliveries of Floggers also indicate that Moscow has dropped previous reservations about the risks of military technology being transferred from North Korea to China and Pyongyang's possible military adventurism against the South.

Since Brezhnev's death in 1982, moreover, the Soviets clearly have been testing the waters and looking for ways to counter closer ties between the United States, China, Japan, and South Korea in order to correct their own isolation in the region. The adverse Asian reaction to the shooting down of a Korean Airlines commercial flight in September 1983 led the Soviets to woo the North Koreans. In the following month, for example, Moscow absolved Pyongyang of any blame for its attack on the South Korean political leadership in Burma in 1983 and renewed an invitation to Kim Il-Sung to visit Moscow at some unspecified time. Soviet accounts of the subsequent talks between premiers and foreign ministers of the two countries emphasized that a mutual interest in strengthening "international security" had created a "reliable basis for their mutual cooperation." Soviet treatment of the USSR–North Korean defense treaty in 1985 also was warmer than usual and focused on the theme of Soviet economic assistance to Pyongyang.

The delivery of MiG-23s is particularly noteworthy because the Soviets had made no serious attempts to improve relations with Pyongyang throughout the 1970s. The Soviets recognized that the North Korean tilt in the direction of Beijing had historic and cultural roots and therefore would be difficult to counter. At the same time Moscow believed that any North Korean move in the direction of the USSR could be only tactical and opportunistic. During the late 1960s, when Moscow had made a decision to improve relations with the United States, the Soviet leadership was particularly leery about being identified with Kim's adventurism against Washington and, as a result, gave no support to Pyongyang in the wake of the *Pueblo* seizure in 1968 or the downing of the EC-121 reconnaissance aircraft in 1969. (The Soviets, moreover, condemned the North Koreans in 1976 when they murdered two U.S. Army officers in Panmunjon.)

The improvement in Soviet–North Korean geopolitical and military relations is merely the latest in a series of steps that have enhanced Moscow's strategic position in Northeast Asia. Over the past several years the Soviets have increased their force posture in Asia without drawing down forces deployed in other military theaters, established an independent theater command for the region, built up their forces in the Northern Territories, enhanced their power projection capabilities at Cam Ranh Bay, and—as a result—signaled a determination not to yield to Chinese and Japanese territorial grievances against the USSR. The Soviets are now in a stronger position to challenge the forward deployment of U.S. military power in the region, particularly the introduction of the Tomahawk cruise missile and the increased number of U.S. fighter aircraft.

In addition to the measurable indicators of strengthened Soviet power, there are a number of more subjective benefits that derive from Moscow's enhanced military power and prestige. These include, first, the reinforcement of Moscow's insistence that its voice be heard in regional and international forums and the bolstering of its claims to superpower status with the United States. Second are the indirect benefits that accrue from bolstering states whose foreign policy goals are compatible with the USSR's. In the Middle East a strengthened Syria has been able to frustrate U.S. peace efforts. Castro has been given the tools necessary to pursue policies in the Caribbean Basin and Africa which also serve Soviet objectives. India is in a better position to counter Chinese and U.S. policies in South Asia. Third is the satisfaction of the Soviet elite that it is following a visible and dynamic foreign policy consistent with its military capabilities and supportive of pressing the world correlation of forces in favor of socialism.

Soviet Military Setbacks in the Third World

Although Soviet military capabilities in the Third World have improved significantly over the past two decades, they have not been sufficient to accomplish all of Moscow's objectives or in many cases to satisfy the expectations of its clients. The Soviets did not have the ability to counter the Israeli invasion of Lebanon in 1982, which resulted in an embarrassing defeat for Syria, a major Soviet client. And in spite of their extensive arms deliveries to Syria and their close relationship with Damascus, they are unwilling to give the Syrians a security commitment—because they have neither the capability to fulfill a promised commitment nor the interest to confront the Israelis or the United States. Similarly, they have been reluctant to provide security guarantees to Cuba. There are even greater limits to the projection of Soviet power to Third World areas that are farther away and of lesser geopolitical importance to Moscow.

The unwillingness to extend security commitments has led in turn to setbacks and challenges to the Soviet position in the Third World. The most dramatic setback to the Soviet military (and political) position in the Third World to date was its expulsion from Egypt in 1972, shortly after the Soviet-American summit in Moscow. The Soviets had access to important facilities in Egypt, as well as a sizable physical presence, and the expulsion led to a downturn in the Soviet naval presence in the Mediterranean and in the deployment of Soviet naval aircraft in the Third World. Perhaps most important, the Soviets considered Egypt the key regional state in an area of primary importance and thus lost what they perceived as a major geopolitical advantage.

The Soviets also were expelled from Somalia and the facilities at Berbera following the conclusion of a Soviet-Ethiopian arms deal in 1977. In this case Moscow clearly had decided that Ethiopia had more potential as a client than Somalia and made the choice willingly—although it may have hoped to retain assets in both states. The loss of naval and naval air facilities in Somalia made the Soviets more dependent on less secure facilities in Ethiopia and led to complications for the Soviet naval presence in the Indian Ocean. Somalia—as well as Egypt—also unilaterally abrogated friendship treaties with USSR which had been negotiated earlier in the 1970s.[12]

The difficulty in translating Soviet military capability into political power to influence developments in the Third World is evidenced in several characteristics of Moscow's presence. Even when dependent on Soviet military aid, Third World states have their own goals, capabilities, and independently determined priorities. When interests coincide, Moscow and a Third World leader cooperate; when interests differ, frictions ensue. Continuing strains in Soviet relations with such close clients as Cuba, Syria, and Vietnam illustrate the perplexing difficulty of translating military power into political influence over clients.

Other factors complicate Moscow's efforts to derive advantage from its military capabilities. Many Third World regimes supported militarily by the Soviets are governing extremely weak states and are threatened by insurgent groups that have transformed the USSR into an often ineffective counterinsurgency power. Assisting counterinsurgency programs in weak states, furthermore, places the USSR in the awkward position of supervising a process that generally weakens the economic development of these states. The introduction of Soviet force also may create a series of regional problems for the Soviets, as witness the Soviet diplomatic and political problems in the Middle East and Southwest Asia following the invasion of Afghanistan.

There are also major constraints facing Soviet forces in distant operations. Despite greater access in some areas such as Cuba and Vietnam, the Soviets lack a network of large-scale foreign bases from which to mount and sustain operations. A lack of aircraft carriers and the limited range of Soviet tactical aircraft create problems of tactical air support which are aggravated by the lack of an aerial refueling capability for fighter aircraft and by the political problem of overflight rights. The Soviet naval infantry is small and the amphibious lift capacity of any single fleet of the Soviet Navy is limited, as is the naval gunfire support available for operations against well-armed Third World forces.

These shortcomings have contributed to Soviet caution in crisis manage-

---

[12]Friendship treaties negotiated since 1971 do not require the the USSR defend its Third World partner, but most of them do require that both sides enter into consultations to eliminate a threat to the Third World country concerned. The obligations of these treaties are described in only vague terms, although the contracting parties usually agree not to permit their territory to be used for purposes detrimental to the security of the other.

ment in the Middle East, Southeast Asia, and the Caribbean—and, as a result, to a perception in some Third World states that the USSR is an unreliable ally. The worsening of relations with both Egypt and North Korea in the early 1970s, for example, was related directly to Moscow's unwillingness to take risks on its clients' behalf.

Soviet willingness to use military force on its borders, moreover, does not necessarily indicate a willingness to get involved directly in distant, noncontiguous areas. Soviet airborne forces have participated successfully in every major invasion on Moscow's border since World War II (Hungary in 1956, Czechoslovakia in 1968, and Afghanistan in 1979), but they have never been deployed in noncontiguous Third World areas. The Soviets have sent their air forces into such Third World crisis spots as Egypt in 1970, but major fighter deployments would require access to regional bases that are crowded and often inadequate and could encounter overflight problems. Merchant ships have been used successfully in military supply efforts during Arab-Israeli wars, and military transport aviation has also been used for weapons deliveries in the Third World.

Anti-Soviet Insurgencies

In addition to the major constraints facing Soviet forces in distant areas, the Soviets are having trouble with guerrilla opposition to the governments that they support. In the past they were accustomed to seeing guerrilla armies fight against Western interests—sometimes effectively (in Vietnam) and sometimes not (in Kenya, Malaysia, and Oman). Today some of the most effective insurgencies are being waged against Soviet-supported regimes.

In Mozambique, guerrillas have cut the country in two and are playing havoc with the economy and with government control in much of the countryside.

In Namibia, the guerrillas of the South-West Africa People's Organization (SWAPO) have been increasingly ineffective against the South Africans, despite Cuban and Soviet support to SWAPO.

In Angola, Jonas Savimbi's guerrillas control more than a third of the country, interdict the main transportation lines, and have created a government infrastructure in liberated areas. All this despite the presence in Angola of 30,000 Cuban troops, who have shown no particular skill or stomach for counterinsurgency.

Ethiopia, also well provided with Cuban forces and Soviet advisers, has two separate insurgencies on its hands and is dealing successfully with neither one.

In Kampuchea, the troops of Moscow's Vietnamese allies are mired in combat with various insurgent elements.

In Afghanistan, more than 100,000 Soviet troops have been futilely sparring with guerrilla forces for nearly eight years. Insurgent attacks continue to increase, and there have been major security incidents in Kabul.

Soviet Power Projection

Despite the significant advances in Moscow's ability to project power into the international arena, the USSR has only a limited capability for global operations. The USSR has emphasized the importance of global reach through military aid missions, acquisition of access, and small-scale naval deployments. A comparison of the U.S. and Soviet navies reflects this difference, with the United States emphasizing out-of-area deployment with widespread rights of access and the USSR being far more dependent on sheltered anchorages and naval auxiliaries. Although the Soviet Navy has increased its capability to interdict Western shipping in the event of East-West hostilities, it is more likely that initial Soviet naval operations would involve defensive measures to protect Soviet submarines carrying strategic nuclear missiles and to keep U.S. aircraft carriers away from Soviet territory.

Third World security concerns will remain secondary to Moscow and, even with improvements to Soviet forces, the USSR will be inferior to Western forces abroad in the Mediterranean, the western Pacific, and the Indian Ocean. Moscow almost certainly will try to achieve favorable military balances in the regions close to Soviet borders. The most significant indicator in this direction would be the development of a more viable forward strike posture, which would include construction of air and naval missile storage and handling facilities in key Third World regions, increased production of long-range aircraft and nuclear-powered submarines, the organization of rapid deployment force headquarters with supporting communications units, and the construction of large fuel storage capacities at airfields likely to be used to support Soviet airlifts.

The Soviets already are building and are expected to have operational by 1990 a 65,000-ton attack aircraft carrier, but it is not certain if this carrier will continue to rely on helicopters and vertical short takeoff and landing aircraft or will make use of higher-performance aircraft that require stronger performance characteristics to withstand carrier landings, pilots trained in the art of carrier landings, and perfected catapults to launch planes and arresting gear to stop them at high speeds. Although it will take several years after launch and fitting-out and training with an operational air wing to develop a credible operational effectiveness, the new Soviet carrier will enable the Soviets to extend their operations beyond the umbrella currently provided by land-based aviation. The Soviet Navy thus will be able to extend its influence, but the United States—which currently has fourteen deployable carriers—will be able to send more carriers than the Soviets to global trouble spots for the foreseeable future.

The USSR could also opt for more substantial forward deployment that would include more attack submarines and strike aircraft and could expand the power projection capabilities of its overseas facilities to accommodate greater forward deployment and expanded integrated operations. Soviet forward deployments would be vulnerable in wartime, but in peacetime such deployment patterns would contribute to regional perceptions of a stronger Soviet presence in the Third World. Integrated military operations could help offset Soviet power projection weaknesses, but such exercises would have to be larger, more complex, and more frequent to produce better results. Cam Ranh Bay is now the center of the largest concentration of Soviet naval units outside the USSR, providing the Soviets with a strategic geographic position for monitoring U.S. operations in the South China Sea, Indian Ocean, and Pacific Ocean.

These developments would not ease significantly the vulnerability of Soviet forces abroad; such forces, moreover, would remain susceptible to the decisions of host governments in the Third World which may be unwilling to risk becoming involved as belligerents, particularly in potential Soviet-American confrontations. In the past Soviet deployment activities in the Third World have been curtailed in Egypt, Guinea, and Somalia and have encountered resistance in Algeria, India, and Iraq. Soviet military resources, moreover, may be inadequate for priority missions abroad, and the costs of substantial increases in forward-deployed forces may not be justified by the potential benefits or gains in the Third World. In any event, the Soviets are likely to press for additional basing and overflight arrangements in the Third World and for fewer operational constraints by Third World governments. Moscow will continue to upgrade such potentially useful facilities as those at Aden and Dahlak Island despite the uncertain security situations that prevail there and presumably will try to use its military assistance to secure naval and air access in other key regional states.

The Twenty-Seventh Party Congress and the Third World

The Twenty-seventh Congress of the CPSU and the new Soviet party program appeared to indicate that Moscow's role in the Third World was less important than addressing domestic-economic concerns and improving relations with the United States. Mikhail Gorbachev virtually ignored the Third World and, other than Afghanistan, made only passing reference to various regional conflicts that will continue to be potential problems for Soviet-American relations. Moscow's commitment to persevere in Afghanistan does not appear to be in doubt, but it is nevertheless noteworthy that Gorbachev chose the congress to make the very first Soviet leadership reference to the possibility of a timetable for withdrawal of Soviet forces.

> We would like to bring back the Soviet forces which are stationed in Afghanistan . . . in the nearest future. Agreed with the Afghan side are the dates of their

withdrawal by stages, as soon as a political settlement is reached, which will secure the real termination and reliably guarantee the non-renewal of armed interference from outside into the internal affairs of Afghanistan.[13]

In modifying the public formulation of Soviet policy on Afghanistan, Gorbachev has increased his stake in finding new ways to resolve the conflict. (No other Soviet leader referred to Afghanistan at the congress, and Afghan president Babrak Karmal made no reference to Soviet withdrawal.)

More recently, at Vladivostok in July 1986 in a major address on Sino-Soviet relations, Gorbachev announced that by the end of the year the USSR would withdraw from Afghanistan "one tank regiment, two motorized regiments, and three antiaircraft regiments—along with their established equipment and weapons."[14] This modest withdrawal effort may be no more than one aspect of a skillful public campaign to increase U.S. and Pakistani interest in the possibility of additional Soviet withdrawals from Afghanistan, but it does reflect a Soviet interest in some withdrawal from a situation that Gorbachev described as a "bleeding sore." The Soviets are also encouraging a "broader base" for the Afghan government and creating some confusion with their recent handling of the state visits of Babrak Karmal and Prime Minister Sultanali Keshtmand. Meanwhile the Soviet press has softened its line on Pakistani president Mohammed Zia and become more realistic about the limits on the opposition to Zia. Additional Soviet references to withdrawal are possible, but there is very little likelihood that Moscow will drop the linkage between Soviet withdrawal and the end to "outside interference" and international guarantees about the "non-renewal" of such interference.

In any event, in ignoring such important issues as the Middle East, Soviet-Indian relations, and Central America, Gorbachev was acknowledging at the party congress that he saw little value in highlighting the more revolutionary and internationalist aspects of Soviet foreign policy at this particular juncture. This tactic may reflect merely Gorbachev's current sense of priorities. Gorbachev's references to the Third World paled next to Brezhnev's various references in 1971, 1976, and 1981, which offered numerous examples of Soviet aid to Third World countries, including military assistance. Ambassador Anatoly F. Dobrynin's appointment to the secretariat and the retirement of the chief of the International Department, B. N. Ponomarev, a veteran of the Comintern who had headed the International Department for twenty-five years, also signaled renewed emphasis on the strategic relationship with the United States and the possibility of less attention to Third World matters.

More important, Gorbachev's vague references at the party congress to the

---

[13]The speeches and proceedings of the party congress were reviewed from the daily reports on the Soviet Union of the United States Foreign Broadcast Information Service (FBIS) for the period February 25 to March 14, 1986. They were taken in most cases from TASS reports or Radio Moscow. General Secretary Gorbachev spoke to the congress on the opening day.

[14]*Pravda*, July 29, 1986, p. 3.

Third World and the emphasis on restoring Soviet-American stability caused concern among key Soviet clients who spoke at the meetings in Moscow. Cuban leader Castro reminded Gorbachev that "blood had been spilled" in the Third World and that the task of economic development in the under-developed world was just as important as avoiding nuclear war. Ethiopian leader Mengistu also urged the Soviets not to give the issue of regional conflict a lower priority than nuclear matters, and he put the Soviet leader-ship on notice that Moscow's Third World allies continued to expect Soviet support. Angolan leader Dos Santos also called for more support from Moscow and reminded his Soviet audience that Angola suffered not only from the effects of war but from the deterioriation of the international situa-tion, particularly the economic situation. All of these leaders appeared to be expressing concern that Moscow may back away from its international obli-gations. They also may believe that any effort by Gorbachev to address U.S. concerns over East-West competition in the Third World could weaken the Soviet commitment to the countries of "socialist orientation."

Afghanistan was the only specific Third World issue mentioned in Gor-bachev's speech to the party congress and, in general, the speeches and docu-mentation of the meetings were vague about any Soviet commitment to assisting Moscow's Third World clients. The Gorbachev leadership appeared to use the party congress to stress the importance of domestic economic concerns and East-West relations and to alert Third World leaders to the importance of self-reliance. In 1981 Leonid Brezhnev had presented many examples of Soviet aid to specific Third World countries, including military assistance, but in 1986 Gorbachev balanced Moscow's commitment to left-wing Third World clients with an expression of equal ties with more moder-ate Third World states. Since the party congress the Soviets have made overtures to the Persian Gulf monarchies (particularly Oman and the United Arab Emirates), courted Jordan's King Hussein, and contacted several mem-bers of the Association of Southeast Asian Nations (ASEAN). The Soviets have also made efforts to improve relations with Argentina, Brazil, and Mex-ico and have even held meetings with Israeli officials to soften Israeli opposi-tion to a Soviet role in the Arab-Israeli peace process and improve the atmo-sphere for U.S.-Soviet trade.

Soviet speeches at the party congress also raised the possibility of coopera-tion with the West on North-South issues, which were formerly said to be the legacy and hence the obligation of Western colonialism and imperialism. The general international environment was cited as a problem fraught with grave consequences (presumably for the USSR as well as the United States) and requiring a common solution. This discussion of international security issues reflected greater Soviet interest in participating in global trade, debt settlement, and bilateral economic cooperation with governmental and inter-national organizations. Gorbachev also delivered an unusually strong con-demnation of terrorist acts and pledged to cooperate with other states to combat the problem. In 1981, Brezhnev had been highly defensive on the issue of terrorism at the Twenty-sixth Congress and did not repudiate terrorist acts.

Conclusions and Outlook

The past three decades have seen a concerted Soviet effort to improve the USSR's military position in all areas. Total military manpower has increased by about one-third to its present size of about five million. Weapons production capacity has expanded by nearly 60 percent, and research and development facilities have nearly doubled. The number of deployed intercontinental nuclear delivery vehicles has increased nearly sixfold, and battlefield nuclear forces have more than tripled in size. The Soviet Navy has evolved from primarily a coastal defense force with limited capabilities for operation on the high seas to a force that now demonstrates the global reach of Soviet military power and counters the previously unconstrained Western use of the seas.

In the Third World the growth of Soviet military power has led to increased use of military instruments to gain political ends. Soviet arms sales to the Third World have increased rapidly since their beginning in the 1950s, and the number of Soviet military advisers in Third World conflicts has grown in increasingly active and threatening stages during confrontations in the Third World. Soviet airlifts involve very little risk for the relatively small number of Soviet personnel involved in them, but Moscow has on occasion played a direct combat and combat advisory role on behalf of its clients in the Middle East and Africa.

> In the late 1960s and early 1970s Soviet air and air defense forces were used in the Middle East. In the civil war in North Yemen in the 1960s, Soviet advisers took part in combat operations and Soviet fighter pilots flew operational missions. Soviet advisers manned surface-to-air missile sites on the west bank of the Suez Canal during the war of attrition with Israel in the winter of 1969–70, and in the October War in 1973 the USSR conducted a massive resupply effort to Egypt during the course of hostilities.

> In the mid-to-late 1970s Soviet logistics forces transported and sustained surrogate Cuban forces for intervention in Angola and Ethiopia. In the Ogaden war in 1977–78 Soviet high-level commanders were directly involved in planning comprehensive military operations during a Third World conflict. The leader of that effort, V. I. Petrov, was named first deputy defense minister in February 1985.

> In 1979 Soviet combat ground and air units invaded Afghanistan, marking the first direct involvement of Soviet ground forces outside the Soviet bloc.

The Soviets have exploited the national security vulnerability of Third World states to acquire such tangible military assets as air and naval facilities and such political advantages as pro-Soviet political orientation of non-aligned states in international arenas. The vulnerability of Ethiopia and South Yemen, for example, has led to Soviet military facilities on the Horn of Africa and the Arabian peninsula. Internal instability in Angola and Mozambique has led to an improved Soviet military and political position in southern Africa. Such non-Marxist states as Algeria, India, and Iraq, however, have been far more reluctant to grant privileged military access to the Soviet Union despite their dependence on Moscow for most of their military aid. Nearly all of these Marxist and non-Marxist Third World states have concluded friendship treaties with the Soviets in the past fifteen years, which refer to the need for consultation and cooperation in times of crisis.

Soviet military assistance and support, in turn, has contributed significantly to the military and political success of Moscow's key clients. And the expansion of the USSR's military role in the Third World has led directly to a strengthening of Moscow's global position, an ability to challenge Western interests, and a bolstering of the Soviet economic base by means of hard currency received for arms sales. The number of pro-Soviet regimes in the Third World has increased dramatically since 1955 as Moscow has used its military and national security assistance to capitalize on anticolonial sentiment, regional conflicts, and the search for rapid assistance by emerging nationalist regimes. In return the Soviets have gained allies such as Cuba, Ethiopia, Syria, and Vietnam in key areas of the world. The Soviets have won support for their positions in international forums and have become a recognized factor in most important regional disputes. The USSR has extensive trade relationships with many Third World states, enabling it to earn hard currency, largely through arms sales. The hard currency earned, in turn, enables the Soviets to support their closest clients, particularly Cuba and Vietnam.

The largest Soviet intelligence collection facility outside the USSR is at Lourdes near Havana, Cuba, and enables the Soviets to monitor sensitive U.S. maritime, military, and space communications as well as telephone conversations in the United States. In addition to the Soviets at Lourdes, there are 2,800 Soviet military advisers and a 2,800-man combat brigade in Cuba. Cuban ports and airfields support Caribbean deployments by Soviet naval task forces and long-range naval aviation, including seven deployments of TU-95 Bear naval reconnaissance aircraft and six deployments of TU-142 Bear antisubmarine warfare aircraft in 1985. Cuban and Soviet naval forces, including the 20,000-ton Soviet helicopter cruiser *Lenin*, have joined in recent maneuvers off the southern coast of the United States.[15] According to Raymond Duncan, Cuba is a "key maritime strategic piece on Moscow's global chessboard" as well as a port of call for merchant marine fishing fleet operations, trade activities, and oceanographic work.[16] Among communist

---

[15]*Soviet Military Power*, p. 128.
[16]See Raymond Duncan, *The Soviet Union and Cuba* (New York: Praeger, 1985), p. 7.

countries, only Vietnam and East Germany have received more military aid than Cuba has from the USSR.

In addition to major facilities in Cuba and Vietnam, the Soviets have access in Syria to the ports of Latakia and Tartus as well as to the airfield at Tiyas. Tartus has become the primary maintenance facility for Soviet submarines operating in the Mediterranean, with a submarine tender, oiler, and water tanker located there. The number of Soviet naval combatant port visits and IL-38 May antisubmarine warfare aircraft deployments to both Syria and Libya has risen over the past several years.[17] The Soviets also have access to an airbase outside Aden, South Yemen, with electronic observation and communications facilities essential to Soviet staging, ocean surveillance, and power projection capabilities.[18] The Soviet Navy uses Aden for crew changes, minor repairs, and refueling and replenishment. These facilities complement Soviet access to anchorages off Socotra Island near South Yemen and the facilities at Dahlak Island near Ethiopia.

From a geostrategic point of view, the USSR's greatest successes and most important clients lie in areas adjacent to its most important adversaries—the United States and China. Moscow's strong ties and military presence in Cuba and Vietnam, as well as its close relationship with India, have given it leverage in areas of vulnerability for Washington and Beijing. To the extent that a Soviet client such as Nicaragua can distract U.S. attention and resources from other regions, it serves broader Soviet policy interests. It also provides Moscow with a new foothold for projecting influence in Central America. Although East-West relations, and particularly the U.S.-Soviet strategic relationship, are of primary importance in Moscow's perception of its foreign policy interests, the Soviet Union has refused to accept the concept of linkage and has continued to pursue opportunities to project its power in the Third World despite potential damage to U.S.-Soviet relations.

Soviet military successes have not led directly to commensurate political triumphs in the Third World. Egyptian president Anwar Sadat and Somali president Siad Barre unilaterally abrogated friendship treaties with the USSR in the mid-1970s despite their political and military dependence on the Soviets. Syrian president Assad and Iraqi president Saddam Hussein have often ignored Soviet interests in pursuing their respective interests against the Palestinians and the Iranians. Soviet weaponry allowed an Egyptian return to the Sinai peninsula in 1973 but could not prevent U.S. domination and Soviet exclusion from the Egyptian-Israeli diplomatic process that followed the October War. Indeed, throughout the Middle East and Africa over the past ten years, Soviet military support has not led to political influence or even a political role in the diplomatic process. Moscow played no role in various disengagement agreements and the Camp David process in the Middle East

[17]*Soviet Military Power*, p. 134.
[18]See Stephen Page, *The Soviet Union and the Yemens* (New York: Praeger, 1985), p. 80.

and was similarly excluded from the Lancaster House talks as well as the Lusaka and Nkomati accords in southern Africa more recently.[19]

Moreover, the tendency for dictatorial governments in the Third World to become domestically unpopular, the problem of guerrilla opposition to these governments, and the constraints facing Soviet forces in distant operations have placed limits on Soviet efforts to expand Moscow's influence in key regional areas. Many pro-Soviet clients are heading weak states that have no guarantee of remaining in power and lack consistent support from other Third World countries. The Soviets presumably would have serious doubts about using their own ground forces in support of such Third World regimes in distant areas, despite their willingness to do so on their borders with Hungary, Czechoslovakia, and Afghanistan.

The forces needed to resolve a crisis on the borders of the USSR can be massed and operated along the lines of traditional Soviet military doctrine, but the introduction of military force into noncontiguous areas would generate a series of geographical and military problems due to an absence of sea-based air power, transportation difficulties, and limited naval gunfire support. The writings of the former commander-in-chief of the Soviet Navy, Admiral Sergei Gorshkov, and others have paid increasing attention to the political value of global naval deployments, but Soviet military writings have not discussed the conduct of distant operations nor such operational problems as force deployment, combined arms, coordination, and logistics and communications support.

In the near term the Soviets can be expected to try to capitalize on their comparative advantage in various military instruments of influence, particularly arms sales and military aid, to expand their political influence in the Third World. Instability in Iran and the impasse in the Arab-Israeli peace process should lead to opportunities in the Middle East. Political instability and the black liberation struggle in Africa should continue to make Soviet military assistance essential. The Soviet commitment to upgrade Cuba and Vietnamese military capabilities should assure expanded use of their air and naval facilities. Indian dependence on the USSR for military assistance should allow the Soviets to maintain their position in South Asia over the next few years. Continued Soviet probing for additional military access can be expected, particularly in the Middle East and the Persian Gulf, which is so near to the USSR and so critical to the balance of power between East and West. Southeast Asia is also important because it provides a useful base for exerting pressure on China and Japan and allows access to sealanes to the Indian Ocean and southern African countries that are of significance to the USSR.

The trend over the past three decades has been for increased Soviet military and political involvement in key regional issues and crises in the Third World. The Soviets have provided significant airlifts of arms in flashpoint situations,

---

[19]See Robert Freedman, *Soviet Policy in the Middle East since 1970* (New York: Praeger, 1982).

as well as support for large-scale introduction of Cuban forces armed with Soviet weapons in Third World conflicts. Soviet acquisition of overflight clearances and access to facilities abroad support Moscow's military operations as well as friendly forces. The deployment of Soviet naval and naval air forces protect and defend the USSR's interests abroad, asserting Soviet rights on the high seas and affirming Soviet support of Third World governments. Soviet leaders presumably believe that the presence of their naval forces—as a visible symbol of Moscow's concern and capability—inhibits Western military initiatives in areas of the Third World during periods of tension.

Although Moscow has accepted a measure of risk in introducing forces into conflicts, it has nevertheless exercised a policy that limits the role of Soviet forces and avoids confrontation with the United States. Soviet pilots and air defense units have engaged in combat but have not operated outside friendly territory. Soviet naval forces have established or augmented a presence in regions of conflict but have not engaged in combat. Airborne units have been placed on alert during times of conflict but have not been introduced into noncontiguous areas. Soviet combat ground forces have not appeared in confrontations in noncontiguous areas. In view of the limitations on Moscow's ability to project power into the Third World, the Soviets will probably continue to exercise constraint in the near term in committing their own forces to regional crises.

4

The Soviet Union and the Third World: The Economic Dimension

Abraham S. Becker

Ill-used as the canonical Leninist quotation may be, it still seems a useful starting point from which to overlook thirty years of Soviet economic involvement in the Third World: "Socialism has exerted and continues to exert its main influence on world development through its economic policy and through its successes in the socio-economic field." An optimistic perception of Soviet power and its economic foundations emboldened the Khrushchev regime in the breakthrough in the mid-1950s and encouraged wide-ranging commitments. Economic realism after Khrushchev's overthrow led to a restructuring of Soviet aid, emphasizing greater contributions from recipients. Economic stringency in the last years of Brezhnev and the brief interregnum that followed probably was mainly responsible for limiting the extent of aid to marginal clients. The evident lack of "successes in the socio-economic field" in the USSR, along with the general failure of dirigiste planning and public-sector industrialization in the developing countries, made the Soviet economic model of diminishing interest to the policy makers of developing countries; these factors also seriously complicated Soviet efforts to understand the "laws" of Third World development. Such handicaps are bound to continue to "exert . . . [a] main influence" on the Soviet Union's ability to extend its position in the Third World.

This chapter surveys some of the outstanding issues and changes in the economic dimension of Soviet involvement in the noncommunist Third World.[1] It attempts to pull together the salient features of what we know (in

[1]"Third World," "LDCs" (less developed countries), and "developing countries" are used interchangeably in this paper. The rubric "noncommunist" in U.S. government statistics generally means the exclusion of China, Kampuchea, North Korea, Laos, Mongolia, and Vietnam in Asia, and Cuba in the Western Hemisphere. Afghanistan after 1979 is *not* excluded. In earlier years Albania and Yugoslavia were included in the group of communist developing states, but they will not be dealt with here. Neither is China. Here the term "communist developing states" refers to North Korea, Mongolia, the three Indochinese states, and Cuba.

a personal interpretation, of course), not to provide original research into the basic issues. After reviewing the development of Soviet arms transfer, economic aid, and trade relations, the chapter concludes with some reflections on elements of the balance of Soviet effectiveness and prospects for future change.

Arms Transfers

It was with arms that the Soviet Union began its active postwar involvement in the Third World, and such sales have continued to be the principal instrument of the extension of Soviet influence and presence. Moscow's arms deliveries to the developing countries in the first half of the 1980s roughly equaled, perhaps even exceeded, sales by the United States.[2] Apart from their political-military utility, which falls outside the domain of this chapter, arms sales have made a major contribution to the Soviet hard-currency balance of payments in the last decade; as noted below, they probably bring other economic benefits as well.

Getting a good quantitative picture of Soviet arms transfer relations with the LDCs is not easy because of Soviet secrecy and the general tendency of Moscow's clients to observe their patron's injunctions regarding discretion. The Central Intelligence Agency (CIA) releases estimates in its statistical annual[3] of total deliveries and agreements for noncommunist countries but has published no regional detail since 1980.[4] The Defense Intelligence Agency generally provides only fragmentary information in its annual appearances before the congressional Joint Economic Committee.[5] The arms transfer figures published by the U.S. Arms Control and Disarmament Agency (ACDA) are said to be "estimates by U.S. government sources," qualified as "approximations based on limited information."[6] Because of differences in period and groups of recipients covered, the ACDA data are difficult to compare with the CIA figures.[7] Moreover, it is difficult to distinguish aid from

---

[2]CIA, *Handbook of Economic Statistics, 1986* (Washington, D.C., September 1986), pp. III, 120; U.S. Congress, Joint Economic Committee, Subcommittee on Economic Resources, Competitiveness and Security Economics, *Allocation of Resources in the Soviet Union and China—1985*, Part II (Washington, D.C., 1986), pp. 19–20.

[3]CIA, *Handbook of Economic Statistics*, 19— (Washington, D.C.).

[4]CIA, *Communist Aid Activities in Non-Communist Less Developed Countries, 1979 and 1954–79* (Washington, D.C., October 1980).

[5]See, for example, *Allocation of Resources in the Soviet Union and China—1985.*

[6]U.S. Arms Control and Disarmament Agency, *World Military Expenditures and Arms Transfers, 1985* (Washington, D.C., August 1985), p. 143.

[7]ACDA's definition of developing countries embraces the communist LDCs including China and Yugoslavia. CIA excludes all these countries. If one subtracts Soviet extensions to China, Kampuchea, North Korea, Laos, Mongolia, Vietnam, Bulgaria, Yugoslavia (the latter two also considered LDCs), and Cuba from the ACDA cumulative total for LDCs in 1979–83, the result is $40.1 billion compared to the CIA sum of $44.7 billion, a difference of 12 percent. The reasons for the difference are not known.

sales in Soviet transfers, as U.S. government data provide no clues as to distribution among these elements. It seems prudent, therefore, to speak of military aid *and* trade in discussing Soviet arms transfers.

The U.S. government estimates, as well as those compiled by the Stockholm International Peace Research Institute (SIPRI),[8] have been challenged by Moshe Efrat as substantially underestimated, by factors of 1.5 to 2 or more, according to information he compiled from a variety of Arab sources.[9] It is not possible to assess his critique here, because of the inaccessibility of his sources and the security classification of U.S. government data. Moreover, Efrat provides no regional breakdowns. We have no choice, therefore, but to rely on such U.S. government materials as are available.

Moscow's arms relations with the Third World began with the Czech-Egyptian arms deal in 1955, a $250 million venture. In the decade and a half that followed that audacious breakthrough, Soviet arms supply broadened and deepened, but annual deliveries still averaged only about $350 million (see Table 1). The next sixteen years, however, witnessed an extraordinary surge in Soviet arms supply. The average annual value of agreements and deliveries in 1970–85 was fourteen times as high as in the first fifteen-year period. If Soviet sales averaged $500 million a year in the decade after the Czech-Egyptian deal, the next ten years brought the annual value of agreements to the $5 billion region, and in the late 1970s and early 1980s annual agreements went over $10 billion.

The mid-1970s were clearly a watershed in Soviet arms relations with the LDCs. There had been a considerable upswing as a direct and indirect result of the Six Day War in 1967, but even in that boom the Soviets were still selling second-line equipment to countries with sharply limited budgets. Both conditions changed in the 1970s: the oil price revolution brought the wealth that fueled inflamed demands after the 1973 war; increasing competition with Western suppliers and the demands of clients forced the Soviet Union to offer much more sophisticated, often first-line equipment. New

---

[8]SIPRI, whose estimates are published in its yearbook, draws its information from public (non-Soviet) sources, consisting "mainly of reports from recipient countries, or accounts in the large number of newsletters, journals and reference works which attempt to identify transactions and inventories." The register maintained is of exports of (apparently) major weapons only, which are priced according to the Western weapon most closely matching the Soviet System. SIPRI, *World Armaments and Disarmament: SIPRI Yearbook, 1983* (New York: Taylor & Francis, 1983), pp. 361–62. The actual values of exports estimated by SIPRI are substantially below the CIA figures of deliveries in the period since 1975. Some of the differences may be explained by SIPRI's use of constant 1975 dollar prices as weights, whereas the CIA figures are in current prices, but in 1976–78 alone the CIA figures are almost double the SIPRI estimates. SIPRI, *World Armaments and Disarmament: SIPRI Yearbook 1984* (London: Taylor & Francis, 1984), pp. 214–15; CIA figures from Table 1. The SIPRI figures are not broken down by region or country of delivery. For SIPRI's criticism of U.S. government figures, see *SIPRI Yearbook, 1984*, pp. 180–83.

[9]Moshe Efrat, "The Economics of Soviet Arms Transfers to the Third World," in Peter Wiles and Efrat, *The Economics of Soviet Arms* (London: Suntory-Toyota Center for Economics and Related Disciplines, London School of Economics and Political Science, May 1985).

Table 1. Soviet and East European military aid and trade with noncommunist LDCs: Total agreements and deliveries, 1955–69, 1970–85 (in million current $)

	Soviet		East European	
	Agreements	Deliveries	Agreements	Deliveries
1955–69	5,875	5,060 (86)[a]	935	840 (90)[a]
1970	1,150	995	50	75
1971	1,590	865	120	125
1972	1,680	1,215	155	75
1973	2,890	3,135	130	130
1974	5,735	2,225	600	210
1975	3,185	2,035	635	275
1976	6,140	3,110	355	350
1977	9,645	4,815	650	355
1978	2,700	6,075	560	550
1979	8,835	8,340	750	645
1980	14,860	8,125	895	645
1981	6,535	8,175	2,595	1,330
1982	10,960	8,660	1,775	1,915
1983	2,535	7,495	1,445	1,195
1984	9,155	7,205	965	2,025
1985	2,130	5,530	2,165	1,500
1970–73	7,310	6,210 (85)	455	405 (89)
1974–79	36,240	26,600 (73)	3,550	2,385 (67)
1980–85	46,175	45,190 (98)	9,840	8,610 (88)
1970–85	89,725	78,000 (87)	13,845	11,400 (82)

SOURCES: 1955–69, 1970, and 1971—CIA, *Communist Aid Activities in Non-Communist Less Developed Countries, 1979 and 1954–79* (Washington, D.C., October 1980), p. 13; 1972–73—Department of State, *Soviet and East European Aid to the Third World, 1981* (Washington, D.C., February 1983), p. 4; 1974—CIA, *Handbook of Economic Statistics, 1984* (Washington, D.C., September 1984), p. 109; 1975—CIA, *Handbook of Economic Statistics, 1985* (Washington, D.C., September 1985), p. 109; 1976–85—CIA, *Handbook of Economic Statistics, 1986* (Washington, D.C., September 1986), p. 111.

NOTE: There are slight differences between the cumulative total for 1954–74 shown in the CIA 1985 *Handbook* (the first annual figure is for 1975) and the 1955–74 sum of the entries for this period in the table above, as follows:

	Soviet		East European	
	Agreements	Deliveries	Agreements	Deliveries
1985 *Handbook*	18,910	13,520	2,010	1,450
Table	18,920	13,495	1,990	1,455

The largest difference is of 1 percent in East European agreements.

a. Figures in parentheses are ratios of deliveries to agreements in percent.

opportunities developed in sub-Saharan Africa (Angola, Ethiopia, Mozambique). Soviet supply prices also rose markedly in the heady new market.

Eastern Europe is a junior but not negligible partner in the arms supply business. Its annual average rate of deliveries in 1970–85 was thirteen times larger than in the first fifteen-year period, the rate of its agreements fourteen

Table 2. Soviet military aid and trade with noncommunist LDCs: Agreements and deliveries by region, 1956–74, 1975–79, 1979–83

In million current $	1956–74		1975–79		1979–83
	Agreements	Deliveries	Agreements	Deliveries	Deliveries
North Africa	2,805	665	8,155	6,500	9,000
Sub-Saharan Africa	715	410	3,920	3,120	4,910
East Asia	890	885	—	—	—
Latin America	205	30	765	645	540
Middle East	11,980	9,375	12,465	9,300	20,375
South Asia	2,330	2,130	3,080	2,280	5,250
Total	18,925	13,495	28,385[a]	21,845	40,085[b]
As percentage of total[c]					
North Africa	15%	5%	29%	30%	22%
Sub-Saharan Africa	4	3	14	14	12
East Asia	5	7	—	—	—
Latin America	1	—	3	3	1
Middle East	63	69	44	43	51
South Asia	12	16	11	10	13

SOURCES: 1956–74 and 1975–79—CIA, *Communist Aid Activities . . . 1979 and 1954–79,* p. 14 (the CIA annual total figures for 1975–79, from which the cumulative sums were computed, differ from those given in Department of State, *Soviet and East European Aid . . . 1981,* Table 6, but the largest relative change, for deliveries in 1979, is only 15 percent; hence the structure is not likely to have been significantly affected by later corrections); 1979–83—ACDA, *World Military Expenditures and Arms Transfers* (Washington, D.C., August 1985), Table III.
    a. The actual total is $35 million higher because of rounding errors.
    b. Includes $10 million for Papua New Guinea.
    c. Sum of components may not add to total because of rounding.

times higher. Deliveries are now fluctuating near the $2 billion level annually. For Eastern Europe, too, the mid-1970s saw a jump in sales, but the early 1980s brought even more remarkable increases, primarily in Africa and the Middle East.

The geographical distribution of Soviet arms transfers has also undergone some change (see Table 2).[10] In the last half of the 1970s Africa, North and sub-Saharan, assumed considerably greater relative importance than it had in

[10]The totals in Table 2 are more or less identical with those in Table 1 for the period 1956–74, but there are differences for the other two periods (in million $):

	1975–79		1979–83
	Agreements	Deliveries	Deliveries
Table 1	30,505	24,375	39,765
Table 2	28,385	21,845	38,285
% Difference, Table 1 vs Table 2	7	12	4

the previous nineteen years. This finding is in part a statistical artifact: East Asia disappears from the tabulation because Vietnam is now considered a direct communist ally. However, if East Asia were subtracted from the 1956–74 totals, the relative decline of the Middle East in the latter 1970s would be more marked. It appears that in the early 1980s the Middle East moved back toward its earlier, relatively dominant position; major arms agreements with Iraq and Syria were a principal cause. The increased weight of South Asia recently relative to the 1975–79 period reflects large deliveries to India and Afghanistan.

Although the data are incomplete, it seems clear that Soviet arms deals are still heavily concentrated by value among a few major clients. Through 1981 Libya was the single largest noncommunist Soviet arms client, with some $15 billion of military equipment and supplies purchased, of which half had already been delivered.[11] In the early 1980s Syria took up the number one position. According to the ACDA figures for 1979–83, ten countries (Afghanistan, Algeria, Angola, Ethiopia, India, Iraq, Libya, Syria, North Yemen, and South Yemen) accounted for over 90 percent of total transfers to noncommunist LDCs; 72 percent of the total was directed to five countries (in descending order Syria, Iraq, Libya, India, and Algeria). Despite the reaching out into new regions, Soviet attention remains concentrated on that arc of countries from North Africa to India which are, to cite language made familiar in Soviet defenses of its involvement in the Middle East, "close to the USSR's southern frontiers."[12]

The CIA does not publish figures on Soviet (or East European) arms transfers to communist countries. The only regular U.S. government source for these data is ACDA, whose estimates for selected periods are shown in Table 3. For 1975–79 and 1979–83, the ACDA numbers indicate that arms deliveries to the communist LDCs (excluding China) add 12 and 24 percent, respectively, to the total volume of arms shipments to noncommunist LDCs shown in Table 2. The increase in transfers to communist countries between the two periods was about two and a half times, compared to a growth of 83 percent in deliveries to noncommunist countries. Thus a global arms transfer series would show more rapid growth than is indicated in Table 1. The effect on the pattern of regional distribution, of course, is significantly to increase the shares of East Asia and Latin America at the expense of the other regions.

Soviet military transfers to noncommunist LDCs once had substantial aid elements, even if only in terms of the soft currency with which they were paid. That situation sharply changed in the 1970s too, as Moscow insisted increasingly on hard-currency settlement. Moreover, equipment sales may

---

[11]U.S. Department of State, *Soviet and East European Aid to the Third World, 1981* (Washington, D.C., February 1983), p. 9.

[12]Of course, absolutely small amounts of arms aid can make a significant difference in the less arms-rich environments of certain Third World countries, for example, in Central America.

Table 3. ACDA estimates of Soviet military deliveries to communist LDCs, in million current $

	1967–76	1975–79	1979–83
Kampuchea	5	20	170
North Korea	480	280	210
Laos	15	100	180
Mongolia	30	120	625
Vietnam	2,481	1,300[a]	5,200[a]
Cuba	355	875[a]	3,100[a]
Subtotal	3,011	2,695	9,485
China	191	210	130
Total	3,557	2,905	9,615
Average Annual (excl. China)	337	539	1,897

SOURCES: ACDA, *World Military Expenditures and Arms Transfers: 1967–1976* (Washington, D.C., July 1978), Table VII (col. 1); *1970–1979* (Washington, D.C., March 1982), Table III (col. 2); *1985* (Washington, D.C., August 1985), Table III (col. 3).

a. According to the Defense Intelligence Agency (DIA), *Allocation 1985* (see note 3 above), p. 20, Soviet deliveries to Vietnam and Cuba were as follows (in billion dollars):

	1974–79	1980–85
Vietnam	2.1	4.9
Cuba	1.3	3.9

have benefited from price discounts—at least from a nominal base price—and standard aid features, such as ten- or twelve-year credits at relatively low interest, but other components of arms agreements, support and infrastructure, were much less likely to be supplied on concessionary terms. Not all arms sales to LDCs now require payment in hard currency; Moscow is still prepared to be flexible on terms when political considerations are uppermost. Economics may largely explain the ongoing, massive Libyan connection, but it is doubtful that it explains the Syrian arms deal of 1982.[13] It is, however, not possible to quantify these sketchy qualitative indicators.

I also note in passing that the sharp increase in Soviet arms sales in the 1970s must have had a negative impact on the transportation and distribution network required to transfer weapons, matériel, parts, and supplies from the USSR to purchasing countries. However, economies of scale resulting from high-volume exports could have helped contain the escalation of costs in Soviet domestic military development and procurement. The increase in sales may have also reduced Soviet military inventory costs.

If the 1970s' upsurge in Soviet arms sales is explained in large part by the oil

[13]After the devastating blows to Syrian air defense inflicted by the Israelis in the Lebanon War, as well as to make amends for Soviet inaction during the war, Moscow replaced the losses and upgraded the Syrian inventory, especially with SA-5 surface-to-air missile systems.

price revolution, the recent softening of energy markets may presage an easing of LDC demand. Libyan oil income has dropped precipitously, from about $22 billion in 1980 to about $8 billion in 1985, and signs of belt tightening in both civil and military sectors abound.[14] Saudi Arabia, the financial angel of many Middle East purchases from both the USSR and the West, is also hurting and seems reluctant to continue its largess. On the other hand, the LDC demand for Soviet arms may not be highly income-elastic, and the supply of Third World conflict seems inexhaustible. Also, falling oil prices in the world market and stagnation in domestic Soviet oil production threaten sizable reductions in Soviet hard-currency earnings, underscoring the importance to Moscow of arms exports for hard currency and suggesting the possibility of shaving prices to maintain high volume. Table 1 shows some tendency to decline in deliveries after 1979, although there was an upward spurt in the volume of agreements in 1984. Soviet arms transfers may grow more slowly in the future than they did in the last part of the 1970s, but the Kremlin will probably exert itself to maintain the hard-currency component at high levels.

Economic Aid

Arms transfer was the principal instrument by which the USSR pried open the Third World, but economic aid has been a major supplementary tool. Before there was an Egyptian-Czech arms deal, there were small trade or aid agreements with Argentina and India in 1953 and Afghanistan in 1954. In some countries, at particular times, the economic aid has been more important, although there has been substantial overlap between the two, especially in the earlier years. In any case, economic aid serves some of the same political purposes—demonstrating support, gaining access, helping maintain politically valuable clients. Often enough, however, it also serves economic ends. Perhaps the most important but least known fact about Soviet aid is that the overwhelming bulk of it goes to three communist allies—Cuba, Vietnam, and Mongolia.

In the 1950s and 1960s Soviet economic aid commitments (or extensions) to noncommunist LDCs (see Table 4) were actually larger than counterpart arms agreements, although deliveries were considerably more rapid in arms transfers. Average annual rates of extension of economic aid ran about $400 million in 1954–69, increased some 70 percent in the first part of the 1970s, and jumped sharply in the second half of the decade to a level of over $2 billion. The annual average stabilized in the first half of the eighties at a level considerably lower than the peak levels in 1978–79. Deliveries increased more

---

[14]Gerald F. Seib, "Lower Oil Prices Put the Squeeze on Libya and Its Military Costs," *Wall Street Journal*, October 3, 1985.

Table 4. Soviet and East European economic aid to LDCs: Total commitments and deliveries, 1954–69 and 1970–83 (in million current $)

	Soviet		East European	
	Agreements	Deliveries	Agreements	Deliveries
1954–69	6,565	3,225 (49)	2,790	910 (33)
1970	200	390	195	145
1971	1,125	420	485	190
1972	655	430	925	175
1973	715	500	630	230
1974	815	700	840	235
1975	1,970	500	545	270
1976	1,080	460	985	405
1977	435	535	525	505
1978	3,000	520	1,600	430
1979	3,800	615	645	310
1980	2,605	950	1,345	325
1981	845	920	895	500
1982	1,030	1,340	625	675
1983	3,185	1,640	415	705
1984	2,480	1,475	2,020	720
1985	2,390	1,405	660	530
1970–74	3,510	2,440 (70)	3,075	975 (32)
1975–79	10,285	2,630 (26)	4,300	1,920 (45)
1980–85	12,535	7,730 (62)	5,960	3,455 (58)
1970–85	26,330	12,800 (49)	13,335	6,350 (48)

Sources: 1954–69, 1970, and 1971—CIA, *Communist Aid Activities . . . 1979 and 1954–79*, p. 17; 1972 and 1973—Department of State, *Soviet and East European Aid . . . 1981*, p. 16; 1974—CIA, *Handbook of Economic Statistics, 1984*, p. 109; 1975—CIA, *Handbook of Economic Statistics, 1985*, p. 109; 1976–85—CIA, *Handbook of Economic Statistics, 1986*, p. 111.
NOTE: There are slight differences between the cumulative total for 1954–74 shown in CIA 1985 *Handbook* and the 1955–74 sum of the entries in this table, as follows:

	Soviet		East European	
	Agreements	Deliveries	Agreements	Deliveries
1985 *Handbook*	10,080	5,670	5,830	1,900
Table	10,075	5,665	5,865	1,885

Figures in parentheses are ratios of deliveries to agreements in percent.

slowly than commitments; the average annual rate of deliveries was not much higher in the late 1970s than in the earlier part of the decade. However, they picked up smartly in the first half of the 1980s, probably to fulfill the larger extensions in 1978–80. This pattern is reflected in a fluctuating ratio of deliveries to commitments: deliveries averaged almost half as much as extensions in 1954–69; the ratio jumped to 70 percent in 1970–74, dropped sharply to 26 percent in the second half of the 1970s, and rose markedly again in the 1980s, to 62 percent. By contrast, the arms delivery ratio was generally above 85 percent; only in one of the subperiods shown in Table 1 was it as low as 73 percent. That comparison says much about the immediacy of the typical arms transfer agreement with the LDCs and the long-term character of economic aid deliveries.

Table 4, like those preceding it, is valued in current dollars, that is, gross of price inflation. Regrettably, no estimates in constant dollars are available, but it is useful to remind ourselves that the 1970s saw high rates of increase in the prices of goods traded in the world market. A very approximate indication of the size of this factor may be gleaned by using the Soviet implicit price deflator for trade turnover with all nonsocialist countries, which came to 155 percent in 1983 on a 1975 base.[15] If we take a three-year average centering on 1975 and 1983, the nominal increases in Soviet agreements and deliveries between the two dates are 73 and 168 percent respectively; deflated by the Soviet trade price index, the "real" increases are 12 and 73 percent, respectively. Moreover, the three-year average for commitments centering on 1983 is absolutely lower in both nominal and real terms than the counterpart average centering on 1979. The Soviets appear to have been in a less generous mood in recent years.

If Eastern Europe was a distinctly junior partner to the USSR in the business of arms transfers to the LDCs, it was, in relative terms, a more important partner in the extension or delivery of economic aid. Considering the entire thirty-year history of modern Soviet involvement with the Third World, East Europeans promised and provided roughly half as much economic aid as did the Soviets but committed and delivered only about one-seventh as much in armaments. Over the three decades the sum of East European economic aid agreements is only a tenth larger than its military aid agreements; in contrast, East European military deliveries have been almost 70 percent larger than economic aid deliveries. This observation reflects a very high delivery-to-agreement ratio for East European arms transfers, much higher than for economic aid.

Table 4 indicates fluctuating levels of Soviet economic aid commitments since 1970. Behind these aggregate figures lie some interesting shifts in country and regional composition. The data are not easy to reconcile, but what we know is shown in Table 5.[16]

In its initial, Khrushchev-led period, Soviet aid was heavily concentrated in three countries: Egypt, Afghanistan, and India accounted for 61 percent of the total. India remained a favorite in the first half of the Brezhnev period,

---

[15]Ministerstvo vneshnei torgovli, *Vneshniaia torgovlia SSSR* (Moscow), the annuals of 1976 and 1983, dividing the change in values at current prices by the index of real volume growth.

[16]The totals in Table 5 for 1955–74, 1975–79, and 1980–81 differ from the figures shown in Table 4 for unknown reasons. In Table 5 they are taken from earlier State Department and CIA sources and in Table 4 largely from the CIA 1985 and 1986 *Handbooks*.

but Egypt's relative role, of course, diminished after Nasser's death. Aid was extended in relatively large volumes to Iran, Pakistan, and Turkey. Thus while the overall share of the Middle East and South Asia remained about the same, the country distribution changed significantly. This was the result of Brezhnev and Kosygin's reassessment after Khrushchev's ouster.[17]

In the second half of the 1970s major agreements were concluded with Morocco and Turkey, and the Indian component was sharply lower. Through the end of the 1970s the Soviets had provided $7.9 billion in aid to the Middle East, more than 60 percent of it to Turkey, Iran, and Egypt (Syria and Iraq got an additional 19 percent). About $5 billion was extended to South Asia, with over 70 percent going to India and Afghanistan (another 18 percent to Pakistan). The aggregate volumes of aid to sub-Saharan Africa and Latin America were small, $1.2 billion and $1 billion respectively, but the distribution in these areas was also concentrated: Argentina, Chile, and Columbia received 69 percent of the Latin American total; Ethiopia, Guinea, and Somalia accounted for half the sub-Saharan Africa total. The higher profile of Soviet involvement in black Africa in the 1970s expressed itself primarily on the military not the economic aid side.

In the first half of the 1980s the geographic structure alters distinctly. A sharp decline in the North African and Middle Eastern shares is balanced by very substantial increases in the relative weight of sub-Saharan Africa, South Asia, and Latin America. The CIA data fail to identify the partners for over half of Soviet aid extensions to sub-Saharan Africa, but Angola and Mozambique are presumably involved. Thanks to the $1.2 billion aid agreement in 1985, India's share of the extensions in South Asia is more than half; Afghanistan accounted for another 35 percent.

The scale of the USSR's aid to the noncommunist LDCs is dwarfed by assistance to developing communist allies (see Table 6). Soviet aid commitments to communist LDCs in the period 1954–77, at $19 billion, were 40 percent larger than aid to noncommunist developing countries, at $13.6 billion.[18] In the next seven years, however, the volume of aid to communist clients shot up, according to CIA estimates, to a total of $34 billion. In contrast, aid extensions to noncommunist countries in 1984 were below the 1978–79 level. Over two-thirds of the 1978–84 aid to communist countries went to Cuba and another one-sixth to Vietnam. Aid to Mongolia lost considerably in relative magnitude. In 1981–82 aid to Vietnam alone exceeded

[17]Francis Fukuyama cites Nadav Safran, *From War to War: The Arab-Israeli Confrontation, 1948–1967* (New York: Pegasus, 1969), p. 128, and Lawrence Whetton, *The Canal War: Four-Power Conflict in the Middle East* (Cambridge: MIT Press, 1974), p. 31, as sources for a Kremlin policy reconsideration, in "The Domestic Roots of Soviet Third World Policy," paper delivered at a conference on domestic sources of Soviet foreign and domestic policy, University of California at Los Angeles, October 10–11, 1985.

[18]Regrettably, a change in the scope of coverage of the CIA data precludes use of earlier CIA sources and therefore any attempt at breaking down the 1954–77 period into smaller intervals.

Table 5. Soviet economic aid agreements to noncommunist LDCs by region, selected periods (in million current $)

	1955–64	1965–74	1975–79	1980	1981	1982	1983	1984	1985
North Africa	250	300	2,365	315	—	negl.	277	negl.	356
Algeria	230	195	290	315	—	—	250	—	340
Morocco	—	100	2,000	—	—	—	—	—	—
Tunisia	20	—	75	—	—	—	27	—	—
Mauritania		10				negl.		negl.	16
Sub-Saharan Africa	490	380	335	310	125	696	311	576	216
Ethiopia	100	—	125	—	10	—	266	276	negl.
Others		905		55	15	38	20	182	23
Unidentified		70		255	100	658[a]	25	118	193
Middle East	1,450	2,520	3,895	—	55	3	1,632	1,345	—
Egypt	1,000	440	—	—	—	—	360	—	—
Iran	65	725	375	—	—	—	n.a.	—	—
Iraq	185	370	150	—	—	—	1,000	455	—
North Yemen		143[b]							
South Yemen		204[b]				?	?	?	
Syria	100	360	310	—	—	—	—	820	—
Turkey		2,380[b]							
Unidentified		c. 1,060			55	3	272	70	
South Asia	1,440	2,355	1,185	1,195	100	90	861	237	1,607
Afghanistan	530	300	450	395	25	90	371	237	325
Bangladesh		304[b]			70	—	73	—	82
India	810	1,130	340	800	—	—	140	—	1,200

Pakistan	40	655	225				277	n.a.	—
Sri Lanka	—	158[b]	—	—	—	—	—	—	—
Nepal	—	30[b]	—	—	—	—	—	—	—
East Asia	150	110	negl.	—	5	—	—	—	—
Kampuchea-Laos	—	30	—	—	—	—	—	—	—
Other	—	230	—	—	—	—	—	—	—
Latin America	30	595	340	250	170	176	182	324	211
Nicaragua				—	80	?	?	?	?
TOTAL	3,805	6,255	8,120	2,070	445	965	3,263	2,482	2,390

Percent of total aid agreements[c]

Region	1955–64	1965–74	1975–79	1980–85
North Africa	7%	5%	29%	8%
Sub-Saharan Africa	13	6	4	19
Middle East	38	40	48	26
South Asia	38	38	15	35
East Asia	4	2	—	—
Latin America	1	10	4	11

SOURCES: 1955–78 (North Yemen, South Yemen, Turkey, Bangladesh, Sri Lanka, Nepal)—CIA, *Communist Aid Activities in Non-Communist Less Developed Countries, 1978* (Washington, D.C., September 1979), pp. 7–10; 1955–64, 1965–74, and 1975–79—CIA, *Communist Aid Activities ... 1979 and 1954–79,* pp. 7, 18–20, 39, 1980–81 and Nicaragua 1955–80—Department of State, *Soviet and East European Aid ... 1981,* pp. 17–19; 1982—CIA, *Handbook of Economic Statistics, 1984* (Washington, D.C., September 1984), p. 110; 1983—CIA, *Handbook of Economic Statistics, 1985,* p. 110; 1984–85—CIA, *Handbook of Economic Statistics, 1986,* p. 112.

Negl., n.a. = negligible or not available, according to source.
a. The figure in the source is 660; it has been lowered to fit within the stated total for Africa.
b. 1954–78.
c. Discrepancies between totals and sum of components are due to rounding.

Table 6. Soviet economic aid extended to communist developing countries, 1954–84 (in million U.S. $)

	Cuba	Vietnam	Mongolia	North Korea	Four Countries
1954–77	10,300a	2,610	5,470	665	19,045
1978	2,945	565	690	35	4,235
1979	3,180	865	685	75	4,805
1980	3,465	1,050	835	260	5,610
1981	4,560	1,225	815	145	6,745
1982	4,665	1,015	870	130	6,680
1983	4,260	1,025	865	50	6,200
1984	4,620	1,040	785	55	6,500
1978–84	27,695	6,785	5,545	750	40,775

	Percent of economic aid to four countries			
1954–77	54	14	29	3
1978–84	68	17	14	2

SOURCES: 1954–78—CIA, *Handbook of Economic Statistics, 1985,* p. 113, Table 80. The first column in Table 80 is mislabeled 1954–83; it is actually 1954–82 (see the 1984 *Handbook,* p. 117). The figures for Cuba given in Table 80 are in a few cases different from those shown in Table 81 (on the same page), which provides a distribution of aid to Cuba by type of assistance. The differences come to $105–160 million, 2–4 percent of the smaller totals shown above. I am told the figures in Table 81 are later, revised estimates; 1979–84—CIA, *Handbook of Economic Statistics, 1986,* p. 115.
   a. 1961–77.

Soviet assistance to all noncommunist LDCs, including Afghanistan. Economic aid to Cuba has exceeded by a considerable margin Soviet economic assistance to all the noncommunist LDCs in every year since 1979. North Korea was promised as much aid in 1980–83 as Algeria; only Afghanistan, Iraq, and India were promised more.

In addition to its markedly larger volume, aid to the communist allies has a different character from aid to other LDCs. Development aid to communist allies takes a back seat to trade subsidies. Such subsidies accounted for 85 percent or more of all assistance to Cuba in the last half of the 1970s, and their share in the mid-eighties is still up around 65–75 percent.[19] By the same token, the gap between extensions and deliveries of aid, focused on trade subsidies, will be much smaller for the communist LDCs. Accordingly, if 70 percent of total Soviet economic aid extensions in 1978–84 was directed to communist countries, the noncommunist LDC share in actual deliveries was probably considerably below 30 percent, perhaps less than 20 percent.

By Western calculations and comparative judgment, direct Soviet aid to the noncommunist LDCs is small in scale. The $1.5 billion of Soviet aid

[19]CIA, *Handbook of Economic Statistics, 1986,* p. 115.

deliveries to noncommunist LDCs in 1984 was one-eighth the size of U.S. gross official bilateral transfers to LDCs in the same year.[20] But not so according to Moscow, whose ambassador to the United Nations declared at a July 1982 meeting of the UN Economic and Social Council that Soviet *net* aid outlays to the LDCs in 1976–80 came to 30 billion rubles, roughly $40–45 billion at average exchange rates of the period, and accounted for 1.3 percent of Soviet national output in 1980. Table 4 indicates that Soviet *gross* deliveries on aid agreements in that five-year period came to only $3.1 billion, or about 7–8 percent of the Soviet claim.[21] The claim probably includes aid outlays on the USSR's communist developing allies, excluded from Table 4, but that addition would be quite insufficient to reconcile the two figures. What else is included in the Soviet claim is not known, and the absence of detail does not inspire confidence.[22] Regrettably, there are no publicly available figures on the repayment of Soviet credits. Even making allowances for various debt deferrals or reschedulings, it seems likely that the annual net flow of Soviet disbursements is tangibly smaller than the gross.[23]

Twenty-odd years ago the chairman of the USSR state committee for foreign economic relations bluntly observed that Soviet economic aid to noncommunist LDCs is not charity.[24] Indeed, it is on the average less "concessional" than Western aid, in terms of the general absence of grants (except to communist allies) and in the length of repayment periods—typically ten to twelve years compared to forty years for Western aid—although probably not in magnitude of interest rates. Some Soviet aid agreements carry stiffer interest terms and may not even meet the Western concessionality criteria.[25]

[20]Ibid., p. 116. Soviet aid to communist LDCs would reduce that gap by an unknown amount (CIA publishes data only on extensions to communist LDCs, not deliveries).

[21]British official estimates of the total Soviet gross disbursements are much higher, about $10 billion. *Soviet, East European and Western Development Aid, 1976–1982*, Foreign Policy Document no. 85 (London: Foreign and Commonwealth Office, 1983).

[22]For an effort to reconcile the Soviet claim with other available information which comes up considerably short of the Soviet figure, see Quintin V. S. Bach, "A Note on Soviet Statistics on Their Economic Aid," *Soviet Studies* 37 (April 1985), pp. 269–75.

[23]In a letter to the UN secretary-general, the United States, Britain, West Germany, and Japan accused the USSR and Eastern Europe of taking four times more in UN development aid than they contributed. The Western industrial nations provided over 90 percent of the contribution to the UN's development aid agencies, whereas the communist nations added a paltry 1 percent. Associated Press, July 18, 1985.

[24]S. Skachkov (then chairman of the USSR State Committee for Foreign Economic Relations), "Ravnopravie, vzaimnaia vygoda," *Pravda*, March 29, 1973. At a joint session of the two Foreign Affairs Commissions of the USSR Supreme Soviet, Delegate Stepan Chervonenko stressed that granting Soviet credits is in accord with Soviet interests, because it "stimulates the export of Soviet machinery and equipment, which improves the structure of Soviet exports. The Soviet Union receives from the developing countries in repayment valuable mineral and agricultural raw materials, manufactures and foreign currency." The same point was made by Boris Ponomarev, secretary of the Party Central Committee and head of its International Department. "Sotrudnichestvo vo imia mira, nezavisimosti i sotsial'nogo progressa" (Cooperation for peace, independence and social progress), *Pravda*, November 30, 1984.

[25]A British government estimate places the grant element in Soviet aid at about 38 percent compared with an average 70 percent in Western aid. Bach, "A Note on Soviet Statistics," pp.

On the whole, credit terms became harder in the 1970s compared with the 1950s and 1960s. The character of Soviet aid, although not directly reflecting the degree of grant element in the credits, also contributes to the same impression. There has been increasing emphasis on trade credits rather than project loans (the Soviets rarely provide balance-of-payment loans), and the aid is heavily weighted to promoting sales of Soviet machinery and equipment. Nevertheless, Soviet trade financing continues to feature interest rates considerably below those demanded in Western capital markets; unlike Western governments and lending institutions, the USSR frequently accepts goods in repayment of debts. These features of Soviet economic aid do redress the balance, at least in part.

As noted, the scale of Soviet economic aid to the noncommunist LDCs continued to grow after 1975, although at a reduced pace in recent years, especially when deflated for price change. There is some evidence suggesting that Andropov was not an enthusiastic supporter of economic aid. Francis Fukuyama cites his speeches at the December 1982 and June 1983 Party Central Committee plenums, particularly the following passage:

> Socialist countries express solidarity with these progressive states, render assistance to them in the sphere of politics and culture, and promote the strengthening of their defense. We contribute also, to the extent of our ability, to their economic development. But, on the whole, their economic development, just as the entire social progress of those countries, can be, of course, only the result of the work of their peoples and of a correct policy of their leadership.[26]

Fukuyama believes that this passage indicates that Andropov was skeptical about the utility of the Brezhnev policy and concludes, "when taken together with a number of other critical statements and articles on the Third World written at around the same time, it is evident that a major policy reassessment has been going on in high Kremlin circles since Brezhnev's death."[27] This reassessment does not appear to have had an immediate impact on aid extensions, which tripled in 1983 over the 1982 level, according to the CIA; in 1984–85, however, annual extensions declined by one-quarter.

Gorbachev has not said much about his views on the Soviet role in the developing world,[28] but it is safe to predict that domestic economic stringencies will restrain both the growth rate and the concessionality of Soviet

---

269 and 274 n. 6. For a Soviet counterclaim, see L. Zevin, "Ekonomicheskoe sotrudnichestvo stran SEV s razvivaiushchimisia gosudarstvami—vymysly i deistvitel'nost'" (Economic cooperation of CMEA countries with developing states—fiction and reality), *Mirovaia ekonomika i mezhdunarodnye otnosheniia* no. 7 (1985), pp. 60–72.

[26]"Rech' General'nogo Sekretariia Tsk KPSS tovarishcha Iu. V. Andropova" (Speech of Iu. V. Andropov, general secretary of the Central Committee of the CPSU), *Kommunist* no. 9 (June 1983), cited in Fukuyama, "The Domestic Roots."

[27]Fukuyama, "The Domestic Roots."

[28]But see Francis Fukuyama, "Gorbachev and the Third World," *Foreign Affairs* 64 (Spring 1986), pp. 715–31.

economic aid. One might expect a continued Soviet search for the type of LDC project that also promises to contribute to Soviet development needs, and a hardening of terms—hard-currency repayments, better interest rates—where possible. However, it seems safe to venture that economics will dominate politics no more in the future than in the past. When it comes to maintaining or losing a politically important client, Moscow will surely know how to be flexible, even at a real opportunity cost.

Trade

The value of trade turnover with the LDCs certainly rose rapidly in the past twenty-five years (see Table 7)—about twenty-five times. But the relative importance of these countries in Soviet trade has hardly changed since 1965 and remains fairly low. The main structural change in Soviet trade before 1980 was the rapidly growing relative weight of trade with the industrial West at the expense of trade with the communist countries.

Table 7 follows Soviet statistics and places the communist LDCs in the group of communist countries. If we recategorize China, Cuba, Laos, Mongolia, North Korea, and Vietnam as LDCs, the value of Soviet trade turnover with the LDC group (using Soviet official exchange rates and trade data) rises by the following amounts:

	1960	1970	1980	1984
Billion $	2.1	2.0	10.3	14.3
Percent	233	63	58	64

Table 7. Value and distribution of Soviet trade turnover by partner group, 1960–83 (in billion current $ and percent)

	World	Communist Countries		Developed West		LDCs	
	bill. $	bill. $	%	bill. $	%	bill. $	%
1960	11.2	8.2	73	2.1	19	0.9	8
1965	16.2	11.2	69	3.2	20	1.9	12
1970	24.5	16.0	66	5.3	22	3.2	13
1975	70.5	39.7	56	22.2	31	8.6	12
1980	144.9	77.9	54	49.3	34	17.7	12
1983	172.1	96.5	56	52.1	30	23.5	14
1984	171.8	98.9	58	50.7	30	22.3	13
1985	169.8	103.9	61	45.8	27	20.2	12

SOURCE: CIA, *Handbook of Economic Statistics, 1985*, p. 96, and *Handbook 1986*, p. 98. The figures are derived from annual issues of *Vneshtorg*, converted to dollars at official Soviet exchange rates.

NOTE: Percentages may not sum to 100 because of rounding.

The sharp relative increase in 1960 is explained by the still large volume of trade with China in that year, a level that (in current prices, at least) has not yet been regained. The fivefold increase in the value of communist LDC trade turnover with the USSR between 1970 and 1980 is primarily the result of a fourfold increase in Cuba's trade turnover in foreign trade rubles and an almost 40 percent increase in the dollar exchange value of the foreign trade ruble. However, the findings summarized in the previous paragraph are not altered when we restrict "communist" countries to European members of the Council for Mutual Economic Assistance.

The Soviets generally run an export surplus with the LDCs. The predominantly civil trade identified by country or commodity in Soviet statistics tends to be in deficit, but the sizable unidentified exports—half or more of the total (see Table 8) and believed to consist largely of arms—put overall trade with the LDCs in surplus. Thus the LDCs play a somewhat larger role in Soviet exports than in the USSR's imports (13–15 and 10–12 percent respectively since 1965). Moreover, the favorable balance with the LDCs compensates for the frequently unfavorable trade balance with developed countries or helps finance the deficit in the USSR's capital account with the West.

Until the 1970s the dominant mode of Soviet trade with the LDCs was bilateral clearing agreements and payment in nonconvertible currency. Almost half of Soviet civilian trade with noncommunist developing countries still proceeds in this mode.[29] But in the mid-1970s the LDCs and the Soviets began moving to settlement in hard currency. Hard-currency transactions accounted for substantially less than half of the trade turnover with noncommunist LDCs in 1970 but about 64 percent in 1984.[30] The predominance of hard-currency trade now is true of both exports and imports; the hard-currency share is about the same in both. On the export side, this reflects the huge importance of arms transfers; on the side of Soviet imports, purchases of grain and other food products from Latin America and South Asia were salient in 1980–81, and purchases of petroleum and products from the Middle East and North Africa have grown rapidly in recent years.

Regrettably, we do not have enough published data to provide a picture of the trend in the Soviet balance of payments with LDCs. The aggregate Soviet balance with the LDCs must have turned "hard" in the mid- and late 1970s, assuming a flow of repayments on the debt commensurate with the scale and timing of aid agreements and allowing for the sharp jump in arms exports. In the 1980s the balance of hard-currency trade with the LDCs was clearly positive for the USSR, averaging over $2 billion annually.[31] Considering that

[29]Thomas A. Wolf, "An Empirical Analysis of Soviet Economic Relations with Developing Countries," *Soviet Economy* (July–September 1985), p. 239.

[30]The figures include military deliveries that in the Soviet statistics are not identified by country. The 1984 data are from CIA, *Handbook of Economic Statistics, 1985* (Washington, D.C., 1985), pp. 71 and 96.

[31]CIA, *Handbook of Economic Statistics, 1983* (Washington, D.C., 1983), p. 69; CIA, *Handbook of Economic Statistics, 1985*, p. 71.

Table 8. Commodity composition of Soviet trade with the noncommunist LDCs, 1972–80 (in percent)

	1972	1975	1980
Exports			
Machinery and equipment	33	24	20
Fuel and electricity	4	10	17
Ores, concentrates, and metals	5	3	1
Timber, pulp, and paper	2	4	2
Food and raw materials for food	2	3	1
Industrial consumer goods	1	1	1
Chemicals, building materials, textiles, and other materials	2	5	3
Unidentified residual	51	50	55
Imports			
Machinery and equipment	1	1	1
Fuel and electricity	13	19	14
Chemicals and products	5	4	5
Textile raw materials	17	12	5
Food and raw materials for food	35	44	48
Industrial consumer goods	12	9	7
Ores, concentrates, and metals	4	4	3
Timber, pulp, and paper	1	1	1
Other materials	8	5	7
Unidentified residual	5	3	9

SOURCE: Thomas Wolf, "Changes in the Pattern of Soviet Trade with the CMEA and the 'Non-Socialist' Countries," in *External Economic Relations of CMEA Countries: Their Significance and Impact in a Global Perspective* (Brussels: NATO Economics and Information Directorates, 1983), p. 223.
NOTE: Components may not sum to 100 because of rounding.

the global hard-currency trade balance of the USSR was barely positive in 1981 and ran about $4.5 billion in 1982–83, the contribution from trade with LDCs appears substantial indeed. However, much of that positive balance with LDCs may translate only into debt to the USSR which Moscow would have trouble collecting. There is little information on other elements of the LDC balance, particularly the capital account.

The USSR's trade, like its economic and military aid, is highly concentrated (not surprisingly, because the two categories are closely linked). In the early 1980s trade turnover reached or exceeded $1 billion annually with nine LDCs—Afghanistan (1984), Argentina, Cuba, India, Iraq, Iran (but not in 1984), Libya, Mongolia, and Vietnam, as well as China (in 1984); it was at or over the $500 million mark for four others—Brazil, Egypt, North Korea, and Syria. Together the first ten countries accounted for 62 percent and the four others added 7 percent of Soviet trade turnover with all LDCs, noncommunist and communist.

Arms transfers apart, the most important single component of Soviet exports to the noncommunist LDCs is machinery and equipment (see Table 8). Indeed, the LDCs are by far the major outlets outside the communist world for Soviet machinery—some three-quarters or more of all noncommunist sales in the early 1980s. However, exports of fuel came a close second in 1980. Sales of oil and products rose from $60 million in 1970 to over $2 billion in 1983. On the import side, food has traditionally been significant but accounted for almost half of all imports from the Third World in the year of the grain embargo. Fuel imports were a relatively large factor in the late 1970s and probably became still more important recently, mainly as payment for Soviet arms but secondarily as a consequence of the stagnation of Soviet domestic oil production.

These data are in current prices, which is all one can get from the official Soviet sources.[32] Thomas Wolf in independent calculations estimates that the real growth of Soviet civil exports in the 1970s was rather slow—virtually zero in the first half of the decade and 1.5 to 3.5 percent per year in the second half.[33] It was the unidentified residual in Soviet exports—presumably, largely arms—that exhibited dynamic growth, perhaps 10–15 percent per year, reflecting sharp differences in the price trends for the two components. The prices of Soviet identified exports rose much more than prices of the residual, probably because of the extraordinary increases in oil prices on the world market. Overall, however, it is possible that the prices paid to LDCs for imports rose more rapidly than the prices obtained for all Soviet exports and that the USSR's net barter terms of trade with the Third World declined somewhat during the 1970s. But here too there were structural changes: in the second half of the 1970s terms of trade fell with Third World countries of "socialist orientation" and even more with oil exporters, but they increased with other LDCs. In real terms, therefore, Soviet *civil* exports grew more rapidly in the 1970s to "socialist-oriented" clients and oil exporters than to other LDCs; on the import side, the importance of food made real growth largest with other LDCs.

Despite the importance of arms transfers in selected countries, the Soviet Union has been a dominant trade partner for very few noncommunist LDCs; in most cases Moscow's dominant position weakened in the 1970s. Among countries that report trade with the Soviet Union to the International Monetary Fund, 29 reported a decrease and 26 an increase in the Soviet share in LDCs' exports; the Soviet share in LDCs' imports declined in 42 of 63 cases. Of nine LDCs with significant trade with the USSR but that do not report it to the IMF, six had Soviet shares in their imports or exports as high as 10 percent or more in the early but not in the late 1970s. Wolfe concludes: "What evidence that exists thus does not suggest widespread high Soviet trade shares in the Third World."[34]

[32]*Vneshniaia torgovlia* provides indexes of real volumes of exports and imports for the world total and for the socialist countries' subaggregate; the developing and industrially developed countries are lumped together in a second subaggregate.

[33]Thomas Wolf, "Soviet Trade with the Third World: A Quantitative Assessment," *Osteuropa Wirtschaft* 30 (December 1985), pp. 273–95.

[34]Ibid., p. 287. Of course, the dependence of the communist LDCs is much higher. Ninety

The data supplied here tend to undermine Moscow's official mythology about Soviet trade with LDCs. The LDC share in total Soviet trade has not been growing; payments arrangements may have grown harder. The USSR claims that it is a large market for nontraditional exports, thereby helping LDCs out of their development rut, but in fact raw materials and agricultural commodities are the staples of Soviet purchases.

Another component of Soviet mythology is that developed socialist countries provide stable and rapidly growing markets for LDC exports. Although Soviet demand for LDC exports certainly grew rapidly in the late 1950s and the 1960s, the initial base was insignificant, and the margin over the rate of change of Western demand was small in the 1960s.[35] Wolf compared trade data in 1960–81 for the USSR and West Germany, Japan and the United States, and seven of ten United Nations Conference on Trade and Development (UNCTAD) "core" commodities—raw sugar, coffee, cocoa beans, tea, natural rubber, raw cotton, and jute—plus rice and tobacco.[36] He concludes that Soviet imports of these primary products grew at an above average rate. However, "the USSR cannot legitimately claim that it represents a more stable market than the large market economies, although the relative variability of Soviet imports of primary products, which was statistically significant in the 1960s, has declined over the past two decades."[37]

There is some evidence that the Soviet Union practices price discrimination among all developing countries (including the communist) in favor of CMEA members (Cuba, Mongolia, and Vietnam) and against the group of soft-currency, noncommunist LDCs. However, the result may reflect Moscow's bilateral economic bargaining power in relation with the soft-currency group rather than a conscious exercise of political muscle.[38]

Soviet trade with the LDCs will undoubtedly grow over the rest of the 1980s in real terms; it has never failed to do so previously. However, there is little reason now to believe that the relative importance of Third World trade to the USSR will change much, unless Soviet machinery becomes substantially more competitive or Moscow finds that more of its import needs can be satisfied from LDC sources—for example, the newly industrialized countries (NICs), which may be able to meet some of the requirements stemming from Gorbachev's modernization program. Of course, the prospect of arms sales will exercise a major influence on the absolute and relative course of this trade. As already noted, falling oil prices may take some of the buoyancy out

percent of Cuba's exports are to other communist countries, and 84 percent of its imports originate in that group. CIA, *Handbook of Economic Statistics, 1985*, p. 107.

[35]Egon Neuberger, "Is the USSR Superior to the West as a Market for Primary Products?" *Review of Economics and Statistics* 46 (August 1964), pp. 287–93, and Philip Hanson, "The Size, Growth and Stability of the Soviet Market for Primary Products," *Jahrbuch der Wirtschaft Osteuropas*, Band 3 (Munich: Guenter Olzog, 1972), pp. 189–301.

[36]Wolf, "An Empirical Analysis," pp. 234–38.

[37]Ibid., p. 238.

[38]Ibid., pp. 238–46.

of LDC demand for Soviet arms, although the political instability of these countries and the balance-of-payments importance to the USSR of arms sales guarantee fairly high levels of arms purchases over the longer term.

Elements of a Balance

Despite the thirty-year record of Soviet trade and aid and the voluminous literature on Moscow's activities in the Third World, there does not appear to have been a Western effort to draw up a balance sheet of costs and benefits. Obviously that task cannot be attempted here, but it may be useful to outline the shape of the problem. When and it if is drawn, the balance will have to deal with three major elements—effects on the Soviet position in the Third World and globally, the net benefit to the LDCs, and the net to the USSR.

Enhancing the Soviet International Political Position

The big breakthrough in the Third World came in the mid-fifties. The political motive was virtually the sole raison d'être of the Soviet arms and economic aid program through most of the Khrushchev decade, and the program achieved distinct results. The Western monopoly of influence was broken; a myth of Soviet identification with liberation from colonialism, political or economic, was propagated. No Third World country joined the faith apart from Cuba, whose enlistment preceded the receipt of major Soviet aid, but the tendency of most developing countries to find substantial overlap of international political interests with USSR was born then.

The watchword of the new, post-Khrushchev regime in relations with the LDCs was "mutual economic advantage." In the first decade, political influence was surely not scorned, but it did not appear to be the driving force of policy even though policy continued to be publicly interpreted in terms of the conflict between the two world systems. Political gains were made in the Third World, but there were substantial losses, especially Egypt, and no spectacular new successes.

In the third decade it was not economic aid or civil trade that wrought a difference in the USSR's position but arms transfers and the insertion of Soviet or proxy military forces directly into Third World conflicts. Of the changes in alignment effected in the second half of the seventies, none seems irreversible. Even Afghanistan, on the USSR's doorstep and policed by 150,000 troops, appears to be a bone in the Soviet throat. South Yemen has been wracked by factional strife and a brief but bloody civil war. Secessionist conflict continues in Ethiopia and Mozambique and has intensified in Angola. New opportunities opened in Central America in the early 1980s, but in El Salvador the rebel tide appears to be ebbing and the Sandinistas' authority in Nicaragua is still under challenge; the Marxist episode in Grenada was terminated shortly after it began. The Kremlin probably views the self-proclaimed Marxist-Leninist recruits of the last decade as distinctly less reliable than its major LDC communist allies, Cuba and Vietnam.[39]

If the balance is drawn over the three decades as a whole, the change in the Soviet position is dramatic and significant. However, some of the largest gains came at the inception of the campaign, and the net is considerably more difficult to estimate over recent periods. Military and economic aid did not automatically purchase political influence. Expectations that Soviet penetration of the Third World would inevitably bring about the contraction of the Western capitalist system were revealed as illusions.

Whatever the size of the net Soviet gain in the Third World, Moscow paid a political price for its activism in another sphere of its global activity. Zbigniew Brzezinski declared that SALT II was buried in the sands of the Ogaden. Certainly, Soviet activism in the Third World, in Africa and in Asia, was one of the important factors contributing to the sea change in American public opinion in the mid-seventies regarding the reality and utility of U.S.-Soviet detente.

Economic and Political Benefits/Costs to Third World Countries

A cost benefit analysis for Third World countries goes far beyond the scope of this chapter, but three contradictory factors may be briefly cited. First, the entrance of the USSR onto the scene probably helped improve the scale and terms of Western aid to the LDCs. This was not just a one-time result but a long-term shift in the aid supply schedule. Second, the Soviet Union helped create and actively nurtured the self-assertiveness of the Third World in the international arena. Moscow was not directly involved in the oil price revolution, but it does not seem far-fetched to argue that the West would not have tolerated this extraordinary raid on its wealth if not for the presence and active support of the USSR. In that sense there is something to the Kremlin's claim that Soviet power is the guarantor of the independence of (some) LDCs, although it is highly doubtful that the Soviet Union would have intervened actively in the late 1960s and early 1970s to repel Western economic or military pressures. I leave to others an assessment of the net economic benefit to non-oil producers of the transformation of the international system since the mid-fifties. But a third, related factor seems to have been a net liability to the LDCs. Moscow did not invent the idea of import-substitution-driven industrialization via state discrimination in favor of the public sector, but the USSR's historical example, its active espousal, and its sustained economic support were powerful influences increasing the respectability and

[39]This does not mean that other and better opportunities for Soviet penetration may not appear tomorrow. Among current worries for the West are South Africa, the Philippines, and Pakistan.

popularity of that dogma. There has been a great disillusionment on this score in the Third World in the 1970s, supported by an increasingly vociferous critique by Western economists.[40] Even in the Soviet development literature, some similar notes can be heard.[41] Disillusionment with the performance of the USSR's radical clients is probably a major reason for the cool attitude to Third World involvement reflected in top leadership statements and the highest party documents in recent years.

Economic Benefits and Costs for the USSR

Attention has been focused recently on the costs for the USSR, but surely there have been gross benefits. (Benefits dominated the considerations of observers twenty-five years ago.) Access to raw materials and food on favorable terms, outlets for otherwise unmarketable Soviet machinery, hard-currency earnings badly needed for purchases of food and capital goods, reduction in the cost of producing Soviet machinery and arms, perhaps even some quality improvements in Soviet manufactures resulting from competition in the foreign markets—these are among the elements of a gross gain from economic relations with the LDCs.

On the other side of the balance Charles Wolf, Jr., and associates have attempted to measure the "costs of the Soviet empire" (CSE) in the 1970s.[42] The empire includes Eastern Europe and other communist countries, as well as the various parts of the world in which the USSR is contending for dominion. Most of the costs estimated by the group fall in the category of trade subsidies—in 1980 about 50 percent in current dollars and 65–70 percent in current rubles—and roughly 90 percent is accounted for by implicit subsidies to Eastern Europe. Similarly, trade credits represent another 9–10 (ruble) or 14–19 (dollar) percent of total CSE in 1980, and Eastern Europe (including Yugoslavia) accounts for 53 percent of them. Military assistance and economic aid deliveries to LDCs (calculated, in principle, at opportunity cost but net of aid repayments and arms sales for hard currency) are estimated to total about $5 billion in 1980. The sum of all costs estimated by the Wolf group to apply to LDCs, communist and noncommunist alike, is roughly $13–15 billion.[43]

---

[40]For a brief, succinct summary of the basic arguments, see Deepak Lal, *The Poverty of "Development Economics"* (London: Institute of Economic Affairs, 1983).

[41]Elizabeth Kridl Valkenier has followed the Soviet discussions carefully. See her *The Soviet Union and the Third World: An Economic Bind* (New York: Praeger, 1983), chaps. 2 and 3. See also Jerry F. Hough, *The Struggle for the Third World: Soviet Debates and American Options* (Washington, D.C.: Brookings, 1986).

[42]Charles Wolf, Jr., and others, *The Costs of the Soviet Empire*, R-3073/1-NA (Santa Monica: RAND Corporation, September 1983).

[43]The sum of $1.99 billion of trade subsidies, $2.84 billion of trade credits, $7.14 billion of economic and military aid, $0.50–$1.20 billion of incremental costs for Soviet forces in Afghanistan, and $0.74–$1.93 billion for covert operations in LDCs (an arbitrary one-third of their total estimate).

There are probably estimating errors in both directions in the components of these totals,[44] but if we may take them as a rough indication of magnitude, the figures correspond to about 2 percent of Soviet gross national product in 1980.[45]

At first glance, this estimate of the relative cost of the Soviet involvement in the Third World seems small. But it would be a mistake to dismiss the question of Third World burden on these grounds. Apart from the possibility of underestimation, the figure cited must be viewed in the context of the USSR's well-known resource allocation stringencies. With slow growth, widespread shortage of consumer goods and services, and inadequate and misdirected investment, the Soviet economy also supports a defense sector that accounts for every fifth or sixth ruble of national expenditure, and perhaps an even larger share when account is taken of the other, indirect costs of the priority given to military demands.[46] Even relatively small diversions of acutely scarce resources can have significant effect. The magnitude of the diversion, in addition, is partly obscured by relating it to GNP. In a longer time frame all components of the national output may be regarded as substitutable in use, but the more direct and immediate trade-offs in expenditure on the LDCs are in aggregate much smaller than the GNP. Thus the hard-currency component of aid outlays on the Third World competes with imports of goods and services from the West: every underpriced barrel of oil sold to Cuba, every tank sold on concessional terms to South Yemen, means a forgone purchase of Western technology or grain or other valued commodity. Even the soft-currency aid of trade credits could divert goods and services from useful employment within the USSR. These considerations are difficult to quantify, but if only half of the LDC outlays in 1980 estimated by the Wolf group involved expenditure of hard currency or opportunity costs in hard currency, the resulting sum is almost four times the Soviet hard-currency current account surplus and twice as large as the identified Soviet hard-currency inflow from all sources in that year.[47]

There is ample evidence that Soviet leaders have been conscious of a burden imposed on the economy by the national military effort, although it is not clear whether they know the burden's true size. Similarly, they must also

---

[44]On the one hand, the figures do not include trade subsidies to Vietnam and Mongolia. On the other hand, the economic and military aid component may be too large, in the view of Joan P. Zoeter's estimate that 90 percent of Soviet arms deliveries to LDCs in 1980 were for hard currency ("USSR: Hard Currency Trade and Payments," in U.S. Congress, Joint Economic Committee, *Soviet Economy in the 1980's: Problems and Prospects*, Part 2 [Washington, D.C., 1983], pp. 503–504; Table 1 indicates that deliveries in 1980 were over $8 billion).

[45]Translating to rubles at the average ruble-dollar ratio implied by the Wolf group's total CSE estimates in rubles and dollars and dividing by their ruble estimate of GNP.

[46]See Abraham S. Becker, *Sitting on Bayonets: The Soviet Defense Burden and the Slowdown of Soviet Defense Spending*, JRS-01 (Santa Monica: RAND/UCLA Center for the Study of Soviet International Behavior, December 1985).

[47]CIA, *Handbook of Economic Statistics, 1985*, p. 72.

be aware of the economic drain from their involvement in the Third World. Khrushchev's rash commitments of aid to Egypt and other countries were opposed by some of his Presidium colleagues and may have been a factor in his dismissal. His successors altered the regional distribution of aid, probably because much of it appeared wasted on countries whose political allegiance proved ephemeral. Aid was doled out somewhat ungenerously in the late seventies and early eighties to some of the radical African clients who appeared to be favored in the mid-1970s. Again, it may be that cost-benefit balancing was involved in the decision. Andropov was cited earlier in a mood suggesting skepticism about the value of at least some Third World commitments. Gorbachev seems similarly inclined.[48] Maybe we should treat the very high levels of aid to Cuba, Vietnam, and Mongolia at least in part as payment for services rendered in sub-Saharan Africa, on the Chinese borders, and in the South China Sea. One wonders, nevertheless, whether Moscow would not keep at arms' length another Cuba appearing suddenly on the scene ready to be embraced in the Soviet camp as a full-fledged Marxist-Leninist socialist state but at an annual maintenance cost of another $5 billion. This is not to argue that economics always and everywhere dominates politics in Soviet Third World strategy, only that the logic of economic decision making probably applies extensively to Soviet LDC policy: the rate of return required to undertake an investment project rises when capital resources become relatively scarcer.

Moscow demonstrates a tight-fisted concern about its purse in various international economic forums. It is still not a member of the International Monetary Fund or the World Bank, makes only token contributions to UN aid organizations, and is not a member of the General Agreement on Tariffs and Trade. The USSR has generally supported LDC demands for more aid from the West—for example, at UNCTAD VI in 1983, in Belgrade. But even here there may be a change. At the July 1985 meeting of the International Cocoa Organization, the USSR bluntly warned cocoa producers that Moscow would not agree to any arrangements on production or distribution which did not reduce prices; it firmly supported the tough line of Washington and London.[49]

Finally, there is the currently precarious state of LDC balances of payments. There seems to be no reason to believe that the servicing of hard-currency debt to the USSR should be exempt from the problems the LDCs are experiencing in earning sufficient net export proceeds to keep current on their obligations to the West. Soviet interest rates certainly do not include a risk premium adequate to cover the threat of partial or complete default. That Cuba is unconcerned about this problem is understandable: its debt to the Soviet Union has been restructured on apparently "highly favorable terms."

[48]Fukuyama, "Gorbachev and the Third World," pp. 715–16.
[49]Steve Mufson, "Third World Pleas on Commodity Prices Get No Sympathy in Developed Nations," *Wall Street Journal*, October 2, 1985.

It can pursue its campaign for concerted LDC repudiation of debt to the West while vigorously assuring the foreign banks that Cuba will honor its own obligations.[50] But Moscow appears to support this campaign, at least for now.[51] Whether that support will continue remains to be seen.

Of course, Soviet economic and military involvement in the Third World is too deeply rooted to be in danger of a reversion to the status quo ante Khrushchev. Recent abrupt declines in oil prices will further constrain Soviet hard-currency oil revenues, which are also limited by the stagnation of domestic production. Nevertheless, economic aid levels will probably continue to rise, if only because of the long-standing factors of LDC demand and Western competition. For reasons discussed earlier, Soviet arms sales will probably remain a significant factor in international relations and in the Soviet balance of payments. Trade with the developing countries will certainly grow, in nominal and real terms. Yet if Moscow decides that domestic economic growth requires renewed, large-scale infusions of Western technology, the aggregate share of the Third World in Soviet trade turnover may diminish.

The scale of Soviet economic involvement in the Third World has grown markedly over the past three decades, but it has also been held back by Soviet resource stringency. In relative terms, the constraint appears to have been felt more acutely in recent than in the Khrushchev years. Unless Soviet economic prospects brighten considerably more than now seems likely, limited resources will continue to retard Soviet efforts in the Third World. It is worth emphasizing, however, that economic difficulties, unless they are exacerbated more than seems likely, will not drive the USSR out of the Third World. Soviet competition there will most likely endure for the indefinite future.

---

[50]Roger Lowenstein, "Cuba Is in Good Standing with Bankers Despite Castro's Talk of Canceling Debt," *Wall Street Journal*, July 30, 1985.

[51]A. Zhitnikov and G. Markov, "The West's 'Debt Trap' for Developing Countries," *International Affairs* (Moscow) no. 8 (1985), pp. 35–43.

5

Eastern Europe and the Third World; or, "Limited Regret Strategy" Revisited

ANDRZEJ KORBONSKI

Not much has been written about the relationship between Eastern Europe and the nations of the Third World and, as a result, in the mid-1980s the data base at our disposal remains rather limited.[1] In this chapter I attempt not to fill this gap but to raise some questions with regard to Eastern Europe's policies vis-à-vis the Third World in the past three decades.

The conduct of East European foreign policy in general, as is the case with the foreign policy of any region, has depended over the years not only on the views and ideas of East European leaders, nor solely or mostly on East European history and traditions and the region's strategic and economic interests, but also on the attitudes and policies of other countries or regions toward Eastern Europe. All these influences or conditioning factors apply with considerable strength to an examination of Eastern Europe's relations with the Third World. Anyone investigating this relationship is faced with definitional, conceptual, and methodological problems that must be dealt with before the discussion can proceed.

To begin with, it is increasingly difficult to define Eastern Europe. The eight countries—Albania, Bulgaria, Czechoslovakia, East Germany, Hun-

---

[1] Among the studies dealing exclusively or partly with East European–Third World relations are Michael Radu, ed., *Eastern Europe and the Third World* (New York: Praeger, 1981); Robert and Elizabeth Bass, "Eastern Europe," and William E. Griffith, "Yugoslavia," in Zbigniew Brzezinski, ed., *Africa and the Communist World* (Stanford: Stanford University Press, 1963), pp. 84–141; Christopher Coker, "The Soviet Union, Eastern Europe, and the New International Economic Order," *Washington Papers* 20, no. 3 (1984); Marie Lavigne, ed., *Les relations est-sud dans l'économie mondiale* (Paris: Centre d'Economie Internationale des Pays Socialistes, Université de Paris I, 1985), vols. 1 and 2; and Lavigne, "Eastern Europe–LDC Economic Relations in the Eighties," in *East European Economies: Slow Growth in the 1980s*, vol. 2: *Foreign Trade and International Finance*, Selected Papers Submitted to the Joint Economic Committee, 99th Cong., 2d sess. (Washington, D.C., 1986), pp. 31–61. For what may be the earliest attempt to discuss this topic, see Stanley Zyzniewski, "The Soviet Bloc and the Underdeveloped Countries," *World Politics* 11, no. 3 (April 1959), pp. 378–398.

gary, Poland, Romania, and Yugoslavia—are not only situated in a reasonably well-defined geographical area of Europe but also have many essential things in common, among which are political and economic structures and institutions, patterns of socioeconomic changes, and a similar historical heritage, particularly since the end of World War II. With the exceptions of Albania and Yugoslavia, they are members of two important regional organizations, the Warsaw Pact (WTO) and the Council for Mutual Economic Assistance (CMEA), and are traditionally perceived as forming the so-called Soviet bloc or Soviet empire in Europe.

Although Albania and Yugoslavia are often excluded from discussions of East European international relations, I consider both of them here. Yugoslavia especially has been a leader of the nonaligned movement and as such has had close relations with the Third World. Albania's role has been much less important and visible, but it still deserves attention.

The concept of the Third World also requires clarification. There has been a remarkable reticence about a definition of the concept. Conventional dictionaries are not very helpful: one describes the Third World as a "group of nations, especially in Africa and Asia, that are not aligned with either the Communist or the non-Communist blocs." Another refers to a simple "aggregate of the underdeveloped nations of the world."[2] The former definition is clearly too narrow, the latter obviously too broad, and a different definition is called for.

One possibility is to apply the concept of less developed countries (LDCs), even though that also raises some definitional problems. Hungary and Romania, for example, members of both the WTO and the CMEA, have been officially recognized by some United Nations organizations as LDCs.[3] Rather than become entangled in definitional hair-splitting, I use the terms Third World and LDCs interchangeably in the hope that doing so will not create too much confusion.

The universe to be considered includes four categories of countries: the LDCs, which are truly neutral and nonaligned, countries that are neither members or affiliates of CMEA nor "states of socialist orientation," nor otherwise perceived as Soviet clients; states of socialist orientation; Third World members and affiliates of the CMEA; and Marxist-Leninist members of the so-called Communist Third World. The categories form a continuum. This typology, though arbitrary, has the advantage of being all-inclusive.

Marxist-Leninist Members of Communist Third World	CMEA Members and Affiliates	States of Socialist Orientation	Neutral and Nonaligned States

---

[2]Neither the *International Encyclopedia of Social Sciences* nor the *Encyclopedia Britannica* has an entry for Third World.

[3]See, for example, International Monetary Fund, *Direction of Trade Statistics Yearbook, 1985* (Washington, D.C., 1986), p. 16.

One additional complication is presented by a limited data base, especially in the critical military and economic spheres that are of particular importance in East European–Third World relations. Obviously the nature of military relations precludes full disclosure of arms shipments, training facilities, numbers of advisers, and other forms of military assistance given to LDCs. Even when estimates are available, however, they tend to differ between such sources as U.S. government agencies, the Stockholm International Peace Research Institute (SIPRI), the International Monetary Fund, and East European and CMEA statistical yearbooks. There is also the perennial problem of disaggregating as between the Soviet Union and Eastern Europe figures that often appear under the heading Soviet bloc, Warsaw Treaty, or Council for Mutual Economic Assistance. These difficulties are compounded by the problem of correct valuation of arms exports, which frequently are derived as a residual category in a given East European country's exports to LDCs. Similar difficulties haunt estimates of foreign trade between Eastern Europe and the Third World where several categories of prices are used to calculate imports, exports, and the resulting balance of trade surpluses and deficits. Thus all figures given here must be approached with caution; they should be viewed as suggesting primarily an order of magnitude rather than correct values.

Of the various influences affecting East European international behavior, we may safely discard the impact exerted by Eastern Europe's history and traditions. For many reasons, until relatively recently the region had practically no direct or indirect relations with the Third World. Before World War II the only direct contacts were economic, as some Third World countries supplied Eastern Europe with selected foodstuffs and raw materials. Even these contacts were insignificant. Several East European countries were so poor that they hardly differed from their Third World counterparts and could hardly afford to trade with them. The only country in the region that could be described as industrially advanced was Czechoslovakia, but even its trade with the Third World, except for arms, was marginal.[4]

Today's Eastern Europe is, of course, a far cry from the Eastern Europe of the interwar period. The key factor in the region's transformation was the establishment of Soviet hegemony east of the Elbe and the creation of a Soviet bloc or empire. The relationship of the Soviet hegemon with its East European allies, as well as with Albania and Yugoslavia (which though communist managed to achieve independence from Moscow), has been widely analyzed, and the argument does not need to be restated.[5]

---

[4]Between 1929 and 1938, apparently, Czechoslovakia's share in international arms trade amounted to 12.6 percent, placing it second only to Great Britain as the chief exporter of arms around the world. Vratislav Pechota, "Czechoslovakia and the Third World," in Radu, *Eastern Europe and the Third World*, p. 103.

[5]For a recent expression, see Sarah Meiklejohn Terry, ed., *Soviet Policy in Eastern Europe* (New Haven: Yale University Press, 1984).

For the purpose of our discussion, there is little doubt that the Kremlin exerts powerful influence over Eastern Europe's international behavior, including the region's policy toward and contacts with the Third World. The relationship between the Soviet Union and the so-called East European Six can be viewed as an interaction of a special kind, quite different from the relationship between the USSR and other regions around the world, both communist and noncommunist. Moscow has a special stake in Eastern Europe which, in turn, generates particular objectives and interests for the Kremlin. Its policy toward the Six has been conditioned to a large degree by its perception of the changing international environment. Successive Soviet leaders from Khrushchev to Gorbachev have treated Eastern Europe by and large as an important actor whose strength must be mobilized to help achieve Moscow's broader international goals.[6] Also, the Kremlin has had a veto power over its clients' international behavior, and Moscow alone has been and still is in a position to determine the current threshold of East European autonomy in foreign and domestic affairs. This fact is of paramount importance for any understanding of East European relations with the Third World in the past three decades.

What other countries have had at least some influence over Eastern Europe's attitudes and policies toward the Third World? One category is communist states outside Europe.[7] At some points in the past the People's Republic of China actively competed with the USSR for influence in the Third World, but by the mid-1980s that competition is essentially a thing of the past, with Beijing strongly preoccupied with domestic issues.[8] Cuba, of course, has continued to be most active, especially in Africa, and Havana's often adventurous policies must have exerted some impact on Eastern Europe, including Yugoslavia. Other communist countries in Asia, such as North Korea and Vietnam, have played a lesser role in this respect.

Clearly Eastern Europe's behavior toward the Third World has also been influenced by the United States and Western Europe and less so by Japan. That influence originates from two sources: the U.S.-Soviet global competition for the domination of the world, and the East-West contest for the "hearts and souls" of the neutral and nonaligned countries of the Third World.

Finally, we must also take into account the direct interaction between individual East European countries and their opposite numbers in the Third World. It is difficult to isolate the bilateral relationships and to disentangle

---

[6]Andrzej Korbonski, "Eastern Europe," in Robert F. Byrnes, ed., *After Brezhnev: Sources of Soviet Conduct in the 1980s* (Bloomington: Indiana University Press, 1983), pp. 298ff.

[7]For details, see Peter Wiles, ed., *The New Communist Third World* (London: Croom Helm, 1982).

[8]For an account of the early period in that relationship, see Ernst Kux, "Eastern Europe's Relations with Asian Communist Countries," in Kurt London, ed., *Eastern Europe in Transition* (Baltimore: Johns Hopkins University Press, 1966), pp. 279–306.

them from the influence of the several intervening variables mentioned above. Still, the record shows interesting variations in bilateral relations, due mostly to historical and cultural factors.

To conclude, the relationship between Eastern Europe and the Third World has been and continues to be complex. In a highly simplified form it may be presented diagramatically:

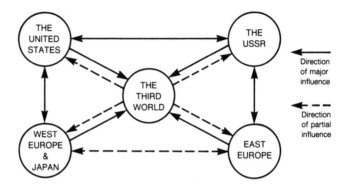

Of the diagram's eight triangles, only one, representing the relationship involving the Soviet Union, Eastern Europe, and the Third World, is examined here in depth. I emphasize that my purpose is not to use the triangle as a single analytical approach comparable to the conceptual "strategic triangle" as applied to analysis of Sino-Soviet-American relations.[9] My goal is much more modest: all I want to suggest is that East European policies toward the LDCs, whether bilateral or multilateral in nature, cannot be treated as an independent variable. In most cases they have been (and still are) a by-product of Soviet foreign policy vis-à-vis the West or the Third World or, at best, they have been influenced to a greater or lesser degree by the behavior of communist countries other than the USSR which harbor their own ambition toward their neighbors in Africa, Asia, or Latin America.

The ways and means used by Moscow to coordinate the Third World policies of its junior East European allies are not well known. The Warsaw Treaty has formally institutionalized its decision-making processes in various ways, including the so-called periodic summit meetings and standing committees of foreign and defense ministers and other devices. The same is true for the CMEA. Moreover, there are ample bilateral contacts between the Kremlin and its East European partners. But whether all these arrangements serve to orchestrate policy is difficult to say. From occasional visible disagree-

[9]For an interesting methodological discussion of the triangular relationship, see Lowell Dittmer, "The Strategic Triangle: An Elementary Game-Theoretical Analysis," *World Politics* 33, no. 4 (July 1981), pp. 485–515.

ments within the WTO with respect to the alliance's policy toward West Germany or the West in general, as in 1984, it may be argued that coordination has not always been perfect, and the same may also be true of Eastern Europe's policy in the Third World. For the purposes of this discussion, however, I assume that the Kremlin is able to control Third World policy to a fairly substantial degree.

The Soviet Union, Eastern Europe, and the Third World

The underlying premise of my analysis, as noted, is that the Soviet Union has shaped the character of Eastern Europe's relations with the Third World in the past thirty years and continues to do so today. Although most of the East European countries are viewed as Soviet satellites, they are, at least in theory, sovereign states. It may be argued that Moscow benefits from the presence of a group of nominally independent states that follow its orders and generally strengthen Soviet aspirations to superpower status. As I show below, the Soviet-engineered and -dominated military-economic alliance system in Eastern Europe has proved a highly useful instrument for closer integration between Moscow and its communist allies in the Third World, such as Cuba and Vietnam, and an equally useful instrument for penetrating other LDCs.

Soviet interests in the Third World can be subsumed under four broad headings: military, political, ideological, and economic. The dividing lines between the four categories tend to be fuzzy, and I use the various labels mostly to identify tendencies in developments affecting East European-Third World relations.

Military Interests

It is a truism that the main institutional arrangement maintaining and safeguarding Soviet security interests in Eastern Europe outside Albania and Yugoslavia has been the Warsaw Pact, which in 1985 celebrated its thirtieth anniversary and was duly extended for another twenty years. Over the years the pact has played three separate but interrelated roles: as a military alliance, as a diplomatic actor on the international scene, and as an instrument of political integration in Eastern Europe. In each case it has been a handmaiden of the Kremlin, which has used and manipulated it for its own purposes.

The Soviet security interests embodied in the WTO include, it is now generally recognized, both offensive and defensive elements. One of the most important aspects of the pact's contribution to Soviet offensive potential has been the apparent willingness of some members to play a role as Soviet proxies or surrogates in the Third World.

Soviet ability to mobilize its junior allies in Europe to act as surrogates in

Africa, Central America, and the Middle East has been one of the most impressive achievements of successive Soviet regimes over the past thirty years. To some extent the growing use of individual East European proxies around the world was a by-product of the USSR becoming widely recognized as a global power, ready to compete with the West and, to a lesser degree, with China for control and influence in the Third World.

So far, junior WTO members have insisted that the Warsaw alliance is valid only for Europe and have opposed its extension beyond the European continent. At the same time, according to some unconfirmed reports, they have over the years successfully resisted Soviet pressure to deploy even symbolic units of their national armies outside Europe, notably on the Sino-Soviet border, in Vietnam, and most recently in Afghanistan. On the other hand, several member-states have appeared willing to become involved in other regions.[10] Some were clearly obeying Soviet orders and acted as outright proxies, others claimed to be motivated strictly by their own national interest, while still others justified their involvement in the Third World by paying lip service to Moscow while pursuing their own objectives.

The first category is represented by Czechoslovakia, which has a tradition going back to the interwar period as one of the principal arms suppliers to the Third World. Prague's public entry into the postwar arms trade was, of course, the Soviet-Egyptian arms deal of 1955, but there is also evidence that Czech arms played an important role in the Arab-Israeli war of 1948 and were shipped to Guatemala in 1954 in support of the Arbenz regime. It is well-documented that for the past thirty years Czechoslovakia has been actively shipping arms to Soviet clients in different parts of the globe.[11]

Romania appears to play a maverick role not only in the Warsaw Pact but also in the Third World. As I show below, its purpose was primarily political and economic rather than military, but because occasionally the policy of Bucharest tends to diverge from and even collide with that of Moscow, this purpose carried security implications.[12]

Much has been written about East Germany's involvement in the military and internal security of the Third World, and Western literature on the subject is replete with references to the Afrika Korps returning to its old haunts and to the heirs of the Gestapo training their counterparts in Africa, the Middle East, and elsewhere.[13] We may assume that East Germany's

[10]Between 1955 and 1968 the USSR supplied roughly 90 percent of military aid to the Third World, with Czechoslovakia providing the bulk of the rest, and marginal amounts supplied by East Germany and Poland. Wynfred Joshua and Stephen P. Gilbert, *Arms for the Third World* (Baltimore: Johns Hopkins University Press, 1969), p. 98. For a more recent account, see Trond Gilberg, "Eastern European Military Assistance," in John F. Copper and Daniel S. Papp, eds., *Communist Nations' Military Assistance* (Boulder, Colo.: Westview, 1983), pp. 72–95.

[11]For details, see Pechota, "Czechoslovakia and the Third World," pp. 77–105.

[12]A comprehensive account can be found in Michael Radu, "Romania and the Third World: The Dilemmas of a Free Rider," in Radu, *Eastern Europe and the Third World*, pp. 235–272.

[13]Elizabeth Pond, "East Germany's Afrika Korps," *Christian Science Monitor*, June 28, 1978. See

motivation has been twofold: first, at least in the 1960s and early 1970s, East Germany had a reputation as the most faithful and loyal ally of the Kremlin, eager to fulfill every demand put upon it and acting as a Soviet proxy in Eastern Europe. Hence it was more than willing to engage in the Third World by sending military and police advisers and instructors. Second, during the same period the GDR was treated as an outcast by the West and many other countries around the world; its activities in some LDCs might be viewed as an effort to achieve at least a modicum of international legitimacy. In the past fifteen years or so East Germany has been granted international recognition, and so it no longer needs to assert its sovereignty, though nothing suggests that this change has affected the GDR's rather extensive involvement in the Third World.

Interestingly, there is no evidence of any major, direct military engagement in the Third World on the part of Poland, Hungary, or Bulgaria. Poland has been shipping tanks and other military equipment to the Middle East to be sure; it has provided training facilities for air force personnel from Soviet Third World clients, and reports indicate that Polish ships have been used to transport military equipment to different Third World countries. But there is no record of Polish military advisers being deployed around the world.[14] Hungary and Bulgaria have also tended to maintain a rather low profile in the military sphere.[15]

Little can be said about the reception given to East European military advisers and hardware by Third World purchasers. Although Czech military equipment has had a tradition of excellence, we do not know much about the quality and performance of equipment originating in East Germany and Poland.[16] In the same vein East German military advisers presumably benefit to some degree from memories of the Wehrmacht, whose exploits in North Africa during World War II were highly regarded by the natives.[17] One may also speculate that all East Europeans were more acceptable to Third World nations than their Soviet opposite numbers if for no other reason than that their behavior was less arrogant than their Soviet mentors'. Possibly the most important reason, however, was that both East European military personnel and equipment came cheaper than Western and even Soviet advisers and hardware and hence were more affordable. There were two likely reasons. One was an inferior bargaining position enjoyed by East Europeans who,

---

also Jiri Valenta and Shannon Butler, "East Germany's Security Policies in Africa," in Radu, *Eastern Europe and the Third World,* pp. 142–168.

[14]Poland apparently has been supplying arms to Iraq at least since the beginning of the Iraq-Iran War. *SIPRI Yearbook, 1984* (London: Taylor & Francis, 1984), p. 198.

[15]This judgment is based on the information contained in successive *SIPRI Yearbooks* from 1976 to 1984.

[16]During a visit to Damascus in April 1977, I heard several complaints about the low quality of Czech and East German equipment.

[17]In the late 1970s the number of East German advisers in Africa was estimated at 3,500–5,000. *SIPRI Yearbook, 1980* (London: Taylor & Francis, 1980), p. 175.

faced with Western and possibly Soviet competition in Third World arms sales, were forced to sell their wares at bargain basement prices, mainly to earn hard currency. The other was Soviet pressure, which compelled East European countries to supply military hardware at discount prices as part of WTO military burden sharing.[18] East European military aid agreements with and deliveries to noncommunist LDCs between 1955 and 1984 are shown in Table 1.

Given these figures, have the East European Six made a major contribution to reducing the Soviets' military aid burden? Although the share of Eastern Europe was not insignificant, it was hardly striking.[19] It may be argued that from Moscow's viewpoint the importance of East European aid was less its absolute quantity or even quality, more its political impact. By marking certain Third World countries as targets for East European penetration, the USSR at least partly avoided the stigma of carrying the East-West conflict directly into the Third World. Even though most of the individual East European countries have for some time been clearly identified as Moscow's puppets, it was often more convenient for the Kremlin to use East Europeans for various purposes, thereby avoiding the suspicion or apprehension that direct Soviet involvement would cause.[20] It was one thing for Washington to become aware of East German military advisers in, say, Zimbabwe, and another to be faced with a large Soviet military mission in Harare.

A good illustration is provided by Soviet behavior in Central America. Moscow has clearly been cautious in Nicaragua and Grenada for fear of putting the United States too much on the alert. According to the so-called Grenada Papers, at the time of the U.S. invasion of Grenada in 1983 there was a small handful of East European, Chinese, and North Korean advisers present on the island but no Soviets.[21] The same is probably true for the rest of

---

[18]For details, see Robert M. Cutler, Laure Depres, and Aaron Karp, "Aspects of Arms Transfers and of Military Technology Transfers in East-South Relations" (paper presented at the XIIth World Congress of the International Political Science Association, Paris, July 1985).

[19]Between 1965 and 1978 Czechoslovakia exported $1.152 billion in current prices to the Third World, making it tenth in the world. The corresponding figure for Poland was $462 million, putting it among the top twenty. *World Military Expenditures and Arms Transfers, 1965–1974* (Washington: U.S. Arms Control and Disarmament Agency, 1976), p. 73, and *World Military Expenditures and Arms Transfers, 1969–1978* (Washington: U.S. Arms Control and Disarmament Agency, 1980), p. 159. For additional details, see *SIPRI Yearbook, 1978* (London: Taylor & Francis, 1978), p. 226.

[20]For example, it has been suggested that East Germany has been active mostly in countries in which the USSR did not desire to play a prominent role. *SIPRI Yearbook, 1983* (London: Taylor & Francis, 1983), p. 367. Also, there seems to be a clear division of labor between the Soviet Union and the smaller WTO partners, with the former concentrating on heavy equipment and the latter exporting small-size weapons and providing mostly training facilities for Third World countries; Czechoslovakia focuses on armor and artillery, Poland on pilot and parachute training, and Hungary on infantry training. Ibid., p. 368.

[21]For examples of contacts between Grenada and Bulgaria, Czechoslovakia, and East Germany, see Paul Seabury and Walter A. McDougall, eds., *The Grenada Papers* (San Francisco: Institute for Contemporary Studies, 1984), pp. 33–40. See also Charles Gati, "Fraternal Assis-

Table 1. East European military agreements with and deliveries to noncommunist LDCs, 1955–74, 1975–84

| | East European | | East European Deliveries as Percentage of Total WTO Deliveries |
| | Agreements | Deliveries | |
	(million current $)		
1955–74	2,010	1,450	9.7%
1975	635	275	11.9
1976	355	350	10.1
1977	650	355	6.9
1978	560	550	8.3
1979	750	645	7.2
1980	870	635	7.2
1981	2,560	1,315	14.0
1982	1,795	1,970	19.6
1983	1,310	1,060	12.9
1984	845	1,845	20.5
Total, 1955–84	12,340	10,450	12.0

SOURCE: U.S. Department of State, *Warsaw Pact Economic Aid to Non-Communist LDCs, 1984* (Washington, D.C., May 1986), p. 19.

Central America, including Nicaragua, where the Soviet presence appears to be nil and where most activities are performed by the Cubans.[22]

What about the military interaction between the East European Six and the communist states in Asia: the People's Republic of China, North Korea, Vietnam, and Afghanistan? There is no record of any extensive interaction in recent years, especially since the end of the Vietnam War in 1978. The East Europeans seem willing to exchange military missions and to offer support on the diplomatic front, in the United Nations and other international forums, but as suggested earlier, they are apparently reluctant to commit their armed forces beyond Europe.

There are indications that some of the East European countries were less than happy with the behavior of fraternal Third World countries such as Cuba and Vietnam. It may be assumed that neither Cuba's military involvement in Africa and Central America nor Vietnam's invasion of Kampuchea enjoyed much support in an Eastern Europe concerned with the overall state of East-West relations and eager to see the resumption of detente—an outcome clearly stymied by the aggressive behavior of Havana and Hanoi, not to mention Moscow's prolonged engagement in Afghanistan.

---

tance: Eastern Europe in Grenada," *Soviet/Cuban Strategy in the Third World after Grenada*, A Conference Report (Washington, D.C.: Kennan Institute for Advanced Russian Studies, Wilson Center, August 1984), pp. 27–30.

[22]There is hardly any reference to East European involvement in the insurgent movements in Central and Latin America in Georges Fauriol, ed., *Latin American Insurgencies* (Washington, D.C.: National Defense University, 1985).

The WTO's role as an instrument of Soviet diplomacy proved limited in scope and character and has been confined to two main areas of activity, both outside the Third World: East-West negotiations on arms control and disarmament in Europe, and the creation of an all-Europe security system. The treaty's most important task, serving as Moscow's tool for the political integration of its domain in Eastern Europe, was also of limited relevance for the Third World. As suggested earlier, the WTO's charter might suggest a model for future integration of communist states outside Europe under Soviet leadership, but so far there have been no indications that this idea was being seriously considered in Moscow, possibly because of strong opposition on the part of an Eastern Europe reluctant to see the WTO extended to the Third World. On the other hand, the East Europeans have continued, albeit reluctantly, to provide aid to Asian communist countries such as Vietnam, some of which aid might have been of a military character.

Political Interests

There is by now a considerable consensus among observers of the East European scene that in dealing with its allies in the region, the Soviet Union has for years been trying to achieve a balance between cohesion and viability.[23] Cohesion implies general conformity of East European domestic and foreign policies to Soviet prescriptions, as well as the rough identity of institutional arrangements between the East European Six and the USSR. Viability, on the other hand, suggests the presence of confident, credible, efficient, and legitimate regimes in Eastern Europe, which would obviate the need for continuous Soviet preoccupation with and intervention in the region.

By the mid-1980s it has become clear that the Soviet Union, faced with the need to choose between conformity and regime credibility in Eastern Europe, has been unable to resolve the dilemma. In the past three decades the Kremlin was forced to grant to some of its clients in the region concessions in both the domestic and the foreign political spheres. Thus Poland, for example, was allowed to keep a large private agricultural sector and maintain relatively friendly relations with the Catholic church, whereas East Germany and Romania succeeded at different times in pursuing an autonomous foreign policy vis-à-vis both the West and parts of the Third World, such as Africa.[24]

Romania's maverick stance and errant behavior have been extensively discussed elsewhere, and there is no need to go over the details again. The origins of Romanian deviation are obscure. Most likely they had their roots

---

[23]The concepts of "cohesion" and "viability" originated, of course, with James F. Brown.
[24]Christopher Coker, "The Soviet Union and Eastern Europe: Patterns of Competition and Collaboration in Southern Africa," in R. Craig Nation and Mark V. Kauppi, eds., *The Soviet Impact in Africa* (Lexington, Mass.: Heath, 1984), pp. 59–85.

in the personalities of Romanian leaders, first Gheorghe Gheorghiu-Dej and later Nicolae Ceaușescu who took over the leadership of the Romanian party and state in 1965. In trying to assert Romania's autonomy with regard to the Soviet Union, Ceaușescu had several options, and he apparently chose the international arena as providing him the best opportunity to pursue the goal of independence, however limited it might ultimately prove to be. Although Bucharest made some overtures to the West and also followed a more or less independent path in a variety of international organizations and forums, its foreign policy was focused on the Third World. In time Ceaușescu's delusion of grandeur was reinforced by the country's economic predicament, which made the LDCs even more attractive as an object of Romania's seeming affection.

The most interesting if not the most publicized relation was Romania's connection with China and North Korea.[25] Bucharest's maintenance of friendly relations with the People's Republic, especially in the 1960s and 1970s, in the face of a boycott by the rest of the East European Six, must have been particularly jarring to Moscow. For its own reasons China appeared to reciprocate Romania's support, and Ceaușescu has been a welcome visitor to Beijing throughout the past twenty years.[26] While Romania's close relationship with China was a good illustration of Bucharest's determination to challenge Moscow's control over its foreign policy, however, the veritable love affair with Pyongyang was most likely due to Ceaușescu's dynastic aspirations. In the eyes of some observers, North Korea became a model to be emulated by Romania in the name of "Socialism in one family."[27] The Soviet Union apparently remained largely indifferent toward the Bucharest-Pyongyang axis, which did not seem to hurt Moscow's global or regional interests.

No evidence points to a Romanian striving to maintain close relations with Vietnam or Cuba. In fact, Romania opposed Vietnam's invasion of Kampuchea, and it is hard to imagine a close personal relationship between Ceaușescu and Fidel Castro. On the other hand, over the years the Romanian leader became a peripatetic traveler and a visitor to capitals of the Third World rivaling only the late Marshal Tito. Kenneth Jowitt has provided us with a perceptive analysis that goes a long way in explaining Ceaușescu's penchant for travel. In Jowitt's opinion, Ceaușescu, aware of the risks associated with his independent stance, attempted to play the game of "safety in numbers" by enlarging the number of Romania's "identity referents"[28] (the

[25]For an account of the origins of Romania's stance, see Stephen Fischer-Galati, "Rumania and the Sino-Soviet Conflict," in London's *Eastern Europe in Transition*, pp. 261–275.

[26]A brief survey of Sino-Romanian relations can be found in George Cioranescu, "Hu Visits Ceaușescu," Radio Free Europe Research, *RAD Background Report/1432*, June 23, 1983.

[27]Kenneth Jowitt, "Political Innovation in Romania," *Survey* 20, no. 4 (Autumn 1974), pp. 132–151. See also Anneli Maier, "Ceaușescu Endorses the Succession Plans of Kim Il-song," Radio Free Europe Research, *Situation Report Romania/13*, September 20, 1984.

[28]See Jowitt's comments in Sylva Sinanian, Istvan Deak, and Peter C. Ludz, eds., *Eastern Europe in the 1970s* (New York: Praeger, 1972), pp. 180–184.

concept refers simply to Romania's multiple membership in various regional and global organizations, groups, and camps). By casting his net wider and by expanding the boundaries of the "World Socialist System" or claiming Romania's membership in the Group of 77 and the nonaligned movement, Ceauşescu clearly tried to accomplish two major objectives: one, to make it more difficult for the Kremlin to put Romania in its place (for fear of creating unfavorable reaction among the non-European communist states and the nations of the Third World); and two, to make it easier for Romania, as one of the LDCs, to receive developmental credits and various trade concessions from the West.[29]

Whether Romania's initiatives yielded many dividends is difficult to say. Some Third World countries were presumably flattered by the attention heaped upon them by Bucharest; others saw through Ceauşescu's game. Some countries were grateful to Romania for speaking on their behalf on such issues as nuclear proliferation; others were probably dismayed by Romania's position vis-à-vis such regional issues as the Arab-Israeli conflict.[30] On balance, Romania's venture into the Third World made very little difference to both Moscow and Washington, although Romania's open disapproval in the United Nations of the Soviet invasion of Afghanistan must have caused considerable embarrassment for the Kremlin. It has been Romania's historical misfortune that few countries have ever taken it seriously, and this attitude goes a long way to explain Moscow's lack of concern for Ceauşescu's policies within the WTO and his peregrinations to the Third World. Interestingly, the United States more than the USSR apparently viewed Romania for many years as an important actor on the international scene.

East Germany also attempted to establish and maintain close diplomatic relations with the Third World. In this case, however, it was much less a matter of Walter Ulbricht's and Erich Honecker's personal ambitions and much more the fact that, as mentioned earlier, at least until 1972 East Germany was largely isolated from and ignored by the rest of the world. To put it crudely, for East Berlin the Third World became "the only game in town."[31]

---

[29]Romania was accorded full membership in the Group of 77 in 1976. It was described by the author of a seemingly authoritative study of the 77 as "a Latin country . . . at a level of development similar to that of some Latin American countries." Karl P. Sauvant, *The Group of 77* (New York: Oceana, 1981), p. 5. See also Kenneth Jowitt, "The Romanian Communist Party and the World Socialist System," *World Politics* 23, no. 1 (October 1970), pp. 38–60.

[30]As is well known, Romania was the only WTO country that refused to break off diplomatic relations with Israel in 1967 in the wake of the Six Day War. It is also generally assumed that Ceauşescu played a major role in arranging the visit of President Sadat to Israel in 1977. In the past few years Ceauşescu has also met with many Arab and Israeli leaders, including President Mubarak of Egypt, King Hussein of Jordan, Yassir Arafat of the PLO, and Prime Ministers Begin and Peres of Israel.

[31]For a comprehensive account, see Hans Siegfried Lamm and Siegfried Kupp, *DDR und die Dritte Welt* (Munich: Oldenbourg, 1976). See also David Childs, *The GDR: Moscow's German Ally* (London: Allen & Unwin, 1983), pp. 296–306; Boris Meissner, "The GDR's Position in the Soviet Alliance System," *Aussenpolitik* (English ed.) 35, no. 4 (1984), pp. 369–389; and Woodrow Kuhns, "The German Democratic Republic in Africa," *East European Quarterly* 19, no. 2 (Summer 1985), pp. 219–240.

Thus the 1960s witnessed East Germany establishing diplomatic relations with several LDCs that, presumably, were interested in some of the things East Germany was prepared to offer in exchange (military advisers and weapons). Those countries were also eager to emphasize newly won independence from their former colonial masters and the United States. Even after 1972, when East Germany was accepted as a bona fide member of the international community and no longer needed the support of the Third World, or at least not as much as before, it continued to make its presence felt in many countries of Africa, by sheer inertia if for no other reason.

A good case can be made that in contrast to Romania, whose forays into the Third World were either treated with indifference or occasionally resented by Moscow, East Germany probably received the Kremlin's blessing for its strong presence and high profile in the Third World. The USSR has fought long and hard to make East Germany legitimate and acceptable, and Moscow welcomed anything that enhanced East Berlin's international standing and prestige. Also, unlike Romania, East Germany was an obedient vassal of Moscow, and we have no reason to suspect that its initiatives in the Third World did not receive the Soviet imprimatur. All in all, East Germany in this particular respect was clearly a major political asset for the Soviet Union.

Other members of the Warsaw Pact appeared in their political relations with the Third World much less active than either Romania or East Germany. The reasons are not clear. To be sure, the leaders of Bulgaria, Czechoslovakia, Hungary, and Poland have paid ceremonial visits to various Third World countries, notably India, Libya, Iraq, and Iran, but otherwise there is no evidence of extensive contacts and what contacts did exist seemed to focus almost entirely on economics. Relations with China and North Korea practically ceased in the mid-1960s and were not resumed until 1986.[32] There is no record of high-level contacts with Vietnam since the end of the war there in 1975. Contacts with Cuba appeared closer, but here again they mostly concerned economics. The various East European countries provided diplomatic support to revolutionary regimes in Angola, Ethiopia, Mozambique, and Nicaragua but relatively little beyond the standard rhetoric voiced in the United Nations and other international organizations.

Outside the Six the story of Albania's defection from the Soviet to the Chinese orbit and its return to total isolation from both is well known, and it probably caused few ripples in the Third World. The influence of the other Balkan country outside the Warsaw Pact, Yugoslavia, was powerful in the past, but it has declined in recent years after the death of Marshal Tito deprived Yugoslavia of its most vocal and forceful spokesman, one who appeared to enjoy great personal esteem and popularity in the Third World.

Yugoslavia's initial influence in the Third World was due, of course, to its being one of the creators of the movement of nonaligned nations, founded in 1954 by Tito together with President Nasser of Egypt and Prime Minister

---

[32]Jaruzelski and Honecker paid official visits to China in the fall of 1986.

Nehru of India.[33] From its very inception the idea of nonalignment and neutrality generated great appeal among Third World countries, and for obvious reasons. Although the United States initially ignored the movement, the Soviet Union after Khrushchev assumed power became keenly interested, and at some point the Kremlin decided that the time had come to penetrate the nonaligned camp and possibly to manipulate it for its own purposes. It was helped in this decision by the deaths of two of the three founders, Nasser and Nehru, and by the progressive decline in international charisma of Tito, who was increasingly preoccupied with Yugoslavia's domestic problems. Moscow found a convenient and willing Trojan horse in the person of Fidel Castro, who in the late 1970s began successfully to challenge Tito for the leadership of the nonaligned movement.[34] The obvious pro-Moscow tilt shown by the camp was greatly aided by the death of Tito in 1980, but a good case can be made that a pro-Soviet stance became inevitable as soon as membership criteria were loosened to admit not only Cuba but several other Soviet clients, not to mention Romania.

To conclude, Eastern Europe's political involvement in the Third World has presented a mixed record from Moscow's standpoint. East Germany's success in establishing bridgeheads in several Third World countries must have been applauded by successive Soviet leaders who most likely remained largely indifferent with regard to Romania's attempt to carve a niche for itself beyond the confines of the Warsaw Pact. Moscow clearly viewed the nonaligned movement spearheaded by Belgrade with considerable suspicion, and even today, despite Yugoslavia's loss of influence in the movement, the Kremlin still sees the neutral camp as less than a reliable potential ally in the U.S.-Soviet global competition.

Ideological Interests

The Soviet Union's ideological stake in Eastern Europe is rooted in the success or failure of a communist political system to become strongly embedded in a given East European society, thus validating, if not legitimizing, the Soviet kind of Marxism-Leninism as a potentially universalistic model. For more than four decades, after all, eight countries in the heart of Europe have existed and grown under communist rule, which may have provided Soviet

---

[33]For a detailed account of the early years of the movement, see Alvin Z. Rubinstein, *Yugoslavia and the Non-aligned World* (Princeton: Princeton University Press, 1970). A more recent treatment can be found in Michael M. Milenkovitch, "Yugoslavia and the Third World," in Radu, *Eastern Europe and the Third World*, pp. 273–300. See also Zdenko Andic, "Nonalignment: From Belgrade to Havana and After," Radio Free Europe Research, *RAD Background Report/195 (Yugoslavia)*, September 17, 1979.

[34]Kevin Devlin, "Castro versus Tito," Radio Free Europe Research, *RAD Background Report/194 (World)*, September 12, 1979, and Slobodan Stankovic, "Tito and the Sixth Non-aligned Summit in Havana," Radio Free Europe Research, *RAD Background Report/197 (Yugoslavia)*, September 17, 1979.

leaders with a proof supporting, in their own minds, their persistent claims that Marxism-Leninism was and is a viable and dynamic doctrine that has universal applicability. Two of the eight countries, Albania and Yugoslavia, are not currently under direct Soviet control, but this does not greatly weaken Moscow's belief that communism is the wave of the future and is available for export primarily, if not exclusively, to the Third World.

Has Eastern Europe proved ideologically attractive to the Third World? With the possible exceptions of Yugoslavia and, interestingly, Albania, the answer is an unequivocal no. The reasons for Yugoslavia's attractiveness are discussed above. Albania today may appear attractive to those countries in the Third World determined not to be linked in whatever fashion to any of the three great powers—the United States, the Soviet Union, and China— and eager to maintain a splendid isolation from the rest of the world. The only Third World country that might conceivably fall into that category is Burma, but it is impossible to say whether Rangoon has modeled itself on Tiranë; most likely the opposite is true, as Burma has maintained its isola- tionist posture much longer than Albania has.

As for the Warsaw Pact proper, its ideological impact on LDCs has been nil. I suggest that the lack of attraction has had little if anything to do with Eastern Europe being communist. For many, perhaps most, Third World countries the label of communism is largely irrelevant, as is illustrated by their attitude toward Yugoslavia. The same is largely true for the institutional and political framework of the East European Six (after all, President Ceauşescu could possibly substitute for Emperor Bokassa, the Poland of General Jaru- zelski has many counterparts in Africa and Latin America, and East Germany could also find its replicas among more advanced countries in the Third World). It has also little to do with official ideologies and economic policies which, as John Kautsky pointed out some time ago, show hardly any dif- ference between communist states and revolutionary one-party regimes—the prevailing mode of government in the Third World.[35]

This is not to say that Third World countries have never found anything in Eastern Europe worthy of admiration and emulation. Some appear initially to have been impressed with an overall economic development strategy that allowed most of the countries in the region to pull themselves up by their bootstraps. Others may have admired the efficiency and esprit de corps of the East German Army, while still others may have liked the quality of Czech weapons. Today, however, the overall perception most likely is strongly negative.

One reason is probably the persistent political, social, and economic in- stability in Eastern Europe. Even though communism may not be a relevant variable, a strong and efficient regime capable of ensuring stability, almost

[35] See John H. Kautsky, "Comparative Communism versus Comparative Politics," *Studies in Comparative Communism* 6, nos. 1–2 (1973), pp. 135–170.

regardless of the means employed, is most relevant. The examples of Hungary in 1956, Czechoslovakia in 1968, and Poland in the past thirty years must have persuaded Third World leaders that Eastern Europe has little to offer as a model of stability and concord. At the same time the widely held perception that most of the East European Six are satellites of the Soviet Union does not enhance the attractiveness of the region. Although the Soviet intervention in Hungary in 1956 was widely ignored by Third World countries, which were preoccupied with the Anglo-French-Israeli invasion of Egypt, Moscow's armed suppression of the "Prague Spring" in 1968 and the Soviet pressure on Poland in 1980–81 were widely noted and commented upon in the Third World and did little to improve the image and global reputation of the USSR. Most LDCs may not like colonialism and capitalism à la United States and may prefer socialism in the Yugoslav version, but they harbor little love for the Soviet Union as leader of a colonial empire in Eastern Europe. This in turn helps explain the attractiveness for the Third World of the neutral and nonaligned movement.

When all is said and done, however, the main reason for the East European countries' failure to make significant inroads in the Third World has been a dismal economic performance throughout the CMEA, especially in the past decade or so. The Third World may have been impressed with the process of industrial revolution followed by rapid economic progress and modernization, but it is hard to imagine that it would be impressed with the more recent decline in economic activity or with the growing inefficiency, shortages, corruption, and general *Schlamperei* that have accompanied the economic downturn. Most of the Third World realized some time ago that the Stalinist central planning system simply did not work and that what Eastern Europe needed was a program of comprehensive economic reforms. Some East European countries, such as Hungary, have indeed undertaken extensive reforms in the past twenty years and proved reasonably successful in implementing them. It is possible that the Hungarian New Economic Mechanism, just like the Yugoslav workers' council system of thirty years ago, may attract the attention of the LDCs, both communist and noncommunist. China, for example, has recently shown interest in the Hungarian reforms.

Economic Interests

It is generally agreed that unlike its security, political, and ideological concerns, Moscow's economic interests in Eastern Europe, except for Albania and Yugoslavia, have undergone significant changes in the past thirty years. In the second half of the 1950s, faced with growing popular discontent in the region manifested in the Polish and Hungarian crises of 1956, the Soviet leadership apparently concluded that, at least for the time being, the economic and thus political viability of the East European regimes had to be given preference over ideological cohesion. As a result, the individual East

European countries were allowed greater autonomy in their economic policies. I stress, however, that the Kremlin did not entirely relinquish control over the economies of Eastern Europe: the rejuvenated CMEA was entrusted with the task of coordinating the economic policies of member-states under Moscow's supervision.

The 1960s witnessed the beginning of economic difficulties that have afflicted Eastern Europe ever since. The Soviet Union, as suggested above, was clearly concerned with the economic viability of Eastern Europe as a precondition of political stability in the region, and the Kremlin opted to continue its earlier policy of supplying its clients with increasing quantities of basic raw materials, mainly oil, at highly favorable prices. In the early 1970s, however, in the wake of the Czech crisis of 1968, Moscow reasserted its previous attitude and decided to use its growing economic leverage to extract greater East European obedience and conformity to Soviet political and economic goals. At the same time, with the USSR assuming the status of a global power, the Kremlin also decided to force its East European allies to act as Soviet proxies in different parts of the world. Moreover, Moscow put increasing demands on its clients to provide resources, such as labor and capital, for the development in the form of joint investment projects of sources of raw materials on Soviet territory and tied the delivery of scarce materials to individual countries' contributions to these projects.[36]

Most East European countries responded to Soviet pressure by seeking alternative suppliers, primarily of oil, in the Third World. For example, in anticipation of Soviet inability or unwillingness to continue supplying its allies with increasing amounts of oil and the resulting necessity to rely more on deliveries of Middle Eastern oil, Czechoslovakia, Hungary, and Yugoslavia, helped by credits from Kuwait, Libya, and the World Bank, proceeded in 1974 to construct the so-called Adria Pipeline, which was to carry oil from the Yugoslav island of Krk to the other two countries. The Adria Pipeline opened formally in December 1979.[37]

It was also in the course of the 1970s that all of the East European countries, including Yugoslavia but excluding Albania and, interestingly, Czechoslovakia, embarked on a major expansion of their trade with the West, stimulated, no doubt, by generous Western credits. Unfortunately, from their point of view, this expansion coincided with the OPEC oil embargo in 1973 and the ensuing increase in energy prices. Both these events had momentous repercus-

---

[36]It has been argued that it was the Soviet pressure for greater East European contribution to joint investment projects that prompted Eastern Europe to seek other sources of raw materials, mostly in Africa. Christopher Coker, "Adventurism and Pragmatism: The Soviet Union, COMECON, and Relations with African States," *International Affairs* (London) 57, no. 4 (Autumn 1981), pp. 618–633. For an opposing view, see Colin Lawson, "The Soviet Union and Eastern Europe in Southern Africa: Is There a Conflict of Interest?" ibid. 59, no. 1 (Winter 1982–83), pp. 32–40.

[37]For details, see "Adria Pipeline Ready: Whose Oil Will It Carry?" Radio Free Europe Research, *Situation Report Hungary/1*, January 22, 1980.

sions for the economies of Eastern Europe and that region's relations with the Third World.

To begin with, the decision to engage on a massive scale in trade and credit transactions with the West resulted in Eastern Europe becoming exposed for the first time since World War II to international economic disturbances and especially the worldwide inflation that followed the OPEC embargo.[38] Moreover, early, ambitious plans to increase imports of Middle Eastern oil had to be drastically scaled down because of the dramatic rise in world market prices, which Eastern Europe could not afford to pay. What followed was a concerted effort to cultivate Middle Eastern suppliers, and in the second half of the 1970s the most eagerly sought after visitors to the various East European capitals were an odd couple: Colonel Qadhdhafi of Libya and Shah Mohammed Pahlevi of Iran, who were both accorded a reception usually reserved for the most distinguished guests from the Soviet Union and other fraternal countries.

The OPEC price rise led to a major increase in oil prices charged by the USSR to East European customers, which put an additional squeeze on ailing economies. Suddenly Eastern Europe in the second half of the 1970s found itself in a highly unenviable situation. On the one hand, the region's demand for oil remained high and, for various reasons, no attempt was made to reduce it through strict conservation measures or a switch to such other energy sources as coal or nuclear power. On the other hand, the Soviet Union continued to be the main supplier of energy to the bloc, charging, after 1975, much higher prices for oil than in the past, thus creating serious problems for its allies.[39] It should be added that the Soviet Union itself faced a dilemma: should it continue supplying its junior partners with previously agreed amounts of energy or cut down on these deliveries and divert at least part to Western Europe, which could pay in hard currency?[40] Another option for Moscow was to maintain pressure on its East European allies to rely more on

[38]For an extensive discussion, see Egon Neuberger and Laura D. Tyson, eds., *The Impact of International Economic Disturbances on the Soviet Union and Eastern Europe* (New York: Pergamon, 1980).

[39]Jan Vanous, "The East European Recession: Did It Come from the West or Was It Sent from Russia with Love?" Discussion Paper no. 78–08 (Department of Economics, University of British Columbia, February 1978). In 1979 energy imports from the Soviet Union accounted for one-half or more of total energy consumption of Bulgaria and Hungary and approximately one-third for Czechoslovakia and East Germany. Ed A. Hewett, *Energy, Economics, and Foreign Policy in the Soviet Union* (Washington, D.C.: Brookings, 1984), p. 208. For detailed statistics, see CIA National Foreign Assessment Center, *Energy Supplies in Eastern Europe: A Statistical Compilation*, ER 79-10624 (Washington, December 1979), and John B. Hannigan and Carl H. McMillan, "CMEA Trade and Cooperation with the Third World in the Energy Sector," in NATO Economics and Information Directorates, *CMEA: Energy, 1980–1990* (Newtonville, Mass.: Oriental Research Partners, 1981), pp. 222–229.

[40]Dina R. Spechler and Martin C. Spechler, "The Soviet Union and the Oil Weapon," in Yaacov Ro'i, ed., *The Limits to Power: Soviet Policy in the Middle East* (London: Croom Helm, 1979), pp. 96–123, and Thane Gustafson, "Energy and the Soviet Bloc," *International Security* 6, no. 3 (Winter 1981–82), pp. 65–89.

Table 2. East European imports of OPEC crude oil, 1970–82 (in million metric tons)

	1970	1977	1978	1979	1980	1981	1982
Bulgaria	.9	.9*	1.3*	2.5*	1.5*	1.5*	1.0*
Czechoslovakia	.4	1.3	.9	.7	.8	—	1.0*
East Germany	1.1	1.4	2.2	2.3	3.2	4.1	5.0*
Hungary	.4	.9	1.5	2.1	.9	.5	1.8
Poland	.8	.4	1.9	3.2	3.1	.4	.3
Romania	2.3	8.8	12.9	13.9	14.5	10.2	9.4
CMEA Six	5.9	13.7	20.7	24.7	24.0	16.7	18.5*
Yugoslavia	2.8	5.5	6.3	7.2	6.0	4.4	4.1
Eastern Europe	8.7	19.2	27.0	31.9	30.0	21.0	22.6*

SOURCE: C. H. McMillan, "Eastern Europe's Relations with OPEC Suppliers in the 1980s," in *East European Economies: Slow Growth in the 1980s,* vol. 1, Selected Papers Submitted to the Joint Economic Committee, 99th Cong., 1st sess. (Washington, D.C., 1985), p. 370.
— negligible or none; * estimate.

oil supplied by the Third World. Not unexpectedly, the Kremlin chose the latter course and, as a result, Eastern Europe had no choice but to continue importing oil from Third World suppliers to fill the gap in its energy requirements.

Eastern Europe's economic difficulties continued through the late 1970s. On the one hand, generous Western credits became largely exhausted, creating a serious credit squeeze and imposing a heavy repayment burden on most of the countries in the region. On the other hand, Eastern Europe still needed oil badly but had little if anything with which to pay for it, especially in the face of sharply rising prices.[41] As a result, East European oil imports from OPEC sources declined sharply after 1979 and the drop continued until 1982, undoubtedly helped by a series of events beyond the control of both the Soviet Union and Eastern Europe: the overthrow of the Shah in Iran, the Iran-Iraq war, and another economic recession in the West caused by rising oil prices. East European imports of oil from OPEC are shown in Table 2.

The decline in oil imports came largely to a halt in 1981–82, and several East European countries began to import more oil from OPEC sources. The main reason was a reduction in Soviet deliveries accompanied by a rise in prices charged by the USSR; the price rise was produced by the CMEA five-year moving average formula, which had been in existence since 1975. In the meantime prices charged by OPEC started to decline, thus narrowing the differential with Soviet prices. Hence, not surprisingly, most East European countries turned once again to Third World suppliers. However, as Carl McMillan points out, Eastern Europe resumed oil imports from OPEC less to

[41] See C. H. McMillan, "Eastern Europe's Relations with OPEC Suppliers in the 1980s," in *East European Economies: Slow Growth in the 1980s,* vol. 1, Selected Papers Submitted to the Joint Economic Committee, 99th Cong., 1st sess. (Washington, D.C., 1985), p. 370.

fill domestic requirements and more for reexport to earn badly needed hard currency.[42]

Still, Eastern Europe was hardly out of the woods yet, and this policy change well illustrates the East European dilemma.[43] Lacking hard currency, the East European countries were forced to engage largely in barter trade, which put them at an additional disadvantage and weakened their bargaining position. Also, despite pious declarations about supporting the quest of the LDCs for economic independence from the West, the East European countries were willing to give exports from the Third World less access to their markets than were the industrially advanced countries of the West.[44] At the same time the technical limitations of East European capital equipment and low quality of consumer goods made it difficult for the East Europeans to increase their exports to the Third World, especially in the face of growing competition from Western Europe, the United States, and Japan, also eager to expand exports to key oil-producing countries. In addition, there was cutthroat competition from the other East European states, almost reminiscent of the "beggar my neighbor" policy of the Depression years, and from such newly industrialized countries as Brazil, South Korea, and Taiwan.[45]

Eastern Europe's only recourse was to focus on those exports which were still finding a market in the Third World: these included weapons, complete factories and other establishments, and labor in the form of technicians, academic personnel, and other experts. Although East European military hardware generally had no difficulty finding buyers, the situation with industrial projects and technicians was different. To export both, East European countries had to accept terms that were, as a rule, rejected by potential suppliers from the West. If East European sources are to be believed, construction workers and other personnel had to endure conditions obviously unacceptable to Westerners. Still, the East Europeans had no choice as long as their efforts generated badly needed hard currency. As a result, paradoxically, the actual return on the effort was often unreasonably low because of very high human and material costs caused by harsh working conditions. This outcome raised serious questions about the economic rationale for Third World transactions, but again the East European countries had no other way out.

In the late 1970s the East European Six, in addition to having the difficult task of penetrating tough Third World markets, were somewhat unexpected-

---

[42]Ibid., pp. 372, 380.

[43]John M. Kramer, "Between Scylla and Charybdis: The Politics of Eastern Europe's Energy Problem," *Orbis* 22, no. 4 (Winter 1979), pp. 929–950, and Coker, "Soviet Union, Eastern Europe," pp. 21–39.

[44]See Colin Lawson and Peter Wiles, "The Soviet-Type Economy as a Generator of Economic Disturbances," in Neuberger and Tyson, *Impact of International Economic Disturbances*, p. 370.

[45]See Kazimierz Poznanski, "Competition between Eastern Europe and Developing Countries in the Western Market for Manufactured Goods," in *East European Economies: Slow Growth in the 1980s*, vol. 2, pp. 62–90.

Table 3. East European economic aid to noncommunist LDCs: Agreements and disbursements, 1954–78 and 1979–84

| | East European | | East European Aid as Percentage of Total WTO Disbursements of Economic Aid |
| | Agreements | Disbursements | |
	(million current $)		
1954–78	9,495	3,510	31.4%
1979	645	305	34.5
1980	1,325	315	27.9
1981	725	485	36.1
1982	560	650	35.3
1983	415	680	32.1
1984	1,750	660	29.3
Total, 1954–84	14,915	6,610	31.8

SOURCE: U.S. Department of State, *Warsaw Pact Economic Aid to Non-Communist LDCs, 1984* (Washington, D.C., May 1985), p. 2.

ly faced with another formidable problem that impinged on their economic relations with the Third World, namely the Soviet Union's emergence as a global power. Stymied in its drive for greater influence in the developed world, Moscow turned its attention to, and became more assertive in, less developed regions.[46] This switch in policy produced two options for the Kremlin: one, help establish closer ties between Eastern Europe and the noncommunist Third World to mobilize the resources of the latter to prop up the faltering economies of the former; two, force the East European allies to help ease the burden of Soviet economic and military aid to Moscow's client states in the Third World.[47] The first option was applied primarily to such countries as Egypt, Iran, and Nigeria, which were supplying oil and possibly other primary products to Eastern Europe. The second affected both communist and noncommunist LDCs, such as Cuba, Iraq, Libya, and Vietnam, which have relied heavily on Soviet and increasingly on East European support.

It soon became apparent that the USSR had picked the first option. Beginning in the late 1970s, the East European countries assumed a new role as providers of economic aid and "loans" primarily to the noncommunist Third World (see Table 3). East European economic aid to Marxist client states was much smaller, amounting only to about 10 percent of total East European aid

[46]For details, see Alexander R. Alexiev, "The New Soviet Strategy in the Third World," N-1995-AF (Santa Monica: RAND Corporation, June 1983).

[47]It is worth mentioning that between 1955 and 1967 Eastern Europe had provided about a quarter of economic aid given by the WTO to the Third World. Joshua and Gibert, *Arms for the Third World*, pp. 98–99. For details, see CIA, National Foreign Assessment Center, *Communist Aid Activities in Non-Communist Less Developed Countries, 1978*, ER 79-10412U (Washington, D.C., September 1979).

to LDCs between 1954 and 1984.[48] The principal form of East European economic aid to Moscow's communist client states in the Third World produces foreign trade surpluses, as shown in Table 4. Although the available data are scarce and often difficult to interpret, the general trend appears unmistakable.[49] Moreover, the data may understate the upward trend and the overall magnitude of the East European economic contribution to Third World countries because the East European Six, like the USSR, most likely have been offering concessionary prices for their exports and/or paying above world market prices for their imports from the Third World.

It may be taken for granted that Eastern Europe greatly resented the Moscow-imposed policy of granting implicit trade subsidies to LDCs in the forms of aid and foreign trade surpluses. To be sure, Eastern Europe has for many years been receiving substantial Soviet subsidies. But in recent years, mostly as a result of a global oil glut and the decline in world market prices for oil, these subsidies have largely disappeared. In fact, there are indications that because of the peculiar price-setting formula in CMEA trade, the price of Soviet oil to members is now higher than that charged by OPEC, and if the East Europeans had any hard-currency reserves it would make sense for them to buy their oil on the open market.[50] Instead, however, they are not only compelled to purchase their energy from the USSR but also forced to reduce the costs of the Soviet empire at a time when their own economies are in disarray and badly in need of outside help.[51]

Clearly the intensity and extent of economic relations with the Third World vary from one East European country to another and are influenced by many factors, such as the country's dependency on foreign trade, its natural resource endowment, the level of its economic development, the history of its economic links with the Third World, product mix available for export as well as its quality, and last but not least the degree of its submission to Moscow's diktats. These criteria identify Czechoslovakia and East Germany as most heavily involved in trading with the Third World. Of the remaining countries, Romania has been active in searching for oil, if only because of the progressive depletion of its own sources and an ambitious expansion of its petrochemical industry. Poland, which was fortunate to have substantial coal reserves, was also seeking oil in the Third World and willing to pay for it with arms and manpower, as presumably was Bulgaria. Hungary, which managed to retain good commercial relations with the West despite

[48]U.S. Department of State, *Warsaw Pact Economic Aid to Non-Communist LDCs, 1984* (Washington, D.C., May 1985), p. 5.

[49]Cf. Coker, "Soviet Union, Eastern Europe," pp. 92–101.

[50]Cam Hudson, "What Do the OPEC Price Changes Mean for Eastern Europe?" Radio Free Europe Research, *RAD Background Report/59 (Eastern Europe)*, March 17, 1983. See also Vladimir Sobell, "The Impact on the CMEA of Declining Oil Prices," Radio Free Europe Research, *RAD Background Report/15 (Economics)*, January 28, 1986.

[51]For an interesting discussion, see Charles Wolf, Jr., et al., *The Costs of the Soviet Empire*, R-3073/1-NA (Santa Monica: RAND Corporation, September 1983).

Table 4. Surpluses/deficits of selected CMEA-six countries in their trade with Cuba, Iraq, Libya, Syria, and Vietnam, 1978–84 (in millions of $)

	1978	1979	1980	1981	1982	1983	1984	Total
Cuba								
Hungary	$9.9	-.7	20.1	-22.9	11.3	51.3	58.1	127.1
Romania	—	-6.0	44.0	63.0	112.0	58.0	58.0	—
Iraq								
Bulgaria	18.8	29.3	39.9	39.9	46.5	43.0	38.8	256.2
Czechoslovakia	55.6	64.7	73.7	73.7	81.5	73.6	66.3	489.1
Hungary	-29.1	22.4	25.7	215.7	270.0	160.5	112.3	777.5
Romania	-399.0	-864.0	-687.0	609.0	511.0	374.0	337.0	-119.0
Libya								
Bulgaria	4.5	-37.3	-22.8	-151.3	-119.7	-86.7	-78.0	-491.3
East Germany	—	—	-27.4	-137.0	-120.6	-95.0	-85.5	—
Hungary	—	41.5	47.0	97.5	-101.4	-268.2	-130.0	—
Romania	-97.0	-280.0	-302.0	-115.0	-140.0	-203.0	-184.0	-1321.0
Syria								
Bulgaria	8.5	25.7	60.8	88.2	41.9	13.3	-.5	237.9
Czechoslovakia	33.8	26.3	27.0	54.6	67.1	60.7	31.7	301.2
East Germany	38.3	32.5	48.9	86.7	29.9	56.9	141.3	434.5
Hungary	13.2	47.4	42.7	54.2	55.5	17.5	37.3	267.8
Poland	20.9	24.5	—	20.2	—	—	3.1	—
Romania	165.0	73.0	-72.0	-90.0	-354.0	-480.0	-363.0	-1121.0
Vietnam								
Hungary	13.6	20.4	33.0	27.4	10.6	1.8	9.8	116.6
Romania	50.0	12.0	43.0	17.0	-3.0	2.0	2.0	123.0

SOURCE: International Monetary Fund, *Direction of Trade Statistics Yearbook, 1985* (Washington, D.C., 1986), pp. 116–117, 150–151, 159–160, 216–217, 326–327, 335–336.
— not available.

the deterioration in East-West political relations, was less interested in LDCs. Finally, Yugoslavia was in a separate category: until recently it was able to maintain extensive trade relations with its partners in the nonaligned movement, but the inflation caused by the energy crisis, as well as its serious economic difficulties at home, have forced Belgrade to reduce the volume of its trade with the Third World and increase its trade with the Soviet Union and the rest of the CMEA.

Insofar as the CMEA's relations with the Third World are concerned, the record shows little progress. Unlike the Warsaw Treaty Organization, the CMEA expanded its original membership into the Third World by recruiting first Mongolia and more recently Cuba and Vietnam. This, in addition to special status to such LDCs as Iraq, Mexico, Nicaragua, and Syria, was used to validate Moscow's claim that in the 1980s the CMEA has become a truly international economic organization. Still, as for many years, a wide gap exists between rhetoric and reality, and for all practical purposes the CMEA has continued to be a paper organization not only in Eastern Europe but also in the Third World.

In sum, although Eastern Europe's economic contacts with and interests in the Third World were more substantial and important than the region's other concerns, for various reasons they showed relatively little progress, especially when compared with earlier plans and expectations.

Conclusion

Having surveyed Eastern Europe's many contacts, links, and relations with the Third world, I find it perhaps less surprising that so little has been written about them in the West. The topic of East European–Third World relations has attracted little scholarly attention so far because the relationship between Eastern Europe and the Third World in the past thirty years has been mostly marginal, a phenomenon that was not likely to cause many ripples in international politics and economics.

To be sure, I have likely raised more questions than I can answer, and this chapter leaves many loose ends. As always, there is also the problem of reliable data and their interpretation. Still, the inescapable conclusion is that unlike Soviet involvement in the Third World, which many observers view as one of the most destabilizing factors in world politics today, the East European engagement beyond the European continent should not be taken too seriously. Like any generalization, this one can be challenged, of course, on the grounds that several East European countries have been harboring terrorists and/or have trained police and military personnel from LDCs, clearly introducing an element of instability into some regions of the Third World. Still, I am prepared to argue that were the East European countries to pull out of the Third World tomorrow, the overall situation there would not undergo a drastic change.

I suggest that one main reason for the paucity of East European involvement in the Third World has been the adoption by the East Europeans, with the exception of Romania, of a "limited regret strategy" in their dealings with the LDCs. Egon Neuberger, who first suggested this concept more than twenty years ago in an attempt to explain slow progress in the CMEA, described limited regret as a "conservative strategy" affected by the presence of "conflicting objectives and constraints" that both the Soviet Union and its East European allies faced.[52]

In the case of the Third World, we find multiple Soviet objectives—military, political, ideological, and economic—and only one or at least the most important East European goal—the possibility of obtaining economic gains and achieving a degree of economic independence from the USSR. Among constraints, the most significant is clearly the built-in conflict between East European countries, which for better or worse are determined to preserve as much of their sovereignty as possible, and the Soviet Union, which seems equally determined to circumscribe those sovereignties by imposing and enforcing bloc cohesion. Additional constraints come from the existence of Soviet-type economic systems in nearly all East European countries, which also inhibits closer economic relations with the Third World. Moreover, the relatively meager East European resources that could be used to expand economic relations with all LDCs tend to be absorbed by Soviet Third World clients.

The adoption of a conservative, "limited regret strategy" by the East Europeans thus makes good political and economic sense. On the one hand, Eastern Europe does more than pay lip service to Moscow's commands and thus avoids, at least to some extent, arousing its wrath; on the other, the strategy, as Neuberger notes, "enables the CMEA countries to reap the benefits of comparative advantage in those cases where the benefits appear so obvious as not to require any serious economic calculations."[53] Although it is clearly not an optimum strategy from the economic point of view, it may well be the only strategy feasible in the circumstances that have existed in the past thirty years. The share of the East European foreign trade turnover taken by the LDCs between 1960 and 1970–83, as shown in Table 5, has not exhibited significant changes, except for Romania and possibly Hungary, providing a tentative confirmation of the limited regret strategy as practiced by the East Europeans.

What net advantages or disadvantages have accrued to the Soviet Union as a

---

[52]Egon Neuberger, "International Division of Labor in CMEA: Limited Regret Strategy," *American Economic Review* 54, no. 3 (May 1964), pp. 506–515.

[53]Ibid., p. 515.

Table 5. Trade with the LDCs as a share in foreign trade of CMEA Six, 1960 and 1970–83 (in percentages)

	1960	1970	1971	1972	1973	1974	1975	1976	1977	1978	1979	1980	1981	1982	1983
Exports															
Bulgaria	3.5	6.5	6.7	6.3	7.2	12.3	10.7	9.2	10.4	11.1	11.3	13.4	17.5	17.2	13.1
Czechoslovakia	11.0	9.0	9.6	8.5	7.6	8.6	8.6	7.6	8.2	8.4	7.8	8.7	9.8	8.4	9.0
East Germany	4.1	4.2	4.4	3.6	3.8	4.2	4.4	4.4	4.7	5.8	5.7	7.2	7.0	8.0	6.5
Hungary	6.6	6.4	5.9	5.7	5.1	6.8	6.4	8.7	9.0	9.3	10.1	11.0	12.2	13.3	13.1
Poland	7.5	7.7	7.1	6.0	5.1	8.0	8.6	8.3	8.4	7.6	8.0	9.7	11.6	13.8	9.3
Romania	5.7	10.0	9.1	10.0	9.5	14.6	22.5	—	—	—	—	—	—	—	—
Imports															
Bulgaria	2.4	4.7	5.7	5.2	5.0	7.4	4.1	4.4	4.5	3.5	3.5	3.9	4.6	6.1	6.3
Czechoslovakia	9.8	6.1	5.7	6.0	6.5	7.3	5.6	5.2	6.5	4.9	4.9	5.5	5.1	4.4	4.1
East Germany	4.2	3.9	3.7	2.7	3.0	5.6	4.4	4.7	5.0	4.7	4.8	6.2	3.8	4.6	5.0
Hungary	4.4	6.2	4.4	5.8	6.4	7.8	6.8	9.4	10.0	8.9	8.3	9.5	8.2	10.3	13.0
Poland	6.8	5.6	5.3	4.7	3.9	4.8	4.9	4.2	4.8	5.4	7.8	9.4	7.0	5.8	4.9
Romania	3.5	6.6	6.6	7.5	7.9	12.2	14.6	—	—	—	—	—	—	—	—

SOURCES: For 1960, Endre Antal, *Die Beteiligung der RWG-Länder am Welthandel* (Berlin: Dunker & Humblot, 1979), pp. 53–54; for 1970–83, *Statisticheskii Tezhegodnik Stran Chlenov SEV (SYSEV)*, p. 342; *SYSEV 1972*, p. 325; *SYSEV 1973*, p. 353; *SYSEV 1974*, p. 333; *SYSEV 1975*, p. 325; *SYSEV 1976*, p. 341; *SYSEV 1977*, p. 325; *SYSEV 1978*, p. 325; *SYSEV 1979*, p. 325; *SYSEV 1980*, p. 373; *SYSEV 1981*, p. 335; *SYSEV 1982*, p. 311; *SYSEV 1983*, p. 315; *SYSEV 1984*, p. 297. The coverage of Romania ceased in 1975.

result of Eastern Europe's involvement in the Third World? On the strength of the foregoing analysis, we can argue that on balance the Kremlin has over the years benefited from Eastern Europe's presence in the LDCs, although the actual benefits were probably less than Moscow had initially hoped for. The chief advantages seem to have accrued in the military and economic spheres through aid, training, and other kinds of help provided by the East Europeans. The costs are more difficult to estimate, but we may take it for granted that Eastern Europe, which itself has been going through hard times, grew increasingly resentful at having to divert scarce resources to the LDCs, with most of the rewards ending up in the Soviet Union. This judgment is obviously impressionistic, but circumstantial evidence suggests that a negative attitude toward some LDCs is quite widespread in Eastern Europe.

Left entirely to itself, I would suggest, Eastern Europe would probably maintain its contacts with the Third World, but the nature of these contacts would be quite different and most likely based on rational economic and political calculations. The East European masses, and possibly even some elite members, perceive the present, fairly extensive contacts as imposed on them by Moscow, and this fact alone makes such links highly suspect and therefore undesirable and resented. It is normally assumed that public opinion has no role to play in Eastern Europe, but I suspect that the ruling oligarchies in the region cannot ignore vox populi entirely and indefinitely, and in this particular case the attitudes of the masses and of some members of the governing elite may be congruent. If this is so, the adoption of the limited regret strategy is even more logical and understandable.

My hypothesis, if correct, does not augur well for the future course of East European–Third World relations. In the early 1970s, when Moscow embarked on its ambitious drive to make friends and influence people in the LDCs, some of its East European allies may have been only too happy to jump on the bandwagon in anticipation of major economic and even political gains. In the mid-1980s the earlier optimism regarding Soviet victories and Western defeats in the Third World has largely given way to a more somber appraisal of the situation. The Soviet drive essentially came to a halt; the West stood its ground and even recouped some of its losses; and the U.S.-Soviet confrontation in the Third World contributed in a major way to the demise of detente. Eastern Europe was a distinct loser in at least two ways: it certainly suffered from the collapse of detente, and it clearly had to pay a price for participating in the struggle for the hearts and minds of the peoples of the Third World. Not only did it gain few advantages from being involved with the LDCs, but the cost of its involvement also proved to be quite high, especially in economic terms. Its difficult situation was further aggravated by growing international tension that resulted in the loss of benefits generated by East-West detente, as manifested in the credit squeeze, the heavy burden of debt repayment, a decline in East-West trade, and other factors.

In this light the continuing Soviet insistence that the East European Six maintain their presence in the Third World, either as proxies or as purveyors of economic and military aid, obviously ran counter to long-term interests of most of the East European countries, which with few exceptions had little to gain from helping prop up insolvent Soviet clients, stirring up instability in regions far from their own borders, and thus creating obstacles for the re-sumption of East-West detente that they greatly desired. It was clearly a no-win situation and another reason why, caeteris paribus, the limited regret strategy appeared the best solution both in the present and in the future.

6

Cuba, the Third World, and the Soviet Union

EDWARD GONZALEZ

Cuba is a privileged ally of the USSR in large part because of its unique role in promoting Soviet political and strategic interests in the Third World. In turn, as Robert Pastor notes, Cuba's capacity as an important, at times decisive, Third World actor has been vastly strengthened by Soviet economic and military assistance to the Castro government:

> Cuba is a small country with a big country's foreign policy. No other developing nation maintains more diplomatic missions, intelligence operatives, and military advisers and troops abroad than does Cuba, not even the oil-producing states that can afford it. The gap between its internal resources and its external capabilities is filled by the Soviet Union, not because of altruism, but because the Soviets are assured that what the Cubans do abroad will serve their purpose.[1]

Yet although Cuba acts within the parameters of Soviet foreign policy, it would be a mistake to think of Cuba as simply a Soviet-directed surrogate in the Third World. As Pastor and others have pointed out, a symbiotic relationship has evolved between Havana and Moscow in their respective strategies toward the Third World in which each needs the other to advance sometimes separate international interests and objectives.[2]

This chapter assesses Cuban strategy in the Third World since 1975, the way

---

This is a revised version of a paper presented at the conference "The Soviet Union and the Third World: The Last Three Decades," sponsored by the RAND/UCLA Center for the Study of Soviet International Behavior and held at the Bellagio Study and Conference Center, Bellagio, Italy, November 11–15, 1985.

[1] Robert Pastor, "Cuba and the Soviet Union: Does Cuba Act Alone?" in Barry B. Levine, ed., *The New Cuban Presence in the Caribbean Basin* (Boulder, Colo.: Westview, 1983), p. 207.

[2] Besides ibid., see Jorge I. Dominguez, "Cuban Foreign Policy," *Foreign Affairs*, Fall 1978, pp. 83–108, and especially Edward Gonzalez, "Cuba, the Soviet Union, and Africa," in David E. Albright, ed., *Communism in Africa* (Bloomington: Indiana University Press, 1980), pp. 145–167.

in which it has been supportive of Soviet objectives, and the potential for recurrent tension between Havana and Moscow over their respective Third World policies. Five major themes are elaborated.

Despite Cuba's resource limitations, Havana's "internationalist" foreign policy has an extraordinary global reach in which the Third World is central to multiple Cuban activities.

Although militarily and economically dependent upon the Soviet Union, Fidel Castro has long had his own motivations, interests, and objectives in pursuing a highly activist foreign policy not only in Latin America but also in Africa and elsewhere in the Third World.

In the mid-1970s there began a greater coincidence of Cuban and Soviet objectives in the Third World, a coincidence that has led to much higher levels of Soviet backing for Cuba and thus to enhanced capabilities for the latter as a regional and global actor.

Despite this recent convergence, Cuban and Soviet interests and priorities in the Third World remain different, thereby providing a basis for such strains in the Havana-Moscow relationship as occurred with the Soviet invasion of Afghanistan in 1979, with Grenada in 1983, and perhaps with Central America in the future.

Since the early 1980s adverse regional and international trends, and now economic priorities at home, appear to be inclining Castro toward more prudent behavior but not toward the abandonment of his "maximalist" objectives and aspirations as a Third World leader.

In conclusion I discuss the policy implications of Cuban behavior for the United States today.

Cuba and Its Third World Activities

The magnitude of Cuba's involvement in the Third World over the last ten years (aided by the Soviets) has been truly astonishing. Beginning in the fall of 1975 Cuba started greatly to expand its military presence in Africa, initially by deploying combat forces to Angola, evidently on its own.[3] With subsequent Soviet logistical support, the Cubans rapidly increased their deployment, according to Castro's "secret speech" of December 27, 1979, to 36,000

---

[3]That Cuba initiated the Angolan operation is the consensus opinion of most specialists who otherwise disagree on or assign different weights to Cuban motivations. See Nelson Valdes, "Revolutionary Solidarity in Angola," in Cole Blasier and Carmelo Mesa-Lago, eds., *Cuba in the World* (Pittsburgh: University of Pittsburgh Press, 1979), pp. 87–119; Gonzalez, "Cuba, the Soviet Union, and Africa"; and William M. LeoGrande, *Cuba's Policy in Africa, 1959–1980*, Policy Papers in International Affairs, Institute of International Studies, University of California (Berkeley, 1980).

at the height of the Angolan civil war in 1976. Then in late 1977 Cuba dispatched another expeditionary force to Ethiopia which, according to the same speech, numbered 12,000 combat troops by 1978.[4]

Cuba's military operations were responsible for the victory of the Marxist Popular Movement for the Liberation of Angola (MPLA), the defeat of the Somalian forces that had invaded Ethiopia, and the establishment of a direct Soviet presence in southern Africa and the Horn. Although since 1984 Cuban troops have been reduced to about 4,000 in Ethiopia, upward of 35,000 are said to remain in Angola in 1986 where they are crucial to the survival of the MPLA regime. Meanwhile, as of 1983 Havana had an estimated 25,000 civilian technicians, teachers, and public health personnel serving in Third World countries, including Nicaragua.

Castro has been constrained from dispatching combat troops within the Caribbean Basin. Still, since 1977 he has actively assisted movements led by Marxist-Leninists in their attempts to gain power. Thus Cuba supplied key material assistance to the Sandinista Front for National Liberation (FSLN) during the anti-Somoza struggle in Nicaragua, including heavy weapons in the spring 1979 offensive. Thereafter, covert Cuban support for Latin American insurgencies intensified. Captured guerrilla documents, together with testimony by guerrilla defectors and past and present insurgent leaders, have recently revealed a far-flung global guerrilla network of which Cuba is the hub, with the Castro regime providing training, logistical assistance, and direction to the Salvadoran and other guerrilla movements.[5]

The Castro government has also played a leading role in helping Marxist-Leninist regimes consolidate their power. After the March 1979 coup in Grenada it quickly stepped in to shore up the regime of Maurice Bishop and his New Jewel Movement. As captured Grenada documents disclose, the Soviet Union and North Korea, as well as Cuba, entered into five secret agreements with Grenada to provide military equipment, security assistance, and political training to the Bishop regime prior to the U.S. invasion of October 1983. Cuba has played an even larger role in Nicaragua since 1979. According to U.S. government estimates, Cuba had 3,500 to 4,000 civilians working in Nicaragua by 1984–85, together with an estimated 2,500 to 3,500 military and security advisers.[6]

Castro has also been active on the political front in developing Cuba's ties with the Third World. He assumed leadership of the Non-Aligned Movement

---

[4]Castro's secret speech to the National Assembly of People's Power was leaked and subsequently published in the West. If his figures are correct, and the context of his speech makes it likely that they are, the Angolan deployment was 50 percent higher than the highest Western intelligence estimates (24,000), while the Ethiopian deployment was 25 percent lower than Western estimates (16,000).

[5]See James LeMoyne, "The Guerrilla Network," *New York Times Magazine*, April 6, 1986.

[6]In 1985 Nicaraguan president Daniel Ortega disputed U.S. claims and put the Cuban military and security presence at 800.

(NAM), hosted its 1979 summit conference in Havana, and addressed the United Nations General Assembly in October 1979 in his capacity as NAM chairman. Havana has also played host to an endless succession of high-level Third World delegations since 1976, especially from Africa, and has sent several party and government delegations abroad, to Africa in particular. By the late 1970s Cuba had also enrolled some 10,000 school-age children from Angola and other African states for study on the Isle of Youth. By 1985 enrollment had swollen to between 15,000 and 22,000 African students, some destined to become the educated cadres and leaders of their countries. Within Latin America, Castro has lately championed the cause of the debtor countries. Calling for a "general strike of debtors," he convened a five-day conference in Havana in July 1985 to promote the debt revolt, with roughly a thousand politicians, writers, and academics from seventeen Latin American countries attending the talkathon.

In these and other ways Cuba identifies itself closely with the Third World. It does so not only in words but also by its commitment of material and human resources that could otherwise alleviate the shortages and hardships that the Cuban population must bear. Moreover, the Castro regime has sacrificed the lives of untold numbers of Cuban "internationalists" in guerrilla and military operations in Latin America, the Middle East, Africa, and Grenada in its attempts to promote "national liberation" and "socialism" abroad.[7]

Because it can provide political, technical, and security assistance, and even military protection, Cuba itself has become a mini-patron state for those fledgling regimes seeking to consolidate their power—notably in Angola, Nicaragua, and pre-1983 Grenada. Such a patron-client relationship entails new responsibilities, burdens, and risks for Cuban foreign policy—as Cuba's continuing military presence in Angola and its defeat in Grenada in October 1983 attest. Indeed, Castro's Cuba stands out as the most fervently internationalist state within both the Soviet bloc and the Third World.

Impulses behind Cuban Internationalism

How is Cuban activism to be explained? One answer might be that, like other radical revolutionary states, Cuba is committed to changing the international status quo for reasons of ideology and security. According to this reasoning, for example, the new Castro regime sought to promote revolution in Latin America in the 1960s because of its ideological commitments to the

---

[7]Save for Grenada in 1983 and Guevara's Bolivian expedition in 1967, Cuban casualties in these operations are not made public. Reportedly, Cuban soldiers wounded in the Angolan and Ethiopian operations have been treated in Eastern Europe. With few exceptions, the war dead who are returned to Cuba are buried quietly and without public fanfare.

"anti-imperialist," "liberationist," and "socialist" struggles of the world and because the emergence of new revolutionary states allied with Cuba could enhance the regime's security and overcome its isolation. But this answer does not appear entirely satisfactory. Like human behavior, a state's international behavior is likely to be driven by a complex set of motivating forces.

In Cuba's case, ideology does not explain why Cuba intervened in Ethiopia to assist the Mengistu regime in its war with Somalia, another socialist state, or in its struggle against the Eritrean liberation movement that Cuba had previously assisted. Nor was Cuba's security enhanced by its far-flung military operations in Angola and Ethiopia, because these incursions halted the process then under way to normalize relations with the Ford and then the Carter administration.[8] Even with the more hostile Reagan administration, Cuba has undertaken in Central America activities that could only heighten tensions with Washington and put Cuba on a collision course with the United States.

Perhaps a more useful way of explaining Cuban behavior is to view it in terms of Castro's particular world view and mindset; his power motivations and strategic relationship with the Soviet Union; and the major institutional interests of his regime. As we shall see, concrete foreign policy goals emerge from these three general sets of motivating forces.

Castro's World View and Mindset

From the very outset of his revolutionary career, Castro has seen the United States as the world's imperialist hegemon and thus as the arch-enemy of Cuba, Latin America, and the rest of the Third World. Although broadly ideological, such a perspective does not constitute a developed ideology in the formal sense. Castro's mindset precedes and predates his adherence to Marxism-Leninism, which later provided the intellectual argument for his emotional animus against the United States. As he recalled in an early interview, with respect to his university days,

> I came to realize more and more clearly that the policy of the United States, and its wholly disproportionate development with respect to Latin America, was *the great enemy* of the unification and development of the Latin American nations; the United States would always do its utmost to maintain the weakness and division on which it based its policy of directing the fate of our peoples as it pleased.[9]

Such a sentiment would subsequently harden, of course, as a result of U.S. support for the Batista regime, antipathy toward the Cuban revolution, and

---

[8]See Edward Gonzalez, "Cuba: The Impasse," in Robert Wesson, ed., *U.S. Influence in Latin America in the 1980s* (New York: Praeger and Hoover Institution Press, 1982), pp. 198–216.
[9]Carlos Franqui, *Diary of the Cuban Revolution* (New York: Viking, 1980), p. 9, emphases added.

efforts to overthrow Castro's revolutionary government and assassinate him during the 1960s.

This anti-imperialism is common among Latin American leftists and ultra-nationalists. But what has consistently set Castro apart from other leaders is that he remains a man of action who is committed to the defeat of the United States, including rooting out its domestic allies in Cuba and elsewhere. Imbued with a sense of historic mission, he sees himself taking on the intensely nationalistic, anti-imperialist legacies of Simon Bolívar and José Martí.[10] In point of fact, he has succeeded where Bolívar, Martí, and contemporary Latin American leaders have failed: not only has he successfully defied the Colossus of the North, but he has also actively challenged "imperialism" internationally since 1959, in the Caribbean, Latin America, Africa, and elsewhere in the Third World.

Castro's personality fits several traditional psychoanalytic concepts that have been applied to other political leaders, such as messianism and narcissism.[11] But his mindset may best be captured metaphorically by conceiving of it in terms of a "hubris-nemesis complex."[12] Such a complex describes a generic type of political leader: Hitler was the archetype, but the term may also fit such current Third World personalities as Ayatollah Khomeini, Muamar Qadhdhafi and especially Castro. Cuba's charismatic *caudillo* is one of those very few and unusual leaders in whom the driving forces of hubris and nemesis are fused together, providing extraordinary energy and messianism as he seeks to fulfill his self-appointed but widely applauded historical role on the world stage.

Castro long ago assumed the role of nemesis of the United States, which itself is the archetype of hubris (as the world's greatest power) and thus, as in Greek myth, attracts nemesis. While fighting against Batista in the Sierra Maestra in mid-1958, for example, Castro revealed his destiny to one of his closest associates, Celia Sanchez: "When I saw [American-made] rocket firing . . . I swore to myself that the North Americans were going to pay dearly for what they were doing. When this war is over a much wider and bigger war will commence for me: *the war I am going to wage against them. I am aware that this is my true destiny.*"[13] Within Cuba, therefore, he has waged a

[10]In his early twenties, Castro recalled, "I was quixotic, romantic, a dreamer, with very little political knowhow. . . . I could not yet foresee distinctly *the great enemies I would have to fight*, but I was already beginning to detect them. The dreams of Martí and Bolívar, as well as a kind of utopian socialism, were vaguely stirring within me." Ibid.

[11]For example, see Jerrold M. Post, "Dreams of Glory and the Life Cycle: Reflections on the Life Course of Narcissistic Leaders," *Journal of Political and Military Sociology*, Spring 1984, pp. 49–60, and Volkan D. Vamik and Norman Itzkowitz, *The Immortal Atatürk: A Psychobiography* (Chicago: University of Chicago Press, 1984).

[12]See Edward Gonzalez and David Ronfeldt, *Castro, Cuba, and the World*, R-3420 (Santa Monica: RAND Corporation, June 1986), pp. 3–32.

[13]Quoted in Rolando E. Bonachea and Nelson P. Valdes, eds., *Revolutionary Struggle, 1947–1958: Volume 1 of the Selected Works of Fidel Castro* (Cambridge: MIT Press, 1972), p. 379, emphases added.

permanent campaign to eradicate U.S. influences and the vestiges of capitalism associated with the former U.S. presence. In March 1968, for example, he launched the Revolutionary Offensive that nationalized what remained of Cuba's small enterprises, taking over even shoe-shine and fast-food stands. Eighteen years later he abruptly abolished a successful six-year experiment with free peasant marketing which had supplied previously unavailable agricultural items to hard-pressed consumers, denouncing it as "a source of enrichment for neo-capitalists and neo-bourgeois."[14]

But it is on the international stage that he has waged an ideological, political, and military struggle to defeat the United States and its allies, not just in the hemisphere but as far away as Africa. Although he denies it, such a messianic role is driven by Castro's own hubris.[15] In his self-appointed role as nemesis of U.S. imperialism he relentlessly pursues power and a commanding role on the world stage. He thus risks overstepping himself, as occurred with the 1962 missile crisis when he overinflated his own role, underestimated the U.S. reaction, and overestimated Soviet resolve.[16] Twenty-one years later a similar miscalculation nearly occurred over Grenada when he ordered Cuban contingents to fight and not to surrender to U.S. forces.

Castro's hubris-nemesis complex largely accounts for the remarkable dynamism, audacity, and global breadth of Cuban foreign policy since 1959. At the strategic level it led Castro to realign Cuba permanently with the Soviet Union as the international adversary of the United States and guarantor of the Cuban revolution. It has also resulted in his unyielding posture toward the United States, in which he vows never to compromise with imperialism no matter what adverse circumstances Cuba may face.[17] And it further impels

[14]*New York Times*, May 20, 1986, p. 6.

[15]In recent interviews Castro has in effect denied being affected by hubris, or excessive pride, by insisting on his modesty. Thus he informed Robert MacNeil and PBS audiences that "you will not see a statue of me anywhere, nor a school with my name, nor a street, nor little town, nor any type of personality cult." Transcript, *MacNeil/Lehrer News Hour*, February 12, 1985, p. 2. The following month he again insisted on the nobility of his purpose: "Money does not motivate me. . . . Likewise, the lust for glory, fame and prestige does not motivate me. I really think that ideas motivate me. . . . If you do not guard against those vanities, if you let yourself become conceited or think that you are irreplaceable or indispensable, you can become infatuated with all of that—the riches, the glory. I've been on guard against those things." "Playboy Interview: Fidel Castro," *Playboy*, August 1985, pp. 58–59.

[16]According to one eyewitness account, "he seemed to have a blind belief in the Soviet military machine and shrugged off any doubts by saying that it was the Russians who were calling the tune. *He felt like one of the powerful, as if he were involved in world-changing events. In any case, he didn't think that there would be a real conflict between the United States and the Soviet Union. And if there were an invasion, it wouldn't be his fault.* Don't forget, Fidel gets his kicks from war and high tension." Carlos Franqui, *Family Portrait with Fidel* (New York: Random House, 1984), pp. 188–189, emphases added.

[17]Thus, at a time when pressures were mounting within the regime to reconsider its policy toward Washington because of Soviet cutbacks in petroleum deliveries and the island's worsening economic situation, Castro declared in August 1968 that "never, under any circumstances—and the comrades of our Central Committee know this; they know this is the line adopted by our Central Committee—never, under any circumstance, even in the most difficult circumstances,

Castro to maintain Cuba's internationalist course even when Washington is conciliatory, as with the Angolan and Ethiopian operations already noted.

Castro's "maximalist" drive, however, does not prevent him from making pragmatic adjustments in Cuban policy. Throughout his political career he has demonstrated a capacity for *tactical* adjustments to buy time, conserve power, and protect gains in order to pursue his strategic objectives later, at a more opportune time. When he was in prison following the Moncada attack, for example, Castro wrote to a fellow-conspirator in April 1954, "much guile and smiles for everyone. . . . There will be ample time later to squash all the cockroaches together."[18] In this respect he exhibits a Leninist commitment in holding firm to his grander, strategic objectives, which have remained remarkably constant over time.[19]

Power and Dependency: Castro's Relationship with Moscow

As a leader imbued with a hubris-nemesis complex, Castro has relentlessly sought to maximize his political power to fulfill his (and Cuba's) destiny. At home he has demanded and held virtually absolute power, as evidenced by his leadership positions in party, government, state, and revolutionary armed forces, while crushing any real or potential challengers, as seen in the Matos (1959), Escalante (1962), and "microfaction" (1968) affairs. Abroad this same power-maximizing imperative has applied. Thus, as former Cuban and Soviet insiders have recently confirmed, he began to work for a preemptive realignment with the Soviet Union as early as fall 1959, not only to ensure the survival of his regime against the United States and to monopolize his power at home but also to gain the power resources with which to act on the international stage.[20]

However, Cuba's dependence upon Moscow invariably constrains Castro's power and freedom of maneuver both at home and abroad. This problem was minimized for much of the 1960s because Castro had leverage vis-à-vis the Soviets owing to Moscow's growing stake in Cuba, the impact of Castro and the Cuban revolution on Latin America and the world, and the skill with

---

will this country approach the imperialist Government of the United States—not even should it one day place us in the situation of having to choose between the continued existence of the Revolution or such a step. Because, gentlemen, that would be the moment at which the Revolution would have ceased to exist." *Granma Weekly Review*, August 25, 1968, p. 4.

[18]Letter to Melba Hernandez, quoted in Luis Conte Aguero, *Cartas del Presidio* (Havana: Editorial Lex, 1959), p. 38.

[19]On Castro's modus operandi over time, see Gonzalez and Ronfeldt, *Castro, Cuba, and the World*, pp. 33–62.

[20]See Franqui, *Family Portrait with Fidel*, pp. 21ff. and 78ff.; Alexandr Alexeev, "Cuba después del triunfo de la revolución," *America Latina*, October 1984, pp. 62–67; and Edward Gonzalez, "Castro's Revolution, Cuban Communist Appeals, and the Soviet Response," *World Politics*, October 1968, pp. 38–64. Although emphasizing Castro's early Marxist-Leninist orientation prior to his assumption to power in 1959, a recent biography of Castro further supports this interpretation. See Tad Szulc, *Fidel, A Critical Biography* (New York: Morrow, 1986).

which Castro himself exploited Soviet interests and vulnerabilities.[21] But after 1970 Cuba's growing economic dependence on and integration into the Soviet bloc, as well as the lessening of revolutionary opportunities in Latin America, deprived Castro of his earlier leverage. As a consequence Cuba became a compliant client that hewed closely to the Soviet line in both its domestic and its international affairs.

Cuban "paladinism" in Angola and Ethiopia thus became the principal means by which Castro regained a measure of leverage over Moscow after 1975. Because these two successful operations proved that Cuba could effectively advance Soviet as well as its own objectives in the Third World, Cuba became a highly valued surrogate in Moscow's eyes. In turn, the value of Cuba's role was heightened because of the expansionist surge in Soviet foreign policy starting in the mid-1970s. At a time when Vietnam and Watergate had weakened U.S. foreign policy, detente and developments in Africa opened up new targets of opportunity for the extension of Soviet influence in the Third World.[22]

Soviet and Cuban interests thus converged. Castro now worked in tandem with Moscow in his role as an international paladin who promoted Soviet objectives in southern Africa, the Horn, and elsewhere in the Third World. By its willingness to dispatch combat troops and maintain a large military presence in Angola and, until recently, Ethiopia, Cuba ensured the consolidation of Soviet gains and the prevention of the sort of reversals that had occurred elsewhere in Africa and most notably in Sadat's Egypt after 1972. Africa was more receptive to Cuba's military presence, and to its security and technical assistance programs, because of Cuba's image as a selfless, revolutionary Third World actor without colonial or superpower designs. Cuba, in fact, had been active in Africa since the early 1960s. The type of Cuban aid and nonracist conduct of Cuban "internationalists" in Africa also helped the country's internationalist image.[23] Because of his African exploits, especially

---

[21] See Edward Gonzalez, "Relationship with the Soviet Union," in Carmelo Mesa-Lago, ed., *Revolutionary Change in Cuba* (Pittsburgh: University of Pittsburgh Press, 1971), pp. 81–104.

[22] By 1980 the Soviets had a direct military presence, including basing facilities, in four Third World countries (Cuba, Angola, Afghanistan, and Ethiopia) while also securing military basing, port, or refueling facilities in six other Third World states (Algeria, Libya, Mozambique, South Yemen, Syria, and Vietnam). See Frank Fukuyama, *The Military Dimension of Soviet Policy in the Third World*, P-6965 (Santa Monica: RAND Corporation, February 1984).

[23] Jorge I. Domínguez observed that "Cuba does not send construction materials; it sends people to build a road. It does not equip a hospital, but it sends health personnel to staff it. It does not provide weaponry, but it supplies military instructors to teach how to use Soviet weapons." Domínguez, "Cuban Foreign Policy," *Foreign Affairs*, Fall 1978, p. 95. According to one Angolan specialist, "the Cubans work directly with Angolans, whatever the task. They seem immensely popular in the country, perhaps because they do not manifest the cultural and racial arrogance of many other foreigners. The Cubans, whose own lifestyle closely approximates that of Angolans, make relatively few demands on the government. . . . [In contrast] the Soviets have not altered the attitudes and behavior that have made them unpopular from Cairo to Conakry and from Mogadishu to Maputo. The very style that earned U.S. citizens the reputation of 'Ugly Americans' during the 1950s and 1960s appears to characterize the Soviets in the 1970s." Gerald J.

in Angola where Cuban troops engaged the South Africans, and his internationalism, Castro emerged as a credible exponent in Third World forums of
the thesis that Soviet bloc countries constitute the natural allies of the Third
World, a line that he advocated (but without success) when he hosted the
Sixth Summit Conference of the Non-Aligned Movement in 1979.

Meanwhile Castro's leverage with Moscow was strengthened in the Caribbean Basin by the ascendancy of his protégé, Maurice Bishop, and the New
Jewel Movement (NJM) in Grenada in March 1979 and the triumph of the
FSLN in Nicaragua the following July. These developments were major setbacks for the United States because pro-American governments—including
the Somoza dynasty that had been the linchpin of U.S. policy toward Central
America for more than four decades—were replaced by Marxist-Leninist
regimes that quickly realigned their countries with Cuba and the Soviet
Union.[24] In tandem with the Soviets, Cuba again played an indispensable
political, technical, and security assistance role in helping both regimes consolidate their power, thereby furthering Soviet interests in the region.[25]

The Nicaraguan revolution in particular appears to have been assessed as a
most significant development by Moscow; its ramifications strengthened
Castro's hand and garnered Soviet backing for his more activist policy after
1979. As acknowledged by such notable Soviet commentators as S. A. Mikoyan in the March 1980 issue of *Latinskaya America*, the Nicaraguan experience
validated the Cuban line of armed struggle and the necessity of forging a
broad but increasingly united military-political front based on an alliance of
the guerrilla organizations and civilian opposition groups. For the first time
since 1960 Moscow thus endorsed the Cuban position as the one to be
followed by the communist parties in El Salvador and Guatemala.[26] With the
FSLN consolidating its power in Nicaragua, and with increasing turmoil and
instability in the rest of Central America, there were now greater prospects
for weakening the "strategic rear" of the United States by stepping up sup-

---

Bender, "Angola, the Cubans, and American Anxieties," *Foreign Policy*, Summer 1978, pp. 10, 11.
In more recent years, however, there have been reports of increased friction between Angolans
and Cuban civilian and military personnel.

[24]The Marxist-Leninist commitment of the Sandinista leadership was well in evidence prior to
the FSLN victory in 1979, and formal party-to-party relations were established between FSLN and
the CPSU in March 1980 during Daniel Ortega's first visit to Moscow. The CPSU entered into a
similar agreement with the NJM in July 1982. On the Marxist-Leninist goals of the FSLN see
David Nolan, *The Ideology of the Sandinistas and the Nicaraguan Revolution*, Institute of Interamerican Studies, Graduate School of Interamerican Studies, University of Miami (Miami,
1984), and Douglas W. Payne, *The Democratic Mask: The Consolidation of the Sandinista Revolution* (New York: Freedom House, 1985). On the Marxism-Leninism of the NJM and Grenadian-
Soviet relations, see Paul Seabury and Walter A. McDougall, eds., *The Grenada Papers* (San
Francisco: Institute of Contemporary Studies, 1984).

[25]See Edward Gonzalez, "The Cuban and Soviet Challenge in the Caribbean Basin," *Orbis*,
Spring 1985, pp. 73–94.

[26]Not all Soviet academicians accepted the Cuban line in their assessment of the significance of
the Nicaraguan revolution. See Jerry F. Hough, "The Evolving Soviet Debate on Latin America," *Latin American Review* 6, no. 1 (1981), pp. 124–143.

Table 1. Soviet economic assistance to Cuba, 1961–83 (in billion U.S. dollars)

1961–70	$3,568	
1971	570	
1972	614	
1973	611	
1974	338	
1975	1,064	
1961–75 subtotal		$6,765
1976	$1,569	
1977	2,270	
1978	2,946	
1979	3,178	
1980	3,463	
1981	4,438	
1982	4,561	
1983 (est.)	4,100	
1976–83 subtotal		$26,525

SOURCES: 1961–70 figures are taken from U.S. Congress, *Cuba Faces the Economic Realities of the 1980s: A Study Prepared for the Joint Economic Committee* (Washington, D.C., 1982), p. 16. The 1976–83 figures are drawn from Directorate of Intelligence, *The Cuban Economy: A Statistical Review,* Reference Aid ALA 84-10052 (Washington, D.C., June 1984), p. 40. Soviet economic assistance includes developmental aid and trade subsidies for sugar, petroleum, and nickel. The U.S. government calculations are based on official Soviet and Cuban sources. From Edward Gonzalez, "The Cuban and Soviet Challenge in the Caribbean Basin," *Orbis,* Spring 1985, p. 77.

port for the Salvadoran insurgency through increased arms shipments, training, and direction by Cuba, starting in 1979. For the Soviets, at a minimum, Central American and Caribbean developments were weakening U.S. hegemony in the region and could divert U.S. attention and resources away from other contested areas of the world. Over the longer term the Soviets could conceivably realize maximum strategic objectives if Marxist-Leninist regimes in Nicaragua, Grenada, and El Salvador provided the USSR with port, landing, repair, and/or basing facilities that would facilitate the Soviet military presence in the Basin, South America, and the South Atlantic.[27]

After 1975, therefore, Soviet and Cuban interests converged in Africa and the Caribbean Basin, and Castro's instrumental value to the Soviets rose as Moscow moved to exploit new targets of opportunity in the Third World. Although correlations do not prove causality, the very fact that Soviet economic assistance to Cuba shot up exponentially in the eight years after An-

[27]Such a development would occur incrementally, over a long period of time, and under ambiguous circumstances, as the Soviet and Cuban build-up occurred in Cuba after 1969, to minimize the risks of U.S. reaction. That the Soviets harbored such a long-term strategic perspective is hinted at by one captured Grenadian document. In a March 10, 1983, memorandum the Soviet Army's chief of general staff, Marshall Nikolai V. Ogarkov, told his Grenadian guest that whereas only Cuba had existed two decades ago, "today there are Nicaragua, Grenada, and a serious battle is going on in El Salvador." "Meeting of Soviet and Grenadian Military Chiefs of Staffs, 3/10/83," in Seabury and McDougall, *The Grenada Papers,* p. 190.

gola suggests that Cuba had become a privileged client of the USSR whose services as an international paladin enabled Castro to command ever-higher levels of Soviet support.

There were military rewards as well for the Revolutionary Armed Forces (FAR). Beginning in 1977 the Soviets sent new weapons systems and military equipment to replace the FAR's obsolete or exhausted inventories, with the first shipment of MiG-23s arriving in March 1978.

Castro's internationalism thus produced multiple payoffs. His policies had resulted in major setbacks for the United States and in greater international prestige and influence for Cuba and for him personally. He also acquired greater leverage and standing with Moscow, thereby securing higher levels of Soviet material assistance for the Cuban economy and armed forces.

Institutional Actors: A Supporting Cast

Although Castro remains the overarching figure in Cuban politics, he must deal with and maintain the support of political elites and institutional forces that comprise his regime and are represented in the party's Central Committee. Although we can only surmise the relative influence of these forces, they appear to carry some weight in the formulation as well as the execution of Cuban foreign policy, whether as political elites (e.g., veteran *fidelistas* and *raulistas* or newer technocrats) or as pivotal institutional actors (e.g., the military, the Ministry of Interior, the Communist party, etc.).[28]

While remaining under the control of *fidelista* and *raulista* elites, institutional forces have become especially important over the past decade. A more institutional order has emerged since 1970 in which major, identifiable institutional interests are represented in the party's Central Committee along functionally specific lines.[29] Also a growth in the professionalism, capabilities, and proficiency of the military, intelligence, and party organs began in the 1970s which has enhanced Cuba's ability to perform on the world stage. Specifically, the realization of Castro's ambitious foreign policy depends on the Revolutionary Armed Forces, the Ministry of Interior, and the Communist party's Americas Department. These three institutions have helped impel Cuban policy along highly activist lines in the Third World, in part because such activism advances their very organizational tasks and interests.

The Revolutionary Armed Forces are headed by Castro's brother, Raul, as army general and minister of the Ministry of the Revolutionary Armed Forces (MINFAR). The top staff and command positions within the military

---

[28]See Edward Gonzalez, "Institutionalization, Political Elites, and Foreign Policies," in Blasier and Mesa-Lago, *Cuba in the World*, pp. 3–36.

[29]See Jorge I. Domínguez, "Revolutionary Politics: The Demands for Orderliness," in Dominguez, *Cuba: Internal and International Affairs* (Beverly Hills: Sage, 1982), pp. 19–70.

and the Ministry of Interior (MININT) are held by veteran *fidelista* and *raulista* officers who fought with Fidel and Raul on the First and Second Fronts, respectively, during the guerrilla war against Batista. Within MININT is the General Directorate of Intelligence (DGI), which works closely with the KGB in foreign intelligence and subversive operations, and the Special Troop Battalion. Serving as Castro's praetorian guard, the Special Troop Battalion is an elite force that played a key role in the first days of the Angolan operation.

The successful performance of the FAR and MININT in Angola and Ethiopia gained Cuba a heightened influence in Third World circles and attracted higher levels of Soviet economic and military assistance. Consequently the FAR, in particular, strengthened its position as perhaps Cuba's premier institution, despite its formal subordination to party authority. Thus in 1980 the first three alternates appointed to the Political Bureau were division-generals, while the combined FAR and MININT membership in the 225-member Central Committee made up the largest single bloc (27.1 percent) in that body.[30] At the Third Party Congress in February 1986 this combined share declined to 19.1 percent of the newly named Central Committee. However, Division-General Abelardo Colomé (also a vice-president of MINFAR), who earlier had distinguished himself in Angola and Ethiopia, was elevated from alternate to full member in the new Political Bureau, the first time a professional soldier other than Raul Castro had achieved full membership.

The professionalization and modernization of the FAR and MININT have strengthened the Castro regime's power projection capabilities well beyond Cuba and the Caribbean. Both organs extend security assistance and technical training to regimes seeking to consolidate their power, as with the FSLN in Nicaragua after 1979. The FAR currently maintains an estimated 35,000 soldiers in combat and advisory roles in Angola to help the MPLA defend itself against both UNITA guerrillas and South African forces. The armed forces' major role has been in Africa; but its presence in Nicaragua and its reported role in directing Sandinista counterinsurgency campaign against the U.S.-backed Contras suggest that the FAR is expanding its international domain. Division-General Arnaldo Ochoa, Cuba's top combat commander and a veteran of the Angolan and Ethiopian campaigns, also a vice-minister in MINFAR, was Cuba's military adviser to Nicaragua between 1983 and 1986.

Founded in 1974, the Americas Department of the Central Committee is headed by Manuel Pineiro, a long-time *fidelista* and formerly head of the DGI. The Americas Department has strengthened the Castro regime's organizational infrastructure for collecting intelligence, carrying out covert operations, training guerrillas, and disseminating propaganda in Latin America and the Caribbean. In directing and coordinating Cuban revolutionary ac-

---

[30]The next-largest group consists of those engaged in "Politics" full time (21.3 percent), followed by "Bureaucracy" (17.3 percent). See Domínguez, "Revolutionary Politics," p. 24.

tivities, the Americas Department works closely with the DGI inside and outside Cuba. A network of guerrilla camps and indoctrination centers on the island, including the party's Nico López Training School, provides instruction in guerrilla warfare, weapons use, and other activities for Latin American recruits. This organizational network enables Havana to maintain close ties with guerrilla forces in Central America, Colombia, and elsewhere.[31]

The organizational tasks and interests of these three institutions have especially inclined them to support Castro's international ambitions provided, of course, that the risks entailed in any operation are not excessive. The organizational missions of the Americas Department and the DGI include directing the "export of revolution," and thus they possess strong organizational incentives to do so. Although both the FAR and MININT hold as their primary mission the defense of the fatherland, they too have strong incentives for extending their global reach and carrying out operations abroad, particularly when detente minimized the security risks to Cuba.

Following its successful African campaigns, for example, the FAR attained a new international stature, particularly within the Soviet bloc, and a universal ranking system and nomenclature was introduced throughout the FAR at the end of 1976 which reflected the military's new professionalism. Also Cuban officers gained invaluable experience in Angola and Ethiopia, especially in the latter where the Cuban expeditionary force served under the strategic command of a Soviet lieutenant general and his thousand-man staff. African military service thus aided career advancement and considerably advanced the combat proficiency of regular and ready-reserve personnel. Above all, the FAR became the recipient of new arms transfers from the Soviets which have greatly enhanced the Cuban military's capabilities since 1976.

Ancillary ministries, such as public health, education, and construction, also have an organizational interest in expanding their roles to overseas operations in Africa, Nicaragua, and the Caribbean. For bureaucratic as well as ideological reasons, these otherwise domestic-oriented ministries can hope to expand their budgets, command additional resources, and gain a role in policy making and implementation by becoming part of Castro's internationalist crusade. Though resources may be siphoned away from their domestic projects, these ministries play supporting roles in Cuban foreign policy.

Cuba's greater outreach abroad has been abetted by an increasingly young and underemployed population. In the mid-1970s the population's age profile started to change dramatically; the number of fifteen- to nineteen-year-olds

---

[31]According to a Nicaraguan defector, as early as July 1979 Cuba had already trained more than two hundred Salvadoran guerrillas attached to the Popular Liberation Forces (FPL), one of the main guerrilla organizations within the FMLN. This was nearly twelve months before the Salvadoran guerrillas began major attacks. Ferman Cienfuegos, of the Armed Forces of National Liberation, was also reported to be in close contact with Cuban intelligence operatives. See Department of State and Department of Defense, *Background Paper: Nicaragua's Military Build-up and Support for Central American Subversion* (Washington, D.C., July 18, 1984), p. 15.

increased by over 339,000 between 1974 and 1980, reaching 1,116,340 in the latter year.[32] With a growing surplus of young men and women, many with technical skills that the island's sluggishly growing economy cannot fully absorb, Castro could thus export combat troops and civilian technicians to fulfill his international ambitions and objectives.

Castro's Maximalist Objectives: New Dilemmas?

Ever since coming to power, Castro has sought to realize a set of minimum interests in his foreign policy while pursuing larger or maximalist objectives. His minimum interests have been to (1) enhance his political power base; (2) assure his regime's security; (3) maintain Cuba's internal autonomy as a Soviet client state; and (4) obtain sufficient levels of Soviet economic support for Cuba's long-term development. These minimum goals have generally been assured by Castro's pragmatic behavior in dealing with both Washington and Moscow. With the major exception of the 1962 missile crisis and, to a lesser extent, the 1983 Grenada conflict, Castro has taken care to avoid precipitating a direct military confrontation with the United States. When he has had no other recourse, he has also yielded to Moscow's pressures, guaranteeing economic support by conforming to the Soviet line on domestic and foreign policy issues since 1968.

Over the years Castro has also pursued maximalist, strategic goals that impart an offensive quality to his international behavior and that stem from his hubris-nemesis complex.

(1) To lead the Latin American and Third World struggle against "imperialism" in order to erode the power and presence of the United States.

(2) To extend Cuba's influence and presence in much of the Third World through an active diplomatic, political, technical, and military presence, including the support of revolutionary movements in target countries. At the very least, Cuban activism compels affected governments to take notice of Havana.

(3) To promote the rise of radical-left or Marxist-Leninist regimes in the Caribbean Basin by means of armed struggle, coups, or other means, in order to develop a core of radical states aligned with Cuba.

(4) To increase Cuba's power potential as a regional and global actor through the infusion of higher levels of Soviet economic and military support.

(5) To increase Cuba's freedom of maneuver on the world stage through reverse leverage over Moscow even while acting within the parameters of Soviet foreign policy.

[32]Sergio Diaz Briquets and Lisandro Perez, *Cuba: The Demography of Revolution* (Washington, D.C.: Population Reference Bureau, April 1981), p. 22.

These goals have remained constant, but their realization has largely depended not only on Cuba's domestic situation but also on Castro's reading of three critical variables affecting the international correlation of forces—the availability of new targets of opportunity in the Third World, the strength and disposition of the United States, and the strength and disposition of the Soviet Union. The last variable has been for Castro the most important: the Soviet Union has been not only the essential guarantor of regime survival but also the principal setter of parameters for Cuban foreign policy. Whether or not the Soviet Union is in an expansionist mode can thus determine whether Castro will realize his maximalist ambitions in the Third World.

In terms of these three variables, the 1975–83 period was most favorable for the realization of Castro's maximalist objectives. Beginning with his Grenadian setback in October 1983, however, both regional and international trends not only appear to be working against further maximalist gains but could also augur potential risks for Castro and strained relations with the Soviets.

The Golden Years: 1975–83

In retrospect, Castro's maximalist posture was greatly favored by developments and trends that started to alter the correlation of forces in the mid-1970s. In the Third World, new targets of opportunity opened up in southern Africa and the Horn, the Eastern Caribbean, Nicaragua, and then elsewhere in Central America where prospects heightened for a regional revolution, particularly in El Salvador. The triumph of the Nicaraguan revolution was perhaps the high point in this period of revolutionary maximalism because, for the first time, Cuba's strategy of armed struggle was vindicated and a new Marxist-Leninist ally was gained in the Caribbean Basin. Elsewhere there were signs of growing Third World solidarity and assertiveness that Cuba could exploit.

U.S. power was constrained during this period by the aftermath of Vietnam and Watergate and by Washington's concern with its allies, the Soviet Union, and detente. Not only was the United States unable to respond to Cuban incursions in distant Africa, but it also found that its traditional hegemony over Latin America was being eroded. This erosion became evident in the more assertive, independent behavior of Latin American governments toward pre- and post-1979 Nicaragua and in the increasing involvement of Western Europe in Central American affairs. The ebbing of U.S. power and presence was symbolized by the sharp decline of U.S. military personnel in the Basin, plummeting from a high of over 25,000 in 1968 to fewer than 16,000 in 1981, a time when both Cuban and Soviet military capabilities in the region were increasing dramatically.[33]

[33]For example, the Cuban armed forces jumped from 117,000 personnel (1974) to 175,000 (1976) as a result of the African operations and then increased further to 225,000 (1981), despite the easing of tensions with the United States during much of this period. With the acquisition of

With their large military build-up, the Soviets attained rough nuclear parity with the United States, thereby redressing the strategic and conventional power imbalance that had affected the outcome of the 1962 missile crisis. Emerging as a genuine global power with a blue-water capability, the Soviets established a military presence in Cuba and the Caribbean with their electronic monitoring facility at Lourdes, outside Havana, and with the Soviet Navy's routine port calls. The Soviet equity in Cuba greatly increased, as evidenced by large aid and trade subsidies, which jumped from $1.6 billion per year in 1976 to $4.6 billion in 1982, and by upward of 13,000 Soviet military and civilian advisory personnel stationed in Cuba. Most critically, the Soviets started in 1975 to embark upon an expansionist surge that carried them, directly or indirectly through Cuba, into Africa, Nicaragua, Central America, and Grenada. Thus, as noted earlier, this period was characterized by a considerable coincidence of interests between Havana and Moscow as each pursued an offensive strategy toward the Third World.

In Afghanistan, however, Soviet behavior abruptly undermined Castro's Third World policy and stature. The Soviet invasion of December 24, 1979, dealt a blow to Castro's Third World leadership aspirations while demolishing his claim that Soviet bloc countries were the "natural allies" of the developing countries. On the verge of winning the Latin American seat on the Security Council, Cuba was forced in January 1980 to withdraw from the race because of the loss of Third World backing. In the General Assembly vote of January 14 calling for the removal of all foreign troops from Afghanistan, Havana was also isolated from most of the Third World as it was compelled to vote with the Soviet bloc against the resolution.[34] Eleven months later, at the Second Congress of the Communist Party of Cuba, Castro publicly endorsed the Soviet action on grounds that the "USSR had to help save the [revolutionary] process and preserve the victories of the April 1978 [Communist] Revolution."[35] Hence Cuban and Soviet interests were not always destined to be mutually reinforcing but could in fact diverge, as developments in Grenada would soon demonstrate.

The Grenadian Watershed: Setback and Divergencies

Events in Grenada in October 1983 provided a major setback for Castro and Cuban policy in the Caribbean Basin, and not simply because of the murder

---

MiG-23s, medium-range airlift capabilities, and some naval ships, the FAR also began to develop a modest offensive regional capability by the start of the 1980s. Meanwhile, in Cuba, the Soviets had established their largest electronic surveillance facility outside the USSR, and over twenty Soviet flotillas paid port calls to Cuba between 1969 and 1981. See Joseph H. Stodder and Kevin P. McCarthy, *Profiles of the Caribbean Basin in 1960/1980: Changing Political and Geostrategic Dimensions*, R-2058-AF (Santa Monica: RAND Corporation, December 1983), pp. 47–61.

[34]Of the eighteen that voted against the resolution, Angola, Ethiopia, and Mozambique among the African countries joined with five other Soviet Third World clients—Afghanistan, Grenada, Laos, South Yemen, and Vietnam—in voting with Cuba, the Soviet Union, and other members of the Soviet bloc.

[35]*Granma Weekly Review*, December 28, 1980, p. 14.

of Castro's protégé, Maurice Bishop, and the dismantling of a Marxist-Leninist regime closely allied with Havana. Grenada also demonstrated Cuba's
limitations as a regional power in aiding a client-regime engaged in a direct
military confrontation with the United States. Although armed Cuban construction forces on the island were ordered to resist the U.S. invasion, and
did, Castro decided against sending reinforcements because he feared a direct
U.S. attack on Cuba itself.[36] Afterward he conceded that Nicaragua, like
Grenada, would have to look to its own defenses in the event of U.S. aggression. Meanwhile Cuban diplomacy in the Caribbean was damaged not only
by the Grenadian setback but also because captured Grenadian documents
revealed that Cuba had served as a conduit for the intensification of ideological conflict and the further introduction of a Soviet presence in the Caribbean.

As with Afghanistan earlier, Castro must also have been profoundly disturbed by Soviet behavior in Grenada before and after Bishop's demise. As
some Western analysts have pointed out, the Grenada papers revealed that
the Bishop government "received a back-of-the-hand treatment from Soviet
political authorities. Its relationship with Soviet officials was confined to low-
level functionaries."[37] Moscow reacted suspiciously to Bishop's confidential
meeting with the U.S. national security adviser, William Clark, in the spring
of 1983.[38] It then appears to have worked at cross-purposes with Havana.
Soviet backing for Bishop cooled even though Castro himself threw his
personal support behind his protégé just prior to the power struggle that
consumed the New Jewel Movement.[39] Worse still, some observers believe
that Moscow may have cultivated Bernard Coard as a more reliable,
orthodox, aparatchik leader, thereby actively undermining Bishop's position
within his own regime.[40] In any event Grenada demonstrated that Moscow
will not commit Soviet power to ensure the survival of its clients in the Basin
if the United States decides to move against them militarily. It thus showed

---

[36]Because "a large-scale Yankee aggression against us" was imminent, Castro notified his
military detachment in Grenada that "it is not the new Grenadian Government we must think of
now, but of Cuba." Accordingly, "sending reinforcements is impossible and unthinkable." Instead, Cuba would join with other countries to promote "a strong campaign" to counter U.S.
threats against Grenada. "Statement by the Cuban Party and Government on the Imperialist
Intervention in Grenada," *Granma Weekly Review*, October 30, 1983, p. 1.

[37]See Seabury and McDougall, *The Grenada Papers*, p. 182.

[38]A Soviet Foreign Ministry official queried the Grenadian ambassador at length regarding
Bishop's meeting with Clark, insisting that is would have been courteous of the Grenadians to
have informed the Soviets of the visit. Seabury and McDougall, *The Grenada Papers*, p. 205.

[39]Before returning to Grenada after his unproductive trip to Eastern Europe in October 1983,
Bishop stopped over in Havana where he was given a gala reception by Castro, his brother, and
six other members of the Political Bureau of the Communist Party of Cuba. Soon afterward,
Castro heatedly denied that he had been interfering in internal Grenadian affairs. See Seabury
and McDougal, *The Grenada Papers*, pp. 327 and 334.

[40]See Jiri and Virginia Valenta, "Leninism in Grenada," *Problems of Communism*, July–August
1984, pp. 20–22.

the precariousness of Cuba's and especially Nicaragua's geostrategic position.[41]

Cuban-Soviet Collaboration and Potential Friction in Nicaragua

Indeed, Grenada revealed that Soviet and Cuban priorities and interests in the Basin remain fundamentally different. Although acclaimed by Moscow for its new revolutionary potential, the region remains peripheral to the Soviet Union's vital interests, which lie in Eastern Europe and the Middle and Far East. Hence the Soviets have moved to exploit openings in the distant strategic rear of the United States primarily for geostrategic gain in the East-West struggle. Fearing overextension in the Basin or elsewhere in Latin America, the USSR is careful not to commit itself politically, economically, and especially militarily to new Marxist-Leninist regimes, as in Nicaragua as well as Grenada.[42]

In contrast, the Basin is of vital importance to Cuba's security and political interests. Castro continues to harbor maximalist ambitions in the region in that he wants not only to erode U.S. hegemony but also to extend Cuba's power and presence, creating a core of revolutionary states that are aligned with Cuba. Although he carefully operates below the threshold that would provoke a U.S. military attack on Cuba, he is prepared to commit Cuban resources and prestige to the revolutionary movements and governments of the region. Unlike the Soviets, Cubans fought and died in Grenada.

These disparities in Cuban and Soviet interests can be seen in Nicaragua. There the large contingent of Cuban military advisers assume command-and-control functions in the Sandinista army, operate sophisticated weapons systems, and serve down to the company level. In contrast, Moscow has pursued a more cautious, low-risk, low-profile approach. As Peter Clement notes,

the Soviets have demonstrated a clear preference for using intermediaries in the delivery of arms (at least until now): indeed, not only such trusted allies as

---

[41]Moscow has minimized its security commitments to Cuba as the latter remains outside the Warsaw Pact and has no mutual defense treaty with the USSR. Instead, stepped-up arms transfers to Cuba since 1981 are to enable the FAR to deter U.S. aggression, as Castro and Cuban and Soviet leaders have stated.

[42]Cole Blasier argues that Moscow has "no intention of investing heavily in Latin America beyond the huge amounts now sustaining Cuba, nor of assuming new strategic risks in the area. Soviet leaders are not sure they can afford the luxury of another Cuba, nor have they forgotten the lessons Khrushchev learned during the 1962 missile crisis. In any confrontation with the United States in Latin America, the Soviet Union is handicapped by the fact that the region has a relatively high priority for the United States and a relatively low one for the USSR. The United States is prepared to go to great lengths to have its way there, but the USSR is not ready to go very far." Blasier, *The Giant's Rival: The USSR and Latin America* (Pittsburgh: University of Pittsburgh Press, 1983), pp. 150–151. For a similar view, see also Augusto Varas, "Ideology and Politics in Latin American–USSR Relations," *Problems of Communism*, January–February 1984, pp. 35–48.

Bulgaria, East Germany, and Cuba, but seemingly more neutral shippers, like Algeria, have been utilized when possible. Although there is a large Cuban advisory presence in Managua, the Soviets themselves have some 200 military and civilian advisers—a far cry from the numbers of advisers in Angola or Mozambique, for example.[43]

However, developments since the mid-1980s suggest that the Soviets have a growing equity in Nicaragua, even though their direct presence remains small. The Soviet bloc extended $200 million in credits to President Daniel Ortega during his visit to Moscow and Eastern Europe in April 1985. The Soviets have also been helping in the construction of Nicaraguan airfield facilities and the dredging of Nicaraguan ports on both the Caribbean and the Pacific coast.[44] Meanwhile, throughout 1985 and 1986 the USSR increased its arms flows to Nicaragua, supplying hundreds of SA-7 surface-to-air missiles and a dozen or more Mi-24 helicopter gunships. Hence Moscow seems determined to provide its new client state in Central America with the wherewithal to consolidate its position and defeat the U.S.-backed Contras.

Yet the closer the Sandinista regime comes to consolidating its power, militarily as well as politically, the greater the possibility that the United States might intervene directly. Such a development would create a Grenadian dilemma for Castro, in which not only would he stand to lose Nicaragua but he could also confront grave risks to Cuba's own security.[45] Because they have carefully limited their role in Nicaragua, however, the Soviets are not likely to intervene to protect a budding Marxist-Leninist regime there any more than they did in Grenada. Hence Nicaragua could be a source of tension between Havana and Moscow as long as there remain serious prospects of direct U.S. intervention.

A Less Favorable Correlation of Forces

Since the Grenada setback, meanwhile, the correlation of forces, both regionally and internationally, appears to have shifted in ways that could severely inhibit Castro's maximalist ambitions in the Third World. In Africa

---

[43]Peter Clement, "Moscow and Nicaragua: Two Sides of Soviet Policy," *Comparative Strategy* 5, no. 1 (1985), p. 82.

[44]The Soviets and Cubans are helping Nicaragua build an airbase at Punta Huete with a 12,000-foot runway, which could accommodate any type of aircraft in the Soviet inventory and complement the Soviet use of air facilities in Cuba. For example, Soviet TU-95 reconnaissance/electronic aircraft could be launched from Siberia; catching the jetstream, they could then fly along the west coast of the United States, and refuel at Punta Huete before going on to Cuba. The deepening of Nicaragua's shallow harbors could also extend the range of Soviet naval operations by providing Soviet ships with offshore anchorages or port-of-call facilities in the eastern Pacific at Corinto and in the Caribbean at El Bluff.

[45]After Grenada, Castro indicated that Cuba would not send combat troops to Nicaragua in the event of U.S. military intervention, although Cuban forces already in Nicaragua would be ordered to resist the U.S. attack. Despite this limited Cuban commitment to Nicaragua, the United States might still decide to ensure the security of the sea-lines of communication in the Caribbean, and thus the success of its Nicaragua military operation, by neutralizing Cuba's air and naval forces.

continuing political violence and state repression in South Africa open up opportunities for Cuban involvement politically but probably not militarily because of the logistical difficulties and military risks that would be entailed were the FAR to engage South African forces. Meanwhile Castro has used the South African issue to justify Cuba's continued military presence in Angola, announcing that Cuban troops will not be withdrawn until apartheid disappears from South Africa.[46] In Angola, however, Cuban troops continue to be tied down in a protracted counterinsurgency war as a result of the insurgent threat posed by the UNITA forces of Jonas Savimbi.

In Central America the Sandinista regime now faces a critical two or three years during which it must defeat the Contras while discouraging direct U.S. military action. In neighboring El Salvador the insurgency appears stalemated, with military as well as political trends since summer 1984 favoring the Duarte government. In Guatemala the assumption of power in 1986 by a reformist civilian president, Vinizio Cerezo, has lessened the appeal of the armed left in that country. Thus Havana faces smaller prospects of revolution spreading throughout Central America, unlike say in 1979, and higher risks of being drawn into a Nicaraguan conflict and/or losing an ally.

Elsewhere in Latin America, Castro has tried to capitalize on the schism within the Catholic church, especially the emergence of a radicalized clergy and the theology of liberation movement. Thus he has urged a broad united front among Marxists and left-wing Catholics, which he evidently aspires to lead.[47] But his leadership over such a coalition would certainly be suspect and difficult to reconcile with his role as first secretary of the Communist Party of Cuba. Although it may make some headway in leftist Catholic circles, such a gambit is not likely to yield major revolutionary breakthroughs in Latin America.

In 1985 the continent's worsening debt problem did give Castro a potent issue to exploit against the United States and in favor of Latin Americanism. However, the Argentine, Brazilian, Mexican, and Peruvian governments have not followed his lead on the debt issue. On the contrary, in an interview published in the September 25, 1985, edition of *Le Monde*, Peruvian president Alan García sharply rejected both Castro's call for a Latin American debt strike and his pretensions to lead the Latin American movement:

> I have great respect for Fidel Castro. At one point in history Cuba represented a very important departure. But when you claim to be a revolutionary the essential thing is to suffer the consequences of the decisions or wishes you express. . . . Our position is realistic. We are part of an interdependent world. *Those who advocate total refusal to repay the debt have a childish, unrealistic, and extremist attitude* [emphasis added].

[46]*Granma Weekly Review*, September 15, 1986, p. 9.
[47]See Castro's extensive interview with a Brazilian, Friar Betto, which was published as a book in Brazil and Cuba in late 1985, bearing in Portuguese and Spanish the title *Fidel and Religion: Conversations with Friar Betto*.

Meanwhile the redemocratization of much of Latin America in recent years, which has seen civilian governments succeed military ones in Argentina, Uruguay, Brazil, and most recently Guatemala, further tends to isolate Cuba politically (though not diplomatically) in the region.

There remain other targets of opportunity for Castro in the Caribbean Basin. Among these are Panama, Puerto Rico, post-Duvalier Haiti, the Dominican Republic, and Jamaica, all of which are beseiged by political uncertainties and serious economic problems. But though Castro may be able to acquire political capital in some of these countries, he may not be able to achieve the revolutionary breakthroughs that occurred in Grenada and especially Nicaragua.

Mexico and Chile loom as the major exceptions. Mexico's deep economic crisis, demographic pressures, and corruption and misrule by the governing party, the PRI, could begin to unravel the heretofore stable Mexican system by the late 1980s or early 1990s. Were a leftist revolution to sweep Mexico, the development would be a "plum" for Castro and especially the Soviets in their respective struggles with the United States. However, Cuban assistance to leftist revolutionaries would irreparably damage Castro's long-standing ties with the PRI government while increasing the chances of direct U.S. retaliation against Cuba. If a right-wing, military-civilian regime were to emerge from the ashes of the PRI, on the other hand, Mexico might well cut its ties with Cuba for security reasons. For the Castro regime a crisis-ridden Mexico could thus prove to be a double-edged sword.

Cuba is not likely to be constrained, however, toward Chile, where there are signs of growing political opposition to the repressive Pinochet regime. Cuba's identification with the ill-fated Allende government, the international opprobrium that attends the Pinochet regime, and the fact that Chile is a less sensitive security issue for the United States—all strengthen the Castro government's subversive proclivities. Hence Cuba reportedly is actively supporting the Manuel Rodriguez Patriotic Front, the armed wing of the outlawed Communist Party of Chile, and has been implicated in supplying the large cache of arms—including nearly 3,400 automatic rifles—discovered in northern Chile in September 1986.

In the United States the Reagan administration, including the president himself, remains viscerally committed to a "rollback" strategy toward communism, as seen first in Grenada and then Nicaragua. Unlike its predecessor, moreover, the Reagan administration is also less susceptible to manipulation by Havana: despite the signing of a U.S.-Cuban immigration agreement in December 1984, for example, and an extraordinary public relations blitz by Castro in the U.S. media during the months that followed, the Reagan administration persisted in putting Radio Martí on the air in May 1985, much to the Cuban leader's surprise and outrage.

American military power has been greatly strengthened in the 1980s while tensions have not receded significantly between Washington and Moscow.

The basis for future U.S.-Cuban military conflict thus survives: because of its position commanding vital sea lines of communication in the Caribbean, Cuba could become a military casualty in the event of either a U.S. invasion of Nicaragua or a U.S.-Soviet crisis involving conflict in a third area. Castro is thus likely to wait out the end of the Reagan presidency in 1989, or at least await its expected weakening by the Iranian arms transfer and Contra scandal that began to unfold in late 1986, before embarking on new expansionist ventures.

In the Soviet Union, after years of leadership crisis, the ascendancy to power by Mikhail S. Gorbachev promises to infuse Soviet policy with a greater sense of direction at home and abroad. The Soviets may be less inclined to resume their expansionist surge in the Third World, however, not only because of the closing off of new targets of opportunity, save potentially in South Africa and the Philippines, but also because of the multiple problems they face on the international and domestic fronts.

Moscow remains absorbed with Afghanistan, concerned over disturbing political and economic trends in Poland and elsewhere in Eastern Europe, and preoccupied with the larger strategic stakes at issue with the United States. At home Gorbachev must wrestle with economic and administrative inefficiencies in virtually all sectors of the economy except the military. In turn Moscow appears less forgiving and more demanding of its East European and Cuban clients. The Soviets are pressing heretical Eastern bloc governments not only to limit their liberalizing economic reforms but also to fulfill their trade commitments with the USSR, supply better-quality goods, and invest in the Soviet oil and gas industries.[48]

For Castro, Gorbachev's new priorities will probably mean not only more limited Soviet largess for the Cuban economy but also renewed Soviet pressure for Havana to put its own economic house in order. At the end of 1984, in fact, Castro launched an "economic war of all the people" to improve the performance of the trade sector, particularly in the sugar and other export industries, with the stated purpose of overcoming the island's bleak outlook for the years ahead. During the last half of 1985 incompetent *fidelista* veterans were removed from their ministerial positions and, at the Third Party Congress in February 1986, from their membership in the party's Political Bureau as well.[49]

---

[48]The new Soviet line was highlighted by *Pravda* on June 21, 1985. See the comprehensive analyses by Robert Gillette in the *Los Angeles Times*, August 26, 1985, and Harry Gelman, "East Europe as an Inhibiting Factor for Soviet Policy: Prospects for the Next Decade" (paper prepared for the European American Institute for Security Research workshop "Fault Lines in the Soviet Empire: Implications for Western Security (II)," held at St.-Jean-Cap-Ferrat, France, September 16–18, 1985).

[49]On the other hand, some of the personnel shake-ups and antimarket policies ordered by Castro work against the revitalization of the Cuban economy and are contrary to Gorbachev's own economic line. For details, see Gonzalez and Ronfeldt, *Castro, Cuba, and the World*, pp. 63–89.

Meanwhile Castro may find Soviet support for an activist Cuban foreign policy in the Third World less forthcoming, not only because of Gorbachev's domestic priorities but also because of Soviet attempts to stabilize the more important strategic relationship with the United States. The major exceptions may be in Angola and Nicaragua, where Cuba's services are essential to the consolidation of Soviet client regimes. On the other hand, a crippled presidency in the last two years of the Reagan administration could invite a more venturesome Soviet policy. Until such a change in Soviet policy occurs, however, Castro appears to be confronting "objective" limitations to the pursuit of his maximalist ambitions.

Conclusion: Policy Implications for the United States

Can the United States exploit the latent friction and divergent interests between Cuba and the Soviet Union to wean Castro away from Moscow? Could a less confrontational policy by the administration at least moderate Castro's international behavior along lines less damaging to U.S. interests in Central America and elsewhere in the Third World? Is a more pragmatic Castro emerging today from the constraints and problems facing his regime? The answer to these questions is, I regret, with some qualifications a guarded "no," for several reasons.[50]

First, it obviously makes good sense for Washington to exploit differences in Cuban and Soviet interest which may arise over Africa and especially the Caribbean Basin, with Nicaragua looming as the most likely sore point in the near future. Yet as Castro's post-Grenada behavior toward Moscow has demonstrated, any interest divergency must ultimately become self-limiting because Castro has nowhere else to go but to the Soviet Union if he is to pursue his grand ambitions as a Third World leader. Castro's objectives are contradictory to U.S. interests in Central America, the Caribbean, and Africa in that his gain is likely to be at the expense of the United States. His grandiose goals can be realized only through a close, collaborative relationship with the Soviet Union. The Americans are unable to provide him with the levels of economic assistance that Cuba has obtained from the Soviets over the past decade; much less can they supply the FAR with the kinds of weapons that it has received from the USSR in recent years. Moreover, Cuba's economic integration into the Soviet camp has become so great—85 percent of Cuban trade is now with the socialist bloc—that it would be difficult for Cuba to reorient any significant portion of its trade to the United States, as Castro himself recently pointed out.[51]

[50]For an elaboration of this position, see Gonzalez and Ronfeldt, *Castro, Cuba, and the World*.
[51]"Frankly, the United States has fewer and fewer things to offer Cuba. If we were able to export our products to the United States, we would have to start making plans for new lines of

Second, despite domestic and international criticisms, the Reagan administration's hard-line stance has been, as the preceding analysis suggests, a major factor in closing off targets of opportunity, forcing a retrenchment in Castro's maximalist objectives, and giving Moscow pause in the Caribbean Basin. It was not a conciliatory approach that led to the Cuban and Soviet setbacks in Grenada, nor to the turning of the political-military tide in El Salvador, nor to Havana's potential predicament over Nicaragua. When the Carter administration attempted a conciliatory approach (at some political risk), that policy led to Interests Sections being established in Washington and Havana and to Cuban unrest that ended in the Mariel exodus, but it did not dissuade Castro from resuming his revolutionary offensive in Ethiopia and then in Nicaragua.

Third, although Castro appears to have become more pragmatic in the mid-1980s, the reasons for his behavior may lie more in domestic and international constraints than in any change in his strategic objectives. Because of his hubris-nemesis personality, his commitment to maximum goals has remained, as suggested earlier, remarkably constant over the decades. In turn, because these goals are power-maximizing, they require maximalist behavior except where pragmatic behavior is required at the tactical level—as is the case today. As in decades past, therefore, Castro's political behavior at home and abroad continues to conform to the following syllogism:

(1) Under certain conditions, pragmatism and moderation may be required to buy time, conserve power, and protect realized gains.

(2) Rebellious, radical, and opportunistic actions, however, are the only means by which maximum objectives can be attained.

(3) Pragmatism is thus a short-term tactic that must not stand in the way of resuming the revolutionary offensive when the opportunity arises.

This syllogism explains why Castro was not responsive to the Ford and Carter administrations but instead moved into Africa in the mid-1970s. It explains why today Castro poses as champion of the debtor countries and radical Catholicism in Latin America. And it explains why, in Antonio Jorge's words, Castro's Cuba becomes "a ready and willing abettor and supporter of assorted discontent and disgruntlements throughout the Third World, always on the lookout for potential rewards for its moves."[52]

---

production to be exported to the United States, because *everything we are producing now and everything we are going to produce in the next five years has already been sold to other markets. We would have to take them away from the other socialist countries in order to sell to them to the United States, and the socialist countries pay us much better prices and have much better relations with us than does the United States*" "Playboy Interview," *Playboy*, August 1985, p. 179, emphases added.

[52]Antonio Jorge, "How Exportable Is the Cuban Model?" in Levine, *New Cuban Presence in the Caribbean*, p. 229.

7

*The USSR
and Southwest Asia*

Shahram Chubin

Much of the conventional wisdom that permeates scholarly analyses of the Soviet Union reflects as much the political debates in the United States as insights into Soviet behavior. Perhaps no country is less able than the United States to overcome swings in national mood and to focus on the problems of long-term competition without crude oversimplification or wishful thinking. The nuances of Soviet behavior as well as its continuity tend to get lost in the din of theological debate and in the eagerness to discover novelty, usher in new eras, turn new pages.

The prevailing wisdom in today's Sovietology is one of a superpower in ineluctable decline, faced with a myriad difficulties, structural obsolescence, and painful trade-offs compounded, in foreign affairs, by a genuine great debate about the wisdom underlying and the instruments used in Soviet policies in the Third World. From this perspective, the issue is the management of the Soviet decline; the debate among experts involves assessing the relative importance of one Soviet writer's thesis on what policy *should be* against that of another. There is doubtless something to be said for the elucidation of the Soviet debate about the Third World. The identification of current Soviet problems, constraints, and policy debates may result in new perspectives and help in the prediction of the course of future policies. Current Soviet debate is of precious little value, however, in assessing past Soviet behavior in the Third World, and it is positively mischievous when alleged current and future constraints are applied to previous eras to support the case that Soviet policy in the Third World has always been prudent, risk-averse, and characterized by limited commitments. The record of Soviet involvement in the past thirty years may or may not be an imperfect guide to the next thirty, but in any case the perspective in this essay is narrowly empirical. I deal mostly with what has been done and with what results, not with debates among theoreticians, party hacks, and scholars, nor even with new trends in American Sovietology.

Some of the difficulty we experience today in assessing Soviet intentions or gauging relative success in Southwest Asia stems from a lack of historical perspective. The mid-1950s are less important than the mid-1940s, and the focus should be on Iran as a special but illustrative example. Much of Soviet policy toward Iran in the immediate postwar period had parallels in Turkey. The general issues it raised then about Soviet intentions and goals, and Western perceptions, interests, and appropriate responses, continue to animate and often divide us. Here I seek to summarize some of the issues of that period to set the overall context for the succeeding era. In this later period I analyze Soviet policy and tactics toward the region, with special emphasis on patterns and behavior rather than chronological detail.

Iran is not a typical Third World state. As a border state it is seen by the Soviets as a direct interest, a place of intrinsic importance. However, it is not simply as a defensive buffer but also as a *point d'appui* into the wider region that Iran assumes importance for the USSR, and similarly for our wider discussion.

Soviet policy toward Iran during and after World War II exhibited what have become characteristics of Soviet statements, claims, and actions ever since. During the war Soviet behavior in northern Iran indicated movement toward a de facto integration of Iranian territory into Soviet control. Soviet propaganda claims about "anti-Soviet actions" and "pro-fascist elements" alerted Western diplomats in Charles Bohlen's words to the customary "build-up to justify extreme Soviet pressure." By December 1944 Soviet ambassador Mikhail Maximov would be telling W. Averell Harriman that the Iranian government did not represent the Iranian people. As the USSR knew what the Iranian people wanted, it was proper for the Soviet government to see that this opinion found expression.[1]

As the crisis in Iran developed, it became clear that the USSR wanted predominant influence in Iran's northern provinces, a "friendly" government in Tehran, an oil concession in the north, and Communist party members in the government. It was never clear whether the Soviets supported revolt in Azerbaijan and the Kurdish Mahabad areas as a form of leverage on Tehran to achieve a complaint government or as a form of extra insurance. What was clear was that the Soviets' contempt for their neighbors, mixed with anxiety about their own security, led to policies that were seen as aggressive. George Kennan argued in 1944 that Russia could conceive of its neighbors only as either vassals or enemies, and "if they do not wish to be one, must reconcile themselves to being the other."[2]

The Soviet Union's justification for its actions in Iran (and Turkey) was "security." Pressed for an elaboration, Stalin argued that Soviet troops in

---

[1]Bruce Kuniholm, *The Origins of the Cold War in the Near East* (Princeton: Princeton University Press, 1980), pp. 197, 201.
[2]Quoted in Barry Rubin, *The Great Powers in the Middle East, 1941–1947* (London: Cass, 1980), p. 153.

northern Iran would stop a hostile Iranian government from sabotaging the Baku oil fields. He insisted that the USSR had the right under a 1921 treaty to send troops into Iran if conditions became "disturbed"—and Soviet propaganda campaigns sought to orchestrate such a disturbance. Neither James F. Byrnes, U.S. Secretary of State, nor British prime minister Ernest Bevin was convinced by Stalin's response.[3] Soviet claims varied as to whether Tehran and Ankara represented a threat when they were too weak or too strong; they were consistent only about Soviet rights, to be gained at Tehran's and Ankara's expense. To some extent they reflected a tactical use of the encirclement argument for domestic Soviet political purposes, as Kennan noted.[4] Doubtless they also represented the age-old Russian drive for security, defined expansively.

Whether these security claims were defensive or offensive was much debated and analyzed by Western policy makers. As usual Kennan put it well, observing that the pressure to extend Russia's borders was basically "only the steady advance of uneasy Russian nationalism, a centuries-old movement in which conceptions of offense and defense are inextricably confused." Soviet claims, he continued, would expand until met and stopped, and they would be pragmatically advanced in the interim. He saw the Soviets as "highly sensitive to the logic of force."[5]

In practical terms there needed to be little distinction between offensive and defensive. The USSR used its claims in the Turkish straits and for security in northern Iran as ways of dominating Turkey and Iran.[6] As Harriman observed in a memorandum in September 1944,

> what frightens me . . . that when a country begins to extend its influence by strong-arm methods beyond its borders under the guise of security, it is difficult to see how a line can be drawn. If the policy is accepted that the Soviet Union has the right to penetrate her immediate neighbors for security, penetration of the next immediate neighbors becomes at a certain time equally logical.[7]

Adolph Berle observed that the Soviet definition of "friendly" governments was obscure: "If it is meant that those governments must not engage in intrigue against the Soviet Union, there could be no possible objection: if it is meant that subsidizing guerrilla or other movements, virtual puppet governments are to be established."[8]

[3]Byrnes called it "the weakest excuse I ever heard him make" (quoted in Rubin, *Great Powers*, p. 170); see also Lord Bullock, *Ernest Bevin: Foreign Secretary* (New York: Norton, 1983), p. 207, and Kuniholm, *Origins of the Cold War*, p. 309.
[4]See Kuniholm, *Origins of the Cold War*, p. 334.
[5]Kennan, Memorandum, in *Foreign Relations of the United States, 1946*, 6:696–709, and George Kennan, *Memoirs, 1925–1950* (Boston: Little, Brown, 1967), pp. 308–311, quoted in Kuniholm, *Origins of the Cold War*, p. 311.
[6]See Kuniholm, *Origins of the Cold War*, pp. 334, 360.
[7]Quoted in Rubin, *Great Powers*, p. 153.
[8]Quoted in ibid., p. 154.

In the final analysis Soviet claims of security needs failed to meet the tests of plausibility and credibility despite the considerable initial sympathy they attracted. Soviet actions in the Turkish straits, Kars, Ardahan, the Kurdish areas, and Azerbaijan were not isolated cases. In Lord Bullock's view, "what gave substance to distrust of Russian interest in any particular case . . . was the appearance of a pattern repeating itself not only in the Middle East, but in Eastern Europe as well."[9] While the issues might concern Soviet security in matters of borders, warm-water ports, and the like, ultimately for the Western powers they also concerned, as Kuniholm notes, "the question of great power influence in the area and Soviet respect for the independence and sovereignty of a border country."[10]

British and American strategic assessments did not differ on the importance of Iran as a buffer for the Gulf and on the protection of oil. They essentially agreed on the need for maintaining Iran's independence, assisting in its stabilization, and rejecting any sphere of influence arrangement (which would weaken the defensibility of the Gulf and harm Western prestige).[11] Generally Western officials saw Soviet aims much as Kuniholm later summarized them: "It seems certain that they [the Soviets] sought to secure their southern flank, to rid that region of Anglo-American influence and at the same time acquire a springboard to the Eastern Mediterranean and the Middle East."[12]

Soviet policy toward Iran in the immediate postwar period revealed six characteristics worth briefly mentioning:

(1) the assertion of an open-ended claim on a neighbor based on security grounds, including a territorial buffer and political concessions, that is, "friendly" or compliant government;

(2) the use of an *ostensibly* valid legal justification for certain actions, that is, the 1921 treaty;

(3) the insistence upon, and preference for, bilateral negotiations with weaker neighbors (resisted by the West because of the opportunities such negotiations provided for coercion);

(4) the direct use of the Red Army to influence politicians in Tehran, embolden its adherents in Azerbaijan, and block central government troops;

(5) the use of antigovernment sentiment in the Kurdish areas for its own purpose of detaching Kurdish areas from Tehran and exerting leverage on the government;

(6) the use of the Tudeh party in Tehran and the National Democratic party in Azerbaijan as its local instruments of pressure.

[9]Bullock, *Ernest Bevin*, p. 159.
[10]See Kuniholm, *Origins of the Cold War*, p. 300.
[11]See Rubin, *Great Powers*, pp. 183, 205, and Kuniholm, *Origins of the Cold War*, pp. 363–377; also Bullock, *Ernest Bevin*, pp. 471–473.
[12]Kuniholm, *Origins of the Cold War*, p. 380.

Soviet activity in Iran was blatant in its use of force *directly* ("a full scale combat deployment" in Azerbaijan according to the U.S. consul Robbert Rossow, an eyewitness), in intimidation, in its use of subservient elements, and in propaganda claims.[13] But confronted by solid Western opposition and the prospect of publicity in the United Nations, and expecting to achieve its ends within Iran in any case, the Soviet Union backed down. Although Moscow believed in negotiating from strength and built up its position to do so in Iran, it was unwilling to go all the way. In any event Stalin's policy of unrelieved hostility toward Iran failed, and Moscow, though not a graceful loser, proved pragmatic about it.

How far were Soviet claims on Iran and its postwar aims due to the specific characteristics of Iran and to the unique fluidity of an immediately postwar world in which maps were being redrawn and frontiers were fluid? How far could one generalize about Soviet regional intentions from Soviet policy toward Iran, a contiguous state? How far was Soviet policy toward its neighbors a product of the personality of Stalin (and Beria) rather than a basic Soviet impulse? Even if the Soviet drive for power in the area really existed, might it not be only "regional" in aim (as Kennan was to argue in 1977),[14] necessitating no excessive Western alarm? Should not sensitivity to the geographical proximity of the region to the USSR dictate a more accommodationist policy, particularly in light of the indefensibility of the region, perhaps by an agreement on the neutralization of bordering states?[15]

It seems clear that the Soviet Union views its immediate neighbors quite differently from other states. States on the USSR's southern periphery are in a class of their own, being developing countries that are largely self-reliant for defense. Politically and economically weak, or potentially so, they are not covered by any firm security guarantees. They are important as buffers for Soviet security yet intrinsically unreliable because of their latent or actual instability. The Soviet Union makes claims on these states arising from its geopolitical security needs, from realpolitik, which have nothing to do with ideology. Of course, where ideological elements intrude, as in Afghanistan in 1978–79, they reinforce the exercise of these claims. But even when they do not, contiguity gives the USSR an ostensibly legitimate claim of "security interests" while facilitating the exercise of influence. Unlike other parts of the Third World, where "gains" and "retreats" are more abstract and the ability to influence events is diffused by the distances involved, neighboring regions provide tangible stakes and are susceptible to direct and indirect influence at

[13]Robert Rossow, "The Battle of Azerbaijan, 1946," *Middle East Journal* 10 (Winter 1956), pp. 17–32.

[14]George Kennan, *The Cloud of Danger* (Boston: Little, Brown, 1977), p. 178.

[15]Clement Attlee as prime minister suggested including Turkey, Greece, Iran, and Iraq in such an arrangement. Bevin argued that the Soviets would not match Western withdrawals with concessions but would pocket them and expand upon them. See Bullock, *Ernest Bevin*, pp. 340, 349–351.

short notice. Similarly, these regions are not subject to fluctuating Soviet interest but of persistent concern. Southwest Asia has always ranked first in Soviet Third World interests, ranking globally after Europe and the Soviet-Chinese border.

None of the questions noted above has been definitively answered, for the evidence remains mixed. Western images (a slippery slope, dominoes) may have been overstated, for Soviet successes in one area have not translated automatically into successes in others. Western defeats have not always benefited the USSR; Soviet efforts have not always been rewarded by success. Yet the image of two superpowers with common interests in avoiding crises is assiduously fostered by Moscow, which likes to draw attention to the similar problems that each superpower has in "managing clients." Thus the Soviets tell American diplomats that, for instance, Iraqis "are just crazy people" and that the USSR cannot control them.[16] But whether outside this limited domain, there is a real basis for comparison between the two superpowers is debatable.

A Balance Sheet of Soviet Involvement

The net gains of three decades of Soviet activity in Southwest Asia have to be judged by one overriding criterion: How far has the Soviet Union succeeded in driving U.S. power out of the Eurasian periphery and preventing the emergence of a hostile coalition to replace U.S. power? The dominance of the periphery and the removal of U.S. power from the Eurasian rimland constituted, as Fritz Ermarth has observed, a primary strategic aim for Moscow in peacetime and in war and is directly related to Soviet defense of the homeland.[17]

Even with a relatively clear yardstick there is room for debate. Some analysts point to the distance yet to go, the complications and dilemmas, the regional obstacles, the limits of influence, local resilience, and so forth. There is little point in cataloguing these matters exhaustively; they apply to every region and are in any case intrinsic to relationships between superpowers and regional states. Analysts who emphasize constraints do so to underline the *costs* of involvement, the *risks* of entanglement, the problems of choice, the transitoriness and reversibility of "gain," the impermanence of influence, and the impossibility of control. Risks and costs are, however, relative terms, not always perceived identically, and usually weighed against possible gains.

---

[16]Soviet ambassador Vladimir Vinogradov said this to Bruce Laingen, ranking U.S. diplomat in Tehran, in 1978, according to U.S. documents published in Tehran and in FBIS VIII 13, January 7, 1985.

[17]Fritz Ermarth, "The Evolution of Soviet Military Doctrine" (paper prepared for the International Institute for Strategic Studies annual conference, "Power and Policy: Doctrine, the Alliance and Arms Control," Berlin, September 1985), pp. 3, 9–11.

Western interpretations are as mercurial as U.S. foreign policy, shifting dramatically in response as much to moods as to changes in objective circumstance.[18] Soviet activism can be rationalized away by reference to problems encountered or difficulties that will be experienced.

From the Soviet perspective, the Third World may prove not as hospitable an environment as Marxist-Leninist doctrine leads adherents to suppose; there may be no automatic or natural alliance between Third World states and the Soviet Union subsequent to tactical cooperation against Western colonialism. The result may well be a Soviet pessimism about future relations with these states, generating incentives for more binding institutional ties and deeper involvement in their security and defense.[19] It may even lead to splits among Soviet analysts about the wisdom of supporting regimes simply because they are anti-Western or domestically progressive, and how much weight to assign to either factor.[20]

Furthermore, the USSR may feel isolated from the Middle East peace process, limited to relations with marginal states, less broadly involved in the region as a whole than the United States, and threatened by the Iranian revolution. Does this scenario merit the title "Superpower in Eclipse"? It seems doubtful, for the basis for comparison is not evidently sound.[21] Compared to Soviet aspirations, Soviet performance may leave a great deal to be desired; compared to the Soviet role in Middle Eastern affairs forty years ago, however, the Soviet Union is not so obviously on the decline.

The Soviet Union can point to several gains across the last generation. Britain's withdrawal from the Gulf and the opening of the Arabian peninsula, together with the dealignment of Iran, has weakened the West's military position in the area. At the same time the Soviet Union's new superpower status, worldwide navy, and power projection capabilities have given substance to Moscow's repeated assertion of a right to an "equal say," particularly in areas near its borders. Soviet statements now routinely include the Persian Gulf and Middle East more generally—historically a new claim (and one not often challenged by Western governments). If security interests have been broadened, so has the Soviet regional presence in the Yemens and the Horn of Africa, and in diplomatic ties with Kuwait, the United Arab Emirates, and Oman. Naval visits, arms supplies, and commercial exchanges

[18]This is one of the themes of John Schlesinger's "The Eagle and the Bear," *Foreign Affairs* 73 (Summer 1985), pp. 937–961. See especially p. 956, where Schlesinger observes the shift in view regarding Afghanistan.

[19]See Mark Katz, *The Third World in Soviet Military Thought* (Baltimore: Johns Hopkins University Press, 1982); and Thomas J. Zamostny, "Moscow and the Third World: Recent Trends in Soviet Thinking," *Soviet Studies*, April 1984.

[20]Jerry F. Hough, *The Struggle for the Third World: Soviet Debates and American Options* (Washington, D.C.: Brookings, 1986), especially pp. 52–62, 419–425, 456–466, 495–496 and *passim*.

[21]See Karen Dawisha, "The USSR and the Middle East: Superpower in Eclipse?" *Foreign Affairs* 61 (Winter 1982–83), pp. 438–452.

figure routinely in many of these relations. The general trend has been an expansion of Soviet interests and activities beyond immediately bordering regions, and it is a trend not likely to be reversed.

The USSR seems to have sought to make difficult if not actually reversible two changes in the regional environment, and it may to some extent have succeeded. By insisting on the "unacceptability" of particular courses of action, with the implicit threat of a strong reaction, Moscow has made the emergence of a pro-Western regime in Iran more problematic, inhibited Western support for one, *and* maintained that the establishment of Western military bases in the Arabian peninsula would be provocative and evoke counterreaction.

The initial Soviet entry into the Arab world, through the Czech arms deal with Egypt in 1955, was in some ways linked directly to the Western decision to set up a regional defense organization including Turkey and Iran. Soviet policy in the broader Middle East and in other parts of the Third World should be seen as the building up of positions for counterleverage and possible exchange. In the Soviet view the value of a particular asset is measured not simply by its direct worth to Moscow but by its value—nuisance or otherwise—to Moscow's principal adversary. Soviet investments in Central America and the Lesser Antilles, for instance, could provide the basis for subsequent "exchanges" between the superpowers.[22]

In Southwest Asia as elsewhere the only durable gains come from complete control, and here as elsewhere the costs of complete control in terms both of assertion and of retention have seemed too high for the Soviets. In a fluid environment the emphasis, rather, has been on tactical exploitation in the *hope* that this will provide the basis for more durable relationships. Exploitation of anti-Western sentiments, insecurity, regional rivalries, and ethnic and sectarian disputes has been the means of starting up relationships. Tactical exploitation, opportunism, and dexterity have been the features of a policy that has been consistent in only one respect: a persistent willingness to get involved in the region's politics. This perseverance may not have achieved as much as Moscow wanted, but it stems from a Soviet belief that only involvement (as opposed to abstention) generates influence and options. And incremental gains rather than sudden breakthroughs may be both a less risky form of competition with the United States and a form more suited to the Soviet system, which is ponderous.

Judged according to the ability to translate short-term alliances into durable partnerships as stepping-stones to a Soviet-sponsored regional order, Soviet policy has not performed well to date. But judging by adaptability in using opportunities to insert itself into the region or administer setbacks to

---

[22]Henry Kissinger reported a Soviet willingness in 1971–72 to link the withdrawal of their advisers in Egypt with those of the United States in Iran in the event of a comprehensive Middle East settlement. *The White House Years* (London: Weidenfeld & Nicolson, 1979), p. 1288.

the West, the Soviet Union has reason to be content. In any case it may be unrealistic to expect any relationships with developing states to be durable and without costs. The nature of domestic and regional politics in the Third World precludes stability, and imabalances in power, quite apart from great-power chauvinism and small-power inferiority complexes, suggest that relationships are bound to be difficult. So a willingness to "stay the course" and to benefit from short-term gains may be the most that can be realistically expected from these relationships.

Iran and Iraq

Soviet policy toward Iran underwent a change after Stalin, but only in tactics, not in aims. Soviet policy here as elsewhere cultivated the anticolonial trend in the Third World but did so without any clear conception about how ultimately to reconcile the trend with Soviet interests. A persistent pattern in postwar Iran was the Soviets' support for antigovernment forces (as in Kurdistan). But this tendency was balanced by the need for good relations with the central government if Moscow was to gain concessions. The upshot was the cultivation of both opposition and government and the use of one as a lever on the other. This pattern even applied with the Communist party, the official but not necessarily the only vehicle for Soviet political influence in domestic politics.

A continuing theme in Soviet-Iranian relations has been the establishment of a balance between Iran's sovereign right to an independent foreign policy that assures its security and the Soviet right to have secure and stable bordering states that do not directly or indirectly threaten it. Soviet efforts to define the USSR's security needs to limit the sovereignty of its neighbors are well-known—elsewhere, indeed, they have become formal doctrine. Less recognized is how persistently Moscow has sought to control the government in Tehran to assure absolute security. Iran, in turn, has resorted to every stratagem, most notably the cultivation of a distant countervailing power, to offset Soviet proximity and power.

Soviet efforts to prevent and then weaken Iran's association with the Western powers, and particularly defense cooperation with the United States, have been persistent. Those efforts have not stemmed from a natural feeling of encirclement arising from a global rivalry with the United States. As indicated earlier, in 1945–46 Stalin was arguing that Iran itself constituted a threat to the USSR. (Later, in the mid-1950s, Soviet leaders "accepted" Iran's assurances of goodwill but pointed to the threat from the United States.) Moscow made every effort to limit Iran's postwar reconstruction, defining as military any construction of railroads or reform of the local gendarmerie and as threatening and unacceptable any attempt to rebuild Iran's shattered military forces. An agreement on U.S. aid to the Iranian armed forces, in April

1952, elicited a formal Soviet note the following month accusing Tehran of "assuming definite commitments of a military nature toward the USA [and thus] setting out on a path of helping the U.S. government to carry out its aggressive plans directed against the Soviet Union." The note pointed out that such actions were "incompatible with the principles of good-neighborly relations" and concluded with a reference to the 1921 treaty and a veiled threat of intervention.[23]

The more Moscow exercised pressure on Iran, the more the Shah saw it as his duty to align with the West. The USSR was unable to stop either Iran's membership in the Baghdad Pact or the signing of a bilateral security agreement in 1959 (an executive agreement). Though the facts are still unclear, it appears that Moscow offered Iran a nonaggression treaty but insisted on the detachment of Iran from the West as its price, which the Shah found unacceptable. By 1962, however, the USSR had concluded that Iran was an unlikely site for intermediate-range ballistic missiles after all (especially with the U.S. shift to a sea-based deterrent) and chose to accept Iran's long-standing assurances in this regard.

After 1962 Iran-Soviet relations developed mainly through the intensification of economic relations and joint ventures in the border region. This trend was accelerated by Khrushchev's successors, who concentrated their energies on their southern neighbors and sought by the development of economic ties to demonstrate the Soviet Union's benign motives. While Moscow, impressed by the Shah's stability, prepared to do business, the Shah sought to reclaim a balance between the two superpowers now that the threat from the north appeared to have diminished. Substantive cooperation replaced the rhetoric and insults of the previous decade.

For the USSR, the lessons of that previous decade had been mixed. First, Soviet support for the Tudeh party had not been total in 1951–53 because it would have entailed direct military assistance against the Iranian Army. At the time the notion was unthinkable. Second, Soviet pressure through notes, threats, propaganda, airspace incursions, and military maneuvers had hardened and may even have pushed Iran into the Western camp. Third, Soviets' penetration of the military and the establishment of cells had alerted the Iranian authorities to the "threat within."[24] It must have been clear to Moscow that its ability to influence Iran's domestic politics during periods of internal stability and strong government was limited.[25]

---

[23]Royal Institute of International Affairs, *Documents on International Affairs, 1952* (London, 1955), pp. 334–350.

[24]In August 1954 some six hundred officers were arrested after the discovery of Communist infiltration in the armed forces.

[25]For an excellent summary of this period, see Firuz Kazemzadeh, "Soviet-Iranian Relations: A Quarter Century of Freeze and Thaw," in Ivo J. Lederer and Wayne S. Vucinich, eds., *The Soviet Union and the Middle East: The Post-World War II Ear* (Stanford: Hoover Institution Press, 1974), pp. 55–78.

Ditching the Tudeh and embracing the Shah were for the Soviets tactical maneuvers reflecting the times not the goals. Even with improved relations, differences with Tehran persisted. The most serious of these related to Iran's arms build-up and regional foreign policy. The Soviet Union revived the argument that an Iranian military build-up threatened it directly. It appeared to mean that the substitution of Iranian for British power in the Gulf complicated the situation and deprived the Soviet Union of the leverage that should naturally have accrued to it. Soviet diplomats were brutally frank in telling Iranians that they would match Iran's military build-up with aid to Iraq. When direct Soviet interests were at stake, as in the escape of a Soviet pilot who sought asylum in Iran in 1976, Moscow reverted to a mailed-fist approach. (In this case it warned the Shah that it would support Iranian opposition groups if the pilot was not returned.) Iran's attempts to organize the Persian Gulf and Indian Ocean states into regional groups, emphasizing security as well as economic relations, competed with Soviet conceptions as well as such Soviet proposals as Brezhnev's Asian Security proposal of 1969.[26]

Despite rather threatening language privately (and occasional public pressure, including MiG-25 overflights and requests to use Iranian airspace to supply Arab clients in 1973), Soviet policy remained restrained in comparison to the 1940s and 1950s. Arms *were* provided to Iraq and support *was* given to liberation movements, but not on a scale calculated to be decisive. The Soviet press was even silent on Iran's dispute with some Gulf sheikhdoms on the disposition of the islands of Abu Musa and the Tunbs; the Soviet Encyclopedia marked them as Persian.

This Soviet modus vivendi with the Shah was disrupted by the revolution, which came as a surprise to Moscow. The Soviets, like the West, found themselves reacting to it. Unequipped to understand religious movements, the Soviets underestimated the religious component of the revolution, nor did they find this aspect congenial. However, Soviet policy was quick to adapt. In November 1978 Moscow staked its claim to become the protector of the revolution. Subsequently, whatever the ideological doubts and disdain in Moscow, the prospect of gains against the West proved alluring. The Tudeh was reactivated, the National Voice of Iran (in Baku) resumed operations. Moscow sought to use the postrevolutionary chaos to advantage, identify the Tudeh and the USSR with the revolution, and accelerate and intensify the "objectively progressive" anti-Western trends within it. It did so by undermining the moderates within the revolution, supporting the extremist clerics, exacerbating the hostage crisis, and raising the specter of an American military threat.

I emphasize that the opportunities offered by the revolution to weaken the West were far more tempting and stronger than anxieties about the ultimate

[26]A. Kunov, "Developing Good-Neighborly Relations," *International Affairs*, May 1977, pp. 21–29.

effects of the revolution on Soviet interests. Analysts who portray Soviet interests as primarily defensive, as having stable neighbors, entirely miss the point.[27] The Soviet *definition* of defensive interests and stable neighbors is the critical issue: states cannot be stable until they are Marxist-Leninist, nor can they be other than aggressive until they are on the Soviet side.

Soviet policy speaks for itself. Between 1978 and 1982 the USSR encouraged the revolution in its cruelties and sought to woo it, aware all the time of the dangers of doing so. The zero-sum attitude vis-à-vis the United States took precedence over any attempt to restore tranquility and a stable border region. Here as elsewhere the Soviets preferred *uncertainty* and the *prospect* of gains to certainty and more limited gains. It was one thing to accept the revolution and, content with its anti-Western and anti-U.S. orientation, seek to build good relations with it; it was quite another to seek to intensify this orientation by identifying with radical factions to make irreversible the gains of the revolution—and in so doing contribute to forces that subsequently hurt Soviet interests, eliciting cries of outrage from Moscow.

If Soviet opportunism vis-à-vis the revolution should occasion no sympathy for Moscow's problems today, it is worth noting the retention of several Soviet levels of influence.

In 1979 the Iranians accused the Soviets of assisting the Kurds against the central government. Presumably other groups could also be helped.

In 1980 and 1983 Tehran accused Moscow of conspiring with the Tudeh party and establishing cells in the armed forces for a coup d'état.

In 1979–80 the Tudeh party forewarned the regime of coup attempts in the armed forces; presumably it learned about them from contacts with the KGB. Withholding similar information in the future may be important.

The Tudeh party (again possibly from the Soviets) forewarned the regime of Iraq's impending attack in August 1980.

The USSR has cultivated ties with one of the fedayeen factions, has links with the mujahedeen, and is active in provinces bordering Soviet territory.

Soviet assistance in providing transit facilities and in various economic projects is important. The withdrawal of Soviet technicians from Iran in July 1985 on the grounds of insecurity resulting from the continuation of the war was interpreted in Tehran as a form of pressure.

Soviet propaganda attacks on the regime of "Islamic Despotism," including calls (through the National Voice of Iran) for an uprising against the regime, demonstrate to the clerics the costs of enmity with Moscow.

---

[27]See Malcolm Yapp, "Colossus or Humbug? The Soviet Union and Its Southern Neighbors," in E. J. Feuchtwanger and Peter Nailor, eds., *The Soviet Union in the Third World* (London: Macmillan, 1971). See also Yapp's chapter in Adeed and Karen Dawisha, eds., *The Soviet Union and the Middle East* (London: Heinemann, 1982).

The Soviet Union has occasionally retaliated for Iranian assistance to Afghan "rebels" with hot pursuit and the bombing of Iranian villages, a matter that Tehran does not choose to publicize.

Soviet policy in the Gulf War is illustrative of similar opportunism and of a theme emphasized earlier: a belief that only involvement begets influence. Some analysts have emphasized Soviet interest in containing the war, in seeing that no decisive victor emerges, in preventing hostilities from escalating into an East-West confrontation, and in preventing the establishment of an American military presence on the Arabian peninsula. But the other side of the coin is equally interesting. The USSR has positioned itself as a supplier of arms to both combatants. It cut off Iraq between 1980–82 judging, correctly, that Baghdad had "nowhere else to go" and subsequently resumed supplies to punish Iran for taking the war into Iraq's territory. At the start of the war arms from the Eastern bloc were of minimal importance, but now they account for some 50 percent of Iran's arms supplies.[28] The USSR has positioned itself to control the supply of arms to both combatants, whether by outright denial of arms or by supplying arms to only one country. It is now in a position to offer a tempting Czechoslovak arms deal–style offer in the postwar period, when both states will be restocking arms. Iran, in particular, with its untrained forces, may find Soviet arms more appropriate than complex Western equipment. Again, whatever the purported Soviet interest in ending the war, Soviet policy in practice is to position itself to emerge in a strong position. The ending of the war, in brief, is not an end in itself. Similarly, the USSR has resisted U.S. suggestions that it limit arms to the combatants, arguing that it will do so only when the United States ceases arms supplies to *other* Gulf states, for example, Saudi Arabia.[29]

The Gulf War has not ended, and it is too soon to assess its consequences for the USSR. Early Soviet assistance to Iran (the supply of jet fuel, the offer of arms aid) suggested that Moscow was tilting in Tehran's favor. In the event of a widening of the war, it is still possible that elements within Iran might seek to "protect the revolution" by calling in the USSR. The USSR has kept in reserve the all-purpose 1921 treaty, refusing to accept its denunciation by Tehran and leaving open the option of invoking it at will rather than in its narrowly intended circumstances. In the post-Khomeini period some contrived invitation may be forthcoming or could be patched together, providing the kind of legal fig-leaf that Moscow likes to maintain to protect the eyes of the prurient while "saving socialism." Besides preventing a slide "back-

[28]See testimony of Richard Murphy in U.S., House, Committee on Foreign Affairs, *Hearings: Developments in the Persian Gulf, June 1984*, 98th Cong., 2d sess., June 11, 1984 (Washington, D.C., 1984), pp. 19–20.

[29]The Soviets told this to Western "academics" who have held government posts, as an "unofficial" means of relaying their views to Washington. Private interviews with participants, Ditchley Park, England, May 1985.

ward" to the Western camp, the Soviets would like to ensure Iran as a friendly state, first with a nonaggression treaty and later with a harmonization of foreign policies. If the immediate future looks bleak, it is important to note a discernible weakening on the part of the Iranian leadership regarding the USSR. Any reconciliation in the near term will be on Soviet terms.

Soviet interest in the other Gulf states is qualitatively different from its interest in Iran, but Soviet policy is not altogether different. Admittedly these relations possess neither the intensity nor the depth of those with Tehran, but in other ways they reveal similar patterns. Soviet involvement in Iraq started with the revolution in 1958, which Moscow offered to protect: Khrushchev offered troop maneuvers on the Turkish border to deter Western clients that might wish to destabilize the new republic. Thereafter the USSR sought to cultivate nationalist anti-Western forces of different stripes, reacting to domestic changes within Iraq. Although keen on advancing the Iraqi Communist party, Moscow never did so at the expense of relations with the central government. Similarly, though not especially enamored of the various governments in Baghdad, especially the Ba'ath in 1963, the USSR chose not to promote the Kurdish separatist forces of Mostafa Barzani which it had assisted. Nor, it might be added, did Soviet support for Barzani translate itself into control over the Kurds, who remained stubbornly independent.

Moscow used Iraq's ambitions in the Arab world and its need for arms to start a relationship that grew despite setbacks and adversity. The USSR was unwilling to support Iraq's claims on Kuwait, to choose between Egypt and Iraq's claims to Arab leadership, to renounce ties with the Iraqi Communists and Kurds, or to support Iraq in its rivalry with Iran. Iraq's ambitions and extremism marginalized the country in Arab politics after 1967 and virtually isolated it from the Gulf states. Unable to match its capabilities to its ambitions, and domestically weak, it was Iraq that set the pace in relations with the USSR, increasing its dependence on Moscow and formalizing it in a treaty of friendship in April 1972. If the Ba'athists believed that this treaty implied a Soviet commitment to Iraq against Iran, or a preference for Iraq over Syria, they were to be disappointed. The USSR in turn was disappointed by its failure to revive the Iraqi Communist party.

By the mid-1970s Iraq was a major recipient of Soviet arms (indeed, by 1982 Iraq was the largest recipient of Soviet arms in the Third World, all the more important for paying in hard currency).[30] However, greater domestic stability, larger revenues from oil, and increased pragmatism increased the

---

[30]Arms supplies grew from some $200 million (1955–60), then dropped to $100 million (1961–64), returned to $200 million (1965–69), jumped to $2 billion (1970–74), and more than doubled again to $4.5 billion (1975–80). See "Soviet Arms Trade with the Non-Communist Third World in the 1970s and 1980s," *Wharton Econometric Forecasting Special Report* (1984), p. 93, and Robbin Laird, "Soviet Arms Trade with the Non-Communist Third World," in Erik Hoffmann, ed., "The Soviet Union in the 1980s," *Proceedings of the Academy of Political Science* 35, no. 3 (1984), pp. 196–213.

Ba'ath leadership's options from the mid-1970s, leading to a diversification of arms supplies, a rapprochement with Iran, and greater communication with the Gulf states and the West, especially France. The Ba'ath found more to criticize in Soviet policy, from Soviet support for communist parties and interference in domestic politics to assistance to the Ethiopian government against Eritrean forces seeking autonomy, culminating in the intervention in Afghanistan, which the Iraqi leadership saw as a sign of Soviet willingness to rig military coups and interfere to produce compliant regimes on the door-step—the analogies with their own situation was not lost on them.

Once war began with Iran, and even after the USSR chose a neutral policy (which in practice favored Iran), Iraqi leaders had little alternative but to maintain links with Moscow. The war increased Iraq's dependency on Moscow, and in the medium term Baghdad had no practical alternative source for arms supplies. Saddam Hussein observed that it had been a Soviet arms embargo that forced Iraq to the conference table with Iran in March 1975. Some analysts, however, attribute Soviet involvement in the war against the Kurds supported by Iran as a major reason for Iran's willingness to negotiate in 1975.[31] Be that as it may, the Soviet Union risked little in wooing Iran in the Gulf War, switching suppliers even in peacetime is a lengthy process; Baghdad cannot replace Soviet arms during the conflict. Nor are there many suppliers both willing and able to supply arms quickly and on a sufficient scale.

Whatever Iraq's views of Soviet dependability, therefore, the country's choices are significantly constrained in the foreseeable future. Moscow re-started supplies in 1982 and has imposed no limits since, including surface-to-surface missiles in its deliveries. However, it has done so while (indirectly) providing similar equipment to Iran. It has also sought (and obtained) Iraqi support for its diplomatic formulations, which refer to the "inadmissibility of military intervention in the region under the pretext of protecting the free-dom of navigation" and are clearly designed to serve notice on the United States.

In its policies toward Iran and Iraq the Soviet Union has not lost sight of the big picture, the need to weaken the West, eliminate its presence, erode its footholds and prevent their reestablishment. This much Moscow has per-sistently and consistently pursued. If it has led regional states to find a certain perversity in Moscow's refusal to take sides definitively, or to commit itself fully; to identify a willingness to hedge and diversify relationships both be-tween governments and oppositions and between governments and their regional adversaries; and to see a comtempt for the regimes themselves ex-emplified on the one hand by an ever-present willingness to insist that the

---

[31] Alvin Rubenstein, "Air Support in the Arab East," in Stephen S. Kaplan, ed., *Diplomacy of Power: Soviet Armed Forces as a Political Instrument* (Washington, D.C.: Brookings, 1981), pp. 504, 507.

superpowers are not to be equated and on the other by a tendency to pursue regional politics with one eye cocked in the direction of Washington; then it is because these states do not understand the stakes involved. The stakes transcend the fate of any one nation and concern the global rivalry of two systems.

The Arabian Peninsula

The Soviet Union finds commitment much easier in the Arab-Israeli zone, where polarization is clear and the relative value of alignment is sharper than in the Arabian peninsula. Here the stakes are much smaller, conflicts are intramural, the benefits of alignment are less clear, and there are fewer incentives for clear commitment. In this context the Soviet Union has sought to broaden normal diplomatic relations by demonstrating its indispensability while emphasizing the dangers from the West. Soviet grand strategy is to weaken the West, but it is constrained by its limited presence in the region. Therefore, while building up relations with states with which it has ties— Iraq, South Yemen, the Yemen Republic, Kuwait, and lately Oman and the United Arab Emirates—it seeks to bring those states together in cooperation to form a critical mass sufficient to enable it to become a significant regional power.

The Soviet Union's closest relations have been with states that are marginal or peripheral, weak or dependent. It has therefore sought to widen its base of operations by wooing the principal state, Saudi Arabia. How it has sought to do so is revelatory about Soviet tactics. First, aware of the Saudis' sensitivity to the Arab consensus, it has tried to convert its "positive" role on the Arab-Israeli issue into currency for its relations with Riyadh. Second, it has attempted to convert its diplomatic relations with Kuwait (since 1963) into a model of what such ties can be. In the process Kuwait has become a showpiece; it has also become the base for an outsize Soviet diplomatic presence and espionage establishment. In addition, Kuwait has become a sort of lobbyist for the Soviet Union among the Gulf states,[32] a role that it finds congenial for distinguishing itself from its cousins in Riyadh. Third, without alienating the target state the Soviet Union seeks by a blend of intimidation and blandishment to communicate its importance in the affairs of the Arabian peninsula.

Soviet interest in the Arabian peninsula and the Red Sea area requires little emphasis; Soviet intervention in the Yemeni civil war, first indirectly and after 1967 directly, testifies to this proposition. The persistence of Soviet effort over eight years, the first clear-cut use of Soviet pilots in the Third

---

[32]See Christopher Dobson, "Red Desert Fort," *Far Eastern Economic Review*, December 29, 1983, pp. 30–32.

World, and the first case of military assistance by a communist state to a noncommunist one, all were features of Soviet involvement. Bruce Porter's words, "the Yemens' civil war, in fact, is one case in which Soviet arms shipments reversed a local balance of power and achieved a decisive outcome in a Third World conflict."[33] It also demonstrated an understanding of the indigenous causes of conflict while depicting the West as the enemy, a tendency to act in areas where a Western response is unlikely, and a willingness to make incremental rather than apocalyptic encroachments on the international system.[34]

Subsequent relations with the PDRY demonstrated in 1978 a commitment to maintain in power a friendly regime and a willingness to react firmly in a situation where Moscow did not expect Western opposition.[35] At the same time the USSR sought to encourage cooperation between the PDRY, Ethiopia, and Somalia to recoup what it could in the Horn of Africa. Despite an obvious strategic interest and commitments in this region, the USSR demonstrated an unwillingness to support fully the PDRY in the provision of assistance to the Popular Front for the Liberation of Oman. It provided indirect, limited assistance both to upstage China (with which it was then competing) and to "stay in the game," to remind the Gulf states (including Iran) of its potential nuisance value. But it did not provide sufficient assistance to make a decisive difference. Why it did not do so we may attribute more to a desire not to antagonize important Gulf states such as Iran and Saudi Arabia than to a miscalculation about imminent success.[36] In any event this episode illustrates a continuing pattern in Soviet relations with the Gulf states, namely, a desire to threaten and intimidate those states sufficiently to encourage them to enter into relations with Moscow (to buy restraint, as it were) without in the process antagonizing and alienating them by an *excessive* commitment to radical forces and militants.

The importance of this balance is the greater because the Soviet Union has concluded that it must work through the states in the region rather than await an imminent revolutionary breakthrough on the Arabian peninsula. Time and again the USSR has sought to demonstrate that it pays to have relations with Moscow. Kuwait is a long-time believer in this form of insurance policy, both vis-à-vis Iraqi territorial claims and against indigenous leftist opposition. Similarly, the restraining role of the USSR in the Yemeni clashes of 1979 may have underscored for the Saudis the benefits of Soviet goodwill.[37] Certainly the Soviets have not concealed the price for the exercise

[33]Bruce Porter, *The USSR in Third World Conflicts* (London: Cambridge University Press, 1984), pp. 83, 23, 66.

[34]Ibid., pp. 219, 221, 240–242.

[35]See Stephen Page, *The Soviet Union and the Yemens* (New York: Praeger, 1985), pp. 77 and *passim*.

[36]Notwithstanding Mark Katz, "Soviet Policy in the Gulf States," *Current History*, January 1985, pp. 26–27. See Page, *Soviet Union*, p. 132.

[37]See Page, *Soviet Union*, pp. 88–89, 140.

of restraint on militant forces in the region. Andrei Gromyko is reported to have told the Kuwaiti foreign minister that it was not reasonable to expect the USSR to relieve tension in the Arabian peninsula without first establishing diplomatic relations.[38] It may be that Oman's decision to establish diplomatic relations in October and that of the United Arab Emirates in November 1985 derived from a mixture of calculations similar to Kuwait's and bait offered by the Soviets.

Certainly the regional environment in some respects favors the USSR. Disillusionment with the West, frustration with Israel, and a desire for conspicuous evenhandedness argue for the establishment of ties. All societies have leftist opposition forces, all states have regional foes, that Soviet pressure might restrain if Soviet goodwill were forthcoming. Regional conflicts have proved a particularly useful entry point for Soviet breakthroughs elsewhere. Soviet involvement with the PDRY and latterly in a more intensive way with the Yemen Arab Republic (YAR) may increase pressures on the Saudis. So too will relations with Oman, never very friendly toward Riyadh.

The Soviet Union's position on the Arabian peninsula is by no means a strong one—although it has grown. In the upper Gulf it is much stronger than on the peninsula itself, while in southern Arabia it is more solid. Indeed, as Stephen Page notes, "since 1967 the USSR has moved from being in an extremely weak position in Southern Arabia to being the strongest outside power involved there."[39] It has done so by responding to circumstances. Whether it can convert this position and the prospect of a strong Yemen into a formidable point of pressure on Saudi Arabia remains to be seen. But there can be no doubt that apart from Iran, Saudi Arabia is the Soviet Union's principal target in Southwest Asia.

In the meantime Soviet diplomacy works to increase the constraints on any formalization or strengthening of U.S. relations with the Gulf states. Like Iraq, the YAR has agreed that "the two sides oppose interference by foreign forces in the internal affairs of the countries of this region under any pretext, including the pretext of ensuring freedom of navigation."[40] Although treaties of friendship have proved to be unreliable in extremis, the USSR maintains a passion for legal form and counts the PDRY, the YAR, Iraq, and Afghanistan as current friends. Possibly these friendships might in time be converted, like the Iran-Soviet 1921 treaty, into a fictional or pseudo-legal right to intervene

---

[38]Saudi Arabia's foreign minister, Prince Sa'ud al-Faysal, in an interview with *Ukaz*, May 26, 1981, quoted in Aryeh Yodfat, *The Soviet Union and the Arabian Peninsula* (London: Croom Helm, 1983), pp. 137, 160. This book is the best treatment of the issues. In some respects the issue of sequence here recalls the problem of Soviet inclusion in regional peace talks. Should the Soviets' goodwill *precede* their involvement or will it be enough to bet on its being the consequence or *product* of their inclusion?

[39]Page, *Soviet Union*, p. 212.

[40]See the YAR-USSR communiqué in *Pravda*, October 12, 1984; *Current Digest of the Soviet Press* 36, n. 41 (November 7, 1984), p. 8.

when circumstances displease Moscow, or at least into a club with which to threaten friends and deter enemies.

Afghanistan

On the face of it the USSR had all it could want in its relationship with Afghanistan in the decades prior to invasion.[41] Here on its southern border was an independent state leaning toward the USSR in a "special relationship" composed of dependence and deference. The USSR was not only that state's sole supplier of arms and primary source of economic assistance but also its principal transit route. From the mid-1950s the West had recognized the primacy of the USSR in this wild, mountainous land and had made no effort to keep Afghanistan nonaligned. By 1979 Western economic assistance amounted to one-fifth of that of the USSR ($532 million versus $2.5 billion). As significant, perhaps, were the infrastructural links between the two neighbors and the Soviets' qualified support for Kabul's claims regarding Pushtunistan as against Western-supported Pakistan. By the late 1970s, in brief, the USSR had in its southern neighbor what appeared a model dependent ally in a relationship recognized and unchallenged by the West, an ally that afforded it the means, if necessary, to bring pressure to bear on the less compliant regime in Pakistan.

The transition from this situation to invasion and bitter conflict is a complicated one. All its details need not detain us, but certain themes require emphasis.

(1) As a bordering state Afghanistan was an object of continuing Soviet interest and, it was generally conceded, legitimately so. But Soviet definitions of security were not static. Contiguity generated demands and also facilitated the exercise of power.

(2) The domestic situation in Afghanistan was in turmoil, and Soviet influence could not guarantee outcomes. Soviet aims progressively demanded greater certainty, implying direct control.

(3) The international context provided both the stimulant for Soviet anxieties and the permissive environment in which the Soviets could resort to force at low risk.

In retrospect the principal events are relatively clear. In January 1965 the People's Democratic party of Afghanistan (PDPA) was founded under the

[41]This section relies principally on Robert Litwak, "Afghanistan, Soviet Policy and the Security of South-West Asia" (paper presented at the Wilson Center, Smithsonian Institution, Washington, D.C., April 30, 1985). See also Marvin Weinbaum, "Soviet Policy and the Constraints of Nationalism in Iran and Afghanistan," in Yaacov Ro'i, ed., *The USSR and the Muslim World* (London: Allen & Unwin, 1984), pp. 226–260; "Forum: The War in Afghanistan," *Orbis* 29 (Spring 1985), pp. 5–71; and Amin Saikal, "Soviet Policy toward South-West Asia," *Annals of the American Academy of Political and Social Science* (September 1985), pp. 105–116.

leadership of Nur Mohammed Taraki. In July 1967 the PDPA split into two main factions: Khalq ("Mass") led by Taraki and Parcham ("Banner") headed by Babrak Karmal. This schism stemmed as much from personality as from ideological differences. In June 1973 the monarchy was overthrown by Mohamed Daoud, possibly with PDPA aid. In any event, once in power Daoud reduced his dependence on the military and the Communists and in due course sought better relations with Iran and Pakistan. This move implied a reduction in regional tensions and, insofar as it would open up alternative transit routes and new sources of economic assistance, a reduction in Soviet influence.

In mid-1977 the Parcham and Khalq factions were at least temporarily reunited, apparently at Soviet insistence, setting the scene for the PDPA military coup against Daoud in April 1978. The Soviets could deny their indirect role in this affair less easily than in its 1973 antecedent. They provided advice, technical assistance, and advisers. Even if the affair was "purely" domestic, however, fortuitously favoring the USSR and spontaneously welcomed by Moscow, it is remarkable how quickly and how warmly the new regime was embraced and its predecessor calumniated.

Soviet public pronouncements lauded Afghanistan under PDPA rule along with other Third World states (Angola, Ethiopia, Mozambique) of a "socialist orientation." Numerous Soviet advisers were brought into key sectors while institution building along Marxist-Leninist lines was emphasized as a means of ensuring long-term influence. Despite the growth of ties on several dimensions and particularly in the economic and security fields, including the signing in December 1978 of a friendship treaty, the situation worsened. The rise of the Khalq faction of Taraki saw a rapid removal of the rival Parcham faction and a radical program of social reform, heavily ideological in content. Such changes in turn stimulated resistance in a traditionalist society, particularly as these reforms reeked of godless communism. As early as 1978 resistance movements were forming, some in Pakistan.

Whatever doubts the Soviets had about this state of affairs they kept hidden or rather subordinated to the exigencies of the bilateral relationship. The pattern of agreements between the two states exhibited unparalleled coordination even as Taraki's radical domestic restructuring deepened rural resistance. Throughout 1979 Soviet military delegations came and went, always confronting the choice of withdrawing and allowing events in Afghanistan to take their course or deepening the commitment to Taraki's experiment. When a Soviet-supported attempt to oust Hafizollah Amin (a radical from the PDPA leadership) to consolidate the power of the more pliable Taraki failed, the Soviet protégé was killed. By September 1978 the Soviet hope of reconciling Khalq and Parcham had evidently failed, and confronting Soviet policy in Kabul was the "loose cannon" of Amin. In late December 1979 Moscow took a direct and unprecedented hand in deposing Amin, replacing him with Babrak Kamal, and sending some 80,000 troops into Afghanistan, allegedly on that government's request under the 1978 friendship treaty. The USSR emphasized not only legal form but also the international precipitants, namely, the prior intervention of the United States, China, and Pakistan, as threats to the Republic.

It is generally recognized that the Soviet invasion was in some sense "defensive," that is, an attempt to prevent a major debacle. On one level it was a desperate attempt to protect a Marxist regime from imminent reversal. To have allowed the overthrow of a regime tied so intimately and so publicly to Moscow would (it was feared) have encouraged similar reverses elsewhere and permitted the very notion of reversibility to gain general currency. On another level the Soviet coup and invasion were preclusive, preventing Amin from taking the "revolution" in any direction other than that prescribed for it by history and by Moscow. On both levels Soviet interests and legitimacy could be undermined by the defection of a state tied closely to Moscow.

Afghanistan's location as a bordering state gave the USSR "legitimate rights" (seldom contested by the West) transcending the question of ideology. Phrases such as "in close proximity to" and "cannot remain indifferent to" serve as a code, alluding to some undefined rights vis-à-vis bordering states. Afghanistan's contiguity to the USSR made the issue of "irreversibility" doubly sensitive: it magnified Soviet security concerns to the extent that Western and other imperialists were actually believed to be involved, while at the same time it gave the USSR the means denied it in more distant locations to resort to forceful measures.

The international context made the Soviet decision easier and more likely. On the one hand, the newly intensified rivalry with the United States, and suspicions about the Sino-American relationship, heightened the sense of the stakes involved in Afghanistan, increasing the need for decisiveness. On the other hand, U.S. preoccupation with Iran and the hostage crisis reduced the risks of U.S. reaction to Soviet moves in Afghanistan.

A final consideration relevant to the Soviet decision to invade Afghanistan is the broader matter of Islam and the Iranian revolution. If there was a delay in Moscow's recognizing the role of religion in Iran's revolution, it was due to ideological distortions that underestimated that role rather than to tactical considerations. From early 1979 Soviet support for the Iranian clergy and the clerical (as opposed to secular) elements in the revolution was unstinting. Soviets showed no sign of concerns about a spillover into the USSR of a Muslim "revival" in Iran or indeed about inevitable Muslim support for the opposition in Afghanistan. If Moscow worried about events in Iran in relation to Afghanistan, it seems to have been concerned that a generalized instability, a new fluidity in the region, provided opportunities for realignments and should be used accordingly. It seems doubtful that the USSR reacted to events in Afghanistan out of a sensitivity to the issue of Islam. The issue, rather, was support for a client regime beseiged by "reactionary" domestic forces. That these forces happened to be Muslim made their opposition more tenacious, but opposition from any quarter would have been equally unpalatable.

Whatever the precise mixture of motivations, the USSR effectively moved its boundaries southward and broadened its military capabilities in the region. Its offers (for example, in 1980) to seek a negotiated settlement have been region-wide, linking Afghanistan with Persian Gulf security. Despite heavy investment, casualties, and seven years of war, the USSR appears no closer to controlling Afghanistan now than it was on the first day of the invasion. Moscow remains reluctant to tie itself too closely to a particular regime because of the problems of extrication and the loss of flexibility that a definitive commitment would imply. Of course, several factors make the withdrawal of the USSR, the maintenance of the current regime, and the stabilization of the country mutually exclusive objectives.

What does Soviet policy in Afghanistan tell us about Soviet goals in Southwest Asia? How far is the record of Soviet behavior indicative of future Soviet policy? First Soviet security interests appeared substantially to have been met in the looser relationship that existed with governments prior to 1978. Over time, however, "influence" was seen as inadequate and "control" preferable. As events in Afghanistan after 1978 (and in South Yemen in January 1986) demonstrate, however, control is not possible in complex, faction-ridden polities without actual physical occupation, which sets in motion opposing forces. So while a preponderant power may exercise influence from a distance, it does so at the risk of setbacks and defeats and without the benefit of guarantees. Once it seeks such a guarantee, indirect control is no longer feasible; it must opt for the occupation without which definitive preponderance and control are impossible. The Soviet Union today wants a "friendly government" guaranteed in Afghanistan, but without military occupation. Its need is indistinguishable from control, and it is doubtful that it is possible without military occupation. Yet the problems of occupation are such as to make "indirect control" attractive again, even if indirect control is now more unrealistic than ever.

Second, the Soviet definition of security has rarely been flexible in relation to its neighbors, even if policy has exhibited realism in regard to the correlation of forces. An overemphasis on global factors led, in the case of Afghanistan, to a correct reading of international forces (that is, to an accurate estimate of the military risks vis-à-vis the West) but to a misreading of local forces. The superpowers, who each give primary attention to the others' policies, rarely read domestic and regional constraints accurately.

Third, the principal catalysts for Soviet activism in Afghanistan were domestic, drawing the USSR further than had been customary into internal squabbles. There are no grounds for assuming that such opportunities, which must appear tempting, are unique; Iran after Khomeini may offer such openings. At the same time the international setting imposed few constraints—rather the reverse, as general mood and the conjunction of other crises made for a permissive environment. No power was in a position militarily to challenge the USSR. Tensions in the Persian Gulf increased the sense of crisis and distracted attention, making the Soviet action in Afghanistan part of the generalized crisis, rather as Suez had deflected attention from the suppression of dissent in Hungary in 1956.

Fourth, the issue of risks and costs, elusive in any analysis, is doubly difficult when risks and costs are being assessed in relation to an adversary's presumed hierarchy of values. The tendency to indulge in "mirror imaging" in such analyses needs to be avoided. For the Soviets, the costs of an invasion have to be measured not only against the costs of doing nothing and the probable increase in costs at a later date but also against the more general question of how Moscow looks at "security," the long-term perspective on border issues, and the sensitivity to "reputation" as an element in power. The risks of a Western reaction were contingent on numerous factors that the Soviets were careful to minimize by, for example, incremental involvement, fabricated invitations, claims of defensive interests, and so forth.

The Soviet invasion of Afghanistan was neither typical of Soviet behavior in Southwest Asia nor an indicator of future policy. But it did reflect a tendency to see security issues in a certain way and to act in their defense with great persistence and decisiveness when necessary. The Soviet definition of security interest, the pattern of increasing involvement, the legal fictions accompanying the relationship, the Soviets' growing demands in terms of controlling outcomes, the variety of reasons adduced for Soviet commitment to the regime in Kabul, and the manner in which the ultimate decision to resort to force was made—all should act as reminders against any notion that the United States and the USSR are at all comparable in their notions about the Third World.

The Regional Environment

Southwest Asia is characterized neither by one dominant issue nor by regional polarization. The variety of issues and cross-cutting alignments militates against any simple breakthroughs on regionwide terms. As colonialism has receded, agitation against the Western power has declined. Although anti-Americanism may have increased for various reasons (including Washington's conspicuous power, its alignment with Israel, and the need for its demonization by peoples who feel impotent and frustrated), the former colonial powers, Britain and France, are now more acceptable partners. And the West is more attractive to the rich and now independent Arab states.

The consequences of wealth are by no means stabilizing, but in the short term wealth has provided these states with greater options in terms of the goods they buy (including arms), the education they have, and the ideas they imbibe. The region is now better defended by indigenous forces than it has ever been; and states can, at least in theory, increase their political control by more efficient internal security mechanisms. Dissidents can be coopted, differences smoothed over, objectors bought off, and opponents dispatched to sinecures. Even threats can be reduced by appeasing their source or at least renting one's good behavior.

The Soviet Union does not find any of these observations working ineluctably in its favor. As is generally recognized, its peacetime assets are few and its ideology does not evoke the spontaneous enthusiasm among the young that Moscow might wish. There is in addition the more general problem of the applicability of Marxism-Leninism, a product of Western thought reflecting Western conditions, to non-Western societies.[42] Many of these societies are passing through an uneasy period of self-discovery and renewal, in some cases inflamed by a militant form of Islam that identifies atheistic communism with the West as much as it does materialistic capitalism. Furthermore, in Iran and Turkey and possibly, as a result of recent experience, Iraq, there is no automatic tendency to equate imperialism with the West or to believe that the threat need necessarily come from the sea to constitute imperialism. If Islamic revival persists in the region, the USSR will have to be sensitive to its own Muslims and to how regional developments affect its own growing community. Some observers attribute Soviet policy in Afghanistan to a hypersensitivity to this issue. But the danger of analysts' exaggerating or condoning Soviet exaggeration of this issue is that it will provide another all-embracing pretext based on "security" to interfere in the affairs of neighbors.

An additional factor in regional politics is the capacity of local states to compete with the USSR in certain fields. Saudi Arabia and Iran in the mid-1970s used their oil revenues to woo the militant poor (radical states such as the PDRY) with some success. Similarly, the Gulf states have redistributed some revenues to ensure that the poorer sheikhdoms (such as Ras al Khaimah) do not feel excluded. Bilaterally, Iran tried to do the same with Afghanistan before 1978, and Saudi Arabia with the YAR. (If such assistance is insensitively supplied, of course, it may increase the recipient's discontent and open it up to Soviet influence, as has happened in the YAR.)

Another complicating factor for Moscow has been the growth of cooperation on the regional level. The Soviet Union opposed the Shah's various schemes envisaging a collective security system in the Persian Gulf and South Asia. His notions offered a rival attraction to nonaligned states and threatened to weaken the influence of the USSR. Similarly, the USSR opposed Saudi Arabia's sponsorship of a conference on the Red Sea as an "Arab Sea" in 1977 and Iraq's Arab National Charter proposal of 1980. Indeed, the USSR has always opposed schemes intended to increase cooperation among regional states. It has never favored independent integration schemes. It did not approve of "Arab nationalism" or the various Arab unity schemes; it opposed

---

[42]See Kazemzadeh, "Soviet-Iranian Relations," p. 66.

the Sa'dabad Pact that included Iran, Turkey, and Afghanistan in the 1930s and similarly the Regional Cooperation for Development scheme among Iran, Turkey, and Pakistan in the 1960s and 1970s. By the same token it is hardly enthusiastic about the Gulf Cooperation Council that has developed since 1981.

Generally speaking, Soviet opposition to the schemes revolves around three criteria: the orientation of these states in foreign and security policy; the security content of the arrangement; and whether the association is "open" or "closed," that is, whether it includes the USSR. If the regimes are pro-Western (and armed by the West), they are accused of creating a "closed military bloc." In theory, economic cooperation among truly nonaligned states would be acceptable, but defense integration, which has been mooted for the Gulf Cooperation Council, is obviously anathema.

The Soviets do not want regional institutions or arbiters in competition with their schemes. Their own overarching Asian security scheme of 1969 was to be supplemented by a series of bilateral friendship treaties. Cooperation among Soviet friends was in some cases (as in the Horn of Africa) expressly encouraged. Similarly, the USSR is clearly behind the PDRY-Ethiopia-Libya treaty of August 1981, apparently constructed as a rival to the Gulf Cooperation Council. Nor does the USSR have any objection to cooperation among rejectionist states, Syria and Libya and now Iran which allows for an indirect channel of communication and a conduit for arms.

The Soviet scheme for Asian security has not amounted to much. But it has served notice of the Soviet Union's presence as an *Asian* (as well as a European) power. Similarly, Brezhnev's proposed Oil Consumers' Conference of 1980 was designed to emphasize that the USSR has a role to play in any discussion of Persian Gulf and oil security—a role that it wants formally acknowledged and accepted.

Soviet Tactics and Patterns of Behavior

Soviet policy in the past three to four decades reveals recurrent patterns of behavior that are worth summarizing. To begin, the Soviets have been persistent in emphasizing their legitimate interests in the region, their right to a say in its destiny, and in their efforts to widen the perimeter of real estate about which they "cannot remain indifferent." At the same time, the USSR has sought to cast doubts on the reality of Western interests in Southwest Asia and to depict these as artificial—particularly those of the United States.

Soviet concern for legal and formal cover for involvement stems not from mere pedantry but from a conscious construction of a base for future actions. Soviet policy appears to involve the slow transformation of perceptions as to the *relative* balance of interests in the region, which, if successful, can decisively affect the credibility and resolve of the superpowers during crises.[43] Related to this point is the phenomenon of the alternation of pressure and reasonableness, of crisis and offers of crisis management, to create a psychological atmosphere that will demoralize the adversary.[44] Moreover, Soviet policy in the region is zero-sum and superpower-oriented. The adversary is depicted as the West, the problems of the region stem from the West, the answer proposed is to shun the West. Soviet policy is undertaken with the other superpower principally in mind.

Soviet commitment to particular states has been limited and contingent. The Soviet pattern has been to use the militant or radical states as an entree into a region (without giving them a total commitment) and then to broaden the base of regional operations by not antagonizing but rather wooing and intimidating more important states. This pattern limits Soviet incentives for provoking crises but not for responding to them quickly. Indeed, the desire to impress recalcitrant states with Moscow's importance may dictate an *activist* policy.

Soviet policy makers have been oblivious to any embarrassment from being on several sides at once; choice is not seen as a dilemma but as one of the fruits of power. Soviet relations with the YAR, PDRY, and Oman, and with Iran, Iraq, and Syria are only regional manifestations of a similar approach to international politics. By hedging and investing in several places, Moscow insures against overreliance on any one asset and protects itself from permanent reverses. More positively, the coordination and vectoring of these various assets could, under some circumstances, lead the Soviet Union to the position of regional arbiter it so ardently seeks.

Soviet risk taking, in terms of confronting the West or overriding regional sensibilities, has been distinctly limited.[45] It has been a feature of Soviet policy to choose areas where advances will be unopposed (for example, the Yemens). In risking the alienation of both clients (Syria and Iraq) or in providing strong commitment to a regime under siege (witness the embattled Alawi regime of Hafez Assad in autumn 1980), Soviet policy is altogether different. In these cases the USSR is shrewd enough to know when its clients have few options or when commitment is worthwhile—whence the signing of a treaty of friendship with Assad rather than his unceremonious "dumping."

---

[43]The point is an important one. More decisive than details of the military balance in crises are the perceptions of the two parties as to their respective interests. See Hannes Adomeit, *Soviet Risk-taking and Crisis Behavior* (London: Macmillan, 1983), pp. 338–340.

[44]Ibid., p. 319. The same characteristic of applying and relaxing pressure, demanding maximum objectives and settling "reasonably" for something less, is evident in Soviet-Iranian relations.

[45]I agree with Steven David's broader remark that Soviet operations in the Third World have been low-risk affairs designed to challenge neither regional sensibilities nor important U.S. interests. "Third World Interventions," *Problems of Communism*, May–June 1984, p. 66.

The Soviets have been reasonably successful in adapting to the needs of regimes in the area. They have become adept at blurring the fuzzy line between "internal" and "external" security problems (a line that moralistic-legalistic Americans uphold). They can supply an ideology for a one-party system, and arms and assistance to keep friends in power.

Finally, Soviet policy is to discourage any form of bilateral or regional cooperation not sponsored or controlled by Moscow and to substitute in its place arrangements that link various states directly to the USSR. A parallel policy is to maintain bilateral diplomacy, lest the creation of multilateral instruments dilute Moscow's advantages in diplomacy.

Some may be impressed by how little Moscow has to show for thirty years of effort. Others may note that the currently weaker Western position at least improves the Soviets' position in comparison with the past. However, even if a relative weakening of the West's position does not translate into a Soviet advantage but reflects an era of greater indigenous control of the region's dynamics and destiny, there are grounds for caution. Soviet miscalculation and overexertion are as likely to come from frustration as they are from optimism and confidence. In the past three decades Soviet pragmatism and caution have emerged not spontaneously but rather from a recognition of the existing military balance and a perception of Western will. If these are seen to be diminished, eroded, or no longer applicable, there is no assurance that pragmatism, incrementalism, and caution will continue to prevail. Similarly, if the Soviets come to see the area not simply as a place to be destabilized for the weakening of the West but rather as a place involving Soviet vital interests requiring deep involvement and stabilization, calculations about risk taking will inevitably alter. The most likely place for such a shift is Iran.

Dialogue, Common Responsibility, and Coordinated Responses

In the past five years Western dependence on Gulf oil has decreased, and the prolonged war in that region has underscored the reduced vulnerability of consuming states to the political problems of the area. With the end of the oil boom attention has shifted elsewhere, while the costs of quick-reaction, interventionary Central Command forces earmarked for the Gulf appear to be too high—for some—to be justified primarily by reference to the defense of the Gulf. In addition, Soviet passivity in the Third World underlines for some observers the difficulties that Moscow has encountered there, the problem of Afghanistan (now Russia's quagmire), and the overreaction of the West to the unique circumstances of Afghanistan.

Soviet inactivity can be explained more persuasively, however, by reference to the triple succession crises, the problem of Poland, and concentration on European and arms control issues such as the INF and the Strategic Defense

Initiative. Moreover, Soviet restraint is due precisely to the crisis of 1979–80, which saw a stiffening of American resolve, the enunciation of the Carter Doctrine, and the improvement of the U.S. military position in the region as a whole. There is no reason to assume a diminution in Soviet attention to Southwest Asia, which in the future will assume renewed importance both for its oil assets and for the Islamic revival that it is undergoing. The region will remain the primary theater of Soviet activity in the Third World, the obvious arena for expanding Soviet influence and of secondary importance only in relation to the European and Chinese sectors of the Soviet border.

Soviet policy is of course conditioned by its central relationship with the United States. Jerry Hough has argued that most Soviet analysts see Soviet Third World policy as essentially part of policy toward the West, which could be moderated to improve ties with the West.[46] The same could be said of Western policy; concern for the Third World rises and falls with perceptions of Soviet malevolence there. Periodically the concern becomes alarm, which then subsides into relief and an attempt to ensure that alarm does not recur. Soviet policy, as I have tried to demonstrate, is under no illusion that at least this part of the Third World is dispensable, that its interest is temporary or contingent on any particular factor. Although Soviet activism is conditioned by the USSR's relationship with the West (and the degree of stability of the regional states), increasing in periods of fluidity and crisis and moving to incrementalism and indirection in more normal times, its focus remains constant.

Soviet-American rivalry in the Third World reflects as well as stimulates the superpowers' rivalry, exacerbating difficulties of agreement on arms control and contributing to a general distrust that accumulates. There is an obvious interest, as a result, in seeing how this rivalry might be limited and (in some cases) how it might be decoupled from the issue of arms control. Suggestions have ranged from ambitious rules to govern reactions to crisis (as in the Nixon-Kissinger efforts of 1972) to specific proposals suggesting linked solutions to analogous regional problems.[47] Sometimes analysts go overboard in their empathy for the other superpower, suggesting for instance, a Soviet withdrawal from Afghanistan in exchange for a neutralization of virtually all of its neighbors.[48] (As a method of conflict avoidance, neutralization has obvious attractions, but it is rarely as simple as it sounds.)[49] Soviet interest in Southwest Asia is not necessarily demonstrated exclusively in policies within the region. Soviet policy in Central America may well be a means of gaining

---

[46]Hough, *Struggle for the Third World.*

[47]Such as Zbigniew Brzezinski's suggestions on Afghanistan and Nicaragua. See *International Herald Tribune,* October 7, 1985.

[48]Notably Selig Harrison, "Cut a Regional Deal," *Foreign Policy* 62 (Spring 1986), pp. 126–147. See also note 15 above.

[49]Cyril Black et al., *Neutralization and World Politics* (Princeton: Princeton University Press, 1968).

leverage for an accommodation on Afghanistan or on U.S. aid to Pakistan. But what sort of arrangement would be truly symmetrical vis-à-vis Iran?[50] It is tempting to envisage a formal arrangement governing Iran. This country, after all, is the most difficult case, bordering the USSR and yet constituting the first line of defense for the Gulf. Historically, Britain and Russia competed in the country but composed their differences (as in 1907) when necessary. A partition agreement or condominium was feasible at that time but probably is not today because of the political mobilization of the indigenous population. A sphere-of-influence arrangement, perhaps separating northern Iran from Western interests in the Gulf, is conceivable, but how it could be enforced in practical terms is another matter. Neutralization is also a possibility, but it would require both agreement by the Iranians and a degree of stability in the country which might not be forthcoming.

Formal arrangements do not appear realistic. What of the informal variety? Obvious interests (at least theoretically) ensure that indigenous instability in a region of overlapping interests does not bring the superpowers to inadvertent confrontation. Dialogue on means to assure that each takes the other's sensitivities into account and does not contribute to superpower tensions is a normal—and continuing—process. Since 1980, and especially since the beginning of the Gulf War, the question of arms shipments, naval deployments, and the like have figured in an informal superpower dialogue. Another important issue concerns respective rights, responsibilities, and constraints in the event of turmoil and political competition in a post-Khomeini Iran.

Crisis management for reassurance is one thing, however; cooperation is another. As the Gulf War has shown, similar interests in the retention of the status quo and the prevention of a decisive victory by either side do not necessarily lead to cooperation.[51] The USSR arms both side, the United States neither; the USSR constantly berates the United States for a nearby naval presence. Neither arms nor rhetoric have been limited. The key issue has been not how coordination might damp down the war but who might benefit from the war and its aftermath.

I do not see that a formal agreement with the USSR governing this area will be feasible unless the USSR changes its conception of its security fundamentally or the United States decides to cede the area to the Eastern bloc. Any agreement requires an acceptance of limits to rights, limits that would have to

---

[50]Many discussions compare Iran and Mexico vis-à-vis their respective superpower neighbor. The analogy is false geopolitcally in that the United States needs access to the Eurasian rimland; the same cannot be said for the USSR and America. Measures envisaging naval arms control in the Indian Ocean under the Carter administration reflected the erroneous view that a balanced reduction of naval forces would have symmetrical effects; they were oblivious to Soviet territorial advantages.

[51]While acknowledging Neil MacFarlane's general point, I do not see Soviet policy in the Gulf War, Iran, and Afghanistan in quite the same way he does. See his "Soviet Conceptions of Regional Security," *World Politics* 37 (April 1985), pp. 295–316.

be accepted on one side and rigorously enforced by the other. Those who advocate agreements with the USSR appear to see them as vehicles for finessing the incessant competition, but agreements are not self-enforcing. Improved communication, to clarify commitments and to establish over time certain rules of behavior toward the region, is, of course, to be welcomed. But improved communication is neither a substitute for military power nor an invitation to relax vigilance. Above all, it should not be construed as the adoption of a common perspective on the region.

8

The Soviet Union in the Middle East after Thirty Years

GALIA GOLAN

Soviet policy in the Middle East may be examined in terms of both Soviet behavior and the factors influencing or determining such behavior. After a brief look at the evolution of Soviet interests in the area over the past thirty years, therefore, I examine the tactics employed by the Soviets in pursuit of these interests, tactics that include creation of national fronts, friendship treaties, Marxist-Leninist vanguard parties, radical blocs of states, and the exploitation of internal and interstate conflicts. I also examine risk taking in overall Soviet Third World policy and the specific (internal and interstate) conflicts in the area. The relationship between risk taking and changes in tactics is examined for correlations suggesting a periodization of Soviet policy. Among the factors influencing Soviet policy, regional factors include the problems of Arab unity, nationalism, and Islamic fundamentalism; I conclude with global factors, primarily the influence of detente, and an analysis of the role of Soviet-American competition and Soviet willingness to engage in the Middle East in a cooperative rather than confrontational relationship with the United States.

Interests

Soviet interests in the region are well-known, but any attempt to draw conclusions from thirty years of Soviet involvement must nonetheless reiterate the shifts in priorities which have taken place in these interests. When the Soviet Union decided to undertake a more active policy in the Third World, after Stalin's death, it chose the areas closest to its borders. The overtures to Iran and Turkey made by Stalin's first successor, Georgii Malenkov, were manifestations of a logical concern for secure borders and friendly governments on these borders evident in earlier periods of Soviet foreign policy and undoubtedly operative today. One difference in 1953 was in priorities, that is,

Soviet willingness to forego its previously dominant ideological interest, which had dictated a confrontational, revolutionary policy. As the new Soviet leadership now perceived risks in such a confrontational policy in the nuclear era, Moscow adopted the Leninist position of cooperation and compromise with nonsocialist regimes and political groupings to ensure friendly, if non-communist, partners for the Soviet Union. A second difference in policies after Stalin's death was the move beyond the immediate border area, a move dictated by the elevation of another interest, the political global interest,—implicit in past policies but now to be pursued in a more pragmatic and competitive but less confrontational way. This new interest was given priority over the longer-term ideological interest and went beyond the narrow concern with border defense. In what may have been perceived as the beginning of the end of the Western colonial era, with the blooming of Third World nationalism, the Soviets now sought to dislocate the West from major areas; in the case in point Iraq, Syria, and Egypt were pursued with no less vigor than were Turkey and Iran. The nonalignment movement was encouraged, and the idea of Third World neutrality—indeed, the idea of a "Third World"—was supported for its anticolonial, anti-Western implications.

In time military and economic interests were joined to these primarily political interests. To be sure, there was always an element of military interest in traditional border security and in the access route through the Dardanelles to and from the Black Sea. In the 1960s, however, the military interest took unprecedented priority, primarily as a result of the expansion of the Soviet Navy, its forward deployment strategy, and efforts to counter America's and develop its own SSBN capacity. By no means limited to the Mediterranean and, later, the Indian Ocean, this change in size, posture, and role of the Soviet Navy brought with it a need for land-based facilities, that is, overseas air as well as naval bases, port facilities, and support systems to service, protect, and complement the fleet. Even with the changes in Soviet military doctrine in the 1970s emphasizing theater (especially European) warfare, Soviet military planning maintains the importance (though possibly reduced) of the Mediterranean down to the Red Sea as part of the southwestern theater TVD.[1] This doctrinal shift reduces the strategic importance of the Indian Ocean–Persian Gulf area somewhat, the southern TVD being of less importance or danger. Yet continuing SSBN requirements in the Indian Ocean, the importance of the southern sea route, and the traditional concern for a Western (that is, U.S.) move in the Gulf dictate a continued Soviet military interest in the area, perhaps of even higher priority than the eastern Mediterranean.[2]

---

[1] See Michael MccGwire, "Soviet Military Objectives," draft, 1985. Although MccGwire argues that the reduced SSBN—seek and destroy—role of the navy in favor of TVD warfare reduced the importance of Egypt, even that TVD role should accord importance to the Mediterranean Fleet.

[2] MccGwire attributes the continued SSBN role in this area to a compromise struck between the commander of the navy, Admiral Gorshkov and Defense Minister Grechko in 1974.

The Gulf holds an additional interest for the Soviet Union, that of trade or economics. If the Khrushchev era subordinated economic to political interests, often at some cost for the Soviet Union, in its efforts to penetrate the Third World, by the late 1960s and particularly the 1970s Moscow was much more concerned with a return on its investments.[3] This new concern was reflected in the balance of payments and trade figures with the Middle Eastern countries, the Soviet share improving and trade returns rising with the richer Gulf states.[4] Just what part the sale of Soviet arms played in this improvement is not documented, but it is clear that the Soviets began to demand hard-currency payments for arms deliveries in the early 1970s, and these sales are said to represent roughly 20 percent of Soviet hard-currency earnings.[5] The absence of any significant Soviet purchases of Middle Eastern oil, despite Soviet difficulties in meeting its own and Eastern Europe's energy requirements, strongly suggests that oil was not a major part of Soviet economic interests in the area and has not become one even as economic interests have risen in importance.[6] With this rise and the relative reduction of the military interest, the political interest has once again emerged as primary, undoubtedly because of the real progress made by the United States in challenging Soviet influence in the Middle East. This by no means excludes the other interests; indeed, a characteristic of Soviet policy as it has emerged over the past thirty years is its greater sophistication or multidimensionality. Nor does competition necessarily mean confrontation, as we shall see in our discussion of tactics and risk taking. It does, however, reflect the Soviets' perception of the vulnerability of all their interests when the political is left in a subordinate position.

Tactics

The above conclusion may be derived, at least in part, from the evolution of Soviet tactics in the pursuit of various interests over the past three decades.

---

[3]Elizabeth Valkenier, "Soviet Economic Relations with the Third World," in Roger Kanet, ed., *The Soviet Union and the Developing Nations* (Baltimore: Johns Hopkins University Press, 1974), pp. 215–236.

[4]See Gur Ofer, "Economic Aspects of Soviet Involvement in the Middle East," in Y. Ro'i, ed., *The Limits to Power* (London: Croom-Helm, 1979), pp. 67–95.

[5]Roger Kanet, "Soviet Military Assistance to the Third World," in J. Cooper and D. Papp, *Communist Nations Military Assistance* (Boulder: Westview, 1983), pp. 39–63; U.S. Arms Control and Disarmament Agency, *World Military Expenditures and Arms Transfers* (Washington, D.C., 1982).

[6]The energy issue has been discussed voluminously elsewhere. As for the claim that the Soviet interest in oil is political-strategic (i.e., the possibility of access denial for the West) rather than economic, (1) the Soviets are far from possessing sufficient control over the oil-producing states and, in any case, could interfere in oil shipping without a large presence in the area; (2) such interference would be a *casus belli*, undoubtedly deemed worth avoiding; and (3) Western dependence on the Middle East has long been viewed as a temporary situation while alternative sources were sought and found.

Whether the ideological interest was reduced in importance because of concern for a less confrontational policy in the nuclear era or whether its reduction was deemed tactically more expedient because of the obstacle of local nationalism (and religion) may be moot. In fact the major tactic for Moscow's competitive move into the Middle East was cooperation with "bourgeois nationalists" (some of whom, such as Nasser, had previously been called "fascist lackeys"), often at the expense of local Communists. Broad political fronts were encouraged as providing means for cooperation, ostensibly creating a basis for communist participation in societies and regimes that were unreceptive to Communists, sometimes to the point of persecuting and outlawing the party. But in fact such cooperation was more suspect in the eyes of the communist parties than the regime parties, for these broad fronts usually served to subordinate and restrain the growth and influence of the Communists. Thus the Soviets might acclaim the achievements of such fronts in Iraq and Syria in the early 1970s or even in the Iranian revolution, but in no case did the front prevent the persecution of Communists; in the case of Syria it led to a split in the party, in Iraq and Iran to virtual destruction.[7] In the case of Egypt, the idea of cooperation led as far as the actual dissolution of the Communist party, although it is not clear that such was the intention of the Soviet Union.[8]

National fronts were the overt form of what the Soviets presumably hoped would be increased communist influence; clandestine penetration and politicking obviously were also employed. Often this meant taking sides in political infighting, as in the Jedid-Assad rivalry in the Syrian Ba'ath, or the nurturing of the Ali-Sabry group in Egypt, or the support of Mossadaq in Iran. Often it included penetration of security and army forces as well. The client regimes tended to guard their independence, however, and the Soviets themselves discovered that personalities were an unreliable anchor in the swirling sea of Middle East politics. It may have been this realization, particularly after Nasser's death and the arrest of Ali-Sabry, which led to a new Soviet tactic, the contracting of treaties of friendship and mutual assistance. Urged by Gamal Abdul Nasser over the years to enter such an agreement, the Soviets reversed themselves in 1971 and pressed Anwar Sadat into a treaty.[9]

[7]See John Cooley, "The Shifting Sands of Arab Communism," *Problems of Communism* 24, nos. 1–2 (1975), pp. 24–42; Robert Freedman, "The Soviet Union and the Communist Parties of the Arab World," in R. Kanet and D. Bahry, eds., *Soviet Economic and Political Relations with the Developing World* (New York: Praeger, 1974), pp. 100–134; Jaan Pennar, *The USSR and the Arabs: The Ideological Dimension* (London: Hurst, 1973), pp. 29–61.

[8]Mohamed Heikal claims that there were differences of opinion within the Soviet Politburo on this issue; certainly there was opposition among some Middle Eastern Communists. Heikal, *The Sphinx and the Commissar* (New York: Collins, 1978), pp. 156–161. See also Shimon Shamir, "The Marxists in Egypt," in Shamir and M. Confino, *The USSR and the Middle East* (Jerusalem: Israel Universities Press, 1973), pp. 292–319.

[9]Heikal claims that the treaty was Sadat's idea, but inasmuch as the Soviets had earlier rejected similar proposals by Nasser, one may assume that at the very least something had changed in the Soviet view of the idea. Moreover, Sadat indicated that it was the Russians who insisted on the treaty (Heikal, *Sphinx and Commissar*, p. 227).

Thus they went beyond the neutrality encouraged in the 1950s and 1960s to seek a more formal allegiance. Presumably the major motivating factor was Soviet fear of losing military facilities in Egypt, but the subsequent campaign to obtain similar treaties with other Third World countries suggests that Moscow now perceived such treaties as a possibly more binding vehicle for securing friendly relations, particularly in countries where there were Soviet facilities but also in countries, such as India, which held more general political-strategic importance.

Whether the Soviets had such a treaty, as with Egypt, or lacked one, as in the case of Syria (which refused to sign one until 1980), Moscow upon occasion had to revert to a more direct tactic: arms blackmail. Attempts to use this tactic occurred, for example, when Sadat expelled Soviet advisers in 1972. Moscow removed (refusing to sell or leave) important equipment as well as personnel and suspended arms deliveries completely for three months and almost completely for another four to five months. The tactic failed totally, and arms deliveries were resumed without any change in Egyptian policy or positions.[10] Similarly in 1976 the Soviets suspended arms deliveries to Syria in opposition to that country's invasion of Lebanon. In this case, too, deliveries were resumed without any change on the Syrian side.[11] Other possible cases may have involved Iraq as early as 1963 in response to anticommunist massacres and, reportedly, in 1975 when Iraqi-Syrian relations deteriorated badly.[12]

Marxist-Leninist Vanguard Parties

For the Soviets, none of these tactics succeeded in winning a degree of control over these countries sufficient to protect Soviet interests, influence local policies, or prevent anticommunist or even anti-Soviet behavior. Indeed, it was probably the defection of Egypt which led the Soviets to rethink their entire Third World strategy in the 1970s. They now seriously doubted that cooperation with bourgeois nationalists, or even revolutionary-democratic regimes, which were by definition not yet Marxist-Leninist, could lead to the desired results. A solution was sought in a new tactic—which some have interpreted as the reinstatement of the ideological interest—in the form of seeking to build Marxist-Leninist ruling parties.[13] From the Soviet point

---

[10]See Galia Golan, *Yom Kippur and After: The Soviet Union and the Middle East Crisis* (Cambridge: Cambridge University Press, 1977), pp. 25–42; Golan, "Decision-making in the Yom Kippur War," in J. Valenta and W. Potter, *Soviet Decisionmaking for National Security* (London: Allen & Unwin, 1983), pp. 192–196.

[11]*Al-Akhbar* (Amman), March 15, 1976; *Ruz al-Yusuf* (Cairo), July 26, 1976; *An-Nahar Arab Report*, August 30, 1976; Iraqi News Agency (INA), July 15, 1976; Deutsch Agence Presse (DPA), August 18, 1976. See also P. E. Haley and L. Snider, *Lebanon in Crisis* (Syracuse: Syracuse University Press, 1979), p. 221.

[12]Cf. Francis Fukuyama, "The Soviet Union and Iraq since 1968" (Santa Monica: RAND Corporation, 1980), p. 25.

[13]Ibid., p. 56.

of view, it was not only the reliance upon certain personalities that led to failure or at best ephemeral success, but also the failure of these personalities to build a stable political organization based on the principles of scientific socialism.[14] Soviet theoretical works were full of the necessity to build such a party, and the 1978 coups d'état in Afghanistan and South Yemen, the apparent coup attempt in Iraq, and clear Soviet pressure on the Ethiopian Dergue to convert itself into a Marxist-Leninist vanguard party, all seemed to attest to such a switch in tactics. Indeed, Moscow had never abandoned the belief that ultimately the most loyal ally was a communist one, and even as ideological interests declined, Soviet tactics had retained parallel activities—at the government level and the party level. Even when it meant dealing with parties such as the Ba'ath or coalitions and national fronts, or at the extreme, as in Egypt, dissolution of the Communist party, communist activity and the development of Marxist-oriented revolutionaries had continued. The change now was one of priorities, that is, a demand for the conversion of the revolutionary-democratic parties to Marxist parties or the elevation of Marxist parties themselves. There was a good deal of debate among Soviet Third World specialists, including party figures, over this tactic, however, some expressing doubts about its timeliness or applicability.[15] By the early 1980s leadership pronouncements suggested a skepticism that a prematurely organized Marxist-Leninist party could ensure eventual scientific socialism. Such skepticism was apparent in pronouncements by Leonid Brezhnev and especially Yuriy Andropov, suggesting less than full support for the tactic and possible retreat from it altogether.[16]

Looking at Soviet policies specifically in the Middle East, one sees little actual change or evidence of the introduction of a new tactic. The purported coup attempt in Iraq was probably little more than Saddam Hussein's hostility to and concern over the usual Communist activities (which may have increased somewhat in magnitude but never achieved the proportions of a coup).[17] The 1978 coup in Afghanistan does not appear to have been a Soviet-engineered affair, though the Daoud regime was no longer to be counted amongst Moscow's "positively neutral" parties. The coup in South Yemen, replacing a leftist regime with a more militant Marxist one, did receive Soviet aid, but it may have been no less anomalous and fortuitous (in potential) than the Communist-supported coup attempt in the Sudan in 1971. In no way was it reflected or repeated elsewhere. Cooperation with existing regimes, some revolutionary-democratic, some more nationalist or bourgeois or even tradi-

---

[14]This is pointed out in R. A. Ul'ianovskii, "O natsional' noi i revoliutsionnoi demokratii: puti evolutsii," *Narody Azii i Afriki* no. 2 (1984), pp. 14–16, and K. N. Brutents, *Osvobodivshiesia strany v 70-e gody* (Moscow: Politizdat, 1979), p. 68.

[15]On this debate see Valkenier, "Soviet Economic Relations," and my forthcoming "The Soviet Union and National Liberation Movements," chap. 4.

[16]*Pravda*, June 16, 1983, and Moscow domestic radio, April 22, 1982 (*FBIS* III, April 23, 1982, R-7), Andropov; *Pravda*, February 24, 1987, Brezhnev.

[17]See Fukuyama, "Soviet Union," p. 59; Karen Dawisha, "Moscow's Moves in the Direction of the Gulf" (Washington: Wilson Center, 1980), pp. 9–13.

tional, continued; it included not only Qadhdhafi but even hopeful support, as long as possible, for Khomeini. Whatever the Soviets hoped or planned for a possible future coalition in Iran, they made no attempt to exploit the turmoil there for communist power or to convert the revolution into a Marxist one. Soviet interests and perhaps realism dictated this course of action, but the policy provides no evidence for the theory that the Soviets had shifted to a more ideological orientation or abandoned the tactics of cooperation with non-Marxist regimes.

Even if cooperation with non-Marxists was generally continued and revolutionary activity was not undertaken everywhere, however, it is still possible that the events of 1978 did represent an attempt to apply a new tactic. Those events coincided with another Soviet tactic designed to further Soviet interests in the Middle East, that is, an effort to forge a bloc of radical Arab states, particularly following the Camp David accords in the fall of 1978, though it was in evidence since the mid-1970s. This tactic was familiar, employed many times over the past thirty years, usually in the name of promoting Arab unity. In fact, such unity was not always the most desirable objective for Moscow, particularly when pan-Arabism threatened to fortify positions independent of Moscow, as in the late 1950s. It was, however, encouraged when Soviet allies in the area were pitted against one another in battles that offered the Soviets few options acceptable to all concerned (often embarrassing Moscow or forcing it to take sides). It was also encouraged when tactically useful to counter American inroads, as in the post–Camp David period. But the effort to forge a radical bloc in 1978 was no less temporary than previous efforts, giving way in the 1980s to a stepped-up attempt to improve relations with the moderate states in the area (including even Israel to some degree). And if the radical bloc was only a temporary tactic that failed, perhaps the more revolutionary thrust of 1978—if that is what it was—also was only temporary, with Brezhnev's 1981 Congress speech signaling a rethinking.

Exploitation of Conflicts

Still another tactic employed in the Middle East, as elsewhere, was the exploitation of conflicts. Such conflicts have never been lacking. The major one providing the Soviets an entree into the region has been the Arab-Israeli conflict, but there have been others as well: those of various minorities (the Kurds, the Dhofars, the Eritreans) and those among states, as in the Yemeni crises. Yet a closer examination indicates that the Soviets neither consistently nor indiscriminately encouraged conflicts for their own sake; nor did they necessarily view a situation of conflict as ipso facto beneficial. The Kurds and Eritreans are two cases in point. Although most Communists in Iraq, for example, are Kurds and the Iraqi Communist party at least once split over the matter, the Soviet Union has only intermittently supported the Kurdish struggle and, on occasion, even assisted the Iraqi government to put down the Kurdish rebellion by force. Similarly, Moscow supported the Eritrean struggle prior to the 1974 revolution in Ethiopia but assisted the central government in fighting the Eritreans after the revolution. Less dramatic but similar has been Soviet support for the Kurdish and other minority struggles in Iran; the Arabs in Khuzistan have apparently never received Soviet support. The key to the Soviet attitude toward these minorities' conflicts obviously lay in what the Soviets deem their greater interest in relations with the state involved. When Soviet-Iraqi relations were uncertain, Moscow was willing to assist the Kurds, perhaps even encouraging them so as to destabilize an unfriendly government in Baghdad. In periods of good state-to-state relations, conversely, the Soviets proved their loyalty by active military assistance against the minority.[18] Support for the Dhofars was and is apparently determined by regional rather than exclusively local considerations, while Soviet concern over Iranian reaction has been the determining factor regarding support of the minorities inside Iran proper, particularly since the revolution of 1979. I return to the regional factors below but must note here a further refinement of Soviet positions. Officially the Soviet Union opposes separatist movements. This opposition is consistently expressed in Soviet literature and was reiterated by Brezhnev in his April 1981 Rules speech.[19] Outside observers have suggested that this opposition stems from Soviet concern over the stability of its own federal system,[20] though it may simply be respect for a consensus in the Third World regarding the borders of new states. Whatever the explanation, Moscow not only officially opposes secessionists, it actually limits the support it gives to what are in fact separatist movements, to advance the objective of autonomy or self-determination within some sort of federal relationship rather than full independence. The Soviet definition of self-determination contains the *right* to statehood or secession but not the necessity of such a solution (the good of the whole or the proletariat's interests being the ostensible criterion).[21] When Moscow supports the objective of independence, it is careful to characterize the movement in question as purely anticolonial rather than separatist. The result is no less pragmatic; Moscow does occasionally find it expedient, as in the cases of Oman and Bangladesh, to support a separatist movement, but on the whole it has been *relatively* consistent in opposing secession as such even when supporting what are in fact secessionist movements.

---

[18]Fukuyama, "Soviet Union," pp. 37–40.

[19]TASS, April 27, 1981.

[20]E.g., Ilya Levkov, in Y. Alexander and R. Friedland, eds., *Self-Determination within the Community of Nations* (Leiden: Sijthoff, 1967), pp. 52.5; U. Umozurike, *Self-Determination in International Law* (Hamden, Ct.: Archon, 1972), pp. 161–168.

[21]See, for example, A. A. Gromyko and G. B. Starushenkó, "Sotsial'nye inatsional'nye faktory razvitiia osvobodivshikhsia stran" *Sotsiologicheskie issledovaniia* no. 1 (1983), pp. 5–7; Gleb Starushenko, "International Law and National Liberation," *International Affairs* no. 2 (1983), p. 84; V. F. Gryzlov, "Protiv fal'sifikatsii antikommunistami FRT leninska teorii o prave narodov na samoopredelenie," *Nauchnyi kommunizm* no. 3 (1977), p. 113; R. Ulyanovsky, *National Liberation: Essays on Theory and Practice* (Moscow: Progress, 1978), pp. 136–145.

Interstate conflicts have been even more problematic for the Soviets. Egyptian-Iraqi rivalry may at times have served Soviet purposes, either to limit Nasser's pan-Arabist ambitions or to play one state off against the other in hopes of gaining a greater foothold. Anti-Egyptian behavior was certainly encouraged after Camp David. On the whole, however, such hostilities—for example, between Syria and Iraq, Syria and Jordan, Iraq and Iran, Iraq and Kuwait, even on occasion the two Yemens—have not been welcomed (nor been initiated) by the Soviets. The reasons presumably are: (1) such internecine fighting prevents any type of united policy favoring the Soviets against the West or provides an opportunity for the West to exploit the situation for polarization; (2) these struggles place the Soviets in the uncomfortable position of having to choose sides, often between two allies or at least between states with whom Moscow hopes to maintain correct, even good relations; and (3) these conflicts can erupt, escalate, and spread into all-out war and serious risks for the Soviets, which at the very least place Soviet credibility in the balance. Examples are the Syrian move into Jordan in September 1970, with or without Soviet knowledge but opposed at least after the fact because of the America-Israeli threat; and the June 1976 Syrian invasion of Lebanon, opposed because it strengthened Assad's stubborn independence vis-à-vis Moscow, linked the Syrians and Americans (at least temporarily), pitted the Syrians against a Soviet ally, the PLO, and threatened all-out war between Israel and Syria. The Soviets were so disturbed by this conflict that they even condoned a peace mediated by the Saudis. Even as circumstances and opponents changed in Lebanon, the Soviets remained concerned over the possibility of an all-out war and, later, confrontation with the United States.

Perhaps the most compelling example of undesirable conflict is the Iraq-Iran war, between two states with whom the Soviets had hoped to maintain positive relations. Originally the Soviets, though formally allied with Iraq, took what was in effect a pro-Iranian "neutral" position. They halted Soviet arms supplies to Iraq, which had been increasingly unfriendly to the Soviets prior to the war, in hopes of impressing the post-revolution regime in Iran. Although they thus exploited the conflict, the Soviets cannot have been pleased to further the deterioration in Soviet-Iraqi relations and, in any case, were accused by each side of favoring the other by proclaimed neutrality (inasmuch as both sides sought an *active* Soviet position). Moreover, the conflict threatened to unite the Gulf states behind Saudi Arabia in a pro-Western alliance or at the least to provide an excuse for the West to increase its military presence in the Gulf for the purpose of containing the conflict (and protecting the Gulf states). When Soviet-Iranian relations deteriorated, the Soviets shifted back to Iraq. They still sought a resolution to the conflict, however, in part because they had not abandoned the possibility of better relations with Iran but also in part because the conflict split the Arab world, complicating relations with pro-Iranian Syria in particular. Moreover, the war still had the potential for escalation and an increased U.S. presence.

This is not to say that the Soviets never favor or benefit from interstate conflicts in the region. Moscow probably welcomed the (albeit brief) Syrian-Iraqi rapprochement of the late 1970s and the 1975 Iraq-Iran agreement that halted the Kurdish war. In the former case, however, the Soviets exhibited little enthusiasm, perhaps because they feared a more independent, more demanding, and more aggressive Syrian-Iraqi alliance. Regarding the latter, Moscow (and the local Communists) clearly lost ground with Iraq once Baghdad no longer needed Soviet assistance against the Kurds and Iran. Nonetheless, given the complications and risks of conflict, the Soviets may not have viewed the benefits as outweighing the costs or potential risks of continued conflict.

Use of the Arab-Israeli Conflict

Nowhere is the use of conflicts more salient or, perhaps, controversial than in the central conflict of the region, the Arab-Israeli conflict. It is undeniable that the Soviets exploited this conflict to facilitate their entry into the region in the 1950s, supplying arms, training, and political assistance to the Arab states involved while emphasizing the American commitment to Israel. The most blatant attempt at manipulation of the conflict to further Soviet interests was perhaps the incitement of Egypt and Syria in 1967 leading (probably unexpectedly for Moscow) to the Six Day War. Designed to strengthen the Atassi regime in Syria and forge a more vibrant anti-American front between Egypt and Syria, exacerbation of the conflict was perceived as beneficial—and also, presumably but mistakenly, as controllable. Although the war did provide Moscow with an opportunity to obtain the naval and air bases it had sought in Egypt since 1964, the Soviets had no reason beforehand to believe that a massive Arab defeat would in fact be the result of the war. Indeed, there were signs that the Soviets were fearful that war would actually break out, persuaded the Egyptians that Israel would not strike, and were both embarrassed and angry over the results once fighting commenced.[22] The Soviets used the conflict to gain the position of Arab representative in the ensuing negotiations (the two-power and four-power talks), but there are signs that when this position became too dangerous, as in the 1969–70 war of attrition, the Soviets sought to defuse the conflict rather than fan the flames to increase Arab dependence.

In fact, particularly in the interwar period, it was not entirely clear that the conflict was not manipulating the Soviet Union. The Arab states, which had always guarded their independence to some degree, became even more independent, in part because of aid from oil-rich states; in part, in Egypt, because

---

[22]Tunis radio, April 12, 1974; A. Horelick, "Soviet Policy in the Middle East," in S. Alexander and P. Hammond, eds., *Political Dynamics in the Middle East* (New York: American Elsevier, 1972), pp. 581–591.

of the rise of Sadat; in part, perhaps, because the Soviets began to demand hard-currency payments for arms and generally more profitable economic relations. If the Soviets ever had really controlled the conflict, their control was virtually eliminated (as demonstrated before and during the Yom Kippur War). If control of the conflict was in question, continuation of the conflict became all the more risky, particularly given the American involvement and Washington's advances after 1973. The conflict could and still can be used to discredit the United States (as Israel's chief ally) and to remind the Arabs of their need for a superpower supporter. However, fewer and fewer Arabs are convinced that the Soviet Union has to be that superpower and that the United States is so inaccessible. Thus Soviet gains have been limited, the risks increasingly high. This tactic probably is no longer perceived as optimally useful in cases where other tactics can be used to preserve Soviet interests.

In the Arab-Israeli context one alternative has been the Soviets' pursuit of participation in the peace process, that is, a role in achieving and securing, as co-guarantor, a settlement of the conflict so as to remain in the region through internationally agreed upon arrangements that legitimize and formalize Soviet interests there. These two tactics, exploiting the conflict and pursuing its settlement, need not be mutually exclusive. Such was the case in 1970, when the Soviets engaged in peak activity at the military level with 20,000 military advisers present in Egypt and Soviet pilots flying combat missions but simultaneously presented their most forthcoming proposals vis-à-vis Israel's borders and a peace settlement.[23] A situation of conflict thus can be exploited, even exacerbated, to persuade the United States and Israel of the necessity of Soviet inclusion in the negotiating process (as the party able to control the Arab side and, therefore, the war option). Yet this tactic has been not only risky but decreasingly effective, and there are signs that the Soviets, perhaps as a result of their change in leadership, are seeking other means to prove their indispensability—specifically to Israel. If between the Yom Kippur and Lebanese wars the Soviets sought to play the Palestinian card tactically, to embarrass the Americans, after the Lebanese War temporary American inroads into the Palestinian camp may have been behind Soviet overtures to Israel and hints regarding the Syrian front as the only front where the United States has as yet no leverage.[24] At the same time, as already mentioned, the attempt to create a radical bloc has given way to a wooing of the moderate Arab states in hopes generally of broadening Soviet options and specifically of gaining the moderates' and Israel's agreement to include Moscow in discussions on the Middle East, through the vehicle of an international conference. Inasmuch as these moves toward the moderate states have

[23]Evgenii Primakov, *Pravda*, October 15, 1970, cited by L. L. Whetten, *The Canal War* (Cambridge: MIT Press, 1974), p. 115.

[24]According to the alleged contents of talks between the Soviet and Israeli ambassadors in Paris (see *Jerusalem Post*, July 21, 1985).

occurred despite Syrian opposition, one may conclude that the broadening of Soviet options and inclusion in the peace negotiations outweigh Soviet concern over effects on Moscow's present relationship with Syria.

Risk Taking

The overriding consideration with regard to any and virtually all of the above tactics has been the matter of risk taking—just how far the Soviets are willing to go to secure their interests in the Third World, specifically the Middle East. Soviet theoretical literature has undergone numerous changes and exhibits a wide spectrum of opinions on such questions as the importance of the Third World, the type of assistance the Soviets rather than indigenous local forces should render, the conditions created by detente and Western posture, power projection, limited war, and the possibility of escalation. Views range from interventionist (expressed by the need to combat "the export of counter-revolution") all the way to nearly isolationist (expressed by the need to bolster the Soviet Union first), and to fulfill its international function merely by serving as an example for the rest of the world.[25] Detente has been interpreted as creating favorable conditions for Soviet involvement at lower risk, variously as a restraining factor on the West or as obviating any need for intervention because of Western restraint.[26] Similarly, Western hostility (the absence of detente) has been emphasized as justifying a need actively to protect interests in the Third World or warning against high-risk interventionist policies. Chronologically, "Soviet Union first" was one of the attitudes that emerged from the post-Khrushchev debate of the late 1960s, presumably playing a role in what Elizabeth Valkenier then pointed out was a shift to economically more beneficial policies in the Third World.[27] Signs of this attitude appeared throughout the 1970s, but the Soviet role was increasingly defined in interventionist terms. Beginning in 1981, however, what had been occasionally expressed positions appeared to become a new policy line, a return to the Soviet Union–first idea.[28] This line emerged side by side

[25]These differing positions are covered in my forthcoming "Soviet Union and National Liberation Movements," chap. 5.

[26]For the latter attitude see, for example, Brutents, *Pravda*, August 30, 1983, or Brutents, *Osvobodivshiesia strany*, p. 128.

[27]Valkenier, "Soviet Economic Relations," pp. 215–236.

[28]K. N. Brutents, "A Great Force of Modern Times," *International Affairs* no. 3 (1981), pp. 83–84; An. Gromyko, "XXVI s'ezd KPSS i zadachi sovetskoi afrikanistiki," *Narody Azii i Afriki* no. 4 (1981), pp. 3–13; Gromyko, "Sovetskaia politika mira i Afrika," p. 2; A. Gromyko, "The Imperialist Threat to Africa," *International Affairs* no. 7 (1981), pp. 47–53; G. Kim, "Sovetskii soiuz i natsional'no-osvoboditel'noe dvizhenie," *Mirovaia ekonomika i mezhdunosodnye otrosheniia* no. 9 (1982), pp. 29–30; Iu. S. Novopashin, "Vozdeistvie real'nogo sotsializma na mirovoi revoliutsionnyi protsess: metodologicheskie aspekty," *Voprosy filosofii* no. 8 (1982), p. 6; P. Ia. Koshelev, "Ekonomicheskoe sotrudnichestvo SSSR s afiikanskimi gosudarstvami," *Narody Azii i Afrika* no. 2 (1982), pp. 8–9 (cited in F. Fukuyama, "Moscow's Post-Brezhnev Reassessment of the Third World" [Santa Monica: RAND Corporation, 1985], p. 30); Iu. A. Krasin, "Uzlovaia problema strategii kommunistov," *Rabochii klass i sovremennyi mir* no. 1 (1977), pp. 35–49.

with an increasingly pessimistic view of the West and "imperialist aggressive-ness," appearing first at the end of detente and after the Afghanistan invasion and mushrooming in the first year of the Reagan administration. Soviet military writing did not follow this sequence, however; rather, it reflected a variety of sometimes contradictory appraisals not only of Western aggressive-ness but of the whole issue of escalation connected with the concepts of limited war and power projection. There were those, throughout the 1970s and into the 1980s, who upheld Khrushchev's belief in the inevitability of escalation of local conflicts and, therefore, the high risk of power projection in the Third World.[29] Yet there were also those who viewed escalation as having a relatively low probability and advocated power projection even in local conflicts to combat the export of counter-revolution.[30]

The indecisiveness of the military literature may indicate continuation of the debate, connected perhaps with more general questions of military doc-trine, to the present. Leadership pronouncements, however, suggest conclu-sions closer to the trend apparent among academic and party theoreticians.

Views of the Political Leadership

The Twenty-fourth Congress of the CPSU in 1971 reflected the rethinking about the Third World of the late 1960s, with its Soviet Union–first theme. The change could be seen both in speeches by Brezhnev and Gromyko and in an article by Ponomarev on the Congress, in which he quoted Lenin to the effect that the Soviet Union's economic example is its main influence on the world revolutionary process.[31] Yet Brezhnev also struck a relatively optimis-tic note regarding the potential for socialism in the Third World. This note appeared to be reinforced when, obviously in response to Castro's position during the latter's 1972 visit to Moscow, Brezhnev and Kosygin introduced

[29]See Rajan Menon, *Soviet Power and the Third World: Aspects of Theory and Practice* (New Haven: Yale University Press, 1986); Maj. Gen. A. Skrylnik, "Under Lenin's Banner," *Soviet Military Review* no. 4 (1984), pp. 5–7; Gen. C. Svedin, "Real Socialism and the Leninist Peace Policy," ibid., pp. 3–4; N. Nikitin, "Nekotorye operativnotacticheskie uroki lokal'nykh voin imperializma," *Voenno-istorcheskii zhurnal* no. 12 (1978), p. 6; Col. E. Dolgopolov, "Razobla-chenie burzhuaznykh i maoistskikeh falsifikatorov istorii lokal'nykh voin," ibid. no. 6 (1980), pp. 58, 62; V. L. Tiagunenko, et al., "Vooruzhennaia bor'ba narodov Afriki za svobodu i nezavisimost'," Ministerstvo oborony SSSR (Moscow, 1974), p. 409.

[30]See Mark Katz, *The Third World in Soviet Military Thinking* (Baltimore: Johns Hopkins University Press, 1982), p. 97; Maj. Gen. Ye. Dolgopolov, "On Principle of Equality," *Soviet Military Review* no. 1 (1984), p. 49; Maj. Gen. D. Volkogonov et al., *Voina i armiia: Filosofsko-sotsiologicheskii ocherk* (Moscow: Voenizdat, 1977), pp. 248–249, 353–354; Lt. Gen. D. Vol-kogonov, "The Soviet Army," *Soviet Military Review* no. 2 (1984), p. 3; Col. G. Malinovskii, "Lokal'nye voiny v zone natsional'noosvoboditel'nogo dvizheniia," *Voenno-istoricheskii zhurnal* no. 5 (1974), pp. 97–98; and, with some ambivalence, Gen. I. Shavrov, "Lokal'nye voiny i ikh mesto v global'noi strategii imperializma," Part I, ibid. no. 3 (1975), pp. 57–66; Part II, ibid. no. 4 (1975), pp. 90–97.

[31]*Pravda*, March 31, 1971 (Brezhnev); *Pravda*, April 4, 1971 (Gromyko); Boris Ponomarev, "Under the Banner of Marxism-Leninism," *World Marxist Review* no. 6 (1971), p. 1.

the idea of the divisibility of detente, that is, detente between states but the continuation of revolutionary activity in the Third World.[32] This line became most explicit with the Twenty-fifth Congress in 1976, when Brezhnev declared that detente and revolutionary activity were not contradictory, promised every kind of Soviet assistance for Third World struggles, and cited Angola as an example of such aid.[33] Virtually all Soviet officials, with the notable exception of Andropov, echoed this more enthusiastic attitude.[34]

The Twenty-sixth Congress in 1981 was apparently the peak for the CPSU of Brezhnev's interest in the Third World. Here Brezhnev advanced what may be interpreted as the line of greatest Soviet involvement: the commitment to fight the export of counter-revolution. Yet he was also decidedly less enthusiastic about the Third World's potential than he had been at the 1976 Congress.[35] Thus while the theoretical literature was advocating the Soviet Union–first position, and the military appeared undecided, the leadership was still advocating an activist albeit less optimistic position. Shortly after the Congress, however, in his April "Rules" speech, Brezhnev articulated a definitely more restrained position, proposing as it were limits for both superpowers in the Third World. He followed in the fall of 1982 with a call to both NATO and the Warsaw Pact to refrain from activity in the Third World.[36] Shortly thereafter Brezhnev held a meeting with his military commanders in which he outlined the country's economic difficulties—a warning perhaps that they should expect some curtailment of their more ambitious plans?[37] This position became dominant as Andropov and then Gorbachev put their stamp on foreign policy. Both Andropov and Gorbachev dropped the promise to combat the export of counter-revolution, offering no more than "sympathy" for Third World peoples.[38] At the Twenty-seventh Party Congress in 1986, Gorbachev mentioned only the opposition to counter-revolution in a paragraph on international terrorism, and the new CPSU program, while condemning the export of counter-revolution, repeated the Soviet Union–first theme and the force of the Soviet example. If the major factors contributing to the change in Soviet thinking were the Soviets' economic situation and the need for detente, as well as a high-risk appraisal of the Reagan administration's policies and, possibly, the setbacks actually experienced in the Third World, little has occurred in any of these spheres to warrant a shift in Soviet thinking.

---

[32]*Pravda*, June 28, 1972 (Brezhnev); *Pravda*, July 4, 1972 (Kosygin).

[33]*Pravda*, February 25, 1976.

[34]For Andropov see, for example, *Pravda*, April 23, 1976 or February 23, 1979.

[35]*Pravda*, February 24, 1981.

[36]TASS, April 27, 1982; TASS, September 20, 1982. See Fukuyama, "Moscow's . . . Reassessment," p. 30.

[37]TASS, October 27, 1982.

[38]*Pravda*, November 23, 1982; *Pravda*, June 16, 1983; *Pravda*, March 12, 1985. See Stephen Sestanovich in *Washington Post*, May 29, 1984.

Soviet Behavior

To what degree were Soviet thinking and leadership pronouncements reflected in actual Soviet risk taking in the Middle East? It is, of course, difficult to delineate risk taking inasmuch as heavy involvement, even intervention, may not signal greater risk taking if the Soviet estimate of a confrontational Western response is low. Table 1 charts Soviet behavior in Middle East crises over the past fifteen years, indicating how much the Soviets were willing to become involved.

If we characterize actual use of force as the greatest degree of risk taking, the Soviets were willing to take the greatest of risks on only one occasion—Afghanistan in 1979. They did so at a time when Soviet theoretical works were already hesitant about overseas involvement but before the leadership changed its attitudes. More to the point, probably, they did so at a time when, despite the demise of detente (or perhaps because this demise meant there was little to lose), U.S. policy was not perceived as particularly confrontational. Certainly the Soviet estimate regarding the risks involved must have been low, with Jimmy Carter in the White House and U.S. policy bogged down in the Iranian hostage crisis. Yet this was the first case of Soviet military intervention in the Middle East since the 1945–46 occupation of parts of Iran. An extreme measure, the Soviet Armed Forces were not used in any of the other Middle East crises. Nor has actual force ever been used to preserve a Soviet presence in the Middle East, for example, when this presence was threatened by the client regime in Egypt in 1972 or Iraq in 1978. Indeed, the Soviets have not used actual force anywhere else in the Third World. Therefore one may conclude that this was a special case, probably more akin to Soviet interventions to preserve Marxist regimes on its borders in Europe than to a policy of power projection in the Third World or specifically the Middle East.

If the Soviets have been unwilling to use direct military intervention to secure their interests, they had available to them another step that could be termed a high-risk action: the threat of intervention. Aside from veiled warnings, less than ultimatums, a direct threat to intervene militarily has come from the Soviets only once in the past fifteen years: on October 24, 1973, at the close of the Yom Kippur War. The only other such threats to the area also came at the close of Arab-Israeli wars, in 1956 and in 1967, although in the former case the threat was clearly a propaganda bid, coming after the crisis was almost over. Again, the example is isolated, not only for the Middle East but for the Third World as a whole. In 1973 the threat came at a time of increasing Soviet interest in the Third World, though not necessarily in this part of the Middle East. It was an uncertain time of actual warfare and a clear American commitment to Israel. But the threat also came after the major fighting had halted, when the outcome was clear and cooperation with the

United States was such that Moscow felt assured that Washington could and would restrain Israel, precluding any need to implement the threat.[39] There was great risk involved, but nowhere near the degree of risk had the Soviet threat come at the height of the battle (when Israel was gaining the upper hand over Syria and then Egypt) and prior to Henry Kissinger's trip to Moscow.

Why was the Soviet Union willing to take even this limited risk (in three Arab-Israeli wars, although not in the war of 1982) when it had not previously—nor has since—taken such a step in any other Third World crisis? One assumes that the answer lies in the fact that the stakes were high, all of Moscow's interests in the area being threatened (which was not the case in Lebanon in 1982) in what was probably perceived as a zero-sum game vis-à-vis the United States should the regimes fall in Egypt and possibly Syria. The risk of Western intervention was still perceived as too high to warrant direct military intervention but not so high as to rule out the threat of such action. Moreover, it must be emphasized, only in the Arab-Israel context have the Soviets been willing to go as far as a direct threat even though, or perhaps because, this conflict, unlike the others, is so directly connected with superpower interests and global strategic rivalry.

If the Horn of Africa is viewed as an extension of the Middle East, one notes the use of intervention by proxy on one occasion in the area. Even if we assume Cuban willingness to act on other occasions, the paucity of actual cases suggests that intervention by proxy is also perceived as high-risk behavior. In the Middle East, as distinct from Africa, the American commitment—and the presence of the Sixth Fleet—may account for a different appraisal of risk. Presumably for this reason, proxy participation in the Middle East has never gone beyond the service of small numbers of Cuban and North Korean advisers (probably negotiated independently with Soviet approval). With regard to national liberation movements, proxy action has been even less direct: in the case of Eritreans and Palestinians, Cuban activity was probably totally independent; in the case of Dhofar it was probably merely a Soviet response, of an extremely low-risk nature, to a PDRY request for logistical assistance, rather than use of PDRY troops as proxy.

The use of military advisers (though limited in numbers), Soviet or other, even to the point of active participation in certain combat positions, would appear to be the borderline of risk taking for the Soviets. From this activity through direct arms supplies to diplomatic political activity, one sees an increasing Soviet willingness to act in interstate crises, and in internal crises limited to the case of Yemen (also in 1967), indicating probably a declining

---

[39]For analyses of this threat see Golan, *Yom Kippur*, pp. 1118–126; Golan, "Decisionmaking," pp. 209–212; and Frank Fukuyama, "Nuclear Shadowboxing: Soviet Intervention Threats in the Middle East," *Orbis*, Fall 1981, pp. 579–605.

Table 1. Soviet behavior in the Middle East, 1970–1985

	No activity	Propaganda activity	Political involvement (covert or other)	Diplomatic political activity	Military supplies	Participation of military advisers	Naval activity	Intervention by proxy	Threat of direct intervention	Direct military intervention
Interstate Conflicts										
Iraq-Iran (1969)	x									
Israel-Egypt (1970)		x	x	x	x	x	x			
Syria-Jordan (1970)		x	x				x			
North-South Yemen (1972)	x									
Israel-Egypt-Syria-Jordan (1973)		x	x	x	x	x	x	1	x	
Iraq-Kuwait (1973)	x									
South Yemen-Oman (1973–76)		x	x	x	x		x			
Greece-Turkey (1974)		x					x			
Syria-Lebanon (1976)		x	x				x			
Greece-Turkey (1976)	x									
Egypt-Libya (1977)		x					x			
Ethiopia-Somalia (1977–88)		x	x	x	x	x	x	x		
Israel-Lebanon (1978)		x								
North-South Yemen (1979)		x					x			
Iran-Iraq (1980–)		x			x (1982–)					
Israel-Lebanon (1982–85)		x	x	x			x			
Libya-United States (1986)		x								
Total (out of 17 cases)	4	13	7	5	5	3	10	1	1	
Internal Conflicts										
Jordan (1970)							x			
Somalia (1970)		x	x				x			
Sudan (1971)		x	x	x						
Afghanistan (1973)		x	x(?)							
Lebanon (1976)		x	x			x(?)	x			
South Yemen (1978)		x	x							

	No support	Political activity	Indirect arms supplies	Direct arms supplies	Training in bloc or third country	Military advisers	Naval activity	Intervention by proxy	Threat of intervention	Direct military intervention
Afghanistan (1978)		x		x(?)						x
Iran (1978–79)		x								
Afghanistan (1979)		x		x	x					
Lebanon (1983–)		x		x	x					
South Yemen (1986)		x		x			x	x		
Total (out of 11 cases)	0	10		7–9	2		1–2	5	0	1
National Liberation Struggles[2]										
Ananya (Southern Sudan)	x									
Khuzistan (Iran)	x									
ELF-EPLF (Eritrea)	x (post-1974)		x (pre-1974)		x (pre-1974)			1		
Kurds (Iraq)[3]	x (post-1972 Iraq)	x (pre-1971–72)	x	x (pre-1971–72)	x (pre-1971–72)					
PLO (Palestine)		x		x	x			4		
Dhofar (Oman)		x		x	x			5		
Total (out of 6 cases)	4	3	1	3	4	0	0	0	0	0

SOURCE: Much of the data for this chart is based on Michael Brecher's *Data Bank of International Crises*, Jerusalem, forthcoming.
1. Participation of proxy advisers (N. Koreans and/or Cubans) but not actually third state intervention. Though not certain, Cubans or Koreans act as proxies.
2. Some overlap with Internal Conflicts category.
3. Soviet assistance to Kurds or other minorities in Iran, such as Baluchis, is hard to confirm. There were reports of renewed support after 1978.
4. Unconfirmed reports of Cuban advisers prior to 1982.
5. Helped transport PDRY troops but not as proxy forces.

perception of the risks involved. The fact that the number of occasions is still not great suggests that the Soviets do perceive some risk (indeed, the use of Soviet pilots in the 1970 war of attrition or the placement of extremely advanced weapons systems in Syria in 1983 did carry some risk). Again, higher-risk activity was almost exclusively within the Arab-Israeli context.

At the other end of the risk scale one finds naval and propaganda activity. The high frequency of such action in interstate conflicts suggests a very low estimate of risk (even for the movement or augmentation of the fleet). The Soviets have been considerably more cautious about naval activity regarding internal conflicts, possibly considering such activity too provocative for such conflicts, though they are still more ready to use it than overt involvement (such as diplomatic activity, military advisers' participation, or military supplies). Although this tendency may be connected less with risk taking than with tactical political considerations, the fact that the Soviets have quite readily provided political involvement and propaganda in the case of internal conflicts suggests that they seek to limit their overt role to an indirect one only.

If Soviet behavior is cautious regarding internal conflicts, it is even more cautious regarding national liberation movements. For some movements, all of them separatist, the Soviets have given no or only periodic support, and the support that has been given has always been limited to political training *abroad* (in Soviet bloc or other third countries), arms supplies, and some political support (particularly and especially for the Palestinians). Aside from transporting South Yemeni fighters to join the Dhofar rebellion, probably a sign more of commitment to South Yemen than to the rebels, the Soviets have never taken the higher-risk course of military advisers or military intervention even through a proxy. The choice probably reflects simply a lower level of commitment rather than a greater concern over the risks of acting. Even in the case of acute danger to the movement involved and the greatest commitment (to the Palestinians), the Soviets have never taken any form of military action or threatened to assist; they have been unwilling to take virtually any risk.[40] Nor, it might be added, and this is probably connected with the Soviet desire to minimize the risks associated with these struggles, has Moscow been an enthusiastic supporter of armed struggle (including terror). It has also exercised caution, arousing much resentment in the movements, in its supplies of arms and the type of training offered. It is noteworthy, however, that the highest risk taking by the Soviet Union has been connected with the Arab-Israeli conflict (including the Palestinian) and South Yemen, suggesting the priority of Soviet strategic interests.

---

[40]When direct or proxy assistance has been rendered, as for example in Angola, the Soviets have been careful to stipulate that this aid came after independence and was, therefore, aid to a government not a movement.

Risk Taking and Changing Tactics

It is difficult to determine a direct relationship between actual risk taking and apparently changing Soviet tactics in the Middle East, or Moscow's attitudes toward the Third World as they appear in the debates and official pronouncements, or its changing perceptions of the West. Official pronouncements can be characterized by period: 1970–75, rising interest; 1976–80, peak interest; 1981–84, declining interest. The second and third periods begin decidedly earlier in theoretical discussions. The periodization of official pronouncements corresponds roughly to a perception of the West as increasingly restrained in the 1970s, peaking in 1975–79 and reversing to a more apprehensive view at the end of the 1970s and particularly 1981 onward. The late 1970s and early 1980s were also characterized by severe economic problems and the succession issue, military doctrinal inquiry, and troubles in Poland. The three highest risk-taking activities of the Soviet Union in the Middle East occurred in the 1970s, the most aggressive, the invasion of Afghanistan, during the peak perception of Western restraint (likewise the use of proxy intervention in the Horn). Yet the second most dangerous Soviet act, the threat to intervene in 1973, occurred shortly after the beginning of the detente era, when the Soviet perception of the United States was probably one of relative restraint (although similar, possibly less credible, threats had been used before the detente period in 1956 and 1967). Similarly, the cases of military adviser participation were also spread over the 1970s, from 1970 to 1978 in the South Yemen coup.

In these actions there does not appear to have been a significant difference, with the exception of Afghanistan, between the 1970–75 and 1976–80 periods. These may be examples, and proof, of a greater Soviet willingness to become involved, coupled causally or not with a view of a restrained West to lower the perceived risks. One cannot overlook the fact, however, that almost the same willingness to become involved in the Arab-Israeli and Yemen contexts was apparent in the pre-detente 1960s. That such risk taking occurred at all is probably more significant than the limited number of occasions involved. Nonetheless, Soviet behavior in the Middle East generally was no more nor less aggressive in the 1970s, if one considers all cases. Nor does there appear to be any deviation in the 1980s. So far there are *no* examples of high-risk behavior, involvement in the internal Lebanese crisis being very little different from that in 1976, involvement in the Iraq-Iran war being only somewhat greater. These actions do not represent significant risk taking, however.

The two incidents that do suggest some movement are the relative Soviet inaction in the Israeli-Lebanese war of 1982–85 and the supplying of advanced weapons to Syria in 1983. The latter, while not as high on the risk-taking scale as intervention, threat, proxy, and even adviser participation, is nonetheless a provocative act similar to the only Soviet precedent in the area, the supply of

SAM-3s to Egypt in 1970. What appears to be a commitment to Syria's air defense resembles Soviet moves in Egypt (albeit with fewer advisers and apparently no pilots) and suggests no less a desire for involvement in the area today than in the 1970s, whatever the perception of the West or the attitude toward the Third World. By the same token, Soviet inaction in the Lebanese War may have reflected less a fear of an aggressive America and second thoughts about the Third World than merely the cautious behavior characteristic of the Soviets even in the 1970s when *no* Soviet client-state was threatened with all-out destruction. Lebanon was not an ally, Syria was not threatened, and the PLO, like all other national liberation movements, has never elicited any Soviet risk-taking behavior, whether in 1970, 1976, or 1982. In other words, this may not be proof of a retreat or change in Soviet behavior. Yet a retreat may be evidenced by the fact that experiences in the PDRY and Afghanistan have not been applied elsewhere, possible opportunities in the Gulf have not been exploited. If anything, the pattern has held: some, albeit limited, Soviet involvement in the course of the South Yemen crisis of January 1986 (the political involvement came after the crisis was under way, the naval activity was primarily for evacuation of civilians); no Soviet involvement in the U.S.-Libyan crisis of April 1986.[41] But this tells us nothing about future Soviet action in the sphere in which its risk taking has always been higher, the Arab-Israeli conflict.

Role of the Region

If the Soviet Union has used regional conflicts and rivalries in tactical ways, obviously the region has played a role in Soviet calculations and capabilities. Beyond these tactical elements, however, are three important regional factors that have influenced Soviet behavior in the Middle East over the past thirty years and are applicable also to the future: Arab unity (or lack thereof), Arab nationalism, and Islam (particularly Islamic fundamentalism). To this list we may also add the stability of local regimes, which is often connected with these three factors.

Arab Nationalism

Arab unity, perceived originally by the Soviets as a solid front rejecting Western imperialism, has actually proved to be of far less certain value to Moscow. It can be beneficial or detrimental to Soviet interests depending upon the fulcrum of this unity, which usually determines its over-all orientation. Nasserite pan-Arabism or Saudi reconciliation conferences have had the

---

[41]See David Pollock, "Moscow and Aden: Coping with a Coup," *Problems of Communism* 35, no. 3 (1986), pp. 50–70.

opposite effect of, for example, the post–Camp David Steadfastness Front or Baghdad summit of 1978. Unity of the Gulf states has posed problems for Moscow as long as these states have been predominantly pro-Western. When coupled with Islamic unity, Arab unity has been all the more problematic for the Soviets, at least in the case of the response to the invasion of Afghanistan. Similarly, solidarity within the Arab world, as we have already noted, enabled weaker states (and movements such as the PLO) to maintain their independence vis-à-vis Moscow. Thus there clearly have been cases when Arab unity operated against Soviet interests, disruption and dissent being preferable to cooperation.

Nonetheless, such disruption and dissent have on occasion been an irritant, even an obstacle, to the pursuit of Soviet interests both regionally and globally. Regional rivalries and conflicts between Soviet clients or would-be clients and the kaleidoscope of changing intraregional alliances, complicated by the instability of some of the regimes themselves, make it difficult for the Soviets to forge a consistent policy in and for the region. Moscow is unable to count on consistency, loyalty, and steadfastness against what the Soviets portray as the common enemy. Clearly the Soviets are better off when the area is united against a pro-West Israel or Egypt, or unencumbered with Iraqi-Iranian or Syrian-Iraqi conflict or state-supported splits within the PLO. Certainly they would be better off if all the countries in the area would agree—and stick to—one clear position regarding, for example, negotiations with Israel and Soviet participation. Moreover, the perpetual uncertainty created by this lack of unity, itself the result of the instability of intraregional relations, confronts the Soviets with continuous insecurity regarding their presence and influence in the region. Thus they are perpetually haunted by the specter of defection of one client or another to the West—and to some degree manipulated by these possibilities. Such insecurity could presumably be reduced significantly by a unity of the region—provided, of course, it assumed the desired orientation, a condition for which there is no guarantee.

Such guarantees are absent not only because of the instability of the region but also because of the strength of local nationalism (Iranian as well as Arab). A force that the Soviets hoped to harness against the West in the 1950s, nationalism has also stood with surprising consistency as a bulwark against Soviet control. A notable case has been the Ba'ath regimes in Syria and Iraq. For all their radicalism and socialism, these regimes are fiercely nationalistic and have jealously guarded their independence. Each has appeared to falter upon occasion, when in particular need of outside help, but neither has relinquished its independence nor granted the Soviet Union sufficient influence for the latter to impose its interests or policies. Like Egypt before them, both regimes on occasion move against pro-Soviet elements, often balk at applying Soviet policy preferences or obeying Soviet commands, frequently find fault with and even defy Soviet policies elsewhere, and intermittently dabble in improved relations with the United States.

Even in the absence of fundamentalism, Islam has been and is sufficiently wound into Arab nationalism that it continues to contribute to Arab (even Iraqi Ba'ath) concern over the evils of communism. The Soviet Union, though free of the imperialist stigma of the Western powers, is nonetheless perceived as the purveyor of an alien culture and an atheistic ideology. Pragmatically tolerated, even actively sought when necessary, Soviet involvement is still perceived as an outside influence ultimately inimical to the values of Arab and Muslim society if not to Arab interests. There are exceptions. Marxist regimes in Yemen and Afghanistan may be said to have overcome nationalism. But the tenacious rebellion in Afghanistan, indeed the very need for the Soviets to invade in 1979, attests to the strength of nationalism there, while the case of the PDRY remains to be judged (particularly as the North Yemen–Soviet rapprochement coincides with rising Saudi influence in the area). Indeed, an appreciation of the continued strength of nationalism has probably prompted the Soviets to concentrate on the more pragmatic side of their relationship with the Middle Eastern countries, seeking formal alliance rather than revolutionary conversion or ideological unity to secure their interests.

Islamic Fundamentalism

The rise of Islamic fundamentalism introduces a more than purely incremental problem for the Soviets. It is not simply a question of "more Islam," that is, more intense religiosity. This in itself poses problems, of course, insofar as it makes Islam a still more central element of society, elevating to a supreme position that which is irreconcilable with communism. Some experts on the Soviets' own nationality problem believe that this change alone is having an effect on Soviet Muslims and is, therefore, a source of concern for the Soviet Union.[42] There is disagreement on this Islamic danger, but the rise of what is to the Soviets basically a hostile ideology on its periphery must be of some concern, particularly inasmuch as this movement is not merely intensely religious but also messianic with an all-encompassing social, economic, and political as well as moral dogma.[43] Its aspirations extend far beyond the purely spiritual needs of the local flock, for the Islamic state envisaged by Khomeini (or for that matter Qadhdhafi) encompasses much more. Nonfundamentalist states in the region are also concerned about these aspirations, not only for their own sovereignty but also for the growing appeal of fundamentalism within their own borders, among their own peoples (including the Palestinians). This concern is creating a certain impatience

---

[42]E.g., A. Bennigsen and M. Broxup, *The Islamic Threat to the Soviet State* (New York: St. Martins, 1983), pp. 100–117; Helene Carrere d'Encausse, "Domestic Roots of Soviet Foreign Policy" (paper, Berkeley, University of California, 1985).

[43]See Martha Olcott Brill, "Soviet Islam and World Revolution," *World Politics* 34, no. 4 (July 1982), pp. 487–504.

or sense of urgency, at least within the Arab-Israeli context, contributing to an apparently greater willingness to compromise for the sake of an American-mediated solution to at least some of their problems. In other words, the fear of fundamentalism may, from the Soviet point of view, drive some Arab elements into the arms of the Americans, as King Hussein and Yasser Arafat worry that further prolongation of the conflict will find them unseated by the rising tide of fundamentalism. A similar concern has already prompted a basically pro-Western alliance of the Gulf states in the face of Khomeinism and the Iraq-Iran war.

Unwilling to alienate the vast numbers of Muslims and, more specifically, the anti-Western and potentially friendly Khomeini regime, the Soviets found a way to accept the new phenomenon. Even as they adjusted to the perceived threat with a stepped-up atheist education campaign in their own Muslim republics and took other practical steps,[44] the Soviets enunciated a theoretical basis upon which to build a relationship. Long having allowed for a progressive as well as a reactionary side to Islam, Soviet theoreticians now elaborated on these more positive aspects. Middle East expert and then Oriental Institute head Evgenii Primakov, for example, referred to the ideas of an "Islamic state" or an "Islamic economy" as positive, "albeit utopian," alternatives to the exploitative system of economy and state known in the West.[45] Such precepts of the Koran as "people's power," "Islamic justice," and "Islamic paths of development" could be positive if interpreted or implemented by revolutionary rather than reactionary elements and could take an anti-capitalist direction. That social issues were taking precedence over or were at least commensurate with religious ones was thus seen as a positive trend provided that the revolutionary potential was developed. Another theoretician, referring to Algeria, observed that Islam was "closely associated with the egalitarian concepts of social justice" and therefore could be used positively "to mobilize believers for fully secular undertakings."[46] The Iranian revolution extracted a pronouncement on Islam by Brezhnev, too, in 1981 at the Twenty-sixth Congress of the CPSU. Presumably expressing the party's official line, Brezhnev took the positive approach that Islam was to be seen as potentially progressive and conservative at the same time, depending on the specific content.[47]

There were less optimistic views, however, which became more vocal as policies in Iran became more anti-Soviet. Rostislav Ul'ianovskii spoke quite early, for example, of the "highly contradictory . . . politization of Islam"

---

[44]Ya'acov Ro'i, "The Task of Creating the New Soviet Man: Atheistic Propaganda in the Soviet Muslim Areas," *Soviet Studies* 36, no. 1 (January 1984), pp. 26–44.

[45]E. M. Primakov, "Islam i protsessy obshchestvennogo razvitiia stran zarubezhnogo Vostoka," *Voprosy filosofii* no. 89 (1980), pp. 60–71.

[46]A. Malashenko, "Religioznaia traditsiia i politika revoliutsionnoi demokratii," *Aziia i Afrika segodnia* no. 9 (1979), p. 21. See also E. S. Troitskii, "Kritika neokolonialistskikh fal'sifikatsii idei V. I. Lenina po problemam natsional'no- osvoboditel'nogo dvizheniia," *Voprosy istorii KPSS* no. 7 (1980), p. 77.

[47]*Pravda*, February 24, 1981.

with the increasing strength of the conservative wing in Iran, and the totally counterrevolutionary character of Islam in a country such as Afghanistan.[48] Aleksander Bovin was more to the point when, upon receipt of the Order of Lenin, he told an interviewer that the Islamic revival was "an attempt to return to those times when Islamic dogmatists determined the character and system of political life." This was, he said, in essence a "theocratic renaissance."[49] An earlier discussion of religion in *Narody Azii i Afriki* had classified Islamic revivalism (along with those of Buddhism and Hinduism) as "heir to popular heresies and sectarian rebellion . . . messianic and eschatological, millennistic movements."[50] Evgenii Primakov and his deputy Georgii Kim also began slightly to shift their emphasis to the negative aspects of Islam in articles they wrote in 1982, the latter referring to the stirring up of "political extremism."[51] And increasingly the daily press took on a more critical line in specific references to Khomeinism.

There is every sign that Islamic fundamentalism as a regional force will continue to affect Soviet policy in the Middle East, forcing it to toe a delicate line between Khomeinism and Islam itself. Soviet policy must find its way through the labyrinth of potentially dangerous Muslim extremists supported by Iran or pro-Iranian regimes without alienating its allies among them or, for that matter, foreclosing the still-hoped-for relationship with Iran. At the very least, Islamic fundamentalism will be a persistent irritant for Soviet plans in the region; potentially it could be a powerful obstacle. Although some observers believe it may actually become a threat to Soviet stability, there are few signs that the Soviet Union believes so.

Role of Global Factors

It is, as we have seen, to a large degree global factors that determine Soviet interests, tactics, and risk taking in the Middle East. Generally the local or regional threat combined with the estimate of global response guides Soviet behavior, but both of these factors are ultimately determined by the challenge to global interests as such, that is, the political and strategic global balance. One could trace the link between virtually every move of the Soviet Union with regard to the Middle East and its interests vis-à-vis the West, in later years specifically the United States, from the first arms deals with Egypt and

---

[48]R. Ul'ianovskii, "O natsional'nom osvobozhdenii i natsionalizme," *Aziia i Afrika segodnia* no. 10 (1980), pp. 3, 6.

[49]*Literaturnaia gazeta*, January 1, 1981.

[50]B. S. Erasov in "Religiia v stranakh Azii i Afriki: Kruglyi stol," *Narody Azii i Afriki* no. 1 (1980), p. 43, as cited in Y. Ro'i, *The USSR and the Muslim World* (London: Allen & Unwin, 1984), pp. 157–158.

[51]*Pravda*, August 11, 1982 (Primakov); G. Kim, "Razvivaiushchiesia strany: usilenie sotsial'no-klassovoi differentsiatsii," *Aziia i Afrika segodnia* no. 11 (1981), p. 5.

Syria (or before that in the creation of the state of Israel) up to the recognition of the PLO and the recent Soviet–Abu Dhabi civil air agreement. The competition with the West in the Middle East is a given, and the global strategic-political aspects of this competition generate a priority for an area so close to Soviet borders. But to what degree do the Soviets' global relationships or policies affect their Middle East policies? Could detente become a factor; could a less competitive policy emerge?

In a study conducted in the 1970s I found no direct link between the progress of detente and the East-West relationship in the Middle East.[52] Aside from the obvious though not total connection between Soviet threat perception and risk taking, which we have already examined, global cooperation has had strikingly little effect on Middle East policies. Following the breakdown of detente in the Middle East, as it was perceived by the United States but not the Soviet Union, with the Yom Kippur War (indeed, the Soviets cite U.S.-Soviet cooperation for a ceasefire as an example of detente cooperation!), no amount of "breakthroughs" or agreements at the superpower level could reverse the decline of cooperation in the area. The Soviets, on the losing end of the post-1973 competition with the United States, invoked detente as a framework or basis for cooperation. The United States was unwilling, and the Soviets for all their invocation of detente were also unwilling, to link the Middle East with other issues in any kind of trade-off.

A salient example of this "compartmentalization" is the 1975 Helsinki Conference, the height of detente from the Soviet point of view, which was followed within a short period by the U.S.-negotiated Israeli-Egyptian Interim Agreement, which the Soviets bitterly opposed. Competition was no less keen in other areas of the region, from the Red Sea to the Persian Gulf. Momentary cooperation was involved in the 1977 joint Soviet-American statement prior to what was to have been a reconvening of the Geneva Conference on the Arab-Israeli conflict. It has been claimed that a trade-off was involved here, the joint statement in exchange for SALT II. Although it is true that SALT II was somewhat more beneficial to the United States than SALT I had been, this was not as such a Soviet concession. Indeed, it was the Soviets who sought U.S. agreement and ratification, just as it was the Soviets who sought American agreement on their inclusion in the Middle East negotiations.

Whatever the verdict regarding linkage, detente has had some relevance for the global relationship in the area itself. Although the West perceived Soviet behavior in the 1973 war as a clear violation of detente, the Soviets' own interpretation of this policy was clearly different. For Moscow, detente, sorely needed primarily for economic reasons, was an atmosphere, a frame of mind or an environment conducive to cooperation and minimizing the risks of superpower confrontation and armed conflict. It was never perceived as a

---

[52]Galia Golan, "The Arab-Israeli Conflict in Soviet-U.S. Relations," in Ro'i, *Limits*, pp. 7–31.

substitute for policy or even for competition. Competition, rather, was to be conducted in a safer environment, one that prevented hostile polarization and thereby created the conditions for cooperation in the realms of trade and arms control. Moreover, the Soviets' view was of a rather elastic detente, one that could be stretched without snapping. The Soviets clearly stretched matters when they resumed arms deliveries to an Egypt preparing for war in 1973 and resupplied Cairo during the war itself. But we may assume that the Soviets' opposition to Egypt's war plans and their efforts to gain a ceasefire from the early hours of the war were at least partly motivated by the Soviet desire to minimize the damage to detente as well as the risk of superpower confrontation. Their conception of detente and that of the Americans were, however, quite far apart. For the Soviets, their inclusion in the 1973 Geneva Conference was the result of detente, their subsequent exclusion the failure to apply detente to the Middle East. Their interpretation, of course, overlooks the fact that their behavior was no less competitive and was in some areas actually confrontational in the same period.

This is not to say that detente has relevance for the Middle East only in the Soviet mind or in Soviet propaganda. It is hard to imagine superpower cooperation such as that of the Geneva Conference or the 1977 joint statement without some degree of detente or global relaxation. Even if detente itself is not a sufficient condition, the total absence of detente—that is, cold war and global hostility—would hardly be conducive to cooperation in any area, including the Middle East. Thus some degree of detente is a necessary, though clearly not a sufficient, condition for cooperation. The Soviets, as already noted, have been on the losing end of the competitive relationship in the Middle East, at least since 1972, and for this reason if for no other have advocated Soviet-American cooperation. To some degree they do so as part of a need or desire for broader superpower cooperation. If one looks at the two major works published by Soviet scholars on the issue of international conflicts, one by Primakov and Zhurkin in 1972, the other by Gantman in 1983, one finds a clear preference for such cooperation.[53] Both studies divided conflicts into (1) those involving the two social systems in the world arena; (2) those in which imperialism attempted to suppress national liberation movements (also defined as local or regional conflicts); and (3) those of a purely interimperialist nature. Both saw the second category as the most likely both to occur and to trigger a broader conflict of the first type. This argument was the inevitability or high probability of escalation I have already discussed in the local war risk-taking context. It was used as the basis for an argument favoring cooperation, advocated by these and other scholars including Americanists Arbatov, Kremeniuk, and Burlatskii but also Middle

---

[53]V. V. Zhurkin and E. M. Primakov, *Mezhdunarodnye konflikty* (Moscow: Mezhdunarodnye otnosheniia, 1972), pp. 19–25; V. I. Gantman, *Mezhdunarodnye konflikty sovremennosti* (Moscow: Nauka, 1983), pp. 4–5, 63, 79, 257–292.

East expert Primakov.[54] Indeed, Zhurkin specified the Arab-Israeli conflict as threatening global conflict and therefore most in need of crisis-prevention through superpower cooperation.[55]

Among those who do not believe in the inevitability or even high probability of escalation and, presumably, the antidetentists, however, there are clearly others who see neither the need nor the desirability for such cooperation. Thus some, as we have seen, spoke of the divisibility of detente, presumably ruling out cooperation in even the prevention of Third World conflicts, including the Arab-Israeli conflict. The Soviet leadership, as we have seen, expressed a generally interventionist position, particularly from 1976 to 1980, a position precluding the cooperation advocated by official Soviet plans and pronouncements regarding the Arab-Israeli crisis. The oft-repeated Soviet call for an international conference to include the Soviet Union in the negotiating process appeared to be an exception in a highly competitive posture regarding the Third World. Whether this was simply a tactical Soviet position or genuinely reflected Soviet concern that the Arab-Israeli conflict was too risky (with too little return) is not at all clear.

Soviet Policy in the 1980s

By the 1980s the overall Soviet line exhibited greater consistency, with Brezhnev's Rules speech suggesting a less confrontational, cooperation-oriented position. Andropov, who as we have seen always appeared to reject the more competitive Third World policy, argued directly against confrontational behavior.[56] To what degree Andropov was actually ready for crisis-prevention cooperation is now moot (as are the views of Chernenko). Gorbachev, at least in his Middle East policies to date, remains certainly competitive but not necessarily confrontational. The challenge to the United States of the past few years, which continues with Gorbachev, has been in the Gulf and among the moderate Arab states. That this challenge is to be combined with an effort at cooperation in the Arab-Israeli context is suggested by intensified Soviet efforts to hold an international conference (including the detailed plan presented by the Soviets in July 1984), talks on the subject initiated by the Soviets with Washington in 1984–85, the effort to elicit a commitment to Soviet participation in negotiations from even the pro-American Arab states, and hints to Israel of renewed diplomatic relations or at least improved

---

[54]*Pravda*, July 22, 1973, and Soviet television, November 24, 1980 (*FBIS* III, December 11, 1980, CC-10 Arbatov); V. A. Kremeniuk, "Sovetsko-amerikanskie otnosheniia i nekotorye problemy osvobodivskikhsia gosudarstv," *SShA-ekonomika, politika, ideologiia* no. 6 (1982), p. 17; F. Burlatskii, *Literaturnaia gazeta*, January 28, 1981; Primakov, "Osvobodivshiesia strany," p. 20.

[55]V. Zhurkin, "Razriadka i mezhdunarodnye konflikty," *Mezhdunarodnaia zhizn* no. 6 (1974), pp. 95–104.

[56]E.g., *Pravda*, April 23, 1978; November 23, 1982; June 16, 1983.

relations in exchange for an international conference.[57] These signs are not necessarily evidence of some new Soviet commitment to international cooperation. As in the past, they may simply be the result of Soviet conclusions that confrontation with the United States, even competition, in the Arab-Israeli conflict runs too high a risk for what has become too low a return, indeed offering little chance for success. More than ever it appears to be the result of the Soviets' deteriorating position vis-à-vis American success, a deterioration not necessarily matched in other areas of the Middle East.

If Gorbachev, unlike his predecessors, sees cooperation on the Arab-Israel issue as a prelude to or bait for broader cooperation along the lines of detente remains to be seen. Certainly detente is of great importance to him; it would also be helpful in the regional effort, but like his predecessors he appears to be operating on both levels simultaneously, without necessarily requiring any connection between them. Moreover, he may view competitive behavior outside the Arab-Israeli context as beneficial to the Soviet position within this conflict as well as in the regional-global sphere.

The Soviets appear to be pursuing a competitive posture in the Middle East outside the Arab-Israeli context, both to fortify their position in this context *and* to improve their general position vis-à-vis the United States politically and strategically (just as they did to compensate for their losses in the Arab-Israeli area in the early 1970s). Nothing in Gorbachev's policies suggests that this competition will become confrontational; Gorbachev appears to ascribe to the noninterventionist, detente-oriented position, possibly even the Soviet Union—first, minimalist position. Just how much he is committed to detente or how far he is willing to endanger it by competition is by no means clear, however. Nor is it clear whether he would view some sort of crisis-preventing cooperation as interfering with his competitive objectives. Domestic factors, most of which I have mentioned, will play a major role in Gorbachev's policies. Not only apparent differences of opinion within the Soviet elite over detente in general and the issue of Third World involvement and risk taking in particular but also the issues connected with changing military doctrine, and above all the exigencies of the faltering Soviet economy, will probably play a major role in determining the Soviet view of the global as well as the regional factors involved, Soviet interests, and Soviet behavior itself.[58] The lessons of the past thirty years suggest that the Soviets will appreciate the lack of control and lack of stability in their relationship

---

[57]See the comments allegedly made at the July 1985 meeting between Soviet and Israeli ambassadors to France, *Jerusalem Post*, July 21, 1985.

[58]Aside from the alleged reference in 1985 (see note 57 above), no link has been detectable between another Soviet domestic issue, the Jews, and Soviet policies in the Middle East. See Jonathan Frankel, "The Soviet Regime and Anti-Zionism: An Analysis" (Jerusalem: Soviet–East European Research Center, Hebrew University, 1984), and "The Anti-Zionist Press Campaign in the USSR 1969–1971: An Internal Dialogue" (Jerusalem: Soviet–East European Research Center, Hebrew University, 1972). This issue has been used, however, in Soviet-U.S. relations.

with their Middle Eastern clients and also the regional and global obstacles to greater permanency and authority. If past behavior is any guide to the future, Soviet policy will be generally cautious, with greater obstinacy concerning the Arab-Israeli conflict and, possibly, the Red Sea but also with a willingness to attempt a cooperative approach to the Arab-Israeli conflict in order to maintain some foothold. The Soviets have been willing in the past to take greater risks in this context. But there is still much doubt that the Soviets will risk direct military intervention, and with it confrontation with the United States, for this area or any other, such as the Persian Gulf, where the United States is fully committed.

9

The Soviet Union and South Asia: Moscow and New Delhi Standing Together

ROBERT C. HORN

The thesis of this chapter is twofold. First, I argue that India has been both the primary focus of Soviet policy in the South Asian region and a central concern of Moscow's overall Third World policy throughout the thirty-year period since the 1955 Soviet-Egyptian arms deal. Indeed, that agreement is rivaled in significance as symbol of the USSR's active "emergence" into the Third World by three major events in Soviet policy toward India in the same year. The Russians began the year by signing an agreement to provide the Indians with a loan of more than $100 million to build a steel mill in Bhilai; Prime Minister Jawaharlal Nehru undertook a precedent-setting, sixteen-day trip to the Soviet Union in mid-year, where he was privileged to be the first noncommunist leader allowed to speak his views publicly before Soviet audiences; and the year concluded with a rather spectacular visit to India by Khrushchev and Bulganin, during which the Soviet leaders expressed support for Indian foreign policy, offered additional economic aid, and lavished praise on Indo-Soviet friendship and cooperation.

This emphasis on India has meant that Soviet policy toward all other regional states—Pakistan, Sri Lanka, Bangladesh, Nepal, Bhutan, Sikkim, and the Maldives—has been subordinated to Moscow's concentration on South Asia's largest state. Nowhere is the point more obvious than in the case of Pakistan, the region's second most important member. Deeply rooted historical and religious animosities between India and Pakistan have combined with the regional competition of the two states to make it impossible for outside powers to build close relations with both simultaneously, as both the United States and the USSR have discovered. For virtually all of these thirty years, with the exception of the 1966–68 period, the Soviet Union has recognized both India's overriding significance in the region and the centrality of India's concern with Pakistan; and it has adjusted its policy toward Islamabad so as not to offend New Delhi. For most of the period, therefore, Moscow has not formulated separate policy toward Pakistan or other South

Asian states; rather, it has viewed its relationship with Pakistan as dependent on its more significant ties with India.

The second aspect of this chapter's thesis is that although the relationship between the Soviet Union and India has probably never—or at least not for any lengthy period of time—been as close as Moscow might have liked, it has been far closer and more stable over the past thirty years than any other relationship between the USSR and a Third World country. In the first decade and a half relations were important to each state, if somewhat distant; since the end of the 1960s ties have become more significant for both states and far closer. There have indeed been alterations or fluctuations in the relationship, but these have taken place within surprisingly narrow parameters.[1]

This twofold thesis warrants explanation in two areas. First, what was it about India which attracted Soviet interest in 1955, and what explains the continuing Soviet interest since then? How did and how does India fit into the Soviet Union's foreign policy goals and objectives? Second, what factors explain the nature of the relationship, its closeness and limitations? What factors have been conducive and what have obstructed the establishment of Soviet influence in India?

The bulk of this chapter is devoted to an examination of these two areas. Thereafter I seek to evaluate the future of Soviet policy toward India and Indo-Soviet relations by considering the current outlook and the possibilities for change in that outlook both in Moscow and in New Delhi. What is the Soviet perception of the results of its policies in South Asia? How does the Soviet Union view the benefits and costs, and also the permanence, of any gains? To what extent is India still important to Soviet foreign policy interests? What changes in other areas of Soviet foreign relations could bring about a shift in Soviet behavior in the region? On the Indian side, how is the relationship with the USSR perceived? What changes—within the Indian political or economic system, or both, and in Indian regional or global policies—could significantly alter Indian views? Finally, I evaluate the role the United States has played and can play in the future in Soviet policy toward South Asia in general and in Soviet-Indian relations in particular.[2] What lessons are there here for Washington, and how might these lessons be taken into account in future American conduct toward both India and the Soviet Union?

India in the Context of Soviet Foreign Policy Interests

The USSR's general policy in Asia has had certain foundation stones since the 1950s. Like Soviet policies in all other areas, actions here have been

---

[1]For an extended discussion of the relationship, see Robert C. Horn, *Soviet-Indian Relations: Issues and Influence* (New York: Praeger, 1982).

[2]For an excellent analysis of American policy toward India, see Norman D. Palmer, *The United States and India* (New York: Praeger, 1984).

intended primarily to enhance Soviet security and secondarily (and relatedly) to increase Soviet power. More specifically, the "general line" of Soviet foreign policy, peaceful coexistence, has meant continued competition with the capitalist system, the United States in particular, in economics, politics, and ideology. The crux of this competition has been the need to keep it peaceful. Thus another operational principle of the Soviet approach to the various regions of Asia is the absolute necessity of avoiding a confrontation with the United States. Fundamental to Moscow's perspective also is the conviction that the drive for genuine independence, and even some form of nonalignment or neutralism, in the Third World as a whole and in Asia in particular can coincide with Soviet interests and lead to a sort of alliance between the USSR and these states—a "zone of peace," as it was described by Nikita Khrushchev at the Twentieth Congress of the Communist Party of the Soviet Union (CPSU) in 1956. Finally, Soviet behavior in Asia has been pragmatic rather than rigidly ideological. Thus it is not surprising that the most likely beneficiaries of an ideological approach, local communist parties and guerrilla movements—which usually have been either pro-Chinese or weak and ineffectual, if not both—have received short shrift in Soviet policy. Moscow has built its policies and expectations on dealings with regimes in power and on state-to-state relations.

Within this framework, what were Moscow's basic objectives in Asia? First, the USSR's approach has been dominated by the goal of reducing, if not eliminating, Western influence. A second goal developed slightly later, to reduce or at least to contain China's involvement in the region. Third, the Soviets have sought a presence and influence in Asia which would justify their claim to be both a global and an Asian power. Fourth, Moscow has sought close relationships with certain Third World states, to serve as an entree to the Third World generally and to the nonaligned movement more specifically.

After achieving independence, India entered world politics with its own set of principles and objectives. Fundamental among these was nonalignment, which to Prime Minister Nehru meant avoiding military alliances or being tied too closely to either camp in the Cold War struggle. In his view the Cold War threatened world peace as well as the independence and economic well-being of new states in Asia and elsewhere. Therefore Nehru envisioned an active role for India in world politics: a moralistic, crusading, internationalist approach in which India would play an important role as a spokesman for Asia and indeed for all nonaligned states. India would champion an end to imperialism and colonialism, and the need for peace, stability, and nonviolent change. In addition to nonalignment and independence, India's objectives in foreign policy have also included security from external threats—defense primarily against Pakistan and secondarily against China. A third goal has been to insulate South Asia and the Indian Ocean from great-power activity except where such involvement might be necessary or useful to the pursuit of the first two objectives. It might be permissible also when it conduces to a fourth goal, that of establishing Indian leadership in the region. Last, and highly significant to New Delhi and its other goals, India has sought assistance in economic development. While avoiding dependence, successive administrations have sought substantial aid for ambitious development plans.

Within the changing Soviet perception of the Third World and Asia of the 1950s, India stood out as an important and attractive target.[3] Nehru's oft-reiterated themes of nonalignment and anticolonialism created friction with the Western powers which dovetailed neatly with the Soviet outlook. Nascent Sino-Indian tension, which was to lead to a border clash in 1959, also fitted well with the growing Sino-Soviet rift. India's high-profile position in the Third World, based on its leadership role among neutralist states—the nascent nonaligned movement—held a strong appeal for policy makers in the Kremlin, because a close relationship with New Delhi appeared a convenient vehicle by which the Soviets might attain credibility as a great power globally, in Asia, and in the Third World. Moreover, the USSR's capability to provide economic assistance to such countries as India would not only serve the recipient's needs but also showcase Soviet economic achievements. Finally, India was large in size and population, occupied a strategic location with regard to Soviet borders and the Indian Ocean, was more economically developed than most other new states, and in political terms appeared impressively stable. In short, India was one of the most significant states in the Third World. It fitted with Soviet perceptions and was thus likely to be responsive to Soviet overtures.

This framework of the origin of Soviet-Indian relations in the 1950s has continued operative over the past three decades. Over time, to be sure, there have been fluctuations and shifts. China emerged as more important concern for both states, especially the Soviet Union. The perceived usefulness to the USSR of India's role in the nonaligned movement has certainly increased. Nevertheless, there has been a basic consistency of both Soviet and Indian interests and goals—as well as of the overall environment in which these relations have operated—over the thirty-year period. The elements that attracted Soviet interest in India, and vice versa, in the mid-1950s have remained largely constant and continue to structure Indo-Soviet relations in the 1980s.

Nature of the Relationship: Attracting Factors

Among the factors conducive to the building and sustaining of a close relationship between the Soviet Union and India has been the strong, but not

---

[3]See, for example, Robert H. Donaldson, *Soviet Policy toward India: Ideology and Strategy* (Cambridge: Harvard University Press, 1974); Zafar Imam, *Soviet View of India, 1957–75* (New Delhi: Kalyani, 1977); and Harish Kapur, *The Soviet Union and the Emerging Nations—A Case Study of Soviet Policy towards India* (London: Michael Joseph for the Graduate School of International Studies, Geneva, 1972).

complete, match between Indian needs and Soviet capabilities. In the economic field, for instance, Soviet assistance to India's economic development
has been forthcoming in periodic agreements and in substantial quantity ever
since 1955. Moscow has participated in more than seventy major industrial and
other projects, and by the end of the 1970s it had financed more than 30
percent of India's steel capacity, 70 percent of its oil-extraction facilities, 30
percent of its oil-refining capacity, 20 percent of its power-generating capacity, and 80 percent of its metallurgical equipment production.[4] Moreover,
Moscow demonstrated its economic support for India by offering to finance
public-sector projects (which the West was reluctant to do) and by providing
more favorable terms than the West: lower interest rates, longer repayment
periods, and repayment in Indian currency or goods rather than in convertible or hard currency. In the area of trade the Soviets were also willing and
able to assist India. Trade grew steadily over the years until the USSR became
India's largest trading partner in the late 1970s, with the Soviets buying raw
materials as well as manufactured goods in return for crude oil, petroleum
products, and other industrial products. Although the United States displaced the Soviet Union as India's number one trade partner in 1984, Moscow still accounted for some 20 percent of Indian exports, making it the
largest importer of Indian goods.[5]

Soviet capabilities have also coincided with Indian needs in the military
sphere. The interest that Moscow and New Delhi shared in an arms relationship in the mid-1950s was given substantial impetus by Sino-Indian tensions
in the early 1960s. In 1962 the Soviets agreed to set up a plant for India to
manufacture the MiG-21. Military agreements and assistance followed
throughout the 1960s, prior to the Bangladesh War in 1971, in the 1970s, and
in three major deals worth more than $1.6 billion each in the first half of the
1980s. Soviet weapons are predominant in all three Indian services. Again, the
Soviets have offered attractive terms: lower costs than the West and better
repayment terms. Although precise figures are not available, one estimate
suggests that Moscow currently supplies some $1 billion per year in weapons
to India, representing some 70 percent of New Delhi's weapons imports.[6]

Another factor has contributed to the closeness of Soviet-Indian relations
and, indeed, gives the economic and military ties far greater significance: the
similarity of Soviet and Indian views of the world. Nehru's suspicious attitude toward the West was intensified by American policies that included the
creation in 1954 and 1955 of the anticommunist Southeast Asia Treaty Organization and the Baghdad Pact. Not only did these moves bring the Cold War
into South Asia but they also meant the arming of India's major adversary,

[4]See Horn, *Soviet-Indian Relations*, pp. 169–70.
[5]See Selamat Ali, "It's Roubles to Rupees," *Far Eastern Economic Review*, March 7, 1985.
[6]See Stephen P. Cohen, "South Asia after Afghanistan," *Problems of Communism*, January–
February 1985, pp. 18–31. Also see S. Nihal Singh, "Why India Goes to Moscow for Arms," *Asian
Survey*, July 1984, pp. 707–720.

Pakistan, which was a member of both alliances. India felt compelled to seek a reliable superpower friend, and the USSR realized that India would likely be responsive to its own anti-American global strategy. The U.S. goal of anti-communism had little to do with Indian goals. Only under the Kennedy administration did Washington seek to be more responsive to Indian needs and security concerns; after the autumn 1962 border clash with China, for example, India found the United States very forthcoming with aid and support. With the administration of Lyndon Johnson, however, the growing U.S. involvement elsewhere in Asia and the perceived futility of seeking peace and positive relations with *both* India and Pakistan caused American attention to India again to decline.

Events surrounding the Bangladesh War of 1971 confirmed the close Indo-Soviet relationship and sent Indo-American relations to a new low. Washington was seen to be "tilting" toward Islamabad on the East Pakistan issue; evidence included the continuing arrival in Pakistan of American arms despite a declared embargo, the disastrous summit that Indira Gandhi held with Richard Nixon and Henry Kissinger, and the sending of part of the U.S. Seventh Fleet into the Bay of Bengal at the height of the conflict in December. Meanwhile the Soviets once again demonstrated that their priority was India and that any approach to Pakistan would be subordinated to Indian wishes. Throughout the crisis Moscow stood as New Delhi's reliable ally, substantially increasing its arms deliveries to India, casting three vetoes in India's favor in the United Nations, deploying its own ships (which may have helped to deter the U.S. carrier *Enterprise* and its task force from intervening), and warning other states, China among them, to stay out of the conflict.[7]

Some improvement in relations between India and the United States resulted from the coincidence in office of Jimmy Carter and Morarji Desai in the late 1970s. This slight warming was, however, plagued by such issues as U.S. nuclear fuel shipments and soon ran into the bigger obstacle of the American reaction to the Soviet invasion of Afghanistan. The return to power of Mrs. Gandhi, a leader much less sympathetic than Desai toward the United States, was heartening to Moscow. Moreover, the new American administration of Ronald Reagan was seen in India as more hawkish and confrontational toward the Soviet Union, a throwback to the 1950s. Indians voiced concern about a greater degree of American support for Pakistan and China, as well as an expansion of U.S. power in the Indian Ocean.

Perceptions of the People's Republic of China became an additional thread in Moscow's and New Delhi's convergent views of the world. By the end of

[7]Among others, see Pran Chopra, *India's Second Liberation* (Cambridge: MIT Press, 1974); J. A. Naik, *India, Russia, China, and Bangladesh* (New Delhi: S. Chand, 1972); Bhabani Sen Gupta, "South Asia and the Great Powers," in William E. Griffith, ed., *The World and the Great Power Triangles* (Cambridge: MIT Press, 1975); Robert Jackson, *South Asian Crisis: India, Pakistan, and Bangladesh, and the Major Powers: Politics of a Divided Subcontinent* (New York: Free Press, 1975).

the 1950s China had replaced the United States as the major external factor motivating the Soviet Union's influence-seeking policies in South Asia. The forceful Chinese crushing of the Tibetan revolt in 1959 and the border clashes with India later in the same year signified a basically hostile Sino-Indian relationship. Not wanting to jeopardize relations with so important a focus of their Third World policies as India, and with Sino-Soviet antagonisms escalating by the summer of 1959, Soviet leaders enunciated a position of neutrality on the border dispute and called for talks between New Delhi and Beijing. The Indians were pleased, the Chinese furious. Over the next few years Moscow became increasingly critical of Beijing's attitude toward India, intensified its economic and cultural relations with New Delhi, and initiated a military assistance program. Although Moscow's temporary equivocation during the next major Sino-Indian clash, in October 1962, introduced some coolness into Indo-Soviet relations, the Russians' ultimately neutralist line, pro-Indian in the eyes of both New Delhi and Beijing, clearly indicated the importance of India to Moscow in the context of the worsening Sino-Soviet dispute. Rapidly warming relations between China and Pakistan served only to confirm the significance of the Soviet-Indian relationship. Moscow has made unremitting efforts since to convince India of the danger that China represents to it—directly along the border and through the various insurrectionist groups Beijing is said to be supporting, as well as indirectly through Sino-American "collusion" and China's support for Pakistan economically, militarily, and politically (for example, on the status of Kashmir).

Moscow has been most successful in enlisting Indian support against China when it has been able to demonstrate to New Delhi the connection between Beijing and the threat from Pakistan. It did so effectively in 1971 as the subcontinent moved toward war (and even as early as 1969, when the Indo-Soviet Treaty of Peace, Friendship and Cooperation signed in 1971 may actually have been negotiated); again in 1975 as renewed U.S. arms shipments to Pakistan underlined the threat to India from the Washington-Islamabad-Beijing axis; and, of course, in the aftermath of the Afghan invasion as those same three capitals have tried to coordinate anti-Soviet policies—which, the Russians have sought to persuade New Delhi, are also anti-Indian.

Significantly, India has sought to maintain its independence by at least keeping open the option of improved relations with China. After the Bangladesh War, for example, India began probing some improvement in the bilateral relationship with Beijing. Just as significantly, Moscow reacted emotionally to these very limited signs of Sino-Indian rapprochement—indeed, there was no response from China at all at the time—and denounced Chinese policy in South Asia, for the first time expressing support for India's position on the territorial question with China. Again in early 1976 India made gestures toward normalization with China, culminating in an April 15 announcement in the Lok Sabha, the lower house of Parliament, that New Delhi would restore diplomatic representation to the ambassadorial level and *ex-*

pected that China would follow suit. Moscow's response was manifold, including the dispatch of a deputy foreign minister to New Delhi to obtain reassurance that new ties with China would not be at the expense of Indo-Soviet relations, an agreement to provide India with another advanced version of the MiG-21, and a new five-year trade agreement. There is evidence that during Mrs. Gandhi's subsequent visit to Moscow in June, China was the number one topic of the prime minister's talks with Soviet leaders. In spite of Mrs. Gandhi's assurances to the Kremlin, however, India gave no indication of backing away from its policy change toward China, nor were the Soviets pleased with the situation. Responding to Brezhnev's thinly veiled warnings to be wary of states that "are striving to subordinate other's people to their rule"—meaning China, of course—Mrs. Gandhi simply stated that "each country must act on its own to reduce areas of suspicion and to enlarge areas of goodwill."[8] In mid-1978, when China finally began to respond to Indian feelers, the Soviets again accelerated their appeals to India. They suddenly and belatedly involved themselves in the Indian debate over the acquisition of deep-penetration aircraft, offering an improved version of the MiG-23. When Indian External Affairs Minister A. B. Vajpayee visited Moscow in September, he was treated to a barrage of anti-China rhetoric from Soviet leaders, the polemics ranging from references to the USSR's experience with China to warnings of Beijing's "designs" in normalization. Soviet Foreign Minister Andrei Gromyko was reportedly so emphatic in his attacks on China that he had to reassure Vajpayee that "his use of strong language was not for the love of it but the use of soft language which they might have liked in relation to China would subserve principled Soviet opposition to war."[9]

The visit of an Indian government official to Beijing, which Moscow had long dreaded, finally took place in February 1979 with Vajpayee's trip to China. There appeared to be some positive steps forward in Sino-Indian relations even if all differences were not resolved. Nevertheless, the progress was overshadowed when Beijing chose this moment to launch its previously threatened incursion into Vietnam, a long-time friend of India's. The Soviets, although they could hardly be pleased with Beijing's invasion of their Vietnamese ally, were hugely relieved by this turn of events as they concerned India. Soviet analysts stressed the linkage between this Chinese invasion and Beijing's "perfidious aggression against India" which was still "fresh in people's minds." They pointed out that China occupied some 36,000 square kilometers of Indian territory, supported India's separatists, interfered in Kashmir, and threatened India's security by strategic roads such as the newly opened Karakoram Highway.[10]

[8]Quoted in *Statesman* (New Delhi), June 9, 1976.
[9]Ibid., September 13, 1978.
[10]V. Tretyakov, "Visit Wrecker," *New Times* no. 10 (March 1979), p. 24.

Soviet premier Alexei Kosygin could hardly have asked for a better prelude to his March visit to India. During his six-day stay Kosygin lambasted China in every public statement he made, and probably in each private talk as well. In his address to the Indian Parliament the Soviet leader referred to the Chinese action against Vietnam as "criminal" and sought to align India with the Soviet position: no peaceful country, no honest person, he said, should remain indifferent when the aggressor, "showing brazen contempt for human life, for world public opinion, is trampling underfoot international law, the lofty principles of peace and independence, sovereignty and equality, everything that has become the people's banner in the struggle against domination and oppression." The Soviet Union and India could not allow such an outrage, he urged.[11] Later in his visit Kosygin drew on all the bluntness he could muster when he warned the Indians that "China might want to teach India a lesson at some point in the future, just as it had sought to do with Vietnam in the present."[12] Judging from the language in the final communiqué, India's interest in pursuing normalization with China when "circumstances permitted," despite Kosygin's impassioned performance, remained unchanged.[13]

Soviet sensitivity on the issue of Sino-Indian normalization has remained evident in the years since the invasion of Afghanistan. This has been a difficult period for Moscow: it has needed friends more than ever in the wake of the global condemnation of its invasion and occupation of a nonaligned state, and there have been several meetings, both in New Delhi and in Beijing, by high-ranking representatives of the two governments seeking to negotiate an end to their border dispute and normalize relations. Although Soviet commentary has not had the vehemence of Kosygin's in 1979—probably due both to Moscow's probing for its own normalization with China and to the lack of substantive progress in Sino-Indian talks—Moscow's concern has been apparent.[14] The Chinese certainly have not failed to note the Kremlin's "slanderous" attempt to "sow discord" between India and China. "Moscow's anti-China comment," wrote a commentator in the *Beijing Review*, "is indicative of how much it fears and opposes the improvement of relations between China and India." Indeed, it concluded, "Moscow has been trying to drive a wedge between the two countries and damage their friendly relations for a long time. Ever since the latter part of the 1950s, it has engaged in such behavior."[15]

---

[11]Quoted in *Statesman*, March 10, 1979.

[12]Quoted in Robert Rand, "Kosygin Ends His Visit to India," *Radio Liberty Research*, RL 89/79, March 15, 1979, p. 2.

[13]*Overseas Hindustan Times*, March 22, 1979.

[14]See the discussion in Robert C. Horn, "Afghanistan and the Soviet-Indian Influence Relationship," *Asian Survey*, March 1983, pp. 244–260.

[15]*Beijing Review*, May 31, 1982, p. 11.

Nature of the Relationship: Limiting Factors

The closeness of relations between Moscow and New Delhi, as the above discussion makes clear, has had limitations. In their perceptions of world affairs and foreign policy interests, the Soviet Union and India have indeed shared a broad range of coincidence. However, this coincidence has not been complete.

Perhaps the best example of the coincidence of interests and its limitations is to be found in the role that the "China factor" has played in the Indo-Soviet relationship. Although this factor has been central in relations, and though there has been broad agreement on how to deal with it, between Moscow and New Delhi there has been a major and all-pervasive difference: for the Soviet Union, China has been the highest concern in Asia while for India the number one issue has always been Pakistan. Relations between New Delhi and Moscow, then, have been closest when both capitals have perceived a close link between the Pakistani and Chinese threats. This was the case in 1969–71, in 1975, and again in 1980 following the Afghan invasion. When Indo-Pakistani and Sino-Soviet tension has eased somewhat, however, as in 1972–74 and the post-1982 period, each capital, particularly New Delhi, has probed for an improvement in relations with the other's adversary. In short, New Delhi has not always been as responsive as Moscow would have liked to warnings about relations with China, and to a lesser extent the Soviets have not always been quite as sensitive to Indian concerns regarding Pakistan as New Delhi would like. Times of tension in the region have tended to merge Indian and Soviet foreign policy interest, and these rather subtle differences in priorities have emerged in times of greater relaxation.

This difference in Soviet and Indian foreign policy goals—as well as the overall strength of the relationship—is well illustrated by the nature of ties since the Soviet invasion of Afghanistan.[16] India has not been able to obtain Soviet withdrawal, and the USSR has not been able to obtain Indian endorsement of the Soviet action. Moscow's invasion and continued occupation have not been fully supported by New Delhi, nor have they brought about a rupture in relations (the alternatives that many in the West predicted). On the one hand, India agreed with the Soviet analysis that blamed the situation in Afghanistan on attempts by "some outside power"—Pakistan, China, and the United States in particular—to interfere in the country's internal affairs by training, arming, and encouraging subversive elements. Moreover, New Delhi was particularly sensitive to the repercussions of the Soviet action, the major one being negotiations between Washington and Islamabad which eventually led to a $3.2 billion agreement on military and economic aid. This development, along with plans for the early delivery of sophisticated F-16

[16]See Horn, "Afghanistan," *passim*.

aircraft to Pakistan, greatly raised the level of threat perception within India. Increased American and Chinese involvement in the region, and particularly the rearming of Pakistan, has thus brought Indian and Soviet views closer together.

The Soviet invasion, on the other hand, has also caused strains. Barely a month after the invasion the Kremlin dispatched Foreign Minister Gromyko to New Delhi in the hopes of obtaining an Indian endorsement of the Soviet move.[17] Gromyko failed, and in June, New Delhi sent External Affairs Minister Narasimha Rao to Moscow to try to obtain a pledge of withdrawal, complete with timetable. He, too, failed.[18] This set the pattern for meetings that have continued to the present, in which Afghanistan is discussed with both sides expressing their views and refusing to budge. The fundamental disagreement is substantial enough that Afghanistan is never even mentioned in the final communiqués or joint statements from these meetings, even though the Indians candidly point out that the issue has been discussed. This reality was seen yet again in Prime Minister Rajiv Gandhi's May 1985 visit to the USSR: he reported at a news conference in Moscow that the situation in Afghanistan had been discussed "at some length" and that Soviet leader Mikhail Gorbachev had given him an account of Soviet assertions that Pakistan was backing the Afghan rebels. India's policy had not changed, Gandhi said: "We are not for any country interfering or intervening in the internal affairs of another country."[19] There was no mention of Afghanistan in the very lengthy joint statement published at the end of the summit.[20]

Additional limiting factors from the Indian side have included New Delhi's efforts to develop other options in foreign policy. Recent years have seen the approach to China as well as a certain warming toward the United States. Indira Gandhi visited Washington in 1982, Rajiv in 1985. Both visits, while introducing little in the way of substantive changes to the relationship, greatly improved the atmosphere and seemed to trigger a more positive approach toward India on the part of the Reagan administration. New Delhi's determination to develop its options also led it to refuse to sign the nuclear Non-Proliferation Treaty and to forego the option of developing a nuclear weapon. (Such a device was detonated in 1974.) Finally, India's interest in regional leadership in South Asia has also made for important, if subtle, differences in Moscow's and New Delhi's otherwise closely similar views of the expansion of superpower capabilities in the Indian Ocean.[21]

In sum, although there is a substantial area of similar or even identical

---

[17] See *Statesman*, February 12–15, 1980. The joint statement is found in *Tass*, February 14, 1980.
[18] *Indian and Foreign Review*, July 1, 1980.
[19] Quoted in *New York Times*, May 23, 1985.
[20] *Pravda*, May 27, 1985.
[21] See Walter K. Andersen, "Soviets in the Indian Ocean: Much Ado about Something—But What?" *Asian Survey*, September 1984, pp. 912–930.

Soviet and Indian perceptions, in some areas these views diverge. On some key points, as a result, Soviet and Indian policies do not coincide. India has interests beyond its ties to the USSR, such as developing its relations with China and the United States, asserting its role in the nonaligned world and South Asia, and supporting the principle of noninterference by large powers in the internal affairs of weaker states. These interests sometimes conflict with Moscow's other interests, including its near obsession with China, its varying desire for detente with the United States as well as its competition with it, naval expansion in the Indian Ocean, and the defense and projection of its interests in Afghanistan.

Pakistan since the Afghan Invasion

The Soviet invasion and continuing occupation of Afghanistan have clearly altered the situation in South Asia. For the Soviets, the most significant change has been to raise Pakistan much higher in Moscow's perception of its interest in the subcontinent. This change is due to the increased American military commitment to Pakistan and, particularly, to the fact that Pakistan has become the funnel for military assistance (from Islamabad as well as from the United States and China) to the anti-Soviet rebels in Afghanistan. Pakistan has now taken on an importance for Moscow which is intrinsic rather than merely derivative of Soviet interests and policy in India.

Nevertheless, this development has not changed the fundamental nature of the USSR's policy and relations in South Asia. Indeed, Pakistan's role in the Afghan conflict has in many ways strengthened Soviet-Indian ties, as discussed above. Moscow may be working with New Delhi in a coordinated policy, trying to decouple Islamabad from the United States and China and to bring India and Pakistan together. The Soviets have tried to do so before, however, with not very positive results: the Tashkent meeting in early 1966, at which Kosygin mediated between the two states, led to a policy of balance which lasted only through 1968. Small-scale Soviet military assistance to Pakistan at that time caused such concern in New Delhi that Moscow halted it rather than risk jeopardizing relations with India. Since then Soviet policy has consistently supported India alone. It is difficult to envision developments in the near future which would cause Moscow to alter that approach significantly.[22]

Soviet policy toward Pakistan since the invasion has been two-pronged. On the one hand, Moscow has urged Islamabad to accept realities and negotiate an agreement with Kabul. On the other, it has issued stern warnings to the Pakistanis to stop backing the "counterrevolutionaries" in Afghanistan.

[22]See the discussion in Cohen, "South Asia after Afghanistan."

In mid-October 1975, for example, *Tass* ominously said that Pakistan was "jeopardizing its future" by its policy in Afghanistan.[23] Moscow also has repeatedly denounced Islamabad's collaboration with Washington, arguing that the United States is "transforming Pakistan into a bridge-head for aggression."[24]

In sum, Pakistan is more important to the Soviets now than before the invasion of Afghanistan, but Soviet policy toward the subcontinent has not been altered. If anything, the USSR is more pro-Indian than before. Although Moscow would like Pakistan to halt its support for the Afghan rebels, the conflict is one whose costs the Soviets can apparently tolerate into the foreseeable future. Moscow has not indicated willingness to pay anything of significance—especially in terms of India's interests—to bring about a change in Islamabad. Indeed, Soviet deputy foreign minister Mikhail Kapitsa was quoted near the end of 1985 in a Pakistani English-language newspaper as saying that although "the Soviet Union desires friendly relations with all nations in South Asia," it "will take India's side in any dispute with its neighbors."[25]

Soviet Perceptions and the Future of Indo-Soviet Relations

One insight into the Soviet view of its relationship with India is found in the general secretary's reports to successive party congresses. After only a mild reference to India at the Twenty-third Congress in 1966, Leonid Brezhnev expanded his commentary slightly at the Twenty-fourth. He cited the "inspiring" developments of Mrs. Gandhi's struggle against "right-wing reaction" in India and hailed Soviet-Indian bilateral ties:

> Our friendly relations with India have received considerable development. The Indian government's pursuit of a peace-loving, independent course in international affairs, the feelings of friendship that traditionally link the peoples of our two countries—all this helps to deepen Soviet-Indian cooperation.[26]

This was merely a prelude to Brezhnev's comments to the Twenty-fifth Congress of the CPSU five years later, where he lavished praise on India to an unprecedented degree. After discussing the multifaceted cooperation between the two countries, Brezhnev pointedly said that "we attach special importance to friendship with this great country." Referring to the 1971 treaty, the CPSU leader asserted that "during the past five year period Soviet-Indian relations rose to a new level."

[23]*Tass*, October 15, 1985.
[24]For example, see *Pravda*, October 22, 1985.
[25]*Muslim*, October 11, 1985.
[26]*Pravda*, March 31, 1971.

In even this brief time, its enormous importance for our bilateral ties and its role as a stabilizing factor in South Asia and on the continent as a whole have been clearly demonstrated.

Close political and economic cooperation with the Republic of India is on steady course. Soviet people are sympathetic toward—more than that, they feel solidarity with—India's peace-loving foreign policy and the courageous struggle of that country's progressive forces to solve the difficult social and economic problems confronting it. We wish the people and government of India complete success in their struggle.[27]

Brezhnev's last address, delivered to the Twenty-sixth Congress in early 1981, was somewhat different.

Comrades, a big place in the Soviet Union's relations with the newly-free countries is, of course, accorded to our cooperation with India. We welcome the increasing role played by that country in international affairs. Our ties with it are continuing to expand. In both our countries, Soviet-Indian friendship has become a deep-rooted popular tradition.

As a result of the recent negotiations in Delhi with Prime Minister Indira Gandhi and other Indian leaders, the entire range of Soviet-Indian relations has been taken substantially further.

Joint action with peaceful and independent India will continue to be one of the important areas of Soviet foreign relations.[28]

Two aspects of Brezhnev's comments deserve special mention. One is that, compared to his 1976 description of India and Soviet-Indian relations, his 1981 characterization is briefer, milder, far less enthusiastic. It is apparent that relations in early 1981 did not occupy the same lofty status as in early 1976. The events of the intervening period had caused a certain loss of enthusiasm in Moscow: Indira Gandhi's defeat in 1977 by the more conservative and "pro-Western" Morarji Desai and the Janata, the general increase in instability within India, increased Indian attempts to improve relations with China and the United States, and then India's somewhat disappointing stance on the Afghan issue. The second significant aspect of Brezhnev's analysis, however, is the other side of the coin: India was the *only* country singled out for more than a passing reference in the section of Brezhnev's speech devoted to development of relations with the newly-free countries. It was a highly significant gesture on Moscow's part, indicating that even if relations with India were not quite on the same level as a few years previously, they were still of particular importance and continued to represent perhaps Moscow's most encouraging success story in the Third World.[29]

[27]Ibid., February 24, 1976.
[28]*New Times* no. 9 (February 1981).
[29]Mikhail Gorbachev's address to the 27th Congress in February 1986 provided no additional insights. Although India was not mentioned by name, neither was any other Third World state

Another method of assessing the results of Soviet policy in South Asia over the past thirty years is to weigh the gains or advantages accruing to Moscow against the costs or disadvantages. It seems evident that relations with India have served the Soviet Union quite well, if imperfectly, in the pursuit of its goals in South Asia. New Delhi has shared Moscow's goal of reducing Western and containing Chinese influence, and it has been willing to accord the USSR status as a global and Asian power. Moreover, the model Soviet-Indian relationship has greatly helped the Soviets in their effort to portray the USSR as a friend and supporter of the nonaligned and the Third World. Probably no other relationship has so admirably served Moscow in its pursuit of all these objectives.

Finally, one can get an important sense of gains from the extent to which the Soviet Union has been able to influence—that is, exercise some degree of leverage over—Indian behavior.[30] The record here is very sparse, however, and examples of Soviet influence are difficult to find. Although Moscow may be said to have influenced New Delhi not to go to war early in 1971, for instance, by October the Soviets had come to agree with India about the necessity of a short-term conflict. More recently India has not condemned the Soviets for the Afghan invasion, and Moscow may have influenced New Delhi in this regard by reinforcing past attitudes. Yet India's stance is consistent with past actions (such as on the Soviet invasions of Hungary 1956 and Czechoslovakia in 1968), and in any case the Soviets may have paid for it: Moscow likely contributed to the Indian decision to recognize the Vietnamese-installed Heng Samrin regime in Cambodia in 1980 but perhaps only at the cost of New Delhi going further with normalization with China. The Russians did seem to influence New Delhi's role in the nonaligned foreign ministers' meeting in early 1981 by persuading India to modify its position somewhat on Afghanistan. But when India met resistance from its nonaligned brethren, it reverted to its standard position, and Soviet influence evaporated. Overall, therefore, direct Soviet influence appears to have been limited and short-lived.

The costs that Moscow has borne in pursuing Indian support of these objectives have been substantial but, apparently, within acceptable limits. In terms of economic costs the USSR has been over the past three decades India's main provider of economic assistance, its second-ranking trade partner, and its major supplier of weaponry. If we are to assess the costs to Moscow, however, perhaps more important would be situations where India was able to influence Soviet behavior; these would represent costs or disadvantages to

---

except Afghanistan. Indeed, there was no separate discussion of the Third World at all. The text of the address is in *Pravda*, February 26, 1986. For analysis of the changing Soviet policy toward developing countries, see Francis Fukuyama, "Gorbachev and the Third World," *Foreign Affairs*, Spring 1986, pp. 715–731.

[30]For an extended discussion, see chap. 8, "The Parameters of an Influence Relationship," in Horn, *Soviet-Indian Relations*.

the USSR. There are indeed examples of a weaker state influencing a super-power, but they too are limited in number and significance. For instance, although New Delhi was unable to prevent Moscow from offering arms aid to Pakistan in 1968, the Indians did influence the Russians to stop the program shortly thereafter. India's playing of the China card in autumn 1972 and again in mid-1976 and 1978–79 influenced the Soviets into a variety of concessions: recognizing some of the Indian positions regarding the Sino-Indian border, further aid, rhetorical support, and an offer of crude oil. The symbolic significance of that oil can hardly be overemphasized, for India had been trying since the beginning of the 1970s to obtain Soviet oil. The USSR's own needs, those of its East European comrades, and the hard currency generated by sales to the West held a higher priority for Moscow. Then, in December 1976, when prospects for a Sino-Indian normalization seemed particularly good, the Soviets were suddenly forthcoming. The Soviets used their oil weapon again when Kosygin offered to increase the quantity sold while in New Delhi in March 1979; Brezhnev did the same in December 1980. The first offer followed Vajpayee's mission to China, and the second also was extended when Indian interest in normalized ties with Beijing was again growing. Other Soviet aid packages—such as the economic one in 1977 and the three major military ones in this decade—were also proposed as inducements (often with even better terms than before, or with previously unavailable items, or both) to reinforce Indian behavior, being directed at the new Janata regime in the first case and at the government's interest in buying Western arms and the possibility of change in Indian policy toward the West, China, or as regards Afghanistan in the latter cases.

This assessment points to the conclusion that Moscow has made considerable gains, at moderate costs, in its South Asian policy. These gains have not been tangible—such as obtaining base rights or turning India into a satellite—but they have been highly significant in the competition for global influence with the United States and China. The next question is how permanent these gains are likely to be. What kinds of changes might take place in Soviet and Indian policy to cause either party to reduce its regard for the importance of the relationship?

Looking first at the Soviet Union, it is possible that changes in Soviet relations with either the United States or China could decrease India's importance for Moscow. And, in the mid-1980s indeed, there are such tentative moves under way on both fronts. Nevertheless, in both cases progress will be so gradual, if there is progress at all, that India is likely to remain a significant focus of Soviet policies for a long time to come. Even if Soviet relations with its two major rivals were to improve considerably, moreover, Moscow's interest in India is likely to continue. New Delhi will remain an entree to the nonaligned and Third World; the USSR's relationship with India is a most useful proof of the credibility of the Soviet Union as a "natural ally" of these countries.

What changes in Indian policy might discourage Moscow and lessen its interest? Short of a complete about-face in foreign policy orientation, such changes are also unlikely. Even if New Delhi's relations with Washington or Beijing improved substantially, for example, India would maintain its Soviet connection. That relationship has been stable, both over time and in crises, and it is difficult to imagine what could cause India to jettison it. An increase in the internal instability of the country, due either to economic malaise or ethnic or religious divisions, would likely dampen Soviet enthusiasm, as it has in the past. Unless it led to the total collapse of the country, however, Moscow would most likely try to see it through. Let us turn back then to a drastic change in foreign policy orientation, most likely, presumably, with a change in leadership in New Delhi. Perhaps the most useful historical precedent here, the replacement of Mrs. Gandhi and the Congress (I) by Morarji Desai and the Janata from 1977 to early 1980, provides evidence of the long-term and stable nature of the relationship, a relationship not susceptible to the outlooks of differing leaderships.[31] Desai, to be sure, did not have the same degree of sympathy for the USSR as did Mrs. Gandhi. In addition, he sought to improve New Delhi's ties with the United States and China, and also to diversify India's source of military supplies. Nevertheless, he went barely further in any of these areas than Mrs. Gandhi did before or after his term, and from the beginning he clearly recognized the importance to India of the relationship with Moscow. Economic and military ties continued, perceptions seemed to coincide to a wide degree, and Desai made two visits to Moscow during his brief tenure in office. Although there were changes in the degree of closeness between the states, in short, the fundamentals of the relationship were unaltered. The same has been true since Rajiv Gandhi succeeded his assassinated mother. Although Rajiv's Western orientation has been stressed, his first official visit abroad after becoming prime minister was to the USSR. Relations with the West were to be improved, it is true, but they were to be improved within the framework of the significance of Indo-Soviet ties. After all, as Rajiv pointed out, the Soviet Union "has been an old friend over thirty years."[32] Soviet-Indian relations have continued to develop along these set lines. In 1986 alone, a Supreme Soviet delegation has been to New Delhi, a new trade protocol calling for further cooperation has been signed, a delegation from India's Congress (I) party attended the CPSU's Twenty-seventh Congress, and the Indian minister for external affairs and trade has journeyed to Moscow.[33] Moreover, Rajiv has continued to contrast India's relations with the Soviet Union favorably to those with the United States.[34]

[31] See chap. 6, "The Janata Interregnum," in ibid.

[32] *New York Times*, May 23, 1985.

[33] See respectively *Soviet Review* (New Delhi), February 6, 1986; UPI, April 29, 1986, and Radio Moscow, April 30, 1986, in *Foreign Broadcast Information Service—Soviet Union* (FBIS-SU), May 1, 1986; Mohan Ram, "Come Closer, Comrade," *Far Eastern Economic Review*, January 30, 1986, p. 32; the speech of the chief Congress [I] delegate to the meeting is in *Pravda*, March 3, 1986; and FBIS-SU, June 16, 1986.

[34] *Tass*, March 5, 1986.

Soviet policy regarding India has followed a consistent pattern over the past thirty years. There have been some lags and surges of attention, but these have been limited, which likely helps explain why relations have been so stable, why changes have taken place within such narrow parameters. Other factors may include the success Moscow has had (far greater than Washington's) in convincing the Indians that it was basing its policy on Indian interests as such rather than viewing those interests as only a function of broader strategic concerns. As a general rule, for example, the Soviet leadership has backed away from the China issue when the Indians become clearly uncomfortable with Moscow's diatribes. Also noteworthy are the USSR's material and diplomatic support for India and its efforts at molding Indian public opinion (compared to the United States, the Soviets direct some 50 percent more radio broadcasts to India, their monthly magazine has eight times the circulation and one-third the price, they translate more books, and distribute more journals).[35] The Soviets have been skillful, finally, in managing their relations with India, avoiding crude attempts to apply influence. The result is that the vast majority of Indians perceive the Soviet Union as the most trustworthy of the major powers.

The basic explanation for the nature of the Soviet-Indian relationship lies in the question of *need*. Who has needed whom more? The relationship through the 1970s and into the 1980s has indeed been, as Robert Donaldson asserts, a "shifting balance [of] mutual dependency."[36] India has needed the Soviet Union for support, in times of crisis vis-à-vis Pakistan and in times of uncertainty as the Sino-American rapprochement has developed. India has also needed the economic, technical, and military assistance that the Soviets have been able to provide. Moscow, on the other hand, has needed India against China, and to a lesser extent the United States, as well as to serve as evidence of the USSR's good intentions for the nonaligned movement, the Third World, and Asia. The degree of need that each feels has depended on the importance of the particular issue and the options available. In 1969–71 each state needed the other's support against its main adversary, Pakistan for India and China for the Soviet Union. After the crisis in Sino-Soviet relations passed in 1969, New Delhi's need for support—given the developing crisis with Islamabad over Bangladesh and India's isolation from the United States and China—was the greater. After the Bangladesh War India's stronger regional position greatly reduced New Delhi's dependence on the USSR. Although the relationship stayed close, both sides explored relations with other powers both regional and external. When those cautious efforts collapsed, the symbol being Washington's lifting of its arms embargo against Pakistan, the mutual need was fairly even and the close relationship restored. Moscow apparently became convinced, however, that the April 1976 policy change

---

[35]See *Los Angeles Times*, November 9, 1980, and *Time*, March 9, 1981, pp. 15–17.
[36]Robert H. Donaldson, *The Soviet-Indian Alignment: Quest for Influence* (Denver: University of Denver Monograph Series in World Affairs, 1979).

toward China signified that New Delhi's need was reduced, and the Soviets responded with a wide variety of inducements to India to rein in its search for normalization. The Janata perceived an even smaller Indian need and sought to improve ties with Washington and Beijing. Even Desai's regime, however, realized the fundamental importance to India of the Soviet relationship, and its policy changes were carefully calibrated so as not to jeopardize the essentials of the relationship. Since the end of 1979 the sense of need seems to have heightened in both countries, perhaps more so in the USSR. The two Gandhis' suspicions of the United States and its arming of Pakistan have been counterbalanced by Moscow's need for support in the wake of the Afghan invasion. The Soviet appeal to India before the Delhi meeting of nonaligned foreign ministers in February 1981 to help the USSR out in its "time of trial," as the Soviet Union had helped India in 1971, could not have been a clearer expression of this Soviet need.[37] It is important to note that this mutual sense of need continues to be recognized in both capitals today. As Rajiv Gandhi put it to an appreciative Soviet audience in May 1985, "we have stood together in times of trial, and we recognize that."[38]

This assessment of Soviet-Indian relations has several implications for the future of U.S. policy toward India and toward the Soviet Union in south Asia.[39] First, Washington must recognize that it is not Soviet influence but rather a coincidence of world views that has made the relationship between Moscow and New Delhi so close. The West seems always to assume that a state that looks at the world in terms similar to Moscow's has been influenced by the Soviets. But many factors help explain why Indian perceptions of world politics have resembled those of the Soviet Union more than those of the United States. They include India's colonial experience and foreign policy principles and the USSR's economic development and challenge to the West in world affairs, as well as specific Western policies such as the repeated arming of Pakistan. In other words, the strain in Indo-U.S. relations has not been because of Soviet influence but rather because Washington and New Delhi see South Asian affairs and much of world politics in dramatically different terms. Second, the United States needs to be aware that Indo-Soviet relations are likely to remain close and that Washington will be unable to pull the two apart. Third, we need to recognize that India's influence over Soviet behavior is also limited and that New Delhi will not be able to solve regional problems, such as Afghanistan, involving the USSR.

The United States must also be sensitive to India's interest in developing and promoting options in its foreign policy. Even within the constraints of India's close relations with the Soviet Union, there is room for greater Indo-

[37]This Soviet approach can be seen in Andrei Fialkovsky, "We Rejoice at Your Achievements," *New Times* no. 4 (January 1981), pp. 8–9.
[38]Quoted in *New York Times*, May 23, 1985.
[39]See Palmer, *United States and India*.

U.S. understanding and cooperation. An improved relationship between Washington and New Delhi might help lessen tension and decrease polarization in South Asia. India is no more interested than the United States, in the unbridled exercise of Soviet power in the region and neither country is interested in a fragmented Pakistan. Rajiv Gandhi's 1985 visits to Moscow and Washington characterized well the situation and opportunities for the United States: the Soviet Union was clearly accorded the higher priority, but Rajiv also went out of his way to establish a new tenor of relations with the United States. President Reagan was also interested, the two leaders got along well together, and the United States considered providing sophisticated military assistance and following up on a recent agreement to provide India with various high-technology items in the civilian field.[40] Can the United States find policies that will help build a relationship necessarily mixed but in the interests of both countries, a relationship marked not by euphoria, anger, or benign neglect but by a realistic assessment of the overlap between American and Indian perceptions of national interests? In the past Washington has been able to do so only in very short spurts. The very real limitations to the relationship—New Delhi's perception of its national interests includes close relations with the Soviet Union—will have to be recognized, but the opportunity may be present at least partially to balance the Soviet role.

[40]Among other sources, see Robert Manning, "Rajiv's Winning Ways," *Far Eastern Economic Review*, June 27, 1985, pp. 14–15, and "Rajiv's Dazzling Roadshow," *Asiaweek*, June 28, 1985, pp. 7–8; Li Wenzheng, "U.S. Trip Builds Better Ties," *Beijing Review*, July 1, 1985, pp. 11–12; and *New York Times*, June 14, 1985.

10

USSR Policy in Sub-Saharan Africa

Colin Legum

Soviet policy in sub-Saharan Africa can be properly understood only in terms of the global interests and priorities of the Soviet Union and the constraints on its pursuit of its objectives. Any meaningful analysis must take full account of the historic changes in the balance of world power since World War II, which resulted from the rise of the USSR as a challenging, but still evolving, superpower; the decline of West European imperialism; and the emergence of the United States as the leading superpower. The conjunction of these earth-shattering developments disrupted the old balance of world power and triggered off the East-West struggle to establish a new equilibrium. Western Europe, having lost its hegemonial position over much of the world, was pushed heavily on the defensive and found it necessary to rely increasingly, though not easily, on the United States to retain as much of its former power as possible.

As the new challenger for power, the USSR was bound to take the offensive and to pursue policies that were essentially expansionist—not so much a territorial expansion as an expansion of influence and control by direct and indirect methods. Two other entirely new factors determined the nature of the struggle to establish a new equilibrium: the emergence in the late 1950s of Maoist China as a rival to the USSR instead of as an ally, which created a third dimension in the balance-of-power struggle; and the birth of what has come to be loosely but not inaccurately described as the Third World, with its aspirations to be nonaligned (wishing, that is, not to be involved in the superpowers' rivalries). However, the economic and military weaknesses of most Third World countries made it impossible for them to remain entirely aloof from the struggle.

Superpower rivalry opened up opportunities for developing nations to engage in loose or close economic and/or political alliances with whichever side seemed to hold out more promise for the fulfillment of their national goals while avoiding, as far as possible, joining either camp. This situation produced a pattern of fairly rapid shifts in alliances between particular Third World countries and either the USSR or the West. Characteristic of these alliances was their transitory nature. Shifts depended on two elements: the willingness of the major powers to provide their clients with economic, military, and diplomatic support; and regime changes in Third World countries. These alliances were essentially opportunistic on all sides. Thus regimes or movements that found their interests threatened or obstructed by Western policies either walked the road to Moscow (as exemplified by Nasser's Egypt) or, if it was the Soviets who were perceived as being unhelpful, took the opposite route to the West. However, the preference of most developing countries was to establish a relationship with both the USSR and the West, as well as with China. On the whole the Soviets found it easier to provide military than economic aid, which gave the West a decisive edge—an advantage that grew with the serious deterioration in the economic condition of most African countries after the mid-1970s. The West's position also improved with the final liquidation of the European colonial empires, leaving only South Africa and Namibia in serious contention. The USSR had a distinct advantage in its willingness and ability to support the national liberation movements that, by and large, developed as challengers to pro-Western governments.

In fact, very few Third World governments can be properly characterized as either pro-West or pro-Soviet. Irrespective of their temporary alliances, all are essentially "pro-themselves," that is, nationalist. Analysts of Third World politics can be seriously misled if they rigidly classify the majority of Third World regimes as firmly rooted in either the Western or the Soviet camp.

Objectives of Soviet Policy in Africa

Moscow's African policies show no evidence of following any master plan but appear rather as pragmatic responses to developments in the continent since the onset of independence in the late 1950s. Because pragmatic responses require adjustments to the flux of circumstances in terms of both internal and external policy changes, it is not surprising to find that Soviet policies are shot through with inconsistencies over the past thirty years of Moscow's experience in seeking to extend its influence in the postcolonial world. Overall, Soviet policy can be described as opportunistic in the sense that it has sought to take advantage of opportunities when they have presented themselves. For example, when President Sekou Touré broke angrily with de Gaulle's France, the Soviets rushed forward to support Guinea and, soon thereafter, also its neighbor Mali; when Jaafar Nimeiry staged his military coup in Sudan in 1970, Moscow responded immediately to his appeal for military aid; and a year later, when Idi Amin staged his military coup in

Uganda, the Soviet bloc joined with Libya in becoming the principal armorer of that unsavory dictator's regime. Moscow, though, showed more caution in answering appeals for support from two former French colonies, the Congo and Benin, whose regimes had proclaimed themselves "people's republics." Similar caution was shown in the level of commitment to President Ratsiraka's military regime in Madagascar, which had declared its hostility to the French in particular and the West in general. The most glaring example of Soviet opportunism is provided by policies in the Horn of Africa: in 1967 Moscow adopted Somalia as a client state, after the regime of President Siad Barre had proclaimed itself Marxist-Leninist, and undertook to help the country build a modern army of 10,000 men in exchange for naval and air facilities at Berbera and Mogadishu. But when Somalia's rival, Ethiopia, adopted an anti-Western stand after the downfall of Emperor Haile Selassie in 1973, Moscow quickly shifted its support from Mogadishu to Addis Ababa, where the prize was potentially much greater.

These opportunistic inconsistencies notwithstanding, USSR policy has been remarkably consistent in several major respects.

It has been undeviating in its support of national liberation movements that operate against governments regarded as belonging to the "imperialist camp."

In every case where opportunities have presented themselves, it has sought to secure naval and air facilities from its clients.

It has given general political and diplomatic support to governments and movements identified as struggling against "imperialism" even where those protagonists did not themselves profess to be Marxists or supporters of the USSR. In this respect it has clung to its avowed policy of waging an "anti-imperialist struggle."

It has used every possible opportunity to strengthen its military outreach (particularly naval) to areas strategically located in proximity to the Middle East.[1]

Since 1958 it has worked hard to undermine Chinese influence in Africa. The length to which the Soviets would go in pursuing this last objective is exemplified in two cases. Soviet support for the tyrannical Idi Amin (a professing anticommunist) seems to have been dictated largely by the USSR's need for a foothold in East Africa to counterbalance the perceived influence of the Chinese in Uganda's neighbor, Tanzania. Even more striking was support for the Zimbabwe African People's Union (ZAPU), led by a noncommunist bourgeois of the first order, Joshua Nkomo, in preference to the Zimbabwe African National Union (ZANU), led by Robert Mugabe, a professed Marxist-Leninist. The reason for this strange choice (strange, that is, for an ideological state) was that ZANU's military wing got its major support from the Chinese.

---

[1]In several major respects the geopolitical situation of the countries of north and northeast Africa makes them as much an extension of the Middle East as a part of Africa; this is especially true of the southern littoral of the Mediterranean and the Red Sea littoral countries in the Horn of Africa.

It is possible to draw some broad conclusions from this brief description of Soviet global objectives, the contradictory ways in which it has pursued these objectives, and its focus on target countries. Moscow's strategy appears to be based on a set of priorities that determine the degree of commitment it is willing to make in pursuing its objectives. These priorities can be categorized as (1) *Immediate*: consolidating Moscow's position in Europe and protecting the Soviet Union's eastern and southern flanks. In these areas the USSR is constrained only by the need to avoid direct military conflict with the Western powers, especially in strategically sensitive areas where it is at a severe military disadvantage. (2) *Short-term*: changing the balance of power in Southeast Asia and the Middle East. The Afro-Arab dimension of the Middle Eastern conflicts accounts for the Soviet interest in Egypt, the Maghreb states, and the Horn of Africa. (3) *Medium-term*: strengthening its position in the Red Sea area, which is bound on its western shore by the countries of the Horn. This priority is directly linked to the Soviets' ascending role as a world naval power, involving it in ocean politics (addressed below). Another priority in this category is the Indian subcontinent and the eastern Indian Ocean. (4) *Longer-term*: expanding its political influence and military outreach in southern Africa, with its strategic location in the Indian Ocean and on the South Atlantic sea routes. Another longer-term priority is Latin America and the Caribbean islands.

However, circumstances do arise when the USSR finds itself presented with irresistible opportunities to extend its influence and damage Western interests, as in the case of the former Portuguese colonies of Angola and Mozambique, where Moscow's support for the national liberation struggle produced a favorable situation. Nevertheless, whenever the USSR has responded to windfall opportunities outside its immediate or short-term priorities, the degree of its commitment has been significantly lower than in target areas enjoying a higher priority. This lower commitment is shown by Moscow's failure to fulfill its treaty of friendship obligations to Mozambique, which left President Samora Machel no alternative but to sign the humiliating Nkomati agreement with South Africa in 1984. Regarding Angola, the USSR has held regular consultations with the United States to avoid a damaging confrontation with the West.

The Official View of the USSR's African Policy

Moscow's official view of Soviet interests and policy in Africa, stripped of ideological persiflage, is a useful point of reference to correct for misperceptions and distorting biases.[2]

---

[2]The information in this section is derived from unpublished reports of private talks between Western diplomats and academics with their counterparts in the Soviet Union. These reports

The USSR insists that, like the United States, it has legitimate interests anywhere in the world; but it questions whether either superpower has vital interests in the African continent. However, although the USSR lays no claim to "vital interests," it insists that it has "responsibilities" to its allies in the region. The principal Soviet allies are Ethiopia and Angola; two of the liberation movements in southern Africa—the African National Congress (ANC) and the South-West African People's Organization of Namibia (SWAPO); and, somewhat lower down the list, Mozambique.

South Africa is acknowledged to be the hegemonic power in the region. It is regarded as possessing a strong regime with considerable political, economic, and military power. As yet, no revolutionary situation exists in South Africa, but one is developing, and when it ripens it will happen swiftly. In that event the USSR and the United States will have to decide jointly how to confront the situation. The USSR prefers to see change in South Africa through peaceful negotiations rather than revolution, but it doubts whether this is likely to occur.

The ANC is regarded as the leading force in the struggle against the status quo in South Africa, but it is not the only power. The United Democratic Front (UDF) is viewed as a positive factor in the growth of the national liberation movement. Neither the ANC nor SWAPO is seen by Moscow as a communist organization. It is thought to be wrong to regard these movements, or Angola and Mozambique, as client states of either the USSR or the United States. On the other hand, South Africa is seen as a client state of the West. SWAPO is regarded as the only legitimate representative of the peoples of Namibia.

The USSR accepts the UN Security Council's Resolution 435 as offering an acceptable framework for the resolution of the Namibian conflict, but it does not believe that South Africa has any serious intention of seeing it implemented.

The USSR does not accept Jonas Savimbi's Union for the Total National Liberation of Angola (UNITA) as an independent force but merely as an instrument of South African and American policies. Thanks to external support, UNITA is seen as militarily strong but politically weak. The USSR is pledged to supporting the MPLA government in Angola and therefore cannot ignore threats to security and territorial integrity. Mozambique's decision to sign the Nkomati accord with South Africa is not regarded as a point of conflict with the Frelimo regime of former president Samora Machel. This position is held to be consistent with the basis of Soviet policy, which is to support whatever the Africans themselves accept as being good for advancing their interests.

---

gain credibility from the qualifications of the informants to evaluate the authenticity of what they were told. Corroboration comes from diverse sources and from reference to official Soviet policy texts.

Moscow takes the view that joint efforts by the superpowers in managing regional conflicts (whether in the Middle East, Africa, or elsewhere) can be beneficial in lessening the dangers to wider peace. Any attempt by the Western powers to exclude the Soviet Union from playing a role in southern Africa will be resisted and is unlikely to succeed. The USSR strongly favors joint Soviet-American cooperation to deal with the problems of southern Africa and blames the United States for resisting efforts to achieve such cooperation. But the Soviets reject any idea that the superpowers themselves might seek to impose their views on Africans—which, even if it were attempted, would be bound to meet with rejection.

African Views of Soviet Policy

Although the East-West conflict is obviously important in analyzing Soviet and Western policies in the Third World, it is a profound mistake to regard local actors as merely passive victims, clients, or unsuspecting agents of the superpower blocs.[3] African leaders have skillfully exploited the Soviet-Western rivalry to enhance their own interests, and all the major powers have been compelled to adjust their policies to address these African interests in order to advance their own interests. For a variety of reasons, a large majority of African governments have given their nonaligned policies a Western rather than a Soviet slant, but mostly without aligning themselves as allies of either bloc. Such alliances have usually proved to be of a transitory nature, as already mentioned, dependent on the interests of a particular regime and, especially, on the military and economic advantages to be had from a closer relationship with one bloc or the other.

Anticommunism has been a strong characteristic of postindependence African politics and has been a major determinant in foreign policy making. Even those governments which, at one time or another, have given a pro-Soviet tilt to their foreign relations have remained sensitively suspicious of the USSR. The corresponding attitude to the West has been characterized by a high degree of ambivalence rather than by any sense of deep hostility. After thirty years of African independence the Western powers still retain a predominant influence in the continent. Soviet inroads there have been significantly fewer than in any other continent except, perhaps, for Latin America.

One measure of the Soviet Union's failure to make itself an inspiring leader in the postcolonial world is the remarkable absence of communist parties in African countries. The only two sub-Saharan states with a significant communist party are Sudan and South Africa, and both of these parties emerged in the 1920s, inspired by the Bolshevik revolution. The more recent phenome-

[3]See Colin Legum, "The African Environment," *Problems of Communism*, January–February 1978.

non of Marxist-Leninist vanguard parties appears in only two of the countries that had been involved in a prolonged armed struggle, Angola and Mozambique, and in the peculiar circumstances of postimperial Ethiopia. In the first two cases the vanguard parties have remained weak and have failed conspicuously to create strong centralized institutions structured along Marxist-Leninist lines. Only Ethiopia shows some evidence of developing such institutions; but even there the institutions have been imposed from the top, and the vanguard party still lacks a strong, popular base. Some countries that achieved their independence through armed struggle under a professing Marxist-Leninist leadership have not sought either to develop a vanguard party or to establish Marxist-Leninist institutions, for instance, Zimbabwe, Guinea-Bissau, and São Tomé and Principe. The "people's democracies" of Benin and the Congo and, at one period, Somalia have all failed to go beyond paying lip service to Marxism-Leninism.

Thus far, sub-Saharan Africa has proved to be barren soil for the growth of vanguard parties as advocated by Moscow and the historic Third International. Indeed, the period that has seen the rise of the Third World has also witnessed the final decline of the Third International. The alternative, Moscow-centered world movement of "progressive forces" has significantly failed to provide the kind of ideological leadership that was once provided by the Comintern. The Cominform was largely dormant, and besides it was not concerned with the Third World.

The Soviet Union made its greatest impact on Africa in 1956, when it established itself as the strategic ally of Nasser's Egypt; but ever since its failure to prove itself a reliable ally capable of providing effective military and economic aid, Moscow's influence has steadily receded in the continent. A major reason for this, according to one well-known African Marxist, Abdul Rahman Mohamed Babu, a leader of the Zanzibar revolution in 1964, was that

> the Soviet Union did not evolve a consistent policy of helping newly independent countries in Africa and its economic assistance was thus spontaneous and arbitrary. This led to many unfortunate experiences in Africa which indirectly strengthened reactionary forces in the continent and added fuel to imperialist propaganda. This shortcoming does not seem to have been rectified and there is room for fresh initiative in the area by the new Soviet leadership.[4]

Constraints on Soviet Policy in Africa

The relative lack of success of Soviet policy in the sub-Saharan states is attributable, as indicated earlier, to reasons that include the strength of na-

[4]Abdul Rahman Mohamed Babu, "Gorbachev: What Policy for Africa?" *Africa Events* (London), April 1985.

tionalist feelings against foreign ideologies; the failure of Soviet-Marxist ideology either to understand or to come properly to terms with these nationalist feelings; the instability of many new regimes that, when they change, shift their allegiance away from Moscow if it happens to have been supporting the supplanted leadership; the close economic links between newly independent states and the Western economic and trading system; and the cultural, political, and educational ties between modernizing African elites and former metropolitan powers.

The USSR had a distinct edge over the Western powers in three major respects: its ability and willingness to offer almost unlimited military aid, mostly of recently outmoded weapons; its total lack of involvement in South Africa; and its undeviating support for national liberation movements. (In this last advantage, however, it has been handicapped by the existence of more than one liberation movement fighting for power in particular countries, which has resulted in its making the wrong choice, as in Zimbabwe; and because of the preference of some, for instance, the Frelimo movement of Mozambique, for China over the Soviets.)

Soviet policy in practice has been circumscribed by three major factors apart from the less than favorable political and economic climate in postcolonial Africa: the relatively low priority accorded to the African continent in terms of Moscow's immediate and short-term interests, except for the North African countries because they are seen as a politico-military extension of the Middle East, and the Red Sea littoral states; the logistical limits of the Warsaw Pact's military delivery systems; and the limitations of COMECON's economic and technical resources, which make it difficult if not impossible to extend the pattern of aid relations established with Cuba and Vietnam.

In the first ten years after engaging itself as Egypt's strategic ally in 1956—a high Soviet priority commitment that related directly to the developing power struggle in the Middle East—Moscow's only major concentration in sub-Saharan Africa, besides support for national liberation movements, was on strengthening its influence in three West African allied states that were then still radical—Nkrumah's Ghana, Sekou Touré's Guinea, and Modibo Keita's Mali. The immediate Soviet interest in this region was twofold: to develop a Soviet airlink across the Sahara, running from Cairo to Bamako in Mali and Conakry in Guinea, and thence across the Atlantic to Havana; and to obtain naval facilities in Conakry as a new port for what later became the Soviet Navy's West Africa patrol.

The next Soviet move was a military treaty with Somalia and, very briefly, with Sudan—the two key countries, apart from Ethiopia, in the Horn of Africa. The Soviets traded an offer to train and equip a modern, 10,000-strong army for Somalia's paradoxical "Marxist-Leninist military regime" in exchange for naval facilities in the primitive port of Berbera and in Mogadishu. After their expulsion from Egypt, the Soviets began their airlink across the Sahara to Cuba in Mogadishu and continued, as before, through Bamako and Conakry. At that time the USSR had become particularly concerned over the development of the American air base at Diego Garcia in the southwestern Indian Ocean. Now, for the first time, the Soviet Navy had access to port facilities in the Red Sea. These would have become much more important had the Nimeiry regime's brief flirtation with Moscow not come unstuck within a year because of the alleged involvement of the Sudan Communist party in an attempted coup. Nimeiry claimed that the Bulgarian Embassy in Khartoum had been a center for this intrigue. The Soviet agreement with the Somalis served not only their military interest in the Red Sea area but also a second of their priority interest: countering China's influence in Africa. The Somalis had in fact approached Beijing before Moscow in their search for military aid.

The amount of aid that the USSR had committed to Somalia was relatively small, but when Moscow shifted its allegiance to the Ethiopians, it undertook a considerable military and economic burden that carried a significant element of risk because the revolution, triggered by the downfall of Haile Selassie, was still embryonic and its prospects distinctly unpromising. The Soviet special interest in the Horn of Africa is considered below.

Moscow achieved two important breakthroughs in 1975, in Ethiopia and in Angola.[5] Although Mozambique had achieved its independence at almost the same time as Angola, the Frelimo regime, having received its principal military support from China during the liberation struggle, was at first not favorably disposed toward the Soviets. It changed its stance in 1977 when it felt itself threatened by South Africa and turned to Moscow in the belief that the Soviets would be a more credible strategic ally than Peking.

The severe constraints and limitations that have prevented the Soviets from following up on their initial advantages in Africa are revealed in two ways. The first is their passive acceptance of the call for them to quit successively Egypt, Ghana (after Nkrumah's overthrow), the former Belgian Congo (now Zaire), the Sudan, and Somalia. In none of these countries did Moscow gain the support of either popular forces or reliable political interest groups; their known supporters were swiftly eliminated once the local regime had lost the need to appease the USSR in order to retain its friendship. The second is the Soviet admission that it could not afford to divert substantial resources to sub-Saharan countries despite their treaties of friendship and cooperation, as in Angola and Mozambique. If either of these countries of crucial importance in southern Africa had figured on Moscow's list of immediate or short-term priorities, it likely would not have fared so poorly as a Soviet ally.

Faced with heavy military and economic demands from both these Marxist-Leninist states, Moscow advised them to seek economic aid from the capitalist West. In Angola's case, though not in Mozambique's, the Soviet

[5]See Colin Legum, "Angola and the Horn of Africa," in Stephen S. Kaplan, ed., *Diplomacy of Power* (Washington, D.C.: Brookings, 1980), and "The Red Sea and the Horn of Africa in International Perspective," in William L. Dowdy and Russell Trood, ed., *The Indian Ocean: Perspectives on a Strategic Arena* (Durham: Duke University Press, 1985).

bloc and East Germany supplied substantial amounts of military aid as well as providing subsidies to Cuba to enable Castro to maintain 20,000 combat troops. Moscow's action in pushing Angola into the arms of the West had two predictable results: it weakened the Angolan regime's confidence in the USSR as a reliable strategic ally (as had also happened in Egypt); and it increased Luanda's reliance on Western friendship, causing the MPLA regime to discuss concessions to Washington over Cuban troop withdrawals as part of the negotiations over Namibia's independence.

The weakness of the Soviet bloc position was even starker in Mozambique. Not only did the Soviets fail to produce substantial military support for their treaty ally and only skimpy economic aid, but on three separate occasions Moscow's leaders personally advised President Samora Machel to avoid any situation that would involve open military confrontation with South Africa because, as they frankly admitted, the Soviets would not be able to intervene effectively on his side in such an eventuality. Although the Soviet Navy "showed the flag" on two occasions in Maputo when the country seemed to be under threat, the clear reluctance of Moscow to intervene was well understood in Pretoria. It was when Mozambique found itself unable to resist South Africa's policies of military and economic destabilization and when it finally realized that the concept of a "reliable strategic ally" had no meaning in its case that President Machel found it necessary to sign the Nkomati accord.

The Evolution of the USSR's African Policies since 1956

Soviet policies in Africa have undergone changes since the heady early days of 1956 when, as Mohamed Heikal brilliantly describes, Khrushchev enthusiastically embraced Abdul Gamal Nasser and the Arab cause.[6] "The Russians," Heikal wrote, "failed to understand the strength of nationalism, which is capable at certain periods of history of transcending the class struggle." Thirty years later, Soviet theoreticians are still grappling with this reality and trying to produce a satisfactory Marxist explanation for a phenomenon that contradicts the central importance they give to the imperative of the class struggle.

Although Lenin, Otto Bauer, and other Marxist theoreticians have advanced differing theses about the role of nationalism, none has addressed the question of substructural national constituents—the clan and the tribe—which has always been a significant feature in African political developments, in premodern as in postcolonial societies. It was not until the late 1970s that a Soviet Africanist, R. N. Ismagilova, was able to publish her long years of study on the ethnic problems of tropical Africa.[7] She argued:

---

[6]Mohamed Heikal, *The Sphinx and the Commissar* (London: Collins, 1978).
[7]R. N. Ismagilova, *Ethnic Problems in Tropical Africa: Can They Be Solved?* (Moscow: Progress, 1978).

Study of the experience of African states' development during their years of independence, however, gives grounds for saying that the general patterns of development really are characteristic for Africa. In addition, the specific nature of the African continent, which is manifested in particular in the mixed character of its economy and the survival of many features characteristic of tribal (clan) society put an essential impress on current processes.

The author deems it necessary to stress that many of the phenomena of African reality cannot be understood without taking the ethnic factor into account. It is not simply a question of the complexity of the ethnic structure of most African states, which faces them with all the problems of a multi-ethnic state and makes it necessary for them to tackle various aspects associated with the national question.

Because of a number of specific features of Africa and of the survival of many archaic institutions of the tribal system, the ethnic factor exerts an immense influence on the course and character of socio-economic processes and on the political life of African states, and will probably do so for a long time to come.

The traditional Marxist analysis that led the USSR to put its faith in the strategy of the anti-imperialist struggle has been unfruitful when measured against the optimistic expectations that postcolonial African states would be more inclined to favor the Soviets than "Western imperialist nations." In recognition of this failure, a new concept of "counterimperialism" was adopted. Counterimperialism has been defined as "a strategy of fighting Western imperialism by using the familiar imperialist methods of political and economic influence linked to the Soviet Union by firm ties."[8]

Another new concept in theoretical Marxism was introduced by Moscow in pragmatic response to the realities they encountered on the ground in the colonial states of Africa and in other parts of the Third World: the "non-capitalist path of development." This concept sought to identify countries not yet in the stage of transition to socialism but establishing the basis for such a transition. This rather vaguely defined theory was later refined to "states of socialist orientation" and a "nonrevolutionary path to socialism." By the mid-1970s, thirteen of the nineteen Third World states classified in this way by Moscow were in Africa: Guinea, Madagascar, Guinea-Bissau, Cape Verde, São Tomé and Principe, Algeria, Benin, Congo, Tanzania, Angola, Mozambique, Libya, and Ethiopia.

In the decade since this classification was made, the first six of these states have retreated from, rather than advanced toward, being socialist states in terms of Marxist ideology. Of the other seven states only three (Angola, Mozambique, and Ethiopia) can properly be defined as "socialist-oriented."[9]

By pursuing a policy of counterimperialism (as well as promoting its pri-

---

[8]Richard Lowenthal, *Model or Ally? The Communist Powers and the Developing World* (Oxford: Oxford University Press, 1977).

[9]See Fred Halliday and Maxine Molyneux, *The Ethiopian Revolution* (London: Verso, 1981).

ority interests, mainly strategic) between 1956 and 1971, the USSR showed itself ready to embrace any regime, irrespective of its character, provided only that it declared itself to be antagonistic to the West (especially the United States) and sought Moscow's support. This policy led the USSR to take on as clients military and bourgeois nationalist regimes and even dictators, as in the cases of Idi Amin in Uganda and Macias Nguema in Equatorial Guinea. However, Moscow's experience was that such regimes were more adept at using the Soviets than the other way around. Alliances with such regimes were mostly of a transitory nature, moreover, either because the regimes reverted to depending on Western support or because they were themselves supplanted by anti-Soviet regimes. Hardened by this experience, Soviet policy makers began to pay more attention to the neglected Marxist theoreticians who had been arguing that the best way of making putatively socialist-oriented regimes irreversible was to return to an earlier concept, the central importance of vanguard parties. Strongly backed with Soviet support, vanguard parties could establish conditions for the growth of a "well-organized party uniting representatives of the working people, supporters of the socialist road—a party free of pro-bourgeois and socialist elements, and guided by a progressive ideology."[10] This concept was systematically implemented for the first time in Ethiopia, in the mid-1970s.

Finally, the theoretical basis of Marxist policy, which is to insist that only the Soviet bloc can provide a real alternative to the capitalist West and that this is "the main and decisive condition for the successful development of the non-capitalist countries," has come up sharply against the fundamental reality that the Soviets are, as yet, incapable of meeting this "decisive condition" because they lack the necessary economic and technical resources to meet the needs of even the handful of developing countries that have seriously sought to break out of the Western economic system. Because the West has so much more to offer developing countries in terms of aid, trade, and relevant technical assistance (however inequitable the terms), the USSR has found it impossible to compete except in Cuba and Vietnam. If African and other developing countries are to wait for the day when the Soviet bloc will finally be able to fulfill its "decisive condition" for their successful development, they have a long time to wait. For Moscow this poses a seemingly irreconcilable dilemma; for most African countries the dilemma is more easily resolved, by looking to the West to get not nearly enough of what they need for their economic growth but sufficient to ensure at least their survival. Whether obtaining aid from the West will, in the long run, weaken the ability of socialist-oriented countries to pursue their goal remains moot.

One further recent shift in Soviet policy has been a growing tendency to allocate more resources to organizations rather than to governments. There

---

[10]Yuriy N. Gavrilov, "Problems of the Formation of Vanguard Parties in Countries of Socialist Orientation," *Narody Azii i Afrika* no. 6 (1980).

has been a significant increase in contacts with ruling parties and women's and students' organizations, and in awards of travel grants and scholarships to Africans to train in East European countries. Indeed, Soviet policy has remained consistent only in one major respect: support for national liberation movements. But Moscow has been highly selective in deciding which movements to support, ignoring those which show a Beijing orientation.

Soviet Policy in Ethiopia

The USSR's role in the Horn of Africa reveals two aspects of its global policy: its pursuit of strategic military objectives, mainly in terms of ocean politics; and the implementation of its new political objective of making the process toward "socialist orientation" irreversible through the establishment of a powerful vanguard party with strong Soviet backing. Ethiopia has become the testing ground for the success of this concept.

The Place of Ocean Politics in Soviet Policy

The Russian interest in acquiring ports in the Red Sea goes back to the seventeenth century, when Tsars Alexis and Peter the Great first embarked on the quest, which was later pursued by Tsar Paul and Catherine the Great.[11] Admiral of the Fleet Sergei Gorshkov, the leading advocate of the USSR's role as a world naval power, has described the function of the Soviet Navy as being "capable of dealing with the latest innovations in the enemy camp . . . in any part of the globe."[12] This aim necessitates facilities for warships throughout the strategic seaways. The particular importance that the USSR attaches to the Red Sea region was expressed by V. Sovinskiy, head of the Soviet Foreign Ministry Press Department, in a televised speech in Moscow on February 3, 1978:

> The Horn of Africa is first and foremost of military, political and economic significance. The importance of the area lies in its location at the link-up of the two continents of Asia and Africa. There are a lot of good sea ports in the Persian Gulf and the Indian Ocean. Moreover, there are sea lanes which link oil producing countries with America and Europe.

Moscow's first move into the area, through its treaty of friendship with Somalia, has already been described. Although the treaty enabled the Soviet Navy to obtain facilities along the Somali coast, these were of only limited value because they lacked adequate deep-sea harbor facilities. The situation

[11]For an excellent exposition of the Russians' historic interest in the area, see Edward Wilson, *Russia and Black Africa before World War II* (New York: Africana, 1974).
[12]S. G. Gorshkov, *The Sea Power of the State* (London: Pergamon, 1979).

was only marginally improved by the Soviets' acquisition of facilities in Aden through its treaty of friendship with South Yemen. A much richer prize was the prospect of acquiring facilities in Ethiopia's two excellent ports, Massawa and Assab (both, incidentally, lying in territory claimed by the Eritreans). Ethiopia offered the additional attraction of being a large and potentially rich country strategically located in northeast Africa. Thus a revolutionary Ethiopia firmly planted in the Soviet camp could provide Moscow with both military and political advantages of the kind that the Soviets lack in sub-Saharan Africa.

The great importance that Moscow attaches to achieving its military and political objectives is shown by the high risks it was willing to take in backing the Ethiopian revolution and in the size of its military commitment, which has been greater than anything undertaken in the Third World outside Cuba, Vietnam, and Afghanistan.[13] Having watched developments in Ethiopia during the first two years following the dethronement of Emperor Haile Selassie, Moscow signaled its readiness to come to the assistance of Col. Mengistu Haile Mariam's Provisional Military Administrative Government (the Dergue) in a statement issued in April 1976: "The strength of the Ethiopian revolution lies in its very inevitability in the world revolutionary process. . . . [its] progress puzzles the uninitiated, maddens its enemies and is a source of satisfaction for the true friends of the new Ethiopia."

Three months later, in July, the Dergue sent a delegation to Moscow for exploratory talks about military assistance. By December a secret military agreement had been signed, and by the end of the month the Dergue had formally announced that "the direction and leadership of the Provisional Military Administrative Committee will be along Marxist-Leninist principles." In March 1977 the first Soviet cargo vessel carrying military supplies berthed at Assab. A month later the Dergue severed its military ties with the United States; and another month later the Dergue leader, Colonel Mariam, signed a $400 million arms agreement in Moscow. Soon afterwards the vanguard of a Cuban military force began to arrive in Addis Ababa. These developments were the signal for Somalia to launch its offensive in the Ogaden, on July 23, 1977. In the following months the military situation deteriorated alarmingly for the Dergue as the Somalis pressed their initiative in the Ogaden and the Eritreans besieged Asmara and Massawa. Responding to the Dergue's pressing demands for aid, the Soviet bloc countries launched a massive arms delivery operation, by air and sea, in December; an estimated one thousand Warsaw Pact military specialists under the command of Gen. V. I. Petrov were brought in, and the Cubans sent an expeditionary force of 20,000 combatants.

Particularly impressive from the Soviet point of view was Moscow's dramatic presentation of naval power. The navy provided protection to Soviet

---

[13]See Legum, "Angola and the Horn of Africa."

bloc merchant ships transporting troops and arms, ferried equipment from Aden to Assab and Massawa, and established operational sea control in the Red Sea basin. Soviet naval combatants in the Mediterranean and the Red Sea provided protection to Soviet bloc merchant ships, while the Soviets' Indian Ocean squadron operated in the Gulf of Aden seemingly as an interposition force between the resupply and other, potentially hostile fleets. The sealift involved some thirty-six freighters, and there was also a huge airlift. Altogether the Soviets had delivered over 60,000 tons of military equipment by June 1978.

But for this timely and substantial Soviet bloc and Cuban military intervention, it is most unlikely that the Dergue could have survived the challenge of 1977 without negotiating a political settlement. Thus a major opportunity was lost for the country to seek a constitutional settlement acceptable to all of the constituent parts of the old empire.

The Rise of the Vanguard Party in Ethiopia

Moscow has displayed unusual patience in its difficult dealings with Ethiopia's traditionally xenophobic leaders. While increasing its military support to enable Mengistu's military regime to survive, the USSR showed itself in no hurry to endorse the Dergue's internal policies, choosing to wait until conditions developed more favorable to a "national democratic revolution." In this waiting period the Soviets concentrated their efforts on helping train thousands of cadres schooled in Marxism, to enable them to fulfill the "vanguard role of the working class," and on encouraging the Dergue to move away from being a military regime by establishing an ideological working-class party. Moscow's commitment to this latter objective was not without its risks and provoked severe tensions with the Dergue. The uneasy relationship lasted over seven years before Mengistu finally established the Working Party of Ethiopia (WPE). Although nominally Marxist-Leninist, the party still bore many of the characteristics of a military regime and lacked a popular mass base.

To fulfill the first of the interim objectives, the entire Soviet bloc was enlisted to provide ideological training. Ideological centers were established in Ethiopia; thousands of potential cadres were brought to Eastern Europe for training. The Soviet bloc also embarked on a program of exchanging visits between Ethiopian administrators and technocrats and their East European counterparts. Hundreds of delegations were brought to Eastern Europe, and East Europeans taken to Ethiopia. The mobilization of a vanguard elite was pursued with great vigor.

By the time Mengistu was ready to launch his workers' party in September 1984, he had become schooled in the teachings of Georgi Dimitrov to whom, he said, he owed his understanding of the nature of people's democracies—

"one of the forms of supremacy and dictatorship of the proletariat manifested in countries with special conditions and levels of development."[14]

Soviet policy requirements were reflected in two major aspects of Mengistu's evolving policy. The first was acceptance of the Soviet Union as the "leader of the world's democratic and progressive forces." And the second, in pursuance of this line, was the proclamation of Ethiopia's revolution as part of the "world revolutionary process and national liberation movements." "Imperialism," Mengistu said, "fears the Ethiopian revolution because of its example for the areas round the Red Sea and Africa."

Moscow was less successful in its attempts to persuade Mengistu to accept advice on how to deal with the nationalities question. Drawing on their own experience, the Soviets understood the importance of solving the problems of the nationalities if the Ethiopian revolution were to succeed. They worked patiently to try to conciliate between the Eritreans and Mengistu. But on this core issue Mengistu showed himself as nationalistic as the emperor had been; indeed, he often used the same language as Haile Selassie in defending Ethiopia's boundaries, and in the end he fell back on the emperor's methods of trying to overcome the Eritrean problem by the use of brute military force allied to inducements to those willing to collaborate. The furthest he was willing to go to accommodate his Soviet ally was to set up a special department for the study of nationality issues; but this department never advanced beyond studying how to resolve these issues on conditions predetermined by Addis Ababa. The Soviet bloc members, while hoping and working for a final resolution of the nationalities issue, gave unstinting support to the Dergue's policy of imposing a military solution on the Eritreans, Tigrayans, and other national groups fighting against the Dergue.

The final outcome of the Ethiopian revolution still hangs in the balance and depends in large measure on the regime's ability to resolve the problems posed by the resistance of strong nationalist movements to the idea of a strongly centralized state. There is also still the problem of building genuine, grassroots support for the WPE, which in part depends on the regime's ability to modernize and expand its economy. Although the Soviets have made what is for them a sizable financial commitment to Ethiopia, their effort falls well below what is required for rapid growth of the economy; and although the Ethiopians have sought Western support, they have so far been largely unsuccessful. Their efforts in this direction have been further impeded by the unpopular measures they have taken, forcibly removing people to new collective settlements both as a means of dealing with the country's chronic drought problems and as a means of relocating peasants from the troubled northern provinces.

---

[14]For the text of Col. Mengistu Haile Mariam's statement, see Colin Legum, ed., *Africa Contemporary Record 1975–76* (London, 1976), pp. B224–B225.

If the Ethiopian revolution should in the end prove successful, however, it would undoubtedly be the most important achievement by the USSR in Africa.

The Soviet Role in Southern Africa

The Pretoria regime bases its military and foreign policies on the premise that the USSR is engaged in a "total onslaught" against South Africa. This is not the view taken by any of the major Western powers. Though there can be no doubt that Moscow's interests would be substantially advanced by the advent of an anti-Western, post-apartheid regime, the Soviet Union's actual involvement in current developments in South Africa is rather limited and is concentrated in two areas: support for the external wing of the African National Congress (ANC), in line with its general support for national liberation movements; and support for the international campaign of sanctions against South Africa. The Soviet view of the ANC was expressed in a message sent by the CPSU on the occasion of the movement's seventieth anniversary celebrations:

> The ANC is now rightly recognized as the genuine representative of the South African people and comes forward as the consistent defender of their rights and interests. In conditions where resistance to the apartheid regime in the RSA [Republic of South Africa] has become widespread, your party rallies all opponents of racism into a single liberation front.[15]

Since the armed struggle was launched by the ANC's military wing, Umkhonto we Sizwe, in 1962, the Soviet bloc has provided arms and training for military cadres as well as funds and support for publications and organizational activities. Soviet support is enhanced by the fact that the ANC is the only liberation movement that maintains an open alliance with a communist party (the SACP). Because of this alliance, the ANC is regarded in Pretoria and in some, but not all, Western quarters as being communist-dominated— a judgment repudiated by the ANC. I believe, on the basis of my own studies and intimate knowledge of the ANC, that the movement is still dominated by nationalist elements—such as its president, Oliver Tambo—who are not Communists but who accept the necessity of an alliance with the SACP and of relying to a considerable extent on Soviet military aid because the Western democracies provide no alternative. Nevertheless, the positive support given to the movement by the Soviet bloc and Moscow's consistent enmity to the South African regime undoubtedly produce a generally favorable view of the Soviets among ANC supporters. Whether this gratitude will one day translate itself into a different kind of South African regime, one more favorable to

---

[15]*Pravda*, January 8, 1982.

the Soviets than to the West, is likely to depend on the denouement of the struggle in that country. If the present South African political system were finally to collapse as a result of revolutionary violence, we might predict that the final outcome would be more favorable to the world communist system than to the West; but if fundamental change occurs without revolution, the chances of a Soviet breakthrough in South Africa seem rather remote.

The USSR does not see the present situation in South Africa as having reached a revolutionary stage, as I have noted, although it does not rule it out if a settlement to the country's conflicts proves impossible. What does seem clear is that at present the USSR does not include Southern Africa among its short-term or even medium-term priorities. It is difficult to forecast what would happen if, in the medium term, a situation of catastrophic proportions were suddenly to arise in South Africa. If we recognize the severe military logistical disadvantage of the Soviet bloc as compared with the NATO powers and allow for the Soviets' global interest in wishing to avoid open military confrontation with the United States in areas of major Western interests, then we must judge direct Soviet military intervention as highly improbable. The best Moscow can hope for is a long-drawn-out struggle during which an armed liberation movement would grow in strength and a revolutionary situation develop in South Africa.

For the foreseeable future, it seems unlikely that the USSR will change the low priority it has so far accorded to southern Africa, other than to shoulder its "responsibilities" in Angola and, perhaps, to increase its still marginal military programs in Zimbabwe, Zambia, and Mozambique. Overall, there are good reasons to accept that the USSR is earnest when it claims that its present interest is to share responsibility with the United States in helping resolve the conflicts in the region. The Western powers are in a much stronger position than the Soviet bloc to determine future developments in southern Africa; only if the West blunders in the way it chooses to exercise its influence in the region is it likely that Soviet global policy will be advanced by the break-up of the present political system in South Africa.

Conclusion

The USSR has expanded its influence in sub-Saharan Africa from zero at the end of World War II. But, considering the opportunities that existed in the immediately postcolonial period when many newly independent govern-ments were keen to distance themselves politically from their recent Western colonial masters, it is remarkable how slender Soviet successes have been. Nearly all of the advantages that Moscow gained proved to be transitory and can be described only as setbacks to its aims in the region. The only extant gains are the Soviets' position in Ethiopia (where the outcome of the revolu-tion still remains in doubt), Angola and Mozambique (where the fragility of the Marxist regimes and their precarious economic and security situations make for an uncertain future); and Soviet influence within the ANC, the premier black political movement in South Africa—though not the only major force.

Notwithstanding the generally anticolonial and anticapitalist mood in black Africa, Marxism has so far attracted little support; its proponents remain mostly tiny minorities. Furthermore, even among African Marxists there exist strong divisions; a significant number adopt anti-Soviet positions. In practice the theoretical ideas of Soviet ideologists about how to present Moscow as a credible strategic ally have not worked out. From this disparity have come shifts in Soviet Marxist theories about the nature of developing societies and the application of Soviet bloc resources to the relevant needs of those societies in ways that will strengthen their ties and promote permanent relations favorable to Soviet objectives.

In forging entries in the region the USSR has experienced most success through its ability to provide arms and military training and its unqualified support for liberation movements that challenge regimes perceived as pro-Western. Its economic and technical resources, however, have proved inadequate to substitute for those of the Western community.

Each of the gains made by the USSR has had less to do with African ideological sympathies for Marxism or for identification with the Soviets' international role than with mistaken Western policies, for example, support for Portugal long after it had become evident colonial rule was approaching collapse; an ambiguous policy toward the apartheid regime of South Africa; and the failure to understand the potentialities for revolutionary change in Ethiopia after the downfall of Emperor Haile Selassie.

Although the USSR has managed to extend the range of its military delivery system below the equator, it has been deterred from exploiting this advantage in areas where it cannot, or will not, risk a major military confrontation with the West. This has been significantly demonstrated by its failure to consolidate its initial advantages in Angola and Mozambique. Moscow now faces its biggest challenge in southern Africa, where the developing, violent crisis will predictably lead the Frontline states to seek the military and economic support of reliable "strategic allies."

II

Soviet-American Rivalry in Asia

Donald S. Zagoria

Although Europe remains the critical region of superpower rivalry and the Middle East the most dangerous, one can plausibly argue that the Soviet leadership sees the strategic center of gravity moving slowly but inexorably in the direction of East Asia. Indeed, in the late 1980s and 1990s Moscow faces the prospect of a fundamental shift in the Asian balance of power through Sino-American security cooperation, significant Japanese rearmament, the probability of a successfully modernizing China that will remain a permanent adversary, and a more assertive United States at the head of an informal security coalition including China, Japan, South Korea, the ASEAN countries, and ANZUS.

In no other region of the world is there such a gap between Soviet military power and Soviet political influence. Moreover, the longer-range trends are against the Russians. By the year 2000 Japan is likely to be the second-greatest industrial power in the world, China may have a gross national product of close to a trillion dollars, and the Pacific Community of free market economies may be closer to reality.

The Russians clearly recognize these adverse trends. As recent Soviet commentaries point out, Japan already has the world's fourth-largest fleet in terms of tonnage and is eighth in overall military spending. It could quickly become a nuclear power. Moreover, "any special relationship with the United States may prove to be illusory. . . . Tokyo is following its own program."[1] At the same time the United States and Japan also have "far-reaching plans for South Korea," which is to become "the third member of a Far Eastern NATO."[2]

---

[1] *Izvest'ya*, April 30, 1985, in Foreign Broadcast Information Service, *Soviet Union* (hereafter FBIS-SU), May 3, 1985, p. CI.
[2] *Red Star*, June 5, 1985, in FBIS-SU, June 7, 1985, p. CI.

Even more alarming for the Soviet Union is the growing prospect of a Sino-Japanese entente, a phenomenon that has serious strategic consequences and brings added defense problems in northeast Asia. Commenting on the recent visit to China by the deputy chief of the Japan Defense Agency, *Red Star* argues that China seems to have an "active approach" to the expansion of military ties between the two countries as well as a "positive approach" to the U.S.-Japanese security treaty.[3] Nor is China complaining about the growing U.S. military presence in Asia or the build-up of Japanese military potential.

At the same time, as the Soviets have also noted, Chinese relations with the United States are intensifying. Defense Secretary Casper Weinberger, Navy Secretary John Lehman, and former chief of staff John Vessey have all visited China in the past two or three years; the Chinese minister of defense has visited Washington; President Ronald Reagan went to China in 1984; China's President Li Xiannian visited Washington in 1985; and Vice President George Bush visited China in the autumn of 1985.

What makes these trends in Sino-American and Sino-Japanese relations even more alarming for the Russians is the fact that Sino-Soviet relations have reached something of a plateau. One of Moscow's shrewdest political observers, Alexander Bovin, recently conceded that "internally [the Chinese] are not yet ready to develop relations with the USSR on so broad a basis. The causes of this may be varied, but the fact itself is indisputable."[4] Bovin went on to complain that Beijing "supports the American policy of militarizing Japan" and also favors the deployment of new American weapons in Western Europe. He concluded that Sino-Soviet relations were "full of contradictions."

If the Soviets understand the nature of their Pacific dilemma, there are few signs as yet that they understand their own role in helping to bring that dilemma about. They continue to increase their own formidable military power in the region; they show no signs of substantially reducing their forces on the Chinese border or of returning the disputed northern territories to Japan; they remain determined to consolidate their power in Afghanistan; they continue to support Vietnam's occupation of Cambodia.

Under these circumstances, it would be naive to expect any substantial accommodation in Asia between the Soviet Union and the United States. On the contrary, the United States is presently engaged in building up its own military power in the region. The Seventh Fleet is being equipped with Tomahawk cruise missiles, some of them nuclear-capable; the *Carl Vinson*, a nuclear-powered attack carrier, and the *New Jersey*, a battleship retrofitted with cruise missiles, have been added to the U.S. Pacific Fleet; two additional squadrons of F-16s have been based on Japanese territory; and a second

[3]*Red Star*, May 28, 1985, in FBIS-SU, May 30, 1985, pp. C2–C3.
[4]Interview, in *Mlada Fronta* (Prague), March 15, 1985, in FBIS-SU, March 22, 1985, pp. B1–B2.

battleship group, led by the U.S.S. *Missouri*, will greatly increase American surface strength in the Pacific.

The Soviets will have to contend with the Japanese fleet as well. The Japanese Navy, though it needs to be modernized, is the fourth-largest and, it is claimed, "one of the best maintained and trained fleets in the world."[5] Some 80 percent of that fleet is operational at all times. The Soviet Pacific Fleet has a much lower estimated operational rate, and so the addition of the Japanese fleet to the U.S. Seventh Fleet is not at all insignificant.

The Soviets may have their problems in the Pacific, but the Western position is far from secure. The continuing growth of Soviet military power, the growing economic Cold War between the United States and Japan, the continuing crisis in the Philippines, the unpredictability of North Korea, the uncertainty about China's policies after Deng Xiaoping, and many other challenges will have to be surmounted.

In this chapter I first offer some general observations on the serious internal and external problems facing the Soviets in coming years. If I am right about their gravity, these problems are bound to condition Soviet foreign policy in the years ahead both in Asia and elsewhere. I then examine the superpower rivalry in Asia in some detail, emphasizing the weak links in the Western position in Asia. I conclude with some observations on coping with Soviet power in Asia, including some thoughts on possibilities for reducing regional tensions.

The Global Setting

The late 1980s and 1990s are not likely to be promising for the Soviet Union in its drive to become an effective challenger to the United States in the global arena. The trends in the strategic competition are becoming increasingly unfavorable for Moscow. U.S. strategic modernization programs—the MX, the Midgetman, the new, more accurate Trident submarine-launched ballistic missile, the revived B-1 bomber, the advanced-technology (Stealth) bomber, and Pershing II, as well as ground-, sea-, and air-launched cruise missiles—will soon enhance the American nuclear arsenal. These systems will endanger the large, land-based Soviet ICBM force, which is the cornerstone of Soviet strategic nuclear power. As Arnold Horelick notes, moreover, "superior U.S. technology in such areas as sensors, computers, computer programming, signal processing and exotic kill mechanisms being harnessed in connection with President Reagan's Strategic De-

---

[5]Hisahiko Okazaki, "U.S.-Japan Relations in International Politics," *Japan Society Forum*, June 25, 1985, pp. B1–B2.

fense Initiative is bound to increase Soviet anxiety about the possible shape of the strategic balance in the years ahead."[6]

At home the Soviet Union faces severe economic and social stagnation. Some Soviet intellectuals have been warning that, if present trends are not soon reversed, the "Polish disease," disaffection within the working class, could spread to the Soviet Union. The new Soviet leader, Mikhail Gorbachev, has implied that the Soviet Union, unless it improves its technology and economic productivity, may not be able to maintain its present strategic position in competition with the West. In a brutally frank report delivered on December 10, 1984, three months before he became general secretary of the Soviet Communist party, Gorbachev attributed the "slowdown of growth in the late 1970s and early 1980s" to the "stagnant retention" of "outmoded production relations." He warned that the ills of the system were of "truly tremendous scale" and in terms of innovation and complexity it would be a "titanic task" to deal with them. What was at stake, he concluded, was nothing less than the need to make sure that the Soviet Union could "enter the new millennium worthily, as a great and flourishing power." And in an unusually candid admission he conceded that because of Soviet economic failures, the West was winning not only the economic and technological race but the ideological competition as well.[7]

As recently as June 11, 1985, Gorbachev continued his dire warning. He said that "urgent measures" were required to improve the economy because he could not cut social programs or reduce defense expenditures in the face of the "imperialist threat." He may yet be forced to do one or the other.

Declining trends in the strategic competition and severe economic difficulties at home are not Gorbachev's only problems. The Soviet Union is still bogged down in Afghanistan, and it faces possible insurrection in Poland. Elsewhere in Eastern Europe its economically hard-pressed satellites want greater independence and increased trade with the West. Some of them want to experiment with Chinese and Hungarian-type economic reforms. A harshly worded *Pravda* article has reacted to these stirrings by warning of the dangers of "revisionism" and even of "Russophobia."[8]

In the Far East the Soviet Union is increasingly "odd man out." In Europe, despite clumsy Soviet efforts to split NATO and prevent the deployment of Pershing IIs and cruise missiles, the Western alliance is still firmly intact and the missile deployment has proceeded on schedule. In the Persian Gulf, Iran's revolutionary regime has severed natural gas deliveries to the Soviet Union, greatly increased its trade with Pakistan and Turkey, two American allies, and continues to broadcast revolutionary Islamic propaganda to Moscow's pre-

[6]Arnold Horelick, "U.S.-Soviet Relations: The Return of Arms Control," *Foreign Affairs* 63, no. 3 (1985).

[7]For the full text of this remarkable statement see FBIS-SU, Annex, February 19, 1985, "Gorbachev Report at December Ideology Conference."

[8]O. Vladimirov, "Veduschchii factor mirovogo revolyutsionnogo protessa," *Pravda*, June 21, 1985, pp. 3–4.

dominantly Muslim southern republics. The other major power in the Gulf, Iraq, has been establishing closer economic relations with the West.

In the Third World more broadly, Moscow faces armed insurgents in almost all of its desperately poor client states; the Soviets are almost universally condemned for their policies in Afghanistan and Cambodia; and many less developed countries recognize the limits of Soviet economic assistance and are looking more to the West for aid, credits, technology, and know-how.

In the meantime the American economy continues to recover, and President Reagan has launched the most sustained U.S. military build-up in postwar history.

None of this means that Gorbachev is going to opt out of international competition with the United States. The Soviets continue to add to their already huge military arsenal, and Gorbachev will almost certainly try to exploit differences within the Western alliance and to improve relations with China. Soviet media continue to stress Western Europe's adherence to the spirit of detente and the opportunities thus presented for Soviet diplomacy. But the problems that Gorbachev faces are formidable and deep-rooted; they cannot be solved quickly. It could take a decade just to begin a turnaround in the ailing Soviet economy, particularly since Gorbachev seems to have ruled out Chinese or Hungarian-type market reforms as too risky. Consolidating the fragile Soviet empire in an era of economic austerity will be an equally long-term and uncertain process. As a result Gorbachev needs a long period of calm in relations with the United States while he concentrates on internal and imperial problems.

The need for a breathing space is what the new Soviet foreign minister Edward Shevardnadze hinted at in a speech to the Helsinki Conference in July 1985. Shevardnadze drew an unusual linkage between Moscow's internal and foreign policies, saying that "the foreign policy of any state is inseparably linked to its internal affairs" and that to implement its vast internal plans to improve the economy, "the Soviet Union needs a durable peace."

More important for the purposes of this chapter is that the Soviet Union is now entering a period when, for its own reasons, it requires calm relations with the West. It does not want tension with the United States in Asia or in any other region. This is not a guarantee of peace and stability in Asia, but it is an encouraging element in the overall picture and one that an alert adversary could exploit to help reduce tensions.

The Soviet Stake in Asia

Although Europe remains the region of key concern, the Soviet Union has vital security interests at stake in East Asia. Geography, geopolitics, and economics all contribute to the enormity of this stake.

In geographic terms the Soviet Union, although generally regarded as a European power, is next to China the second-largest Asian power. One third of its vast territory lies east of Irkutsk in east Asian Siberia. Large stretches of Soviet Siberia border on China and Mongolia, moreover, and the Soviet Pacific coastline is close to Japan, Korea, and China. As a result of the Russian conquest of much of Central Asia in the nineteenth century, fifty million people, some 20 percent of the Soviet population, are Asians.[9]

Geopolitics is also critical in shaping Soviet policy in East Asia. The Soviet presence in the region and status as a world power are inseparable from Moscow's global strategic competition with the United States. Yet the United States, by dint of its naval and air power, its bases, its alliance system, and its economic and cultural influence, remains the strongest power in the Pacific.

The Soviets are determined to weaken that U.S. alliance system, to contain China while improving relations with Beijing, and to project their own power and influence in this important region. Moscow's acquisition of new bases in Vietnam in the late 1970s was an important strategic gain, perhaps the most significant strategic change in the Pacific during the past decade. These new naval and air bases will enable the Russians to project their power more readily into the Persian Gulf and the Indian Ocean.

A third factor that shapes Soviet policy in the Asia-Pacific region is economic. In the remaining decades of the twentieth century, and far into the twenty-first, Moscow will seek to develop Siberia, which contains a large proportion of potential Soviet mineral wealth, energy resources, and precious metals. The development of these Siberian resources will become increasingly important in the latter 1980s, when the Soviet Union may be facing an energy crunch.

Finally, Soviet policy in Asia is shaped by certain fears and insecurities, some of them rooted in reality, others in paranoia; some inherited from the past, others rooted in recent developments.

> The Soviets fear having to fight on two fronts if it comes to a general war. They know what might have happened had Japan joined Germany and attacked Russia in 1941 instead of turning south against China and Southeast Asia and then against Pearl Harbor. The Soviet Union would almost certainly have been defeated. As late as the battle of Stalingrad the Russians kept large forces on the Siberian front to guard against such a danger.

> They fear that one day a strong, huge, irredentist China may claim back the territories grabbed from a weak Manchu empire by tsarist Russia in the middle of the nineteenth century. The Russians surely cannot forget what Mao Tse-tung told the Japanese Socialists in 1964, sympathizing with their demands for a

---

[9]For more details see John Stephan, "Asia in the Soviet Conception," in Donald S. Zagoria, ed., *Soviet Policy in East Asia* (New Haven: Yale University Press, 1982).

return of the Kuriles—that China had not yet presented *its* bill to the Soviets for *its* lost territories.

They have a sensitivity about the vast borderlands with China. Is a powerful China likely to accept Soviet domination of Mongolia? The Kazakhstan/ Sin-kiang frontier will also remain a sensitive issue because of the minority races who live on both sides of the border.

The Soviets fear a powerful Japan, already the third-largest industrial power in the world. It is a country with which the Soviets have had an unpleasant history and an intractable territorial dispute.

They are concerned about the geopolitical vulnerability of Siberia, a region that is sparsely populated, a long distance from European Russia, and with long, overland lines of communication that are vulnerable to interdiction.

Finally, the Soviets are uncertain about the loyalty of some forty million Muslims in Soviet Central Asia at a time of an Islamic awakening on Russia's southern border.

An Asian Overview

By and large, Soviet policy in East Asia has been a spectacular failure. The reasons for this failure are varied. Some have to do with the success of American policies, others with the heavyhandedness of Soviet diplomacy, and still others with the extraordinary economic dynamism of the region itself. But a brief overview of the region demonstrates that the basic trends are—with some notable exceptions to be discussed later—extremely encouraging for the West and quite unfavorable for the Soviet Union.

The Asia-Pacific region is one of extraordinary economic dynamism. The Pacific economies have displayed the greatest resilience and the highest rates of growth in the world. The economic output of the Pacific region as a whole now equals more than two-thirds of total U.S. gross national product. U.S. trade with East Asia, which only a decade ago was $42 billion, was $170 billion in 1984 and accounted for almost 30 percent of total world trade of the United States. U.S. direct investment in the Pacific region is now conservatively estimated at more than $30 billion.

Not unrelated to economic dynamism is the fact that the Asia-Pacific region is, with the notable exception of Cambodia, basically at peace. Peace and prosperity are interrelated. Without peace the region would not have enjoyed such economic prosperity. Without economic prosperity the region would almost certainly have been more unstable.

Despite serious trade frictions, the U.S.-Japan strategic alliance remains strong. Under Prime Minister Nakasone, Japan has moved from a passive to an active ally, with joint planning, joint basing, and joint training exercises. Japan is expanding aid to key countries throughout the world, not just to traditional Japanese trading partners but also to some states threatened by instability—Turkey, Egypt, Pakistan. Japan is taking responsibility for the defense of its sea lanes. Public opinion in Japan is more favorable to the Western alliance than ever before. There has, in fact, been a sea change in Japanese attitudes toward the alliance with the United States, borne out in Japanese public opinion polls. Even the Japanese Socialist party, the largest opposition party, is trying to break away from its earlier position of "unarmed neutrality."

China has been embarking since 1978 on a historically significant reform and modernization program comparable to Japan's Meiji Restoration in the nineteenth century. If it continues to be as successful in the next decade as it has been in the last, China, by the early twenty-first century, will have a gross national product approximately equal to that of the Soviet Union today. China's experiment with market reforms is bound to have an enormous impact on the Third World, on Eastern Europe, and on the Soviet Union. It has already affected North Korea, which has instituted a new tax program designed to attract foreign investment. As long as China is absorbed with domestic modernization, it will have a continuing stake in peace and stability in Asia and in expanding its economic and other cooperative ties with the West, even as it simultaneously seeks to reduce tensions with the Soviet Union. In foreign policy China now shares with the West an interest in containing Soviet power, in a strong U.S.-Japan alliance, in improving relations with South Korea while restraining North Korea, in forcing Vietnam out of Cambodia while improving relations with ASEAN, in removing the Soviet Union from Afghanistan while shoring up Pakistan. Over the longer run China will certainly not be anyone's card, but it will remain by reasons of geography, history, and national interest a massive barrier to the spread of Soviet power in the Pacific and a deterrent to Soviet adventurism elsewhere.

Yet another piece of good news is the developing dialogue between North and South Korea. Economic and Red Cross talks have begun; there are discussions about joint hosting of the 1988 Olympics; the North is even suggesting a summit meeting. Such changes portend a significant alteration in North Korean policy which is partly attributable to economic difficulties at home, partly to China's encouragement, and partly to the vitality of South Korea, which now has a gross national product more than four or five times that of North Korea.

In Southeast Asia, since the fall of Saigon in 1975, the dominoes have not fallen. Rather, they have banded together in a unified ASEAN, one of the world's most successful regional organizations.

More broadly speaking, communism as an ideology and moral force, and as a model for development, has with the single exception of the Philippines lost much of its appeal. China's open questioning of Marxism, the enormous successes of free market systems, and the economic weaknesses of communist countries from the Soviet Union to Vietnam and North Korea have put communism on the historical defensive.

Also, despite its substantial military build-up in the Pacific, the Soviet Union has failed to convert its military power into political advantage. It is unlikely to do so in the future. Its policies in the Asia-Pacific region are in fact counterproductive, and it will be difficult to retreat from them. I have in mind the Soviet invasion of Afghanistan and the indications that Soviet troops will remain there; the Soviet-supported Vietnamese invasion of Cambodia; the Soviet military build-up on the northern islands whose ownership is disputed with Japan; the enormous Soviet build-up on the Chinese border, including its forces in Outer Mongolia; and Moscow's crude handling of Asian sensibilities. All of these factors have contributed to a new strategic consensus in the Asia-Pacific region which has developed since 1978.

In the Pacific, as elsewhere, recent years have seen a substantial resurgence of American military power.[10] Then, too, in the Far East as in no other region of the world the East-East conflict helps maintain a favorable balance of power. In Asia today, with the sole exception of the Korean peninsula, which still remains divided along East-West lines, the most serious and bitter confrontations are those between contiguous communist states: Russia against China, China against Vietnam, Vietnam against Communist insurgents supported by China in Cambodia. All the Asian communist states are finding that their most active and dangerous adversaries are not faraway Western powers but neighboring communist states with whom they share disputed and heavily armed borders and a historical record of conflict going back several centuries—a record undiminished by a supposedly common ideology. These East-East conflicts, deeply rooted in history and geography, are likely to endure. Divisions among the communist states contribute to a new balance of power in East Asia, a balance that is more favorable to the West than anyone could have imagined ten or fifteen years ago.

Finally, and not least important, there is growing in the West a recognition of the strategic interdependence of Europe, Asia, and the United States. The Soviet deployment of medium-range ballistic missiles—the SS-20s—has highlighted this interdependence. Japan and China have manifested a clear interest in preventing any redeployment of the SS-20s from Europe to Asia. The West has an equally clear stake in ensuring that any Soviet-Chinese detente does not lead to a transfer of Soviet forces from the Siberian border to the Central Front in Europe.

In sum, for the West the Asia-Pacific region is extremely encouraging. The region is prosperous and generally peaceful, relatively stable and basically pro-Western. The overall balance of power in the region favors the West. For the Soviet Union the region must look quite disturbing.

---

[10]See *Asian Security*, 1984, p. 34.

Moscow's Future Prospects

This generally favorable situation for the West may change. But if such adverse changes are to take place, they will more likely come about as a result not of Soviet actions but of bad management of the Western alliance, political or economic instability in key countries, and so forth. Before we turn to some of these possibilities, let us briefly review Soviet relations with the various countries in the region to expose Moscow's weak political position.

With regard to China, the Soviets are well aware that China is a long-term adversary. The clash between Russia and China is an old-fashioned contest between two huge land empires with potentially unstable buffer zones across their long common frontiers. As a Eurasian empire the USSR has a special concern about China because it has not fully assimilated its own Central Asian peoples and cannot do so. The long-range "China threat" is made even more serious in Soviet eyes by the American strategy of trying to tie down Soviet power in Asia to weaken Soviet capabilities elsewhere. Moreover, there are conflicting geopolitical interests between Russia and China in Mongolia, Indochina, and southern Asia; there is an unresolved border conflict; there are deep-seated mutual suspicions and fears on both sides; and eventually China will modernize its armed forces, particularly its nuclear forces. It will then pose a real threat to Soviet security.

To be sure, a tactical detente now observed will probably continue. It is in the interests of both countries so long as both need to concentrate on internal economic problems. But this detente will almost certainly be limited. Over the long run Russia knows that a more powerful China will be a more dangerous China.

Japan, too, is almost certain to be a long-range Soviet adversary. Soviet relations with Japan are now at one of their lowest points in the entire postwar period and not likely to improve substantially.

A dramatic breakthrough for the Russians on the Korean peninsula seems equally implausible. The visit by Kim Il-Sung to Moscow in May 1984, his first in seventeen years, has produced a new warming trend in Soviet–North Korean relations. Diplomatic contact has increased in the past year, and the Russians have evidently begun to sell MiG-23s to Pyongyang, a break with their past policy of withholding modern aircraft from North Korea. Still, suspicions between the two countries run deep.

The Russians can hardly view Kim as a satisfactory vehicle for expanding their own influence on the Korean peninsula. To begin with, North Korea under Kim has generally been much closer to China than to Russia during the past three decades. Second, Kim has, at least until quite recently, opposed Soviet policy in Afghanistan and Cambodia. He continues to provide a residence in Pyongyang for Prince Norodom Sihanouk, the nominal leader of the anti-Vietnamese resistance in Cambodia, a man whom Russian media routinely describe as a "hireling of the imperialists." Third, Kim has in the past publicly accused Russia of "dominationism" and of efforts to exploit the North Korean economy. Fourth, in the past several decades Kim has developed into something of a state religion his philosophy of *chu'che* or self-reliance, and although he has not been able to realize this philosophy to the extent that he has preached it, *chu'che* symbolizes his determination not to become dependent on the Russians. Despite what have probably been considerable Russian pressures for North Korea to provide Russia with military facilities and to join COMECON, the Soviet-sponsored Council for Mutual Economic Assistance, Kim has so far resisted such pressures. Finally, Kim has frequently involved the Russians in unwanted confrontations with the United States.

Kim is equally suspicious of Moscow. His distrust of the Russians stems from deeply rooted considerations. He does not need to be reminded how close the Russians came to incorporating North Korea into the Soviet Union during 1945–50. He knows only too well how the Russians use their military and economic advisers, troops, and KGB agents to infiltrate governments that they intend to dominate. Moreover, Kim has watched the fate of Russia's neighbors, from Eastern Europe to Outer Mongolia to Afghanistan. And he knows about the Brezhnev Doctrine, by which the Russians have arrogated to themselves the right to intervene in the internal affairs of any "socialist state" that defies Moscow.

For such reasons alone, Kim would keep his distance from Russia. He also saw for himself, during the Korean War, that Russia would not risk war with the United States in order to salvage North Korea. Even when American troops were marching toward North Korea's Tumen River border with Russia, the Russians gave no indication that they were prepared to intervene. Only the Chinese intervention saved Kim Il-Sung's regime from being toppled.

South Korea is tied to the United States and is likely to remain so as long as Korea is divided and surrounded by two giant communist states. Taiwan continues to be economically dependent on the United States and is extremely unlikely to make any moves toward warming relations with Moscow.

The Soviet Union and Southeast Asia

Although Soviet interests in Southeast Asia were marginal in the early postwar period and still remain secondary to Soviet interests in Europe, the Soviets are increasingly shifting their attention to the Asian theater. There are a variety of reasons for their doing so.

First, although in global terms Asia is still in the shadow of Europe—the theater that remains the main focus of U.S.-Soviet rivalry—forces are at work which are shifting the strategic center of gravity slowly eastward. Asia is the most economically dynamic region of the world, and the interests of four great powers intersect there. Both the Soviet Union and the United States are increasing their naval and air forces in the region. Growing Soviet-American rivalry in the Pacific seems inevitable. The United States recognizes that the present balance of forces in the region is highly favorable to it and seeks to secure that favorable balance. Its broader strategic objective is to tie down Soviet forces in the Pacific so as to deter Soviet adventurism in Europe and other theaters. The Soviets, on the other hand, recognize that the existing correlation of forces in the Pacific is highly disadvantageous to them. In recent years Soviet media have repeatedly insisted that the United States seeks to form a Pacific NATO, using Japan and South Korea as its principal bases. The Soviets see U.S. and Japanese efforts to form a Pacific economic community as part of this broader anti-Soviet effort. A high-ranking Soviet official recently told an American academic that the Soviet Union sought parity not only in nuclear weapons and in Europe but in Asia as well. Viewed in this broader strategic context, the minimal Soviet goal in Southeast Asia will be to prevent the six ASEAN countries from joining an overtly anti-Soviet grouping in the Pacific led by the United States. The greater goal is to use growing Soviet military power and widespread suspicion of China as a basis for spreading Soviet power and influence throughout the region.

Second, the Soviet rivalry with China will also lead Moscow to greater involvement in the affairs of Southeast Asia. The Russians know that China, once it modernizes its economy and its military, will become a much greater danger. China already has a modest nuclear capability that could inflict considerable damage on Soviet Siberia. That capability is likely to grow in the years ahead. Soviet deputy prime minister Mikhail Kapitsa recently told one American visitor that Moscow could count on several Asian countries for containing China over the longer run. His list included India, Indonesia, and Vietnam.

Third, the Soviets will also want to increase their influence in Southeast Asia to gain more leverage over Japan, a country that has already become an economic superpower and one that is bound to play an increasingly important role in the affairs of the Pacific.

Fourth, because Southeast Asian waters are an important transit point between the Pacific and Indian oceans, the Soviets will also want to increase their presence in the region to facilitate the projection of their power in the Indian Ocean. Already the Pacific Fleet is the largest of four Soviet fleets. It contains more than one-third of the Soviet Union's general-purpose naval forces and is still growing steadily.

Fifth, now that all of Indochina has come under Vietnamese control and the Vietnamese have entered into a close strategic relationship with the Soviet Union, the Soviets have a big stake in consolidating their position in Indochina. Cam Ranh Bay is already the largest Soviet air and naval base outside the Warsaw Pact, and according to some estimates Soviet economic and military aid to Vietnam doubled in 1985.

Finally, for all of the reasons cited above the Soviet stake in Southeast Asia is bound to grow substantially in the years ahead. The Soviets will have several major objectives in the region: to increase their influence at the expense of the United States and China; to consolidate their position in Indochina; and to institutionalize their presence in the region and become a regional security manager. In the past year or two the Soviets have become much more active in pursuing all of these goals. They have expanded aid to Vietnam; they have launched a major effort to expand political, economic, and cultural relations with Indonesia, Malaysia, and Thailand; and they have offered to mediate a solution to the Cambodian stalemate while carefully probing divisions inside ASEAN between Indonesia and Thailand.

Moscow's Strengths and Weaknesses in ASEAN

The Soviets have strengths and weaknesses in the ASEAN region. On the negative side of the ledger, the six ASEAN countries are authoritarian, free market, basically pro-Western, anticommunist states. Several of these countries remain deeply suspicious of any communist power because of earlier efforts by the Russians and Chinese to sponsor communist insurrections. Indonesia, Thailand, Malaysia, and Singapore all went through long and often bloody struggles with indigenous communist parties in the 1950s and 1960s. In 1965 the Indonesian Communists joined with others in an attempt to take power after murdering several Indonesian army leaders, an episode that has left deep anticommunist feelings within the Indonesian military establishment.

The Soviets, moreover, have very little to offer any of the ASEAN countries in economic terms. Soviet trade with Malaysia and Thailand, for example, is still relatively small and heavily skewed in favor of the Malaysians and Thais because both countries have difficulty finding suitable goods to import from the Soviet Union. All of the ASEAN countries are deeply involved in the pro-Western Pacific economic community. Their principal sources of trade, investment, and markets are Japan, the United States, and other Western countries. Also, of course, the Soviet-supported Vietnamese invasion of Cambodia and the Soviet invasion of Afghanistan have markedly increased suspicions and fears of the Soviets throughout the region.

On the other side of the ledger, however, potential Soviet assets in the region are not as negligible as they are sometimes portrayed. Fear and suspicion of China runs deep throughout Southeast Asia. Anti-Chinese sentiments are widespread within the Indonesian ruling elite, for example, and several Southeast Asian leaders see the Soviet Union as a potential counterweight for China. The present leader of Malaysia, Mahatir, publicly made statements to this effect in the 1970s.

Although the United States has made something of a comeback in the region since the fall of Saigon in 1975, there are deep and residual concerns about American reliability and consistency. A common complaint from

Southeast Asian diplomats, journalists, and intellectuals is that American foreign policy changes from election to election and that America is therefore unreliable. Moreover, uncertainty is growing in Southeast Asia about the export markets in the West on which the region so heavily depends. Growing signs of protectionism in the United States and other Western countries have fed ASEAN's concerns. The Soviets seek to exploit this uncertainty by offering to buy a variety of Southeast Asian commodities.

Throughout the region is a deep longing to be rid of great power involvement and to turn Southeast Asia into a region of peace and neutrality. Since the region is now more intimately associated with the West than with the East, this attitude works against the West.

If Soviet military power in the region continues to grow, some ASEAN leaders may come to feel the need for an accommodation of Soviet interests. Most important, there are deep divisions within ASEAN over how to deal with Vietnam and the Cambodian stalemate. Some Indonesian leaders evidently want a cosmetic solution to the Cambodian issue that would leave Vietnam as the dominant power in Cambodia, because they believe that Vietnam could act as a long-term buffer against China. For the Thais, on the other hand, Vietnamese dominance of Cambodia would be intolerable because it would eliminate Cambodia as a buffer between Thailand and its traditional Vietnamese adversary. If Indonesia looks upon China as a greater long-range threat than Vietnam, however, it will have an important common interest with the Soviet Union, and Indonesia is the largest country in ASEAN.

The coming to power in the Philippines of Corazon Aquino has by no means eliminated the prospects for Marxist revolution in that country. Although there has been a lull in the insurgency since Aquino came to power, the Communists are exploiting a weak and possibly transient government to work within the system through a so-called national democratic front. Left-leaning organizations such as Bayan, Partido ng Bayan, and the labor federation, Kilisant Mayo Uno, are organizing strikes and putting up candidates in local and national elections. The extent of communist control over these organizations is debatable, but officials who lead them say that many of their political programs are similar to those of the Communists—strengthening national sovereignty (a shorthand for anti-Americanism), removing U.S. bases, and implementing a more radical program of land reform.[11] A new moderate and reformist government is bound to take many years to establish itself in the Philippines amid continuing economic, political, and military crises.

The Soviets are exploiting growing resentment among some small South Pacific states over the behavior of American tuna fleets. They have signed fishing and port agreements with Vanuatu and are seeking similar accords

---

[11]See "The Left Seeks New Roads to Socialism," *Far East Economic Review*, August 23, 1986, pp. 32–33.

with other ministates in the area. Moscow is also seeking to block Washington's plan to relinquish its United Nations mandate in Micronesia in return for new compacts that would leave military decisions in American hands.

Finally, serious strains are developing within the ANZUS alliance (the United States, Australia, and New Zealand) as a result of New Zealand's reluctance to provide port facilities for American naval ships carrying nuclear weapons. If New Zealand's "nuclear allergy" spreads to Japan and the Philippines, the naval balance of power in the Pacific will be dramatically affected.

The New Soviet Activism in ASEAN

In recent years Moscow has launched a new campaign of diplomatic activism designed to exploit its potential assets in the region and to "normalize" its relations with ASEAN.

In November 1985 one of the Soviet Union's nine deputy prime ministers, Yakob Ryabov, spent five days in Kuala Lumpur. Ryabov was the highest-level Soviet visitor ever to go to Malaysia. The Soviet minister suggested the establishment of several joint commissions, cultural exchanges, friendship societies, and the like. More generally, two-way traffic between Malaysia and the Soviet Union is growing. In March 1985 the Malaysian deputy foreign minister attended Konstantin Chernenko's funeral in Moscow, and while in the Soviet capital he talked to Soviet Foreign Ministry officials. Somewhat more quietly the Malaysian Air Force chief went to the Soviet Union in 1985 to evaluate a possible purchase of Soviet helicopters. The Soviets are also luring Malaysian tourists to Moscow by offering cheap Aeroflot air tickets. Meanwhile the Malaysian authorities are watching but not interfering with a new publication called *Diplomat*, which carries many Soviet-inspired articles about foreign affairs.

In July 1985 Anatoly Zaitsev, the head of the Soviet Foreign Ministry's Southeast Asian bureau, visited Thailand. This visit was followed by a visit to Bangkok of the Moscow-based Thai-Soviet Friendship Society, which is seeking to open a branch in Bangkok. In late October 1975 a Soviet parliamentary delegation led by Vice President Akil Salminov of the Supreme Soviet and Economic Minister V. G. Ivanovich visited Bangkok. Ivanovich conspicuously visited Thai garment factories and offered to buy more of their products.

In October 1984 Ali Wardhana, Indonesia's economics minister, visited Moscow; *Izvestiya* hailed the visit as the first in twenty years by an Indonesian statesman at such a high level. The Soviet newspaper concluded that Wardhana's visit was proof of a "recently evident evolution" in Jakarta's foreign policy which reflected a desire to make Indonesia more independent. Indonesia, said *Izvestiya*, was unwilling to see ASEAN dragged into a pro-Western military and political bloc. Earlier the same year, in April, during a visit to

Moscow by Indonesian foreign minister Mochtar Kusumaatmaja, *Izvestiya* quoted with approval remarks by the Indonesian Armed Forces commander, Benni Murdani, that Vietnam was not a threat to Southeast Asia. The Soviet newspaper went on to argue that Thailand was chiefly responsible for stoking tension in the region, acting at the behest of Washington.

Soviet deputy foreign minister Mikhail Kapitsa has made annual tours of the ASEAN countries in recent years in an effort to further Soviet objectives in the region. He continues to hold out the promise of better relations between ASEAN and Vietnam and between ASEAN and the Soviet Union if ASEAN ends its support of the Cambodian resistance. More recently, he has been offering a "compromise" solution in which the Cambodian government would be broadened to include some members of the resistance.

In sum, the Soviets are engaged in a steady and long-range effort to increase their influence in ASEAN by expanding economic ties, developing cultural and political relations, exploiting fears of China, capitalizing on uncertainty about the United States, and making use of divisions within ASEAN. At the same time the Soviets seek gradually to improve their relations with China though not at the expense of their ties to Vietnam.

Soviet Relations with Vietnam

Despite recurrent reports of strains in the Soviet-Vietnamese relationship, stemming in part from visible Vietnamese concern about the prospect of improving Sino-Soviet relations, the Soviet-Vietnamese alliance rests on solid foundations. Soviet leaders are providing Vietnam with somewhere between one and two billion dollars of economic aid. The Soviets meet all of Vietnam's oil needs, and the provide all of Hanoi's fertilizer and heavy equipment. They are also building bridges and hydroelectric stations. The Soviets have agreed to reschedule Vietnam's mounting ruble debt.

On the military front the Soviets are also stepping up their assistance. The Russians have begun to supply Vietnam with combat helicopters, SU-22 swing-wing fighter aircraft, missile attack boats, tanks, and a variety of surface-to-air missiles.

In return, the Soviet military presence in Vietnam continues to grow. In 1979 elements of the Soviet Pacific Fleet made only occasional forays into the South China Sea. By the mid eighties the figure had increased to between twenty-five and thirty Soviet vessels at any given time, including six to eight surface combatants and about five submarines. The Soviet air and reconnaissance presence in Vietnam has also grown impressively. Moscow now has in Vietnam a squadron of MiG-23s, which provide air-defense cover for about eight TU-95 Bear D reconnaissance aircraft and sixteen TU-Badger bombers. Ten of the Badgers have cruise missile strike capabilities. U.S. intelligence specialists say that the Soviets may eventually deploy about thirty Badger bombers to Cam Ranh. The combat radius of the Badgers extends over all six of the ASEAN states.[12]

Using their bases in Vietnam, the Soviets now have the capacity to carry out surveillance of submarine and surface shipping in the South China Sea and to give pause to any Chinese planners thinking about administering a "second lesson" to Vietnam.

In addition to their growing economic and military support, the Soviets have given virtually complete diplomatic support to Vietnam's goals in Cambodia. Soviet media have claimed that the "new order" in Cambodia has gained viability. Moscow's strategy in recent years has been to call for an international conference on Cambodia which would provide the stamp of legitimacy to the Heng Samrin government.

With regard to Chinese demands that the Vietnamese withdraw from Cambodia before there can be any breakthrough in Sino-Soviet relations, the Soviets continue to refuse to compromise the interests of "third parties" in order to improve relations with China. Increased Soviet military and economic aid to Vietnam should be interpreted in this context.

Meanwhile both the Soviets and the Vietnamese seem to believe that time is on their side in Cambodia, that the resistance is gradually fading, and that the divisions within ASEAN can be exploited to obtain eventual recognition of the status quo.

While deepening their involvement with Vietnam, the Soviets are also developing their ties to both Laos and Cambodia, and they are doing so independently of Vietnam. Soviet sources recently announced that between 1979 and 1982 the Soviet Union had given Heng Samrin's government in Cambodia some $329 million in aid and $15 million for the construction of satellite communication facilities. In addition, Moscow provided Cambodia with about $150 million in loans. This assistance all went direct to Phnom Penh, not via Hanoi. According to one high-ranking Thai official, Kompong Som, the biggest harbor in southern Cambodia, is already completely under Soviet control.[13] Soviet influence in Laos is also growing. There are reportedly about 4,000 Soviet cilivians, including economic advisers, and about 4,000 Soviet military advisers in the country. Western estimates put Soviet aid to Laos at about $100 million a year, half of all foreign aid received by that country.

To be sure, signs of tactical differences between Moscow and Hanoi are visible regarding Hanoi's policy in Cambodia. The Soviets would evidently like Hanoi to be somewhat more flexible about broadening the government in Phnom Penh to try to reach some accommodation with China. At a more

---

[12]For details on the Soviet military presence in Vietnam, see recent issues of *Asian Security* and also Robert Horn's "Soviet Policy in Asia: The Soviet-Vietnamese Influence Relationship."

[13]*Asian Security*, 1984, p. 47.

basic level the Vietnamese must feel some discomfort at their excessive dependence on the Soviets, which is why they have recently invited a number of
high-level Americans to visit Hanoi and seem anxious for American recognition and assistance.

Still, the Soviet-Vietnamese alliance is based on a conjunction of common
interests that are likely to remain strong in the foreseeable future. Both
Moscow and Hanoi see China as a long-range adversary. Vietnam is highly
dependent on Soviet economic and military assistance and on Moscow's
ability to deter China from future military action against Vietnam. Moscow,
for its part, now has access to important military facilities in a region that is
growing in strategic importance. Under these circumstances it is difficult to
imagine developments that might fundamentally alter the situation. Hanoi
wants to improve its relations with the West, but it almost certainly will not
relinquish its dominance in Cambodia as a quid pro quo for assistance. The
Soviets want to end the Cambodian stalemate so that they can improve
relations with China and ASEAN, but they do not have the leverage to force
the Vietnamese out of Cambodia. Over the longer run Vietnam's plan is to
"Vietnamize" Cambodia. Since 1980 Vietnam has extended its control of
Cambodia to the provincial level by sending a division of troops to each of
the nineteen Cambodian provinces, adopting them as "sister provinces."
Hanoi has also encouraged mass emigration to Cambodia in an effort to
change the country's population structure. According to Chinese sources,
Vietnamese residents in Cambodia now number in excess of 700,000, and
further emigration is planned. In Cambodia's capital city of Phnom Penh,
Vietnamese make up more than sixty percent of the population, according to
these same sources.[14] The Vietnamese are also encouraging mixed marriages,
especially among high-ranking officers. These are all indications that Vietnam's long-range strategy is to dominate Cambodia.

Long-Range Determinants of Soviet Policy

Over the longer run Soviet policy in Southeast Asia will continue to be
shaped by great-power relations. As long as the Soviets aspire to global
superpower status, they will have a strong interest in altering the key regional
balances that now favor the West. In Southeast Asia, and in the Pacific more
broadly, the Soviets will seek to weaken American influence and to increase
their own.

Soviet policy in Asia will also be determined to a significant extent by
Moscow's long-term concern about containing China. As a result of these
two basic rivalries, with the United States and with China, Moscow will want
to consolidate its present position in Indochina and to expand ties with the
ASEAN states, particularly with Indonesia, potentially the largest and most

---

[14]New China News Agency (NCNA), February 17, 1986, FBIS-China, February 18, 1986, p. E1.

influential power in the region and one that shares Soviet concerns about China.

Challenges for the West

Although the basic outlook for the West in the Pacific is extremely positive, several serious problems and challenges do exist. Some of these problems are related to Soviet policies but others, perhaps the most important, are not. Here I discuss some of the more serious potential challenges to Western interests in the Pacific.

Although the United States maintains naval and air superiority over the Soviet Union in the Pacific, the margin of its superiority has been decreasing. In the fifteen years or so before 1980 the tonnage of the Soviet Pacific Fleet more than doubled while that of the U.S. Seventh Fleet was reduced by one-third. The Soviet submarine force is the largest in the world, and the Soviets are currently producing or testing seven different classes of submarine. The trend in major programs for surface warships has been toward larger, more technologically sophisticated ships. Substantial numbers of Backfire bombers now represent a considerable threat to the U.S. Seventh Fleet. At the same time the Soviets, by deploying more than one hundred SS-20 intermediate-range nuclear missiles in Siberia, pose a serious threat to the entire American base structure in the region. In addition, the Soviets continue to maintain fifty divisions of troops opposite China. The danger of this impressive Soviet military power in the Pacific is not so much that Moscow is likely to use it in overt military activity; opportunities for the use of Soviet forces in Asia will probably remain limited. Rather, it is that growing Soviet military power might encourage the Soviets to use coercive diplomacy against their adversaries. That power could also encourage a drift toward political neutralism in Asia, paralleling a drift that has recently occurred in Europe.

There remains the possibility of a backlash against the "open door" policy in China, which could lead to a substantial reorientation of Chinese domestic and foreign policy. The Chinese, successful so far in implementing their ambitious reforms, are running into major problems with inequality, inflation, and corruption. A future, post-Deng leadership may curtail ties to the West and revert to a more traditional, Soviet-style, centralized economic system. If accompanied by continuing U.S.-Chinese frictions over Taiwan and a steady improvement in Sino-Soviet relations, such a change could have an adverse effect on the overall balance of power in Asia.

North Korea is pursuing a double-track policy that is still fraught with uncertainty. On the one hand, it has entered into a dialogue with South Korea for the first time in a decade. On the other hand, it has purchased advanced fighter planes from the Soviet Union, deployed U.S.-made helicopters smuggled into the country, and increased its menacing forward deployment near the demilitarized zone.

South Korea enjoys only a precarious stability. It remains to be seen whether power will be transferred peacefully in 1988 or whether the familiar cycle will repeat itself, with liberalization leading to unrest and crackdown.

Vietnam shows no sign of removing its 180,000 troops from Cambodia or of negotiating a political solution that would be acceptable to China or to ASEAN.

Finally, antinuclear sentiment is rising in the South Pacific. A Labour government in New Zealand is committed to banning from its ports all nuclear-powered and nuclear-armed ships. The policy is imposing serious strains on ANZUS, one of Washington's oldest alliances.

In addition to the economic strains in the U.S.-Japan alliance there is a continuing crisis in the Philippines, which is one of the most serious problems that the United States faces in the region. The realignment of political power since Ferdinand Marcos's departure has not yet produced a stable government. There is growing labor unrest; Aquino's inner circle does not seem to be trusted by the Philippine military; and although inflation has been cut, the economy is still saddled with enormous debt. Nevertheless, Aquino is popular; the new constitution will probably give her a mandate to widen the country's land-reform program; and she has deferred the question of the U.S. bases after 1989 by saying that the issue will be put to a referendum. The future of the American bases in the Philippines will be clouded with uncertainty for some time to come.

The building Soviet pressure on Pakistan and the potential break-up of Pakistan as a result of external and internal pressures represent another serious challenge to Western interests in Asia.

When Pakistani president General Mohammed Zia ul-Haq went to Moscow in March 1985 to attend Konstantin Chernenko's funeral, the new Soviet leadership bluntly warned him: Cut off Pakistani aid to Afghan insurgents or face a new Soviet campaign to goad the disgruntled Baluch minority into breaking away from the Pakistani state. According to one informed analyst, Pakistan's military leadership has led the country into peril by sharply restricting internal political activity and by neglecting the grievances of ethnic minorities. "Together, internal divisions and external pressures are pushing Pakistan to the point at which other Third World countries, such as Cyprus, Lebanon and Pakistan itself in 1971, have fallen apart."[15]

Pakistan's ethnic problems stem largely from the continuing struggle of its three smaller provinces—Baluchistan, the Northwest Frontier Province, and Sind—to resist domination by the far more populous Punjab. The Sind has become a hotbed of separatist feeling since the execution of its favorite son, Zulfikar Ali Bhutto, in 1979. The province's small towns and rural areas erupted in late 1983, and reports suggest that many of the Sind's rural areas,

---

[15]Mohammed Ayoob, "Dateline Pakistan: A Passage to Anarchy?" *Foreign Policy*, Summer 1985.

the most economically depressed part of the country, continue to seethe with resentment. A radical populist movement, the Sindhi Awami Tehrik (Sindhi People's Movement), blending peasant radicalism and Sindhi nationalism, has become extremely powerful.

Baluchistan has been remarkably passive in recent years. According to one Baluch leader, the reason is that the Baluch are husbanding their resources and waiting for the external environment to become favorable before striking Pakistan a deathblow.[16]

Three million Afghan refugees have streamed into the Northwest Frontier Province, and they are heavily armed. The Pushtun people of the province sympathize with their displaced Afghan cousins, but Pakistani Pushtuns resent the new competition for grazing land and jobs. Moreover, some leading local politicians are demanding autonomy for the province and negotiations with Kabul to find a political solution to the Afghanistan problem.

Zia continues to search—so far without success—for a formula to legitimize his authoritarian rule. In 1983 he unveiled a plan for an "Islamic" Pakistan with no political parties, but the proposal triggered new outbursts against Zia's regime. The opposition political parties, now virtually outlawed, boycotted the referendum on Islamization. Meanwhile the Soviet Union has refrained from stepping up its support to Pakistani dissidents, presumably because it still hopes to force Zia into an accommodation with its client state in Kabul. If Zia refuses such accommodation, however, the Soviets may yet escalate their support to provincial separatists.

In sum, although the overall picture in Asia is exceedingly positive, the United States cannot take Asia for granted. The Soviet military build-up in the Pacific, problems of political instability, and Soviet opportunism will continue to pose difficult issues.

Coping with Soviet Power in the Pacific

The problem of coping with Soviet power in Asia can be discussed under four headings: the need to balance Soviet power; the importance of maintaining an effective security coalition; the importance of dealing with the weak links; and finally, the desirability of some limited cooperation with the Soviet Union to manage and prevent crises and to reduce tensions.

During the past decade or more, I have already indicated, the Soviets have made impressive efforts to build up their military power in the Asia-Pacific region. Between 35 percent and 40 percent of Moscow's ICBM forces and ballistic-missile-firing submarines and more than 30 percent of its strategic bombers are now deployed east of the Urals. The Soviets have begun to deploy in the Far East a substantial number of SS-20 intermediate-range

---

[16]Quoted in ibid.

nuclear missiles, which are capable of covering the entire east Asian archipelago from positions in Siberia. The Soviets are modernizing and expanding their Pacific fleet, which is now the largest of their four fleets. They have acquired significant support facilities for this fleet in South Yemen, Ethiopia, and Vietnam. Moreover, the Soviet Union has a large naval construction program under way. That program includes at least eight different classes of surface ship and seven different types of submarine. The Soviet submarine force is already the largest in the world. The Soviet naval aircraft program has kept pace with the ship-building program, and more than a hundred Backfire bombers are now in service with Soviet Naval Aviation. In addition, some 325 long- and medium-range aircraft, some of them now stationed in Vietnam, are committed to reconnaissance and antisubmarine warfare against U.S. Navy ships. The Soviet Union is also adding to the already large number of antiship cruise missiles deployed throughout the Soviet fleet.[17]

Whatever the intentions behind this huge Soviet military build-up in the Pacific, its very existence poses severe challenges to the United States and its allies. As the head of a global maritime alliance and as the world's largest trading nation, the United States has a vital interest in command of the Pacific. Its present strategy in the Pacific is based on a forward deployment of ground and air forces and a substantial naval presence. To such a strategy maritime superiority is indispensable. There may be differences among U.S. military strategists about what kind of forward strategy and force projection capabilities best serve U.S. interests, but all schools accept the need for naval superiority.[18]

Although the United States still maintains naval superiority in the Pacific, the margin of that superiority is declining. Both the quantity and the quality of Soviet surface ships, submarines, and naval aviation are increasing. U.S. naval forces continue to be "stretched so thin," according to Admiral Wesley McDonald, "that very little surge capability exists for rapid responses to additional crises."[19] It has been estimated that approximately 80 percent of the U.S. sealift fleet would be needed to support a continuing military presence in the Persian Gulf.[20] As the commander in chief of the U.S. Pacific Command has noted, moreover, "the Pacific and Indian Ocean basins present a different military challenge than any other theater" because "the vast dis-

---

[17]For details, see U.S. Department of Defense, *Soviet Military Power, 1985* (Washington, D.C., 1985).

[18]Robert W. Komer, *Maritime Strategy or Coalition Defense* (Cambridge, Mass.: Abt, 1984), p. 36.

[19]Testimony of Admiral Wesley McDonald, Commander in Chief, Atlantic Command, before U.S. Senate, Armed Services Committee, *Hearings*: Department of Defense Authorization for Appropriations for Fiscal Year 1985 (1984), pt. 2, p. 115, quoted in "Can America Catch Up? The U.S.-Soviet Military Balance," Committee on Present Danger, updated, p. 50.

[20]U.S. House, Subcommittee on Merchant Marine, *Hearing*, April 30, 1984, cited in Committee on Present Danger, p. 50.

tances influence everything we do" and because our facilities and our allies are widely spread over islands and around the littoral.[21]

One chronic problem is that of credibility. Although the Reagan administration's military build-up has gone a long way toward dispelling doubts among American allies as to American reliability in case of crises, such doubts continue to exist. Recent polls in Japan indicate a basic lack of confidence that the United States would honor its commitments under the 1960 security treaty between the two countries. As the *New York Times* noted, "suspicions that the United States may be a muscle bound giant set in during the hostage crisis in Iran five years ago, and they have not been dispelled by American immobility during more recent episodes."[22]

To meet the Soviet military challenge in the Pacific and elsewhere, the United States is engaged in a long-overdue effort to build a six-hundred-ship navy, which includes fifteen aircraft carriers deployed by 1990. Deployable naval vessels will number 545 in 1985. It will be necessary to sustain these programs in the face of rising public criticism in the United States of allegedly excessive defense spending—not an easy task in a nation where the public mood on defense is highly volatile. It will also be important for Japan to continue quantitative and qualitative improvements of its fleet and to sustain the higher level of cooperation with the U.S. fleet that has developed in recent years.

Finally, more thought needs to be given to the role in Pacific defense of other interested parties—including South Korea, Australia, the ASEAN states, France, Britain, and also China. For example, one can imagine cooperative efforts between the United States and a number of Pacific countries on air defense, intelligence gathering, and so forth. Japan could play a key role in guarding the exits from the Sea of Japan, thereby greatly complicating Soviet defense planning. As long as the Soviet Union is building up its military power in the Pacific at such an impressive rate, the Western alliance will need greater efforts and greater burden sharing.

Building and maintaining an effective coalition to contain Soviet power is the second challenge facing the United States in the Pacific. At a time when relative U.S. economic and military power is declining, when Soviet military power is growing, and when nuclear stalemate reduces the credibility of extended deterrence, the United States needs more than ever the help of its allies. As Robert Komer notes, "the single greatest remaining U.S. strategic advantage over the USSR is that we are blessed with many rich allies while the Soviets have only a handful of poor ones. Most of theirs are a strain on the

---

[21]Statement by Admiral William J. Crowe before U.S., Senate, Armed Services Committee, 1985, mimeo.

[22]*New York Times*, August 6, 1985, p. A8.

Soviet exchequer whereas most of ours pay their own way. They also fear their own forced allies while we fear *for* ours."[23]

The United States has to maintain the Pacific coalition in the face of substantial Soviet efforts to break it up and in spite of equally substantial divergences of interest among its members. Soviet efforts to intimidate Japan can be expected to grow as Japan increases its security cooperation with the United States and adds to its own military forces. Efforts to intimidate may be coupled with efforts to woo. Similar tactics will be employed against China.

The United States will be faced also with the need to reconcile divergent perspectives and interests among its Pacific partners. The conflict with New Zealand over port calls by U.S. nuclear warships exemplifies the difficulties that such a task presents. Dealing too harshly with New Zealand runs the risk of jeopardizing the ANZUS alliance; dealing too leniently runs the risk of encouraging other American allies in the region to follow New Zealand's path.

Other contradictions abound. The United States requires Japanese naval assistance to keep open the Pacific sea lanes of communication, yet other U.S. allies in Asia are extremely wary of the Japanese. Similarly, the United States intends to help China defend itself against the Soviet Union, but other Asian countries fear that the United States may go too far in developing China's military power. It will be the continuing task of American diplomacy to be sensitive to these differences and to prevent them from disrupting the security coalition.

Strengthening the weak links in the U.S. Pacific position will also be difficult. No easy or quick solutions can be promised to the U.S.-Japan trade competition, to the crisis in the Philippines, or to Pakistan's ethnic rivalries. Nor can anyone be sure that China's open door will remain as open in the post-Deng era as it has been over the past five years. Dealing with these issues will require great skill and patience.

With regard to the U.S.-Japan trade issue, we can only hope that Japanese efforts to open domestic markets and American efforts to lower the federal budget deficit, accompanied by continuing economic growth in both countries, will gradually defuse the present inflammatory situation. It is encouraging that, despite the trade issue, the overwhelming majority of Americans and Japanese continue to regard each other as friendly. In a recent survey of 1,569 adult Americans, 88 percent viewed relations with Japan as friendly, 23 percent as very friendly. Similarly, a solid majority of 1,428 Japanese adults surveyed, some 73 percent, described ties between the two countries as amicable.[24] The task for American and Japanese leaders is to make sure that con-

[23]Komer, *Maritime Strategy*, p. 27.
[24]See *New York Times*, August 6, 1985, p. A8.

tinuing trade frictions do not erode these overwhelmingly positive attitudes in the years ahead.

In the first two or three years of the Reagan administration, U.S. relations with China were erratic and tense; since then, by contrast, relations have become much more stable. Washington and Beijing should now be able to weather minor changes in China's open door policy. Technology transfer from the United States to China has grown rapidly in the past two years. Scientific, educational, and cultural exchanges have proliferated. Some thirteen American companies are collaborating with the Chinese in the search for oil. Trade has increased rapidly. And the United States is now exploring ways of helping the Chinese upgrade their antitank and air defense as well as their capacity to wage antisubmarine warfare.[25] With a Soviet military build-up in Siberia, the long and disputed border between Russia and China, continuing geopolitical competition between the two countries in Korea, Indochina, and South Asia, and the past history of relations, it seems likely that China will continue to regard the Soviet Union as its main enemy and will welcome U.S. efforts to balance Soviet power, particularly in Asia. A stable and cooperative Sino-American relationship is as much in China's interest as it is in America's.

In Pakistan, as in the Philippines, there will be no quick or easy solutions to the problems of potential political instability. The United States should continue to increase military assistance to Pakistan as a token of support against Soviet efforts to intimidate. But it also should encourage President Zia to give greater autonomy to the provinces to defuse ethnic unrest. The United States should also seek to enlist India in defusing Soviet pressure on Pakistan, for surely it cannot be in India's interests for Pakistan to be dismembered again.

Finally, it is time to engage the Russians in a broad dialogue on Asian security issues and to offer them a role in helping maintain regional security. It cannot reasonably be denied that the Soviet Union, while an adversary, is also an Asian power with legitimate interests in the region. In Asia, moreover, the United States and the Soviet Union share some significant common interests. Neither wants a new Korean war. Neither wants incidents at sea which could lead to confrontation. Neither wants to see the proliferation of nuclear weapons. Neither wants to see an escalation of the conflict in Cambodia. In sum, the Soviet Union is as concerned as the United States about the dangers of confrontation and escalation and the threat of war. Moreover, the Soviet Union now has a stake in the status quo in certain parts of Asia—for example, Vietnam, Laos, Cambodia, Afghanistan.

The new Soviet leader, Mikhail Gorbachev, has offered to undertake a

[25]Speech of Michael H. Armacost, undersecretary for political affairs, *Current Policy* no. 725 (July 9, 1985).

wide-ranging discussion of Asian security issues with interested Asian powers. It is time for the United States, *after* careful consultation with its Asian allies and friends, to explore this offer.

The Korean peninsula may be the place to begin. The Soviet Union does not want a new Korean war, because it cannot afford to let Pyongyang win or lose. A North Korean loss in a new war would have profound political and psychological consequences among the Soviet Union's other allies and treaty partners. A North Korean victory would risk a Soviet-American military confrontation near Soviet borders, end whatever chances there are for improving Soviet-American relations, carry the risk of Chinese intervention, and lead to great pressure within Japan for Japanese remilitarization—all of which results would be severely detrimental to Soviet interests.

There is a window of opportunity to moderate tensions in Korea between 1986 and 1988—the date of the Olympics scheduled for Seoul. South Korea does not want North Korea to disrupt the Olympics, and North Korea wants to co-host the games. Perhaps an agreement can be worked out to satisfy both sides.

The United States, after careful consultation with Japan, China, and South Korea, could begin to probe the Soviets on the Korean issue. The Soviets, if they so choose, could lend their weight to a substantial reduction of tensions in the peninsula. And if the two superpowers would throw their respective weights into an easing of tensions in Korea, the move would in itself have an extremely beneficial impact on their general relationship.

If the West wants to reduce tensions with the Soviet Union in East Asia, it will have to adopt a policy that combines the important but limited insights of both hawks and doves. On the one hand, it must continue to build up its strength to balance Soviet power. On the other, it must seek, whenever interests dictate, to probe for ways to reduce tensions.

12

The Soviet Union in the Less Developed World: A Retrospective Overview and Prognosis

Harry Gelman

What are the prospects for Soviet policy in the Third World during the Gorbachev era? Does the stagnation of Soviet fortunes in many areas of the world since the heady advances of the late 1970s presage a scaling down of Soviet efforts to advance influence at the expense of the West in the less developed parts of the world? Does the new Soviet leadership believe that past disappointments and internal Soviet difficulties require a qualitative change in Soviet Third World priorities?

When summed up without too much concern for offsetting considerations, the roster of Soviet disappointments in the first half of the 1980s indeed seems imposing. In sub-Saharan Africa the striking advances of the 1970s have been followed by some well-known setbacks. In Latin America the hopes engendered at the close of the last decade that the Sandinista victory was the start of a wave of further revolutionary inroads on U.S. influence— hopes reflected in some rather cocky private remarks by Marshal Ogarkov to the Bishop regime in Grenada[1]—have been eroded by subsequent events in Grenada and by the gradual ebbing of revolutionary fortunes in El Salvador.

In the Middle East the Soviet Union, despite a few recent improvements in its position, remains a secondary actor, maneuvering on the periphery of events. It has yet to recover from the devastating loss of influence it suffered in the 1970s in Egypt, the largest and strongest Arab state; despite some occasional contacts, it has been essentially self-isolated from the strongest regional military power, Israel, a client of the United States; because of Khomeini's hostility it has thus far failed to draw full dividends from the American debacle in Iran; because of the intractability of the many forces involved it has also been unable to register more than modest gains from the

---

[1]See the memorandum from *The Grenada Papers* cited by Edward Gonzalez in his "Cuba, the Third World, and the Soviet Union" in this volume.

expulsion of Western influence from Lebanon and the fragmentation of the country; and because of the difficult choices imposed by the Iran-Iraq war it has lost some ground in Iraq while making little headway in Iran.

In Afghanistan the Soviet Union has been disappointed to find itself committed to a protracted war effort, forced to abandon both the initial hope that the resistance could soon be ended and the initial illusion that it might prove possible to rely on the Afghan Communists to do most of the fighting. And in the Far East the Soviet Union's political position has remained much weaker than its military position for a variety of reasons, notably the adverse reaction of the ASEAN states to Soviet support of the Vietnamese war effort in Cambodia; meanwhile the USSR has remained essentially excluded from the benefits of much of East Asia's economic dynamism.

This panorama seems rather dismal, although, as already suggested, it is not a balanced picture; there is another side to the story, which I shall discuss presently. Meanwhile, there is also evidence, recorded particularly by Stephen Sestanovich and Francis Fukuyama, suggesting the advent in Moscow of a less sanguine attitude toward the Third World, a mood that began to spread in a few circles in the 1970s but that has widened in the Soviet elite in the 1980s and apparently reached at least part of the leadership.[2] This mood has been alluded to more than once in this volume. There is a general impression of somewhat reduced Soviet short- and medium-term expectations and also of somewhat reduced Soviet enthusiasm for Third World commitments. Some reasons are suggested in Soviet writings, but some remain largely a matter of supposition. What is most clear is increased Soviet skepticism about the malleability and long-term reliability of many of the actors and forces involved. Coupled with this is an evidently heightened realization of Soviet resource limitations and of the impediments to the consolidation of Soviet footholds in the Third World that those limitations, and Soviet economic weaknesses generally, often create.

In addition, two other considerations may possibly have some influence in the Soviet elite today, but they are much more conjectural and in my opinion more marginal. One is whether a somewhat greater degree of military risk may now attach to any given Soviet venture because of the overall posture of the Reagan administration. The other is whether the Soviet Union should draw any inhibiting conclusions for the future from the political price that it ultimately paid for its Third World behavior in the 1970s, above all in the long-term response evoked from the United States. These two considerations raise fundamental questions about the underlying priorities of Soviet foreign policy, to which I also return later.

---

[2]Stephen Sestanovich, "Do Soviets Feel Pinched by Third World Adventurism?" *Washington Post*, May 20, 1984; Francis Fukuyama, *Moscow's Post-Brezhnev Reassessment of the Third World*, R-3337-USDP (Santa Monica: RAND Corporation, February 1986). The less sanguine Soviet mood was reflected during Gorbachev's first year in the considerably reduced emphasis given the Third World in the new Party Program, in the semiannual party slogans, and in Gorbachev's speech to the Twenty-seventh Party Congress.

To sum up thus far: there is evidence of a variety of Soviet disappointments and frustrations in the Third World, particularly over the last six years and in some cases much longer, and there is also evidence that at least a somewhat more sour and chastened mood has evolved in Soviet thinking in response to this experience. Less clear is the relative importance of all the factors that could, in principle, tend to inhibit the Soviets' future behavior. Most uncertain of all is how much operational significance recent Soviet experience will in practice have upon Moscow's future decisions if the Soviet Union is faced by changing circumstances with momentous new choices.

In the discussion to follow I explore in greater detail the relative weight of the opposing considerations that are likely to affect Soviet Third World choices in the future. I first touch on certain aspects of the historical background—including events in the Third World, the communist world, and the Soviet Union—which help condition Soviet behavior to this day. I examine those factors in the present world configuration of forces which tend to impart momentum and continuity to Soviet Third World policy and weigh them against those considerations which have been pressing the Soviet leadership in the direction of change. I then draw some net conclusions.

The Stalinist Heritage in Soviet Policy

At least some of the roots of present Soviet Third World policy antedate the Czech arms deal of 1955 and go back to the Stalinist era. It is true that the events of 1955 did represent a major turning point in Soviet policy, symbolizing a shift away from Stalin's rather pessimistic assumptions and conservative priorities toward intensive efforts to explore the anti-Western, anti-American potential of the new, noncommunist leaders of the newly independent states. But it is also true that from the Soviet perspective, some of the decisive changes in the colonial and semicolonial world that continue to affect Soviet calculations to this day occurred a decade earlier, at the close of World War II.

From today's standpoint, it requires an act of will to recall that the Soviet Union started with virtually a blank slate. Stalin evidently perceived the colonial and semicolonial world from which the newly independent states were beginning to emerge as a vast sea in which Western influence was almost totally predominant and Soviet influence and presence virtually excluded, except for the inadequate instruments represented by the local communist parties and the international front organizations. The insurrectionary efforts that he sometimes encouraged in remote parts of the underdeveloped world in the first postwar years were therefore essentially adjuncts to his pressure on Western Europe. At the same time his initial skepticism about the usability for Soviet purposes of the emerging "national bourgeoisie" in newly independent countries such as India was probably not based only on his dogmatic assumptions about the fraudulent nature of Indian independence. It also seems likely that he was influenced by his sense of the Soviet Union's economic weakness and even more by his awareness of the USSR's profound military weakness in all areas of the globe not contiguous with Soviet borders and easily accessible to Soviet land armies. This consciousness of Soviet inability to exercise either economic or military leverage in distant regions tended to reinforce Stalin's predisposition to be pessimistic about his ability to influence elite forces in the underdeveloped world which were not totally under his control—that is, were not already dominated by communist parties loyal to him.

In contrast, at the close of World War II Stalin did seek to register specific gains through the use of Soviet military power in certain parts of the old colonial and semicolonial world that *were* contiguous and now within his reach.[3] Because of a variety of unforeseen circumstances, the long-term results were not brilliant. In Iran a tentative effort to keep hold of the occupied province of Azerbaydzhan was abandoned after Stalin encountered unexpectedly sharp resistance from the United States. In China, then the largest and most important "semicolonial" country in the world, the Soviet Union emerged from the war controlling a loose protectorate over Xinjiang Province in the West, run by a pro-Soviet Chinese warlord, while simultaneously occupying with its own forces the Chinese eastern industrial base of Manchuria, seized from the Japanese in the last days of the war. Both of these gains unfortunately, from Stalin's prospective, had soon to be relinquished to the unexpectedly victorious Chinese Communists. Although Stalin attempted to hedge by retaining from Mao certain Soviet naval and other extraterritorial rights in Manchuria, Stalin's weaker successors soon had to give these up; and as we know, within the next two decades even China's new orientation away from the West and toward the Soviet Union was incrementally reversed.

At the outset, therefore, an immense cumulative subtraction from Western influence in the colonial and semicolonial world was registered; indeed, the Soviets have had reason to believe that the communist conquest of China remains by far the most important change yet to occur in this world. As was to happen on several other occasions in subsequent years, however, the Soviets encountered frustration when they sought to consolidate an initial advantage, partly because of adverse circumstances and partly because of mistakes in judgment.

The significance of this historical background for more recent Soviet policy is twofold. First, it is a reminder that subsequent and recent Soviet setbacks in the less developed world had an early, major precedent. Second, because the impact of the Soviet defeat in China was felt only after Stalin's successors had begun to make new inroads in the underdeveloped world in the mid-

---

[3]This crude and direct use of Soviet military power in contiguous areas of the less developed world was not repeated by Stalin's successors until the invasion of Afghanistan in December 1979.

fifties, all such setbacks could always be interpreted as part of a long-term, continuously evolving flow of rolling gains and losses. The estrangement from China developed in the late 1950s and early 1960s simultaneously with the growth of Soviet influence in India, Egypt, and Cuba; similarly, the almost equally important expulsion of Soviet influence from Egypt in the mid-1970s was soon followed by the arrival of the Soviet political and military presence in Black Africa, Afghanistan, and Indochina. I draw attention to this historical sequence because it has tended over the years to counteract periodic waves of pessimism in Moscow and to foster an assumption that new manifestations of Soviet weakness in the Third World will find eventual compensation in new windfalls.

The Evolving Soviet Response to Adverse Experience

This long-term, overlapping continuity of Soviet gains and losses helps explain the long-term resiliency of Soviet policy and the persistence of Soviet efforts in the face of great handicaps and repeated disappointments. The history of Soviet endeavors in the less developed world is punctuated by misadventures that subsequently were submerged in the continuing Soviet effort to advance. Some of these Soviet misfortunes proved to be of major importance; others, less so.

The two gravest disappointments—the separation from China which began to become manifest in 1960 and the loss of Soviet influence in Egypt since the middle 1970s—have already been alluded to. The next most important setback, probably regarded in hindsight as regrettable but not nearly as damaging, was the loss of the Soviet position in Somalia in 1978 when the Soviet Union chose to assist Somalia's opponent, Ethiopia. Others have included such secondary disasters as the demise of the positions that Khrushchev had once staked out in Guinea, Ghana, and Mali; the 1965 military overthrow of Sukarno and communist influence in the Indonesian armed forces, which rendered moot the previous Soviet effort (only marginally effective, in any case) to cultivate that country through arms sales and other endeavors; and the Soviet inability to prevent Mozambique from yielding to South African pressure in the 1980s. Still others, such as the loss of the Marxist-Leninist regime in Grenada, are likely to be seen in retrospect as relatively trivial.

Probably more disturbing to Soviet leaders than many of these specific defeats has been the pattern of frustration they have often encountered in seeking to maintain long-term relationships in the underdeveloped world. In a good many cases—although not always—the Soviets have been unable to build on relationships established in the 1950s and 1960s and maintain enduring continuity with client regimes. They have found this particularly likely to happen in the Middle East and Africa for a variety of reasons, including

Soviet economic weaknesses, the complexity and multiplicity of the forces involved, the mutual animosities among Soviet client states (notably Egypt, Syria, and Iraq), the vagaries of mercurial personalities (Nasser being one example and Guinea's Sekou Touré another), Soviet vulnerability to the consequences of unpredictable leadership changes (such as the shift from Nasser to Sadat), and occasionally (as my later discussion of the case of Mozambique shows) the limitations on Soviet military reach and on the Soviet ability to support a client under pressure.

Soviet Eclecticism

Over the years the Soviet response has been a pragmatic, trial-and-error search for other expedients while nevertheless preserving older approaches when appropriate. This eclecticism continues to be fundamental for the Soviet Union today; the Soviets have important commitments in the under-developed world across a very wide ideological spectrum. Despite the dem-onstrated fatuity of Khrushchev's early hopes that some weak, radical bour-geois regimes in Africa which the Soviets termed "national democracies" would continue to evolve in a Soviet direction, the USSR has by no means abandoned the courting of selected national bourgeois leaders of Third World states—the heterogeneous assortment of noncommunist leaders typ-ified at the outset, in the mid-1950s, by Nasser of Egypt and Nehru of India. Such diverse states, with diverse relationships with the Soviet Union, as India, Syria, Iraq, and Libya all fall into this category today. Although the Soviets by now lack significant hope that any of these countries will ever adopt "scientific socialism," they nevertheless continue to accept the partial foreign policy benefits they get from each as a basis for a protracted relation-ship.

Moreover, the Soviets during and since the Brezhnev era have enlarged their dealings with states of the less developed world which are even further removed from Soviet control and which are not Soviet clients in any sense. Since the 1970s, that is, the Soviets have sought to expand and diversify geographically—to "globalize"—their economic connections with many bourgeois-led countries of the less developed world where Soviet political influence is as yet quite attenuated or even nonexistent. This tendency has been reflected partly in Soviet economic assistance and credits to such seem-ingly unlikely recipients as Morocco and Turkey but also in a multiplication of purely commercial dealings with such countries as Argentina and Brazil.[4] These trends have evidently been driven partly by economic motives: to improve Soviet access to the benefits of the international division of labor, to

[4]See Abraham S. Becker, "The Soviet Union and the Third World: The Economic Dimen-sion," in this volume. The data presented by Becker suggest that the "evening out" of Soviet economic aid among different regions of the world has been particularly marked in the 1980s.

earn hard currency in some cases, and—as in the case of grain purchases from Argentina—to diversify Soviet sources of supply. At the same time this broadening of the base in Soviet economic dealings with the less developed world clearly is also intended in many cases to plant political seeds for the future, to open up possibilities for the eventual insinuation of Soviet influence in presently barren terrain. This long-term political motive is particularly evident, of course, in Soviet commercial arms sales since the 1970s to such nonclient bourgeois states as Peru, Zambia, Jordan, and Kuwait.

Meanwhile, at the other end of the political spectrum, the Soviets—especially in the years since the fall of Khrushchev—have moved to shore up their relationships with the three oldest, most firmly established small communist states in the underdeveloped world: Cuba, Vietnam, and (most recently and to a lesser extent) North Korea. The Soviets consider these relationships not merely dealings within a closed socialist world but also an integral and extremely important part of their broader operations in the formerly colonial world; and so should we.

Finally, as Fukuyama and others have shown, the Soviets during the Brezhnev era simultaneously sought to find an answer to the problem of building durable relationships with weak radical regimes in the Third World by seeking to induce such regimes to erect Marxist-Leninist party and state structures in the Soviet image.[5] It should be noted that in so doing, the Soviets partially returned to Stalin's policy of seeking to deal with the underdeveloped world through communist parties under his control. For the Soviets, the model and inspiration for these efforts was probably the metamorphosis of Castro's Cuba, which during the 1960s gradually and voluntarily acquired such a Soviet-style Leninist apparatus and in the process was transformed, in Soviet eyes, from a distrusted "radical petit-bourgeois" regime into one more reliably oriented toward the Soviet Union. In the regimes of this type which the USSR has sought to encourage in Asia and Africa, a major Soviet purpose has been to give the Soviet Union multiple long-term channels of influence supplementing and if possible bypassing the original leaders at the top. Although this effort to broaden the base of Soviet influence has worked reasonably well in South Yemen,[6] elsewhere—notably in Ethiopia[7]—it has fostered suspicion and resistance from local leaders wary of Soviet purposes and determined to retain supreme personal control.

In addition, in several such states the Soviet Union has also attempted to

---

[5]See Francis Fukuyama, *The New Marxist-Leninist States in the Third World*, P-7020 (Santa Monica: RAND Corporation, September 1984).

[6]The breadth and inherent strength of the Soviet position in the leadership structure of the PDRY were tested and confirmed by the outcome of the bloody civil war waged between opposing Marxist factions in early 1986. It remains true, of course, that this prolonged military confrontation between opposing wings of a generally pro-Soviet organization was for many reasons highly distressing and embarrassing to Moscow.

[7]See Paul B. Henze, "Communism and Ethiopia," *Problems of Communism*, May–June 1981, pp. 55–74.

ensure stability and pro-Soviet continuity by arranging for stationing of foreign communist military contingents—mainly Cubans—as "praetorian guards" to stiffen Marxist-Leninist regimes. But this gambit has also had major drawbacks, since it has more closely entangled the Soviet Union with weak states that have proved to have grave economic weaknesses and that have in several instances been faced with serious, protracted, internal and external challenges to regime authority.[8] I consider the Soviet reponse to these latter challenges below, in the discussion of the evolution of the Soviet use of military power in remote areas for political purposes.

The Spectrum of Soviet Relationships

On the whole, one is left with the impression of a mixed and diverse picture, with part of the Soviet position in the underdeveloped world quite stable, other parts likely to be subject to continued kaleidoscopic fluctuations over time, and still others in an intermediate status as to the prospects for durability and longevity. These distinctions cut across ideological differences among Soviet clients.

At the pole of greatest stability are two cases where the Soviets have encountered not only success but long-term success. One of these two pillars of Soviet policy in the underdeveloped world is India. There the Soviets have been able to foster a strong and stable relationship over the entire three decades since Stalin, enduring through several changes of Indian and Soviet leaderships, relying particularly upon Soviet ability to take advantage of long-term Indian geopolitical conflicts with Pakistan and China, Indian differences with the United States, and the Indians' felt need for a stable source of sophisticated weaponry. The other pillar is Cuba, where over the last twenty-five years the Soviets have watched evolve an ally that is avowedly communist and immensely valuable to Soviet political and strategic purposes, albeit burdensome for the Soviet Union and by no means passively subordinated to Soviet policy.

In practice the Soviets derive most of the rest of the strength of their present position in the underdeveloped world from a few of their accumulated relationships that are not so effervescent as to be likely to disappear tomorrow yet do not possess the history of stability built up with India and Cuba. These medium-term working relationships are all marriages of convenience; although they have not existed as long as the relationships with India and Cuba, they have typically lasted a considerable time and seem likely to go on considerably longer because of a continuing mutuality of interest. The regimes involved also have a somewhat more secure hold on power than

---

[8]See Francis Fukuyama, *U.S.-Soviet Interactions in the Third World*, OPS-004 (Santa Monica: RAND/UCLA Center for the Study of Soviet International Behavior, March 1985); also Fukuyama, *Moscow's Post-Brezhnev Reassessment*.

some other Soviet clients. For various reasons some of these relationships with the Soviets are much looser and vaguer than others (ranging from that with Libya at one end of the spectrum to those with Syria, Ethiopia, and Vietnam at the other). All are characterized by some degree of mutual distrust, and none is guaranteed to last forever; yet all are useful to Soviet political and strategic interests for medium-term planning.

The Impact of Soviet Economic Handicaps

Cutting across all Soviet political calculations in the underdeveloped world are the economic constraints on Soviet policy that have grown in the last decade. My net judgment is that these constraints are indeed a serious handicap for Soviet prospects but not necessarily an insuperable one.

It must be remembered that any measure of the Soviet cost-benefit ratio is likely to be elusive and inconstant, heavily influenced by personalities and circumstances. Indeed, the issue of whether Soviet costs incurred in the underdeveloped world would be worth the prospective benefits long antedates the recent growth in Soviet economic difficulties.

I have already suggested that a sense of the Soviet Union's profound economic weakness in competition with the capitalist industrialized states was at least a contributing factor in Stalin's skepticism about his chance of making substantial political inroads with the national bourgeoisie of the former colonies of those states. Some years after Stalin's death, when Khrushchev first considered Nasser's request that the USSR assume the burden of building the Aswan Dam rejected by the United States, he apparently encountered particular resistance from certain of his Stalinist colleagues, particularly Molotov and Kaganovich. These Politburo skeptics are likely to have argued, on Stalinist principles that sound familiar today, that the Soviet Union could not afford such a diversion of funds from more important purposes; and that the anticipated political returns from such an unpredictable and unreliable person as Nasser were far too chancy.[9] The dam neverthe-

---

[9]The evidence that Molotov and Kaganovich, and possibly others, objected to the Soviet Union assuming the burden of building the Aswan Dam for Nasser is fragmentary and not conclusive but strongly suggestive. In December 1955 the USSR had proposed participation with Western states in helping build an Aswan high dam. After the West in 1956 declined, Egypt in October 1956 claimed that the Soviets would do so unilaterally; the Soviet Union publicly denied having made any such commitment. Khrushchev, in great personal difficulties at that moment and in political retreat before his adversaries Molotov and Kaganovich because of the disastrous consequences of de-Stalinization, was initially reluctant to take this step. It was not until a year after Khrushchev's defeat of these opponents and the expulsion of the "anti-Party group" from the leadership that the USSR, in October 1958, did sign a formal commitment to build the Aswan Dam. Yaacov Ro'i, *From Encroachment to Involvement: A Documentary Study of Soviet Policy in the Middle East, 1945–1973* (New York: Wiley, 1974), p. 272. Three months later, at the Twenty-first Party Congress in January 1959, Molotov's former ally Maxim Saburov alleged that the members of the "anti-Party group" had obstructed Soviet assistance to unspecified newly independent

less was eventually built, on Khrushchev's insistence. In contrast, a few years later Khrushchev in 1963 decided that North Korea's political behavior no longer justified continued Soviet economic and military assistance; a year after that, with no significant change in the North Korean stance, Khrushchev's successor Brezhnev reversed his decision and offered Pyongyang a new aid package.[10]

In short, it is apparent that quite apart from all objective Soviet difficulties and the objective circumstances in a given client country, the subjective predispositions of different Soviet leaders play a large role in shaping judgments as to what the Soviet Union can or cannot afford in return for a prospective political benefit—that is, as to whether the political payoff is commensurate with the cost. Therefore, while recent Soviet tendencies to retrench should be carefully noted, we have little reason to conclude that those tendencies must necessarily produce Soviet paralysis in cases that a future Politburo may deem particularly important.

The Roster of Soviet Difficulties

At the same time it is clear that the Soviets' objective difficulties in using economic policy to serve Soviet political ambitions in the underdeveloped world have in fact grown substantially, partly because of the adverse trends in the Soviet economy since the 1970s and partly because of the cumulative burden already imposed by overseas commitments assumed in the Brezhnev era. This burden involves, above all, the cost of prosecuting the war in Afghanistan while simultaneously subsidizing heavily the Soviet political and strategic footholds in Cuba and Vietnam. There is evidence that Soviet unhappiness about these costs has resulted in sporadic efforts to constrain the flow of resources to the Cuban and Vietnamese clients and to try to compel both clients to make better use of Soviet inputs. Yet there is little doubt that the Gorbachev leadership will feel obliged to continue to bear a substantial burden in subsidizing these two regimes as long as the Soviet Union continues to receive the present political and strategic payoff from each.

Future, comparably large increments to this bill, however, are clearly another matter. It is quite possible that despite all their difficulties, the Soviets would accept a comparable additional burden for the sake of a sufficiently important new strategic gain; but the measure of what is sufficient strategic compensation for a given economic sacrifice is surely rising. Soviet leaders have obviously become increasingly sensitive to the adequacy of the payoff

countries. *Pravda*, February 3, 1959. In his memoirs, Khrushchev alludes without elaboration to "the grumbling of those skunks, those narrow-minded skunks who raised such a stink and tried to poison the waters of our relations with Egypt." *Khrushchev Remembers* (Boston: Little, Brown, 1970), p. 450.

[10]See Harry Gelman and Norman D. Levin, *The Future of Soviet–North Korean Relations*, R-3159-AF (Santa Monica: RAND Corporation, October 1984), pp. 19–20.

from investments in major new overseas adventures. This heightened sensitivity has been reflected, in the last decade, in the demonstrated Soviet reluctance to assume new economic obligations on behalf of some radical suitors in the underdeveloped world—such as the short-lived Manley regime in Jamaica—whose political viability seemed dubious. A similar parsimoniusness has been displayed toward those existing clients which are considered relatively marginal; they have been encouraged to strive to increase inputs from the capitalist world. This reluctance on the Soviet side to spend money in marginal cases has been matched, among the clients, by a widespread perception of the inferiority of Soviet civilian technology; this perception impels those few clients who have the hard-currency-earning capacity to prefer in any case to import Western civilian goods. Although the Soviets accept and to some extent discount the handicaps imposed by their economic inferiority, they are surely chagrined that in at least one instance, Mozambique, a client has felt obliged to alter its political posture toward the United States to seek American economic assistance.

Another complication is created for Soviet policy in the Third World by the pressure on Soviet hard-currency-earning capacity created by both the growing difficulties in Soviet production of oil—the leading Soviet hard-currency earner—and the recent major decline in world oil prices. These trends will tend over the long term to increase the opportunity costs of some politically motivated gestures—such as supplying oil to favored Third World clients on soft-currency terms—which the Soviet leaders have been selectively employing.[11] In addition, the reduced hard-currency returns to be expected from Soviet oil exports will produce increased economic incentives for Soviet leaders to maximize hard-currency earnings from arms deliveries and therefore to consider reducing further the proportion of arms exports furnished to some clients without hard-currency repayment. At the same time some oil-exporting states are evidently finding it more difficult to allocate funds for such repayment.

Finally, Soviet economic constraints in another area—the labor shortage—hinder Soviet options for action in the underdeveloped world in a different way. Because of the growth in the list of Soviet adversaries over the past two decades, Soviet ground force manpower stationed on Soviet frontiers has been increasingly stretched between competing theaters and missions around the Soviet periphery even as the domestic economy's labor shortage has mounted. This consideration suggests that the continued aggravation of the labor shortage over the remainder of the 1980s will be one factor tending to

[11]Eastern Europe is of course a much more significant burden on the Soviet Union in this respect, followed by Cuba and Vietnam, which are heavily dependent on Soviet oil deliveries and could have their supplies trimmed somewhat if similar constraints are imposed on Eastern Europe. Other politically motivated shipments by the Soviets to the Third World on barter or gratis terms—for example, to India and Nicaragua—probably represent a portion of Soviet exports small enough to remain bearable.

constrain the Soviets' readiness to take on large, new, long-term ground force missions in regions near their borders.

Offsetting Considerations

I stress, however, that all of these considerations are likely to operate upon Soviet behavior as important factors but surely not as binding prohibitions. First, despite the military manpower constraints just mentioned, the Soviets will certainly retain the capability to act in regions near their borders—such as post-Khomeini Iran, for example—if they consider the occasion sufficiently important and the risk acceptable.

Second, some countertrends partially offset Soviet economic handicaps in the Third World. The difficulties that many less developed countries experience in generating hard-currency earnings to pay for imports of Western goods may somewhat increase the attractiveness of barter trade with the Soviet Union, even if the goods obtained are at a lower technological level. The constriction of markets for LDC exports imposed by recent protectionist tendencies in the capitalist industrialized world further increases incentives to sell surplus output to the Soviet Union (a tendency already observable in, for example, the conduct of the PRC and Thailand).

Third, as far as the overall burden of Soviet engagement in the Third World is concerned, it is important to bear in mind that in some cases Soviet opportunities in the Third World may not necessarily bear large economic costs. The political advantages that the USSR has sought through its most recent arms shipments to Libya and its new arms sales to Kuwait clearly fall in this category.

Fourth, as already suggested, in view of the size and diversity of the Soviet economy, the Soviet leaders, despite all their economic burdens, may retain the inclination to make new, external economic commitments if they deem the prospective prize sufficiently great, or even if the prize is not enormous but they consider the political costs of *not* responding excessive. It may be symptomatic, in this connection, that after six years in which the Soviet leaders displayed relative parsimony toward the economic needs of the Sandinista regime in Nicaragua, a marginal and low-priority object of Soviet policy, the Gorbachev leadership in the spring of 1985 was at last induced, by the desperate state of the Nicaraguan economy, to extend considerably greater assistance, notably in guaranteeing Nicaragua's petroleum supply.[12]

And last, Soviet weaponry is still in considerable demand, and despite their heightened need to use arms exports to earn hard currency, the Soviets appear likely to continue to use some subsidized arms deliveries as political "loss leaders" in what they deem to be appropriate cases. Since the advent of Gorbachev, there has been some evidence of the enduring nature of that

---

[12]*New York Times*, May 21, 1985; *Washington Post*, May 21, 1985.

Soviet tendency. During Gorbachev's first year he began deliveries of MiG-23 fighters and SA-3 air defense missiles to North Korea, reversing a fifteen-year ban on significant military assistance to Pyongyang.[13] This shift in policy—part of a broader Gorbachev effort to strengthen the relatively weak Soviet position in the Far East that I discuss later—has brought the Soviet Union political returns in improved relations with North Korea, including in particular permission to overfly North Korean territory when staging military reconnaissance flights from the Soviet Far East.[14] Meanwhile, 1985 is also reported to have seen an increase in the volume of Soviet weaponry supplied to Nicaragua,[15] despite the obvious inability of the Sandinista regime to pay.

On the whole, Soviet judgments as to the relative importance of the economic and the political recompense they get from arms exports to the less developed world appear to remain extremely flexible. The relative weight of these two considerations seems to vary widely. Wherever possible—as with their arms supplies to Angola, Libya, Syria, Iraq, and Kuwait—they seek to obtain benefits of both kinds, trading arms for hard currency or the oil equivalent and at the same time seeking thereby to retain or strengthen existing political/strategic relationships (in Angola, Libya, Syria, and Iraq) or to begin to build a new political presence (in Kuwait). In other cases—as with their barter trade with India—they will forego hard-currency earnings from arms exports to preserve a valuable existing political relationship. In still other cases, economic considerations are even further subordinated. This is not only true of arms supplies to their heavily subsidized clients in Cuba and Vietnam and their smaller flow of arms to Nicaragua. It is also characteristic of their continued arms deliveries to Ethiopia, where adequate repayment seems, to put it mildly, problematical, as well as of the new arms deliveries to North Korea where, historical experience suggests, whatever the nominal terms of the transaction, full repayment may in practice be indefinitely deferred.[16]

In sum, the economic constraints on Soviet activities in the less developed world, while real enough and very important where only minor Soviet interests are involved, have thus far had only marginal effects on Soviet behavior in areas where significant Soviet military or strategic interests are already

[13]*Washington Post*, July 18, 1985; *Sankei Shinbun* (Tokyo), December 26, 1985. This Soviet shift carried out by Gorbachev in 1985 probably followed through on initial commitments entered into the previous year, when Chernenko was general secretary and Gorbachev was already playing a key policy-making role as second secretary. Although the weapons supplied are not the most advanced in the Soviet arsenal, the change is nonetheless dramatic and important.

[14]*Sankei Shinbun*, January 27, 1986. The overflights apparently began in advance of the new Soviet weapon deliveries, in December 1984.

[15]A White House spokesman in the fall of 1985 stated that there had been a "serious increase" in such shipments in recent weeks. *Wall Street Journal*, November 19, 1985.

[16]For a detailed discussion of past events in this economic relationship, see George Ginsburgs, "Soviet Development Grants and Aid to North Korea, 1945–1980," *Asia Pacific Community*, Fall 1982, pp. 42–63.

engaged. Such constraints have not prevented the Soviet leadership from taking vigorous action to defend those Soviet Third World positions under attack (as in Afghanistan and Angola) which Moscow deems of particular importance. Support of major bridgeheads that require long-term subsidization, as in Cuba and Vietnam, seems likely to continue indefinitely. In at least two other recent cases, Nicaragua and North Korea, the advance of Soviet interests has apparently been considered to justify at least modest additional expenditures. In two other cases, weapon sales to Libya and Kuwait, important new efforts to promote Soviet influence have apparently proved possible without any such financial costs. The Soviet readiness to make commitments in new areas involving large fresh expenditures, however, remains untested.

Soviet Military Commitments and Pretensions

The third major aspect of Soviet post-Stalin policy toward the formerly colonial world is a natural adjunct of the first two. Along with their multiplication of political contacts and the dispatch of economic and weapons assistance to the less developed world, the Soviets began to assume direct and indirect military commitments of various kinds at increased distances from Soviet frontiers and thus from the base of Soviet military power. Whereas Stalin had been notoriously reluctant to take on such commitments in noncontiguous areas, and particularly on behalf of regimes or groups that he did not completely control, his successors were to become significantly more venturesome in both respects.[17]

One salient feature of Soviet conduct in the Third World since Stalin's time, however, has been the race between the expansion of Soviet political pretensions as a world actor and the expansion of Soviet military capabilities and readiness to back up such pretensions. Because a gap has always existed between the two, varying degrees of ambiguity have always characterized the real military commitment behind Soviet Third World ventures, the real willingness to take risks. At all stages the Soviets have shown themselves willing on occasion to use this ambiguity to try to extract short-term political profit by implying in advance a greater degree of commitment than in fact they could or would subsequently deliver.

Khrushchev of course was most notorious for this, both inside and outside the Soviet Union. At the time of his ouster in 1964 he was severely criticized by Suslov for the threat of military intervention with Soviet "volunteers" he had raised during the 1956 Suez crisis, a threat that Suslov characterized as having been dangerous and adventurist.[18] Khrushchev's colleagues had ap-

---

[17]It is sometimes said, with only modest hyperbole, that Stalin was unwilling to commit himself "beyond the range of Soviet artillery."

[18]*New York Times*, October 30, 1964.

parently feared that inherent in the Suez situation, there had been escalatory possibilities for a clash with the United States against a background of what Soviet leaders knew to be significant Soviet strategic inferiority.

After the launching of Sputnik in 1957, Khrushchev sought to encourage the myth of a "missile gap" between the Soviet Union and the United States and of a consequent Soviet strategic advantage.[19] He sought to use this supposed central advantage as underpinning for his various efforts to exert pressure against Western positions and his various threats to take unilateral action both in Europe and in the Middle East. It was thus in the late 1950s, long before the Soviet Union actually caught up with the United States in central strategic power in the late 1960s and early 1970s, that Soviet propagandists first began to assert that the USSR, because of its stratetgic advances, had achieved the ability to facilitate the victory of "national liberation movements" by "paralyzing" the response of "imperialist" power. In making this claim, the Soviets were alluding in part to the outcome of the Suez episode, when Khrushchev's threats were widely (if erroneously) given credit for compelling the retreat of Britain and France when those Western states were not supported by the United States.

However, the hollowness of Khrushchev's claims to an ability to exert strategic leverage at a distance in the Third World was incrementally exposed in the early 1960s by three decisive events. First, during the crisis in the summer of 1960 associated with the granting of independence to the Belgian Congo, the Western powers decisively defeated the Soviet Union in its efforts to promote the ascendancy of the local radical Patrice Lumumba and his successor Antoine Gizenga. Second, during the following year the American authorities became aware that the supposed Soviet missile advantage over the United States, and the overall strategic advantage, had been an illusion.[20] Third, in the fall of 1962 the Soviet Union suffered its greatest overseas humiliation when the Americans rebuffed Khrushchev's attempt to restore the impression of Soviet strategic leverage by placing in Cuba nuclear missiles and aircraft capable of striking the United States. The net result of these three events was to make it apparent, by the time of Khrushchev's fall in October 1964, that Soviet military power was not commensurate with the role that Khrushchev had sought to stake out for the Soviet Union as a distant actor on the world scene.

The Post-Khrushchev Changes

Since 1964 Khrushchev's successors have changed this situation in three fundamental ways. First, they have methodically sought to turn Khrushchev's

---

[19]See the discussion in Arnold L. Horelick and Myron Rush, *Strategic Power and Soviet Foreign Policy* (Chicago: University of Chicago Press, 1965).
[20]Ibid., pp. 83–105.

strategic pretense into reality. By the early 1970s their systematic build-up had attained what is generally termed a position of "robust equality" with the United States in strategic nuclear systems, a position that they have since managed to preserve. For the last fifteen years this U.S. loss of strategic superiority has indirectly helped Soviet efforts to defend and improve their geopolitical position in the Third World, by reducing the credibility of the U.S. deterrent where America does not have a conventional force advantage, as in Southwest Asia.

Second, they have simultaneously carried out a more general, all-service expansion of their armed forces since the mid-1960s and as one consequence have greatly improved their ability to insert a Soviet military presence in support of Soviet political ventures and arms assistance programs in noncontiguous Third World areas. In this effort the most mobile Soviet military assets have naturally taken the lead. The Soviet Navy, first deployed in force to the Mediterranean as a counterbalance to U.S. naval forces there, has since penetrated permanently to such distant waters as the Red Sea, the Indian Ocean, the South China Sea, the Caribbean, and the Gulf of Mexico. Soviet long-range naval air reconnaissance has followed to the same remote areas, staging from bases acquired over the years in Cuba, Africa, and Southeast Asia. Soviet-manned bombers have also been deployed to bases furnished by client regimes at three widely separated points in the underdeveloped world, at intervals a decade apart: first briefly in 1962, as an adjunct of Khrushchev's abortive Cuban missile venture; next by Brezhnev to Egypt in 1971, until they were expelled by Sadat in 1972 along with Soviet combat advisers; and third by Andropov in 1983 to Vietnam's Cam Ranh Bay, where thus far they have remained.

Most important politically has been the growth of Soviet airlift capabilities, which Soviet leaders have used on an expanding scale since the late 1960s for both military and demonstrative political effect. Having first sought and failed to obtain Chinese permission to stage such a demonstrative airlift across Chinese territory to Vietnam in 1965, the Soviets found the first occasion to exhibit to the Third World their new airlift capability in 1967, when they staged a massive resupply effort to the combatant Arab states defeated by Israel in the Six Day War. Four years later the USSR mounted an airlift in support of India's 1971 attack upon East Pakistan, and two years after that staged another such effort to resupply Egypt and Syria during the October 1973 Arab-Israeli war. Between 1976 and 1978 these airlift capabilities were for the first time extended south to sub-Saharan Africa, in support of Cuban and Soviet ventures in Angola and Ethiopia. And at the end of the 1970s this capability was used in support of the Soviet invasion of Afghanistan.

One major qualification should be noted, however: growth of this ability to assert a military *presence* in the Third World has greatly outstripped the growth of the ability to project Soviet *power* in distant areas. The distinction is important because the Soviet capacity to deliver large numbers of men or large quantities of firepower to noncontiguous regions in the face of significant opposition, like the operational capabilities of the Soviet Navy in remote waters, is still greatly inferior to that of the United States. What has changed particularly is the Soviet acquisition of an ability to make a rapid, highly visible, but essentially unopposed logistical input to create and support a combat presence in Third World areas where the Soviets have a political stake in local contentions.

Third, despite this qualification, the Soviet leadership since Khrushchev's time has used its new military capabilities in repeated efforts to enlarge the political and military Soviet presence in "hot spots" of the underdeveloped world and to support the military endeavors of Soviet allies and proxies. A chain of such ventures was visible beginning with the participation of Soviet pilots in a Yemeni civil war in late 1967, continuing with the temporary deployment of large numbers of Soviet air defense personnel to Egypt in 1970, following with Soviet-Cuban military adventures in Angola and Ethiopia in the late 1970s, and concluding, in 1979, with the arrival of Soviet naval vessels and aircraft in support of Vietnam at Cam Ranh Bay and then with the outright invasion of Afghanistan.

Post-Khrushchev Bluffing and Risk Taking

But although Soviet Third World efforts had more military substance in the post-Khrushchev years, Khrushchev's successors on a number of occasions repeated his tendency to imply a degree of military commitment greater than the Soviet Union was willing to deliver. This behavior was particularly noticeable during the first eight years of the Brezhnev regime.[21] Thus despite Suslov's 1964 criticism of Khrushchev's adventurism, the Soviet regime's behavior three years later, just before the outbreak of the Six Day War, seems to have been equally deserving of the epithet. False allegations of an impending Israeli attack on Syria, initially disseminated by Soviet representatives in Damascus, set in motion the chain of events that eventually produced war. President Podgorny repeated these allegations to Egyptian representatives in Moscow on May 11, 1967, and Nasser regarded these statements as confirmation of claims to the same effect already being received from Syria. It was on the basis of this information that Nasser dispatched his troops into the Sinai a week later and requested the withdrawal of UNEF forces.[22]

The Soviets had evidently not anticipated or desired that Nasser would react with so dangerous a move as blockading Israeli movement through the Straits of Tiran. Nevertheless, it is noteworthy that even after he had done so

---

[21]For more extensive discussion of this Soviet conduct, see Harry Gelman, *The Brezhnev Politburo and the Decline of Detente* (Ithaca: Cornell University Press, 1984).

[22]Mohamed Heikal, *The Sphinx and the Commissar* (New York: Harper & Row, 1978), pp. 174–176; Nadau Safran, *From War to War* (New York: Pegasus, 1969), pp. 274–276.

and up to the very outbreak of hostilities, they continued to display an ingratiating and calculated ambiguity in some high-level contacts with Arab leaders, behavior that may have misled some Arabs into expecting that the Soviet Union would play an active combat role if war occurred. Nasser's confidant Mohamed Heikal alleges that Marshal Grechko made encouraging statements of this kind to Egyptian defense minister Shams al-Dia Badran at the close of the latter's visit to Moscow in late May 1967. He also credibly implies that Syrian prime minister Nur al-Din Atassi received similar encouragement from Soviet sources during a visit immediately afterward.[23] Given the presence in the eastern Mediterranean of the U.S. Sixth Fleet, however, the Soviet leadership—like Khrushchev during the 1956 Suez crisis—had no intention of allowing itself to be drawn into hostilities. Yet the ensuing disaster to the Arab armies threatened Soviet interests sufficiently that the Politburo in the end felt obliged to threaten intervention if Israel did not cease its drive toward Damascus.[24] It may be argued that the risk involved in this threat was reduced by the fact that Israel had already achieved its essential war aims and was therefore prepared to halt; but the Brezhnev Politburo was surely relieved not to have to make good on its threat.

Two and a half years later, in early 1970, the Soviets incurred an even greater risk of stumbling inadvertently into a clash with the United States after they had sent thousands of Soviet air defense troops to Egypt to defend Nasser against the consequences of his war of attrition against Israel. Before the conclusion of a new Egyptian-Israeli ceasefire in the summer of 1970, Soviet fighter pilots flew patrols ever closer to the Suez Canal; in one well-known incident the Israelis shot down five.[25] Finally alarmed at the escalatory possibilities, and now aware that more and more Soviet combat inputs might be required to deal adequately with Israel, thereby increasing the likelihood of a compensatory U.S. reaction, the Soviets ceased such patrols and showed heightened interest in an early ceasefire.

Thereafter the Soviets never again assumed the same degree of risk in their overseas military commitments, although they continued from time to time to find themselves in potentially dangerous situations. In October 1973, at the close of the Yom Kippur War, they were enticed by a vain hope of shoring up their position in Egypt into issuing a last-minute threat of unilateral military intervention when the United States initially failed to obtain Israeli observance of the ceasefire agreement with Egypt. The Soviets were deeply chagrined when the United States responded by placing its forces on strategic alert, imparting a global dimension to a regional crisis and thus implying the possibility of nuclear escalation despite the Soviet achievement of strategic parity. The Soviets were, however, relieved when the United States pro-

[23]Heikal, *Sphinx and the Commissar*, p. 176.
[24]Lyndon Johnson, *The Vantage Point* (New York: Holt, Reinhart & Winston, 1971), p. 302.
[25]Henry Kissinger, *White House Years* (Boston: Little, Brown, 1979), p. 585.

ceeded to compel Israel to comply with the ceasefire, thus in effect giving the USSR what it had demanded and relieving the crisis.

In the second half of the 1970s most of the more spectacular Soviet military steps taken in the underdeveloped world involved very few open-ended risks. The Soviet-Cuban military interventions in Angola and Ethiopia in the late 1970s implied little risk of military confrontation with the United States, since Washington was doubly deterred by internal political constraints and by the fact that these Soviet actions were deemed acceptable by much of Black Africa. The Soviet invasion of Afghanistan in December 1979 carried a variety of costs but no risk of a direct clash with America.

In early 1979, on the other hand, the Soviets again found themselves faced with the possibility of disastrous conflict, this time with China as a result of Soviet backing for the Vietnamese invasion of China's client, Cambodia. The Soviets were careful to avoid any overt military step during the ensuring Sino-Vietnamese crisis, and they were in the end proved right in their calculation that the Soviet strategic deterrent would dissuade the PRC from responding with a full-scale effort to topple the Vietnamese regime. Yet the Soviets were evidently surprised and embarrassed when the Chinese did respond with a more limited incursion into Vietnam in February–March 1979.[26] If the Soviet calculation had proved mistaken, and if Beijing had persevered in its attack to go on to menace the city of Hanoi and the Vietnamese regime—which was within Chinese capabilities—the Soviet Union would have been faced with a severe dilemma: either accept the grave political losses involved in appearing to abandon its ally, or accept the consequences of an undesired war with China. This episode of Soviet overseas involvement in a local conflict was therefore a gamble, although ultimately a successful one.

Finally, in 1982 the Soviet Union again took a military step in the Middle East which involved some risk of potential escalation, although probably a smaller risk than those assumed a decade earlier. The Soviets decided to supply advanced SAM air defense units and Soviet air defense personnel to help defend Syria after the Israeli advance into southern Lebanon and Israeli-Syrian clashes in the Beqa'a Valley of Lebanon. They were impelled to take this step by a felt need to bolster their position with their principal remaining Middle East ally in the wake of the setbacks to Soviet prestige incurred by failure to react to the Israeli advance or to the PLO expulsion from Beirut, as well as by the recent inability of older SAM equipment supplied to Syria by the USSR to withstand Israeli attack in the Beqa'a. Although the Soviets through this new step assumed some risk of escalation had the Israeli government become involved in further combat with Syria, they correctly calculated

---

[26]See Harry Gelman, *The Soviet Far East Buildup and Soviet Rist-Taking against China*, R-2943-AF (Santa Monica: RAND Corporation, August 1982), pp. 84–105.

that this would not happen, partly because of the deterrent effects of the Soviet presence upon Israel and the United States.

In Africa in the 1980s, the scope of Soviet military actions on behalf of client regimes has been constrained not only by the various costs and risks involved but also by incremental discovery of the continuing limitations on Soviet ability to coerce at a distance. Soviet leaders now appear to have found that in some cases Brezhnev in the 1970s, like Khrushchev in the late 1950s and early 1960s, had entered into relationships that implied more than the Soviet Union can today deliver. That is, the Soviets in the 1970s formed some overseas political attachments that remain beyond the range of effective sup-port from Soviet military power.[27] This limitation on Soviet military reach has so far been most clearly evident in the case of Mozambique, the most distant Soviet client in Africa, where despite private Soviet warnings to South Africa and the dispatch to the area of two Soviet destroyers in 1981,[28] the Soviet Union found itself unable to furnish a credible geopolitical counter-weight against South African pressure on Mozambique sufficient to prevent Mozambique from being compelled to yield to that pressure and to sign an agreement for a supposed modus vivendi on South African terms.[29]

The present Soviet leadership appears, however, to be still attempting to decide through trial and error the effective geographic limits on Soviet ability to support clients acquired in the 1970s, and the circumstances under which the USSR should make a vigorous effort to render such support. In Angola, for example, the Soviets may feel that their interests are more deeply engaged than they are in Mozambique and also that their capabilities are somewhat greater. There is a variety of reasons: because Angola had earlier been the scene of an important, symbolic, geopolitical victory for the USSR over the United States (when the Soviet-supported MPLA triumphed in 1976 over rivals favored by the Americans); because of the Soviet bloc commitment implied in the large Cuban military presence in Angola since then; because the USSR obtains some military benefits from Angola (in the use of Luanda for staging naval air reconnaissance flights to the Western Hemisphere) which it does not receive from Mozambique; and because Soviet logistical access to Angola is more convenient while Angola is somewhat further than Mozambique from the center of South Africa's countervailing military power. Soviet response to an ongoing challenge in Angola has therefore evolved differently from the Soviet response in Mozambique. Although the USSR in the early 1980s was forced to acquiesce in an ephemeral Angolan diplomatic accommodation with South Africa, the Gorbachev leadership has

---

[27]This problem exists entirely apart from the question of the *economic* capacity of the Soviet Union to succor ailing client regimes, already discussed.

[28]See Congressional Research Service, *The Soviet Union in the Third World, 1980–85: An Impe-rial Burden or Political Asset?* (Washington, D.C.: U.S. GPO, 1985), pp. 239–240.

[29]Subsequently the continued operations of the Renamo guerrilla opposition in Mozambique have placed in question South African good faith in signing this agreement.

responded forcefully—with weapons and, apparently, some Soviet combat advisers—to a heightened challenge by UNITA insurgents to the viability of the MPLA regime.[30]

Gorbachev's Attitude toward Military Risk in the Third World

On the whole the new Gorbachev leadership has thus far shown considerable ambivalence in its attitude regarding risk taking in the less developed world. On the basis of the limited evidence available from Gorbachev's conduct during his first year, we can speak of a spectrum of behavior.

Where a real danger of U.S. military involvement has been fairly obvious—as in Central America—the Gorbachev Politburo, like its predecessors, has continued to be selective in the furnishing of weaponry and sparing in the commitment of its own military personnel, leaving the Cubans to assume most of the direct risks of military assistance in Nicaragua.

Meanwhile, although Gorbachev has stepped up Soviet diplomatic and sporadic crossborder military pressure on Pakistan to desist from helping the Afghan insurgency, that pressure has on the whole been sufficiently limited to avoid drawing the United States into an involvement more direct than the provision of military hardware to Pakistan. At the same time the emergence in 1985 of some momentary tribal disturbances on the Pakistani side of the Afghan border—heavily advertised by Soviet propaganda—has suggested that the USSR has begun at least to experiment with efforts to promote internal disruption in Pakistan, a course that could have escalatory potential.

On another plane, Gorbachev's resumption of some sophisticated Soviet military assistance to North Korea implies Soviet acceptance of a marginally greater risk of inadvertent involvement in dangerous conflict in the Korean peninsula, although this is a risk that the Soviets probably feel is still controllable. It is likely that one of the contributing reasons for the Soviet halt in advanced weapons supply to Pyongyang after 1970—along with several other objections to North Korean behavior—was a Soviet conviction that Kim Il-Sung's well-demonstrated adventurist proclivities could some day drag the Soviet Union into unpredictable confrontation with American forces in South Korea.[31] This consideration, although probably still a Soviet concern, has now evidently been downgraded in importance by the Soviet leaders for the sake of geopolitical profit.

---

[30]The Western press has also reported UNITA allegations—sometimes exaggerated but probably not wholly incorrect—of a new participation by Soviet officers in the Angola fighting. *Le Monde*, September 24, 1985; *Washington Times*, September 25, 1985. Heightened Soviet military support to the Luanda regime in 1985 probably was decided on at a Soviet-Cuban-Angolan conference in Moscow in March 1985, presided over by Defense Minister Sokolov. This 1985 effort represented a further increment to a substantial increase in military deliveries begun in 1984. See Alex Alexiev, *U.S. Policy in Angola: A Case of Nonconstructive Engagement*, P-7183 (Santa Monica: RAND Corporation, January 1986).

[31]See Gelman and Levin, *Future of Soviet–North Korean Relations*.

Finally, the most disturbing initiative taken by Gorbachev from the perspective of risk acceptance was the decision late in 1985 to provide Libya with surface-to-air missiles and apparently, at least initially, Soviet advisory personnel to help operate them.[32] The Soviet missile advisers arrived in Libya when Libya's link to a variety of terrorist atrocities had become the occasion for growing confrontation with the United States and its closest Middle East associates, raising a more distinct chance that Libya might eventually come into military conflict with the United States, Israel, or Egypt. Equally important, the new Soviet leaders were surely well aware that Qadhdhafi would also attempt to use the presence of the missiles as a deterrent against U.S. naval and air operations in the Gulf of Sidra claimed by Libya, a matter particularly sensitive to the Soviet Union since armed clashes in the air had previously occurred between the United States and Libya over this issue. The escalatory potential of this Gorbachev decision was thus considerable. Although the Soviet Union subsequently took care to minimize the chance of Soviet direct involvement during and after the April 1986 American air attack against Libya, the Gorbachev step that had raised the possibility of involuntary involvement appears to have been short-sighted.

Soviet Third World Behavior and the Relationship with America

All the phenomena discussed so far have another dimension, which has become more important as the years have passed. Superimposed on such questions as the loyalty and viability of Soviet clients, the limits of Soviet economic and military capabilities, and the limits of acceptable military risk is another, equally important issue that has periodically confronted the Soviet leaders since they became seriously engaged in competition in the formerly colonial world three decades ago. What trade-offs should be made between Soviet efforts to expand the Soviet position overseas at the expense of the United States, on the one hand, and intermittent Soviet efforts to improve the USSR's bilateral political relationship with the United States, on the other?

This question had presented no great problem for Stalin after World War II, because there was little discrepancy between the hostile demeanor he displayed directly toward the West during the Cold War and his demeanor toward Western interests in other parts of the world. (In addition, as earlier suggested, Stalin in practice had only a feeble capability to harm Western interests in noncontiguous areas of the colonial and underdeveloped world.) Nor was this much of a dilemma for Soviet policy makers in those periods during the Khrushchev and Brezhnev regimes—for example, 1957–58 and 1966–67—when the Soviet leadership consensus saw little incentive to at-

---

[32]*Los Angeles Times*, January 2, 1986.

tempt to improve the bilateral atmostphere with the United States. In periods when Soviet leaders have seen it as in their interest to promote a significant expansion of bilateral dealings with the United States, however, they have sometimes been forced to confront the underlying conflict in their priorities. In such cases up to now, the relationship with America has come second.

Such conflicts between opposing Soviet policy interests emerged, in particular, on two notable occasions. The first was the period 1959–60. Six months after Khrushchev's visit to the United States in the fall of 1959 and the Soviet evocation of the "spirit of Camp David," the Soviet Union's Chinese ally launched a ferocious, thinly veiled attack on the implications of Soviet dealings with America. Beijing implied—albeit with scant justification—that Khrushchev, to facilitate his dealings with the American imperialist enemy, was encouraging a weakening of the militancy of revolutionary forces in countries throughout the world in their struggle against regimes associated with the United States. Although couched in Marxist-Leninist ideological jargon, this sustained Chinese assault was in fact an attempt to bend and focus the priorities of the Soviet Union to suit the perceived national interests of the Chinese state.[33] The Chinese Communist leaders in this period saw their national interest in maximizing worldwide pressure on the United States, the ally and protector of Taiwan, and were seeking to harness to this end the Third World policies of the Soviet Union and all the instruments it then controlled, particularly the world communist movement and the international front organizations. Although the Soviets in 1960 vigorously resisted the Chinese attack on Soviet authority, precipitating the Sino-Soviet schism, the substance of the Chinese charges against Khrushchev nevertheless appears to have found some resonance among conservatives in the Soviet leadership. In particular, party secretaries Mikhail Suslov and Frol Kozlov seem to have feared that Khrushchev's experiment with rapprochement with the United States in 1959 had made the Soviet Union more vulnerable to Chinese efforts to usurp Soviet authority in the communist movement and among other anit-American radical and revolutionary forces around the globe, particularly in the Third World.

The growth of this concern among Khrushchev's colleagues reinforced other factors that placed Khrushchev on the political defensive in 1960,[34] induced the Soviets to jettison their initial venture into detente, caused a severe momentary slippage in hierarchy status for Anastas Mikoyan, the man most clearly identified with advocacy of the move toward the United States,[35] and

[33]See Harry Gelman, "Russia, China, and the Underdeveloped Area," *Annals of the American Academy of Political and Social Science*, September 1963, pp. 130–142.

[34]Notably, these other factors included Khrushchev's failure to get concessions from the West regarding Germany after his visit to the United States; the U-2 incident in May 1960; and the humiliating Soviet defeat in the Belgian Congo that summer.

[35]See the discussion in Michel Tatu, *Power in the Kremlin from Khrushchev to Kosygin* (New York: Viking, 1970), pp. 79–84.

produced an upsurge in the Soviets' efforts to refurbish their revolutionary credentials in the Third World. In the near term Khrushchev's concern to offset the Chinese challenge to these credentials evoked such bizarre incidents as Khrushchev's shoe-banging performance at the UN General Assembly in the fall of 1960, when he used histrionics to fill the gap in Soviet Third World accomplishments. Along the same lines Khrushchev put forward a programmatic statement in January 1961 formally enunciating the Soviet commitment to "ideological struggle" and support for "national liberation movements." At the time President Kennedy reacted strongly to this statement, which was interpreted in the United States as a Soviet challenge requiring America to gear up its counterinsurgency capabilities. Throughout the remainder of Khrushchev's tenure in office, even after he returned to some negotiations with the United States in 1963, he was forever seeking to evade the Chinese ideological indictment of his behavior.

The second period when Soviet leaders were forced to confront the underlying conflict between their policy in the underdeveloped world and an attempted rapprochement with the United States was the 1970s, when the circumstances were greatly altered. On the one hand, Chinese pressure on the Soviet Union for a more consistently hostile posture toward the United States had vanished as a result of the militarization of the Sino-Soviet conflict and the consequent Sino-American rapprochement. Chinese competitive pressure on the USSR for greater militancy in the Third World—a prominent feature on the world scene from the late 1950s through the late 1960s—had faded away.

On the other hand, however, more than counterbalancing this change was the fact already described that by the 1970s the Soviet military presence around the world, Soviet military capabilities for Third World intervention, and Soviet political opportunities for such intervention had all significantly expanded. In addition, as I have also noted, the Soviet Union had achieved strategic parity with the United States, finally providing some support for Khrushchev's earlier empty boasts of his ability to "paralyze" imperialist response around the world. As a result, in the 1970s Soviet military involvement in Third World conflicts became the widespread reality it had not been in Khrushchev's day. Whereas Khrushchev had repeatedly threatened to send "volunteers" to intervene in various crises, particularly in the Middle East, in practice, except for the abortive Cuban missile venture, he took no actions whatever to intervene with Soviet military forces in the underdeveloped world. In contrast, Brezhnev's dispatch of a Soviet expeditionary force to Egypt in 1970 became the precursor of subsequent military interventions, alone or in support of the interventionist efforts of Soviet allies, in Angola, Ethiopia, Indochina, and Afghanistan. In sum Brezhnev in the 1970s added a long-missing Soviet combat increment to the political attack on Western interests in the Third World which Khrushchev between 1955 and 1964 had conducted with subversion, propaganda, economic aid, threats, and weapons supply.

At the same time, the 1970s was also the decade in which the Soviet Union repeated Khrushchev's initial, abortive move of 1959 to reach a detente with the United States, and on a much larger scale. The contradiction between the two aspects of Soviet behavior was thus posed for Brezhnev in particularly sharp form. As we know, Brezhnev's response was twofold: on the one hand, unlike Khrushchev, he persisted for several years in maintaining that a detente relationship with the United States was possible despite the competition between the two powers in the world at large; on the other hand, like Khrushchev, he insisted that the Soviet Union would not alter external behavior that America saw as damaging to its interests for the sake of the bilateral realtionship. In practice, however, it proved impossible for Brezhnev's two policies to endure simultaneously. The Soviet leadership found by the end of the 1970s that if the Soviet Union was unwilling to exercise the restraint—in the Third World and in other domains[36]—that the American public regarded as inherent in the detente bargain, then those aspects of detente which the Soviet Union valued could not survive.

Conclusions: Gorbachev's Inheritance and His Third World Policies

The panorama reviewed in this chapter suggests that the Soviets have incrementally achieved a far-flung political and military presence in the underdeveloped world but in the process have revealed—to themselves, to their clients, and to their opponents—manifold weaknesses, particularly in staying power. Their prospects for further advance, and to some extent their ability to consolidate the gains of the past, are particularly hampered by economic weaknesses of which they are now increasingly aware. They recognize the fragility and vulnerability of certain of their clients faced with insurgencies that the United States and other opponents support. And despite their rhetoric about rejecting "linkage," they are surely more keenly aware—having seen the evidence in two traumatic episodes over the last twenty-five years— that further pursuit of Soviet aspirations to supplant Western influence in the underdeveloped world will almost inevitably conflict with any aspiration to improve the atmosphere of the bilateral relationship with the United States.[37] To the degree, therefore, that Gorbachev sees a reduction in the intensity of competition with America as desirable to secure a respite, a breathing space, in which to revitalize the ailing Soviet economy, he is indeed

---

[36]The most important of the other areas in which Soviet conduct tended to undermine detente was of course the nuclear arms race. Soviet leaders in the 1970s took a view of the Soviet Union's requirements in central strategic and European nuclear missile force ratios which the American and Western publics found threatening and unacceptable. See the discussion in Harry Gelman, *The Rise and Fall of Detente: Causes and Consequences*, Occasional Paper OPS-002 (Santa Monica: RAND/UCLA Center for the Study of Soviet International Behavior, January 1985).

[37]For evidence of such awareness in some Soviet circles, see Fukuyama, *Moscow's Post-Brezhnev Reassessment*, pp. 30–33.

likely to perceive major drawbacks in the continued pursuit of expansionist goals.

Does this mean that the Soviet leaders over the rest of the 1980s are likely to see themselves as obliged to tacitly accept the status quo? The prospect appears very unlikely. The notion of significantly contracting Soviet horizons, of relaxing the pressure outward, continues to be intensely disagreeable to any Soviet leadership, including the present one, for many reasons.

The Defense of Positions under Siege

Under present conditions the Soviets are deeply enmeshed in a web of circumstances; they are profoundly engaged in efforts to consolidate the precarious advances of the past, and they cannot disengage from these efforts without accepting setbacks that, however disguised, will be generally recognized as humiliating Soviet defeats. Soviet recognition of this fact has been reflected in such behavior as the refusal to cease support of Vietnam to propitiate China, in the decision to supply advanced SAMs and Soviet SAM personnel to Syria in 1982, and in Gorbachev's decision to increase the Soviet military stake in Angola.

The Gorbachev leadership more generally perceives itself as being engaged in a worldwide struggle to repel American efforts to eliminate a whole series of as yet unconsolidated geopolitical advances in the Third World which the Soviets staked out in the 1970s. Gorbachev's first year saw a growing American inclination to lend support to insurgencies against four newly acquired Soviet clients in Afghanistan, Cambodia, Angola, and Nicaragua. The American political consensus behind this policy trend has varied in strength from case to case, being strongest in the first case and weakest in the last, but the general tendency has seemed clear to the Soviet leaders. Soviet propaganda—guided since Gorbachev's advent by the vehemently anti-American Central Committee secretary Aleksandr Yakovlev, who is a long-time, close associate of Gorbachev—refers to this policy trend as the "new American globalism" and speaks of the United States as seeking "social revanchism" in the underdeveloped world. It seems clear from the evidence already adduced that the Gorbachev leadership is determined to defend Moscow's past geopolitical advances and to this end, despite all its economic difficulties, is prepared to increase its efforts, although to varying degrees in each case.

In the most important and difficult case, that of Afghanistan, Gorbachev has adopted a two-pronged strategy. On the one hand, as already noted, he has increased diplomatic and sporadic military pressure on Pakistan while intensifying Soviet punitive military efforts in Afghanistan. At the same time, as also noted, there seems reason to believe that the Gorbachev leadership on at least one occasion made an effort to subvert Pushtun and Baluchi tribes in Pakistan near the Afghan border, with a view to obstructing the flow of supplies to Afghan insurgents while increasing pressure on the Zia government. Soviet propaganda in the fall and winter of 1985 advertised, and no doubt exaggerated, Pakistan's difficulties with these tribes.[38]

Simultaneously Gorbachev has also escalated a campaign of hints—particularly to Washington and Paris—that he would like to see a compromise settlement of some sort in Afghanistan. But despite Gorbachev's evident discomfort with the war in Afghanistan and the recent Soviet inauguration of a campaign for a negotiated settlement, Soviet leaders are highly unlikely to believe that any government not subject to their will can be created in Afghanistan, after all that has happened since 1978, which will not also be vehemently anti-Soviet. It is also most unlikely that Soviet leaders believe that the United States, or any other outside source, can as part of a hypothetical deal with the USSR induce the Afghan insurgents to cease resisting the Soviet Union and attacking the government in Kabul as long as a Soviet military presence remains in the country or as long as any regime in Kabul remains under Soviet domination. Despite their propaganda rhetoric, the Soviets are not likely to delude themselves that the United States controls the mujahedeen and can turn off their resistance at will. The Soviets apparently do, however, hope to secure a reduction in outside support for the insurgents by holding out the prospect of subsequent Soviet troop withdrawals and a broadened Kabul regime under continued communist leadership.[39]

For this reason alone it seems improbable that in the foreseeable future Soviets will abandon their effort to consolidate their hegemony in Afghanistan. Accordingly, any Soviet agreement to broaden the Afghan communist regime will almost certainly be conditioned by Soviet determination to retain control in Kabul—to embellish the form of Soviet domination while preserving its essence. By the same token it is equally probable that the Soviet leadership does not regard negotiations on the possibility of Soviet military withdrawal from Afghanistan as a search for a mythical compromise between the essentially uncompromisable alternatives of Soviet control and non-control. Rather, the Gorbachev Politburo evidently sees such negotiations as a process through which to weaken external opposition to the fact of Soviet hegemony and particularly to undermine Pakistan president Zia's domestic support for the policy of resisting Soviet control in Afghanistan.[40]

---

[38]See, for example, *Pravda*, December 22, 1985. There has been apparent confirmation that the Kabul regime has given arms to some tribal elements in Pakistan for this purpose. *Los Angeles Times*, March 14, 1986.

[39]See *Washington Post*, December 28, 1985. In January 1986 a spokesman for the Kabul regime specified that even if a peace settlement *were* reached and the bulk of the "limited contingent" of Soviet troops were then withdrawn, several thousand Soviet military "advisers" would still remain to help in the battle against the Afghan rebels. *Washington Post*, January 23, 1986.

[40]It is noteworthy that the important *Pravda* article of December 22, 1985, while endorsing the notion of "compromises" in Kabul "to expand the social base of the revolution" under Communist party leadership, took the occasion to level a veiled threat at Pakistan for showing insufficient enthusiasm for this concession. *Pravda* claimed that Pakistan was suppressing the alleged desire of Pushtun tribes in Pakistan to eliminate "anti-Afghan subversive bases" near the Pakistan-

The Defense of the Soviet World Role

Second, and more fundamentally, a more than marginal change in the leadership's attitude toward the struggle for ascendancy in the underdeveloped world is unlikely because the leadership would see any profound shift as undercutting the Soviet raison d'être. The perpetual effort to press outward (within the limits of prudence) has become enshrined in the leadership's self-image and has also become embedded in the myth about the historic role of the Soviet state which helps justify the party's rule. Short-term compromises, even small retreats, are justifiable and even praiseworthy when absolutely necessary; accepting and legitimizing a long-term derailment of the locomotive of history is another matter entirely.

Reinforcing this pressure on Soviet external behavior created by the Soviet self-image is the felt need to make continual, partial adjustments to the priorities of some of the USSR's key Third World clients. The Soviet increase in military supplies to Nicaragua in 1985, for example, is likely to have been intended in part to assuage Cuba's demonstrated unhappiness at the limitations the Soviet Union had imposed on such military help to Nicaragua.

Moreover, a major contraction of Soviet ambitions on the world scene is very difficult for the Soviet leadership to accept because Soviet presence and influence around the world, though considerably greater than it once was, is still weaker than that of the United States and far weaker than that of all of the Soviet Union's adversaries considered together. To accept and legitimize the present world constellation of political forces is thus to legitimize a permanent position of geopolitical, although not military, inferiority for the Soviet Union. This is not likely to be tolerable whatever the state of Soviet internal difficulties.

Furthermore, Soviet leaders find it difficult to visualize ceasing to press outward because they have yet to extract the political returns they think due to them from the great improvements in their relative military position that took place in the late 1960s and the 1970s. They have long been rather frustrated and aggrieved about this discrepancy, particularly in Europe. It is also noticeable in parts of the former colonial world, notably in the Far East, where Moscow's nuclear advantage is even greater than it is in Europe while its overall political position is on the whole considerably weaker. Under these circumstances it is doubly hard for any Soviet leadership to curtail the long-term effort to find a way to extract profit from the regional balances.

American Vulnerabilities and the "Yakovlev Line"

Finally, the Gorbachev leadership is likely to see itself impelled to keep trying to expand the Soviet world presence because of the many evident or

---

Afghan border. This claim appeared to be a strong hint that the Soviet Union might increase efforts to encourage minority separatism in Pakistan if President Zia failed to accept Soviet terms for a negotiated settlement.

latent political vulnerabilities in the American world position. This attitude is articulated most clearly by Gorbachev's new lieutenant Yakovlev, who is outspoken in his desire to see the USSR strive more vigorously to outflank the United States around the world through more aggressive competition.[41]

The Soviets probably find it difficult to believe that they cannot extract much greater advantages from American political setbacks than they have done so far. They have been given many reasons over the last few years to perceive important vulnerabilities in the American position in the Middle East and Southwest Asia. In this broad area they are likely in particular to see grave weaknesses in the internal political and economic situation of two key American clients, Egypt and Pakistan, strains dramatized by a serious mutiny in part of the Egyptian security forces in early 1986. As a result of conservative Arab desire for a partial offset to the United States, the Soviet Union has recently found it possible to begin building a modest political presence in the lower Persian Gulf, establishing diplomatic relations with Oman and the United Arab Emirates and a growing arms supply relationship with Kuwait. In the wake of the American confrontation with Libya in early 1986 the Soviets found it possible to introduce their naval vessels into Libyan harbors as a complement to the new Soviet air defense missiles.[42] Meanwhile the Soviets undoubtedly remain deeply chagrined that they have been unable to make major political advances as a result of the American debacle in Iran and the fragmentation of Lebanon, two once secure bastions of Western influence which have now been shattered. This, for them, is still unfinished business, particularly Iran, where they are now awaiting the changes that the death of Khomeini may bring.

In East Asia, Gorbachev's search for new competitive opportunities to improve the generally weak Soviet political position has been reflected in a new approach to Japan and in an acceleration in the improved political, economic, and military dealings with North Korea begun in 1984. In much of the Far East the Soviets meanwhile see a confluence of new factors tending slowly to erode the large American political advantage. An American quarrel with New Zealand over the question of nuclear port calls has disrupted the

[41]See, for example, A. Yakovlev, "Sources of the Threat and Public Opinion," *Mirovaya Ekonomika i Mezhdunarodnyye Otnosheniya* no. 3 (March 1985).

[42]Until U.S. armed clashes with Libya actually began in March 1986, the Soviets sought with some success to promote an impression in much of the Arab world that the Soviet posture had deterred the United States from attacking Libya. In January 1986 the Soviet ambassador to Libya stated on Libyan radio that "we will not stand idly by or sit on the fence should events develop further." Tripoli radio, January 11, 1986, *FBIS Daily Report, Soviet Union*, January 13, 1986, p. H-1 The Soviet ambassador to Italy publicly stated that the Soviet Union expects Washington "to carefully weigh the dangerous consequences that could come about if it persists in its policy toward the sovereign Libyan state." ANSA, Rome, January 15, 1986. A Kuwait newspaper alleged that the Soviet Union had told the United States that it would lift any naval blockade imposed on Libya by America. *Al-Qabas*, January 6, 1986. In this period "Middle East diplomats in Washington" were said to hold the widespread conviction that "Soviet support of Libya, now made graphic by warships steaming to Col. Qadafhi's side, has been part of the reason the U.S. had opted not to take military action against Libya." *Wall Street Journal*, January 20, 1986.

ANZUS alliance. The ministates of the Western Pacific have begun to enter fishing treaties with the USSR which will for the first time bring a Soviet political presence to the region. In the Philippines, despite the unexpected victory of the Aquino opposition to Marcos—the Soviet Union miscalculated badly and clung to Marcos to the very end—the Soviets probably see a long-term threat to the viability of the major American naval and air bases, which have been permanently placed on the Philippine political agenda. The central aim of Soviet policy and propaganda therefore continues to be the eventual elimination of the bases, which would have obviously beneficial consequences for the Soviet regional military position. At the same time the Soviets are also likely to retain hopes that the trend of battle in Kampuchea— and growing fears of an ultimate Vietnamese victory—will eventually erode the ASEAN coalition opposing Vietnam, with further adverse consequences for tacit Sino-American cooperation in the area.

Meanwhile the Soviets also must surely hope that the continued exacerbation of the racial conflict in South Africa, even if it never produces an overthrow of the Boer regime, will over time have the side-effect of further weakening American influence elsewhere in Africa. And indeed, they are likely to see concrete evidence that this is already happening, in the angry reaction by some African leaders against the United States in response to the evolution of events in South Africa.

Finally, while greatly concerned at the weaknesses of some of their Marxist-Leninist client states faced with insurgencies that the United States encourages, the Soviets are also likely to be aware of the important American political vulnerabilities latent in a U.S. policy of supporting such insurgencies. Despite the broad U.S. political support for assistance to the Afghan resistance via Pakistan, for example, there is no comparable U.S. consensus for combat support of Pakistan in the event that continued Pakistani help for that resistance eventually produces a serious Soviet-Pakistan clash. In Black Africa, so long as the UNITA resistance in Angola continues to be popularly identified with South African backing, American support for UNITA is likely to encourage a perception of Washington as closely linked with Pretoria, with some adverse political consequences for the United States throughout the continent.

In sum, the momentum of inherited Soviet policy interests appears to exercise great leverage over Gorbachev's ability and inclination to alter the broad pursuit of long-existing policy goals. This framework seems to constrain and channel his options on all sides, so that Soviet language thus far has changed much more than Soviet behavior. Increased caution regarding the Third World may characterize the general mood of the Soviet elite today, and this mood was reflected in Gorbachev's reticence on the subject at the Twenty-seventh Congress of the CPSU. But the inertia of competitive struggle paradoxically continues to dominate many short-term decisions and to propel the Soviet Union into actions that are not very cautious, as in the case of the Libyan missiles. Although Gorbachev would undoubtedly prefer to be relieved of the burden of the Afghan war, he is unlikely to find it politically possible to get out of Afghanistan on any terms that do not perpetuate Soviet hegemony. Although he would like to further improve relations with the PRC, he cannot give up the growing Soviet base at Cam Ranh Bay and stop supporting Vietnam in order to propitiate Beijing. He is surely not oblivious to the dangers that may be latent in closer military association with such unpredictable adventurists as Qadhdhafi and Kim Il-Sung, but he seems impelled to give at least equal priority to other considerations. Overall, he appears well aware of the reasons to maintain prudence in assuming military risks in the Third World and to continue to show caution in assuming new external economic burdens. But he seems equally aware that it is a cardinal sin against Leninist precept and the Soviet political dynamic to ignore any emerging opportunities to advance at what may seem moderate cost and risk.

CONTRIBUTORS

ABRAHAM S. BECKER is a senior staff member of The RAND Corporation's Economics and Statistics Department and Associate Director of RAND's National Security Strategies Program. Apart from numerous works on the Soviet economy, he has written widely on Soviet policy toward the Middle East. His most recent research has been on Soviet policy on trade with the West.

SHAHRAM CHUBIN is on the staff of the Graduate Institute of International Studies in Geneva, Switzerland. Formerly the Assistant Director for Regional Security Studies at the International Institute for Strategic Studies in London, he has written widely on Persian Gulf and related affairs.

FRANCIS FUKUYAMA is a member of the Political Science Department of The RAND Corporation and an associate of the RAND/UCLA Center for the Study of Soviet International Behavior. Formerly a member of the Policy Planning Staff of the U.S. State Department, he is the author of a number of articles and monographs on Soviet policy toward the Third World.

HARRY GELMAN is a senior staff member of the Political Science Department of The RAND Corporation and a former Assistant National Intelligence Officer for the Soviet Union and Eastern Europe. He is the author of *The Brezhnev Politburo and the Decline of Detente* (Ithaca: Cornell University Press, 1984) and has written extensively on many aspects of Soviet foreign and domestic policy.

GALIA GOLAN is Darwin Professor of Soviet and East European Studies and former head of the Mayrock Center for Research on the Soviet Union and Eastern Europe at the Hebrew University of Jerusalem. She is the author of *The Czechoslovak Reform Movement* (Cambridge: Cambridge University Press, 1971); *Reform Rule in Czechoslovakia* (Cambridge University Press, 1973); *Yom*

Kippur and After: The Soviet Union and the Middle East Crisis (Cambridge University Press, 1977); *The Soviet and the PLO* (New York: Praeger, 1980), and a forthcoming book, *The Soviet Union and Third World National Liberation Movements.*

MELVIN A. GOODMAN is Professor of International Studies at the National War College in Washington, D.C. He has been an analyst for the Central Intelligence Agency and the Department of State.

EDWARD GONZALEZ is a professor of Political Science at the University of California, Los Angeles, and a resident consultant at The RAND Corporation. For more than two decades he has focused his research on Cuban affairs, Cuban-Soviet relations, and U.S. policy toward Cuba and Central America. His many articles have appeared in *World Politics, Foreign Affairs, Problems of Communism,* and other professional journals and books. The author of *Cuba under Castro: The Limits of Charisma* (1974) he coauthored a RAND study on *Castro, Cuba, and the World* in 1986.

ROBERT C. HORN is Professor of Political Science at the California State University, Northridge. He has published articles on Soviet policy in Asia in various journals and books and is currently working on a book on Soviet-Vietnamese relations.

ANDRZEJ KORBONSKI is Professor of Political Science at the University of California, Los Angeles, Co-director of the RAND/UCLA Center for the Study of Soviet International Behavior, and Director of the UCLA Center for Russian, East European Studies. Born in Poland and a member of the Polish Underground Army during World War II, he has specialized in East European and Soviet politics, worked as a program officer for the Ford Foundation, been a director of the International Research and Exchange Board (IREX) and the National Council for Soviet and East European Research, and was chairman of the UCLA Political Science Department from 1976 to 1981.

COLIN LEGUM is an independent writer and commentator on African affairs living in London, England. Formerly an associate editor of *The Observer* (London), he is editor of both *African Contemporary Record* and *Third World Reports,* and was co-editor of the *Middle East Contemporary Survey.* He is the author of numerous books and articles on contemporary African affairs.

STEPHEN SESTANOVICH worked as a Soviet specialist on the National Security Council staff from 1984 to 1987. The analysis presented in his chapter is the author's own and does not necessarily reflect official policies of the U.S. government.

DONALD S. ZAGORIA is a professor of government at the Graduate Center of the City University of New York and a fellow at Columbia University's Harriman Institute for the Advanced Study of the USSR.

INDEX

Library of Congress Cataloging-in-Publication Data

The Soviet Union and the Third World.

"A book from the RAND/UCLA Center for the Study of
Soviet International Behavior."
Includes index.
1. Developing countries—Foreign relations—Soviet Union. 2. Soviet Union—
Foreign relations—Developing countries. 3. Soviet Union—Foreign relations—
1945–   . I. Korbonski, Andrzej. II. Fukuyama, Francis.
D888.S65S645 1987   327.470172'4   86-47974
ISBN 0-8014-2032-6
ISBN 0-8014-9454-0 (pbk. : alk. paper)

3584